THE HISTORY OF PARLIAMENT

THE

HOUSE OF COMMONS

1754–1790:

INTRODUCTORY SURVEY

BY

JOHN BROOKE

OXFORD UNIVERSITY PRESS

LONDON   OXFORD   NEW YORK

Oxford University Press

OXFORD   LONDON   NEW YORK
GLASGOW   TORONTO   MELBOURNE   WELLINGTON
CAPE TOWN   SALISBURY   IBADAN   NAIROBI   LUSAKA   ADDIS ABABA
BOMBAY   CALCUTTA   MADRAS   KARACHI   LAHORE   DACCA
KUALA LUMPUR   HONG KONG   TOKYO

First published in Vol. 1 of Sir Lewis Namier and John Brooke:
The History of Parliament: The House of Commons 1754–1790
by Her Majesty's Stationery Office, 1964.

First issued as an Oxford University Press paperback, 1968

FILMSET BY ST. PAUL'S PRESS LTD., MALTA
PRINTED IN GREAT BRITAIN
AT THE UNIVERSITY PRESS, OXFORD
BY VIVIAN RIDLER
PRINTER TO THE UNIVERSITY

FOREWORD

As an historical project, the *History of Parliament* is of long standing. Here, however, it is sufficient to say that the present phase of the undertaking dates from 1951, when a generous annual grant-in-aid for the purposes of the History was provided from public funds. From that time onwards the planning and preparation of the work have been directed by an Editorial Board of professional historians, under the general supervision of Trustees drawn (until 1967 exclusively and since then in the main) from the members and officers of the two Houses of Parliament. Publication of the History, by Her Majesty's Stationery Office, began in 1964 with three volumes covering the period 1754–90, edited by Sir Lewis Namier and John Brooke. Other periods are being prepared.

In accordance with the plan of the History, the volumes for 1754–90 comprise three main divisions: an introductory survey; electoral histories of every constituency in England, Wales and Scotland; and biographical and political studies of all Members of the House of Commons during the period. At the time of Sir Lewis Namier's death in 1960, the typescript of the second and third divisions was nearing completion, but of the introductory survey there were only a few pages in draft. To the new editor, Mr. Brooke, Sir Lewis's senior assistant since 1951, therefore fell the threefold task of completing and revising for press the constituency histories and biographies and writing the introductory survey. It is his introductory survey, with three of its six appendices and its index, all taken from volume I, that are here reprinted.

Readers who wish to know more about the Members and constituencies mentioned in the introductory survey, or about the historical evidence used in its composition, should go to the three-volume edition: Sir Lewis Namier & John Brooke, *The History of Parliament: The House of Commons 1754–1790* (H.M.S.O., 1964). The scope of the History as a whole, its underlying principles, and the methods being employed in its preparation, are indicated in a general foreword and other pages of prefatory matter in the first volume.

CONTENTS

1754–1790

When this period opens George II had been on the throne for nearly 27 years; and Henry Pelham, first lord of the Treasury and leader of the House of Commons, had held these offices for nearly 11 years. The nation was at peace; Jacobitism no longer menaced the Hanoverian dynasty; and no deep-seated party divisions disturbed the House of Commons.

On 6 March 1754, a month before the fourth Parliament of the reign was due to be dissolved, Henry Pelham died; and a new era opened. Pelham was immediately succeeded as head of the Treasury by his brother, the Duke of Newcastle, but the question of who was to hold the key office of leader of the House of Commons remained unsettled and occupied the attention of politicians for the next three years. Connected with this were problems of foreign policy. In 1755 fighting broke out between the British and the French, on the seas and in North America, and after war had been declared Britain was forced to undertake further campaigns in India and Germany. The conduct of the war and the making of peace were complicated by the death of the King in 1760 and the accession of George III, only 22 years old, immature for his age, and untried. The search for a stable Administration in terms of the new reign did not end until 1770; rapidly changing ministries, the growth of personal parties within the House of Commons, and of urban radicalism outside, are symptoms of the disturbed state of politics in the first ten years of George III's reign.

After 1770 Parliament was faced with momentous issues concerning the government of two sub-continents, India and North America. The problem of Britain's relations with her American colonies dominates the period, not only because of its consequence for world history but also because it arose out of claims made by Parliament and was to have important repercussions on the life of Parliament. The American war stimulated a movement to reduce the influence of the Crown and led to demands for parliamentary and administrative reform; and the years after 1782 are largely taken up in the House of Commons with the working out of these themes. The period ends when the outbreak of the French Revolution was about to lead to a new alignment in British politics.

These are the events which make up the parliamentary drama of this period. How individual Members of the Commons responded to them can be seen from their biographies. The purpose of this survey is more general: to describe the various kinds of constituencies, their character and management, the great diversity of electoral qualifications; to analyse the general elections and the House of Commons which resulted from them in the six Parliaments of the period; to consider the economic, social, professional, and other groupings within the House, examining its composition from a sociological point of view; and finally to look at the House as a living institution and to single out the main features of its development during this period, particularly the most significant feature of all, the growth of party.

1 . THE CONSTITUENCIES

Between 1754 and 1790 the House of Commons consisted of 558 Members, elected by 314 constituencies. The 245 English constituencies (40 counties, 203 boroughs, 2 universities) returned 489 Members; the 24 Welsh constituencies and 45 Scottish constituencies returned one Member each.

THE ENGLISH COUNTIES

Each of the 40 English counties returned two Members to Parliament, and the voting qualification in all counties was the same: the possession of freehold property valued for the land tax at 40 shillings per annum (the 40s. freehold). For electoral purposes the term 40s. freehold was widely interpreted: it included leases for lives; annuities, rent charges, and mortgages based on freehold property; ecclesiastical benefices; and appointments in Government service. The number of electors varied from county to county, and owing to the infrequency of polls at elections during this period only approximate estimates can be given. Yorkshire had the largest county electorate (and the largest electorate in the country) with about 20,000 voters; next came Kent, Lancashire, and Somerset, with about 8,000 each; and nine counties had between 5,000 and 6,000 (Cheshire, Essex, Gloucestershire, Hampshire, Leicestershire, Lincolnshire, Norfolk, Staffordshire, and Suffolk). Most of the English counties had electorates between 3,000 and 4,000. At the bottom of the scale were Bedfordshire, Huntingdonshire, Northumberland, and Westmorland, with about 2,000 voters each; Monmouth with 1,500; and Rutland with about 800.

The county electors were the landed classes; they were, in theory, the independent gentlemen of England, supposedly men of property and substance, able to choose their representatives freely. But the practice of the constitution, in this as in other matters, did not match the theory. Many of the freeholders were also tenants, renting land from a large landowner, or were under other obligations to him; many had little political consciousness, or their political horizons did not extend beyond local affairs. The larger landowners, the peers and the country gentlemen, were the acknowledged leaders both of county society and of county politics. Electioneers and politicians always assumed that tenants would vote in accordance with the wish of their landlords, and measured a landowner's parliamentary interest in a county by the number of his tenants and the extent of his acreage. Interest, by this reckoning, meant first and foremost the possession of landed property.

It would be more correct to say, however, that property was a foundation on which a parliamentary interest could be built. The relationship between the landlord and his tenants was much more than a material one: the assumption that tenants voted as their landlord wished from fear of being dispossessed is a caricature of the real state of affairs. Landed property, after all, was primarily a source of income, and any large-scale dispossession for political reasons would have hurt the landlord as much as the tenants. Even Sir James Lowther, 'the tyrant of the north', would not go to this extreme: when he was thwarted by his tenants at Whitehaven in 1780 he threatened to stop their supply of coal, but he drew the line at evicting them. The gentry were the leaders of the county, not its masters; they expressed their wishes to their tenants, not their orders; and the tenants' vote, when used agreeably to the landlord, was a tribute of respect, not an acknowledgement of dependence. It was always possible to rouse the freeholders with the cry that their independence was in danger, as is shown by these lines from an election song current in Somerset in 1768:

> Rich bullies denied
> And would fain set aside
> Our right our own Members to choose;
> They threaten us too
> What mischief they'll do
> Should we their directions refuse.

Some landlords, such as the Duke of Devonshire in Derbyshire, would ask their tenants for one vote only and leave them free to dispose of the second as they wished; while a hard landlord, such as Thomas Cholmondeley in Cheshire, who let his estate at rack-rent, would find his parliamentary interest decline. And when the freeholders felt strongly about a political issue they were able to assert their independence against their landlords, as Lord Fitzwilliam found in Yorkshire in 1784. Fitzwilliam had inherited every acre that his uncle Lord Rockingham had possessed in the county; but while Rockingham had been able to secure the return of two Members of his own political complexion, Fitzwilliam was beaten down by the wave of anti-Foxite feeling. Even a small county like Westmorland, described by Oldfield in 1792 as 'as much under the command of an individual as the most rotten borough in the kingdom', rebelled against the intensely unpopular Lowther in 1768 and returned a candidate against his interest. Social and personal relationships, traditional and hereditary loyalties, counted for a good deal in county elections; and there was an element of goodwill present in every parliamentary interest, the extent of which it is impossible to measure quantitatively though its absence can be readily detected.

Candidates for the county were fixed upon at a county meeting, held about a year before the general election was due, and attended by the leading peers and country gentlemen. Usually the sitting Members were invited to continue, unless one or the other of them had made himself particularly unpopular. The counties disliked changes in their representation, especially if these involved a contest, and would-be candidates incurred some odium if they disturbed 'the peace of the county' without adequate excuse—unless they could plead, as did Admiral Boscawen in Cornwall in 1760, that 'the only honour the county can confer' should not be confined to a few families. If several candidates presented themselves, the county meeting would provide an indication of the amount of support they were likely to receive. Sometimes, as at the Cornwall meeting of 1774, a vote would be taken; but generally the sense of the meeting was made clear without that formality—without support from some of the leading gentlemen a candidate would have no chance. In addition to choosing candidates, the county meeting was also used to question the representatives about their conduct in Parliament or to vote instructions to them.

Having been adopted as candidates, the next step was to canvass the county—to go round and ask the freeholders for their votes. This was a laborious undertaking, hardly to be attempted without the assistance of friends and supporters; but it had the great advantage of enabling the candidates to make a rough estimate of how many votes they were likely to receive, and whether it would be worth their while to continue the fight. Yorkshire in 1784 was thoroughly canvassed by two sets of candidates, one supporting the Fox-North party, the other Pitt's Administration. The two Foxite candidates received promises from only 3,000 freeholders as against 11,000 for their opponents; and on the evening before the election was due to begin they withdrew. A canvass, in fact, was often a bloodless election; it was a device to test the opinion of the county with the minimum of expense—an eighteenth-century kind of public opinion poll.

The chief objection to county contests was their enormous expense. This arose principally from the fact that the voting took place at the county town; and the electors had to be brought there, fed, liquored, and lodged at the candidates' expense. Without this attention and treating, many voters would not attend. The Cumberland election of 1774 was a relatively quiet affair after the expensive fight-to-the-death of the previous general election in 1768: Sir James Lowther and the Duke of Portland, the protagonists on that occasion, had agreed to recommend to one seat each, but their peace and unanimity were disturbed by Sir Joseph Pennington who set himself up as a candidate. Lord Egremont's agent wrote about the election campaign:

Things here are carried on upon a new plan. Not a single farthing spent and the freeholders are to come to the election at their own expense. This, it is imagined, will make a very great many of them decline coming at all, and the objection will increase in proportion to their distance from the place of election.

Still, candidates could be mistaken about the results of a canvass, or even stand a poll although the canvass had been unpromising. In such cases it often happened that a candidate would withdraw after the first day's polling had convinced him he had no chance: thus Sir Sampson Gideon in Cambridgeshire in 1780 and Sir Thomas Charles Bunbury in Suffolk in 1784. But where the candidates were evenly balanced or where party or political rivalries were strong, the poll would be continued until the flood of voters became a mere trickle: the Sussex election of 1774 lasted 24 days (excluding Sundays) and the Cumberland election of 1768, 19 days. In 1785 the maximum duration of county elections was fixed at 15 days, which helped towards reducing their expense; but a bill to enable the poll to be held in more than one place, which would have reduced the expense still more, was defeated.

Figures of election expenses in the eighteenth century must always be treated with caution: still, for what they are worth, here are some for this period. The Essex by-election of 1763 is said to have cost each side over £30,000. The Oxfordshire election of 1754, the last great Whig-Tory battle of the century, cost the Tories over £20,000 and the Whigs can hardly have spent much less. The canvass in Somerset in 1768 cost over £5,000; and at the Hertfordshire election of 1774 the expenses of the county meeting alone, for food, drink, and transport, were estimated by one of the candidates at £4,000. Sums such as these were not met solely by the candidates, though they had to pay a large share: when the candidate stood as the representative of a party or group in the county, a subscription would be opened on his behalf. Thus in Yorkshire in 1780, £12,000 was raised on behalf of the Opposition candidates, Sir George Savile and Henry Duncombe, and in 1784, £18,000 on behalf of the Pittite candidates, Duncombe and William Wilberforce. Subscriptions of this amount were a convincing testimony of support and helped to frighten away opponents. Occasionally the Treasury helped to finance candidates, if political credit was to be obtained from their victory, as in Oxfordshire in 1754, Hampshire in 1779, and Berkshire in 1784. But Government aid was liable to draw odium on the candidates who received it ('treating the county as if it were a rotten borough'), and was never sufficient to replace a public subscription. Nor did it avail much against a popular candidate or cause: in 1780 the Treasury spent £4,000 trying to secure the return of Thomas Onslow for Surrey, but failed miserably. On the other hand, for a popular candidate returned unopposed, a county election could be the cheapest method of entering the House. Sir John Trevelyan's election for Somerset in 1780 cost him only £25, and about the election of 1784, when an opposition was threatened but not proceeded with, he wrote:

We then dismounted from our horses and went into a house with some of the principal gentlemen, when upwards of £10,000 was subscribed in a very few minutes. . . . Whilst I was there Mr. Poulett . . . came to the door and desired to speak to me, assuring me that no opposition was intended against me. . . . The election was gone through as soon as the forms would admit of, and we parted, the town of Ilchester desiring to pay the usual fees of bellringing and chairing. The remainder of the expense was as follows:

Under sheriff	£10.	10.	0.
County clerk	5.	5.	0.
Porter to the county clerk	2.	2.	0.

And then we all departed before dinner, as the town could not produce enough of meat and drink for one tenth part of the freeholders present, none of whom came but at their own expense.

He could hardly have been returned for less at any pocket borough in the kingdom.

Still, Trevelyan would have been prepared to meet the expense of a contest had it been necessary. Why were men ready to spend such large sums to enter Parliament for a county, when they could have got in more cheaply and easily for a pocket borough? In part, the desire to represent one's county in Parliament was a fashion of the times, like planting trees or building country houses, and there is no accounting for fashion. Thomas de Grey told the Norfolk county meeting in 1767 that he was ambitious of representing his native county, but 'would not accept of a borough though invited to it at free cost'; and Sir George Savile, whose parliamentary career is a record of service to his constituents without material reward to himself, was prepared to spend a fortune to come in for Yorkshire in 1754 but refused nomination at York and Higham Ferrers. For these men, to be chosen knight of the shire was a social honour, evidence of their standing in the county and of the approbation of their fellows. They did not go to Westminster to make or unmake governments, to win places or honours for themselves; they went there to watch over the interests of their constituents and to look on political matters with an independent eye. 'Independency, gentlemen, has long been the characteristic of your county,' wrote the *Salisbury Journal* at the time of the Wiltshire by-election of 1772. 'Let us be the last to resign it to corruption and Court influence.' The country gentlemen who were returned for the English counties were the most disinterested group of Members in the House, and a most accurate reflection of the state of political opinion among the landed classes. The position of sons of peers or aristocratic dependants who represented English counties was somewhat different: they sat not in their own right, but as representatives of great families. The motive for election was the same: a Cavendish sitting for Derbyshire or a Stanley for Lancashire was symbolical of the respect and pre-eminence accorded to the Duke of Devonshire or the Earl of Derby by their own counties. But aristocratic knights of the shire had a twofold allegiance: to their constituents and to the great house they represented; and their independence and disinterestedness were qualified.

In the west of England, where pocket boroughs were numerous, there was a strong feeling that the peers should confine themselves to the boroughs and leave the county representation to the country gentlemen.

A meeting of Somerset justices of the peace at Wells in January 1784 passed a resolution that 'no person who is heir apparent of a peer, or is in the immediate succession to a peerage' ought to be chosen for the county. In Cheshire, Cornwall, Devon, Dorset, Shropshire, Somerset, and Worcestershire the county representation was practically monopolized by the country gentlemen; and in these seven counties there were only two contested elections during this period—both in Cornwall, in 1772 and 1774. In Wiltshire, the choice of candidates to be presented to the county meeting was in the hands of a club of the principal landowners, and solid, safe country gentlemen were always chosen. In Leicestershire, where there was only one borough constituency, it was understood that Leicester was to be left to the peers and the county to the country gentlemen, though this agreement was never strictly applied. Other counties free from a dominant aristocratic influence were Essex, Hertfordshire, Norfolk, Northamptonshire, Suffolk, and Warwickshire. In these counties the peers did concern themselves with elections, but usually on behalf of a country gentleman, rarely for one of their own families; and contests were more frequent than in the western counties. Northamptonshire alone of this group was uncontested during this period, and there were ten contests in the other five counties.

In other counties, particularly in the north, there were aristocratic families of sufficient standing and antiquity to be able to command a seat almost by hereditary right: the Duke of Bedford in Bedfordshire; Sir James Lowther (created in 1784 Earl of Lonsdale) in Cumberland; the Duke of Devonshire in Derbyshire; the Earl of Darlington in Durham; the Earl of Derby in Lancashire; the Duke of Northumberland in Northumberland; and Earl Gower in Staffordshire. But this apparent right was really a concession on the part of the country gentlemen and did not extend to both seats. Lord Frederick Cavendish wrote to his nephew the Duke of Devonshire about the election for Derbyshire in 1768: 'The Tory gentlemen acknowledge our moderation and do not deny but that we may have carried two [seats], but that, I think I have said to you before, I hope you will never think of unless drove to.' Lord George Cavendish's seat was not in dispute, and the two country gentlemen who stood, Sir Henry Harpur and Godfrey Bagnall Clarke, each solicited votes for himself and Cavendish. Cavendish was returned head of the poll with over 2,700 votes out of an electorate of 3,000— a lead of nearly 1,000 over Clarke, the second successful candidate.

When contests took place in this type of county constituency (there were eight in the seven counties of this group during this period) they arose usually from an attempt by the aristocratic interest to fill both seats. The great Cumberland contest of 1768 was a revolt of the independent freeholders and smaller landlords against the over-bearing tyranny of Sir James Lowther. With the Duke of Portland as their patron, they adopted two candidates in opposition to the Lowther interest and secured their return, one on petition by the House of Commons. But in 1774 the Cumberland gentry did not deny Lowther's claim to one seat, provided he left the other to their free choice. Similarly in Northumberland in 1774 the Duke of Northumberland's attempt to carry both seats was defeated, but only by a margin of 16 votes. In Durham the Earl of Darlington secured a second seat at the by-election of 1760, and at the general election the following year held both seats—an almost unique achievement in this period.

In other counties the predominance of one aristocratic family, though marked, was not overwhelming. Lincolnshire generally accorded one seat to the family of the Duke of Ancaster and no contest in this period was carried to a poll. In Oxfordshire, after the great contest of 1754, the Duke of Marlborough concluded an agreement with the Tory country gentlemen by which each was to nominate one Member for the county; and Lord Charles Spencer was able to tell Lord Shelburne in 1782 that his seat for Oxfordshire was as safe as if he held it by burgage tenure. But probably the most successful aristocratic interest in county politics during this period was that of Lord Rockingham in Yorkshire. Rockingham was well aware of the independence of the Yorkshire freeholders and of their suspicion of aristocratic interference: indeed, at the beginning of his career he had used anti-aristocratic feeling to oust Lord Holdernesse from the primacy in Yorkshire politics. Rockingham's principle in Yorkshire was to follow the sense of the county, not to lead it: 'I would not give any handle in Yorkshire', he wrote in 1769, 'for Yorkshiremen to say that my politics had led them beyond their intentions or that I had checked their well-founded ardour.' From 1780 onwards his authority was challenged by the Yorkshire Association, a group of country gentlemen who had adopted a political programme much too radical for Rockingham and who were suspicious alike of peers and politicians. By trying to work with the Association, rather than against them, Rockingham preserved his primacy in the county until his death, but could not hand it on to his successor. The independent freeholders of Yorkshire could be led by personality but not overawed by property.

In Westmorland, where the electorate was only about 2,000, Sir James Lowther's property was such that he established his control over both seats. But even in this small county Lowther's interest did not go unchallenged: there were four contests during this period, and Lowther lost a Member in 1768—largely through over-confidence. Three other small counties were controlled by a combination of the two leading peers in the county: Cambridgeshire, by the Earl of Hardwicke and the Duke of Rutland; Huntingdonshire, by the Duke of Manchester and the Earl of Sandwich; and Nottinghamshire, by the Duke of Portland and the Duke of Newcastle. After 1768 the second Duke of Newcastle and the Duke of Portland were always on opposite sides politically, but this did not prevent their close collaboration in Nottinghamshire election affairs. Similarly, Sandwich and Manchester, though politically opposed to each other, worked together in Huntingdonshire, though with a good deal of jealousy and bickering. 'There is no place in England', Sandwich wrote in 1780, 'where the parties are more at variance than in Huntingdonshire; we could not dine together on the election day, and the two Members could not agree to give a joint ball to the ladies.' This was written at the time of an unopposed election, but they could always agree when, as in 1768, there was an opposition to their joint rule.

In Rutland the Earls of Exeter, Gainsborough, and Winchilsea contended for supremacy; while in Monmouthshire, another small county, the allied families of Morgan and Hanbury, traditionally Whig, disputed the representation with the Duke of Beaufort, whose family had a Tory tradition. Gloucestershire in this period recalls Dickens's description of Eatanswill, where 'the very church had a Blue and a Buff aisle': in Gloucestershire everybody seems to have been either a Berkeley or a Beaufort. This division was partly traditional and partly political: the Berkeleys had a Whig inheritance and the Beauforts a Tory, and during the American war the Beauforts supported the Government and the Berkeleys the Opposition. At the contested by-election of 1776, when the House of Commons was deeply divided on the American war, Government and Opposition took sides, Government supporting William Bromley Chester and hailing his victory as a great triumph for their cause. But it would not be easy to say what the two sides were fighting about except whether or not both county seats should be filled by protagonists of the Berkeley family. After a campaign of seven months and a poll of eleven days, Gloucestershire had had its fill of election excitement, and in 1783 the two sides agreed to divide the representation between them. In 1784 an attempt by Winchcombe Henry Hartley, a zealous partisan of Charles Fox, to challenge this agreement came to naught, and Hartley retired after having polled only 20 votes.

In only two English counties did the Government have an important electoral interest. In Hampshire the Government could influence electors employed in the dockyards at Gosport and Portsea, the custom house officers in the numerous ports, and the Crown tenants in the New Forest; and at the contested election of 1779 (the only one during this period) £2,000 was advanced by the Treasury towards the expenses of the Government candidate. But the Government interest was not decisive: in Hampshire, as in Gloucestershire, the gentry tended to align themselves with one or other of two powerful magnates, the Duke of Chandos and the Duke of Bolton; and in 1779, despite Government support, the Chandos candidate was defeated. In Kent, again because of its ports and dockyards, there was also a Government interest, but smaller than in Hampshire, and in an electorate of about 8,000 it was much less effective.

Social and economic developments affected particularly the politics of three counties: Warwickshire, Middlesex, and Surrey. From 1754 to 1774 Warwickshire had no contest, and its representation was in the hands of the country gentlemen. At the general election of 1774 Sir Charles Mordaunt retired from Parliament, and his son John was proposed in his place. But the Birmingham manufacturers felt that Mordaunt was not a suitable candidate to represent their interests, and they proposed Sir Charles Holte of Aston. Thomas George Skipwith, the third candidate, was accepted by both parties; and the contest was really between Holte and Mordaunt, or between Birmingham and the rest of the county. In the hundred of Hemlingford, where most of the county's industrial development had taken place, Holte polled 1,175 votes against only 315 for Mordaunt, and was eventually successful by 1,845 votes to 1,787. In 1780, when both Members retired, an advertisement appeared in the *Birmingham Gazette* for a meeting of freeholders to choose a candidate as Holte's successor, whom they would then propose to the county. A correspondent wrote from Birmingham to Lord Dartmouth:

The various commercial regulations so frequently made by the legislature affect the trade and manufactures of this place very much, and render it an object of great importance to its inhabitants that gentlemen may, if possible, be chosen for the county who are connected with the people and not entirely uninformed of the particulars in which their interest consists.

Sir Robert Lawley was selected and returned unopposed both in 1780 and 1784. Thus Birmingham, itself unenfranchised, had established its claim to choose one of the county Members; but it should be noted that neither Holte nor Lawley was a business man—both were country gentlemen, of a type indistinguishable from others who sat for the county.

The growth of London, and its expansion into the neighbouring counties, is reflected in the politics of Middlesex and Surrey. Until 1768 Middlesex chose country gentlemen, one Whig and the other Tory, and the success of John Wilkes, a bankrupt outlaw convicted for blasphemy and libel, at the general election of that year astonished all parties. The increasing urbanization of the county had led to political changes— the growth of radicalism, emanating from London, unobserved by the politicians until Wilkes provided a focus for the social and political discontents of the smaller business men and shopkeepers. Throughout the rest of this period radicalism was the strongest political force in Middlesex. Similarly, in Surrey, the expansion of Southwark led to the spread of radicalism, and in 1775 Sir Joseph Mawbey, a Southwark distiller, became the first radical to be returned for the county. By the end of this period national politics had come to be the critical factor in Surrey elections. No such effects as these are to be observed in Essex and Kent, the counties adjoining London on the east. Perhaps London had not expanded in that direction to the same extent as it had done westwards; in any case, since both counties had large electorates, the effects of urbanization would be much less felt. Moreover, both Essex and Kent were sea-bordering counties, with thriving ports of their own, not dependent on London for an outlet for their trade. Geography, as well as the social structure of a county, was an important factor in determining its politics.

Altogether there were 50 county elections carried to a poll during this period: 37 at the six general elections (out of a possible 240); and 13 at 123 by-elections. County polls were more likely to occur at general elections than at by-elections; but (as will be shown) county elections as a whole were less likely to go to a poll than those in large boroughs. The most contested counties, each going to the poll at four elections, were Hertfordshire, a very independent county; Middlesex, largely because of the Wilkes affair; and Westmorland, trying to escape from the

control of Sir James Lowther. Essex, Herefordshire, and Surrey each
had three contested elections; seven counties had two; fifteen counties
had one; and twelve counties never went to the poll during the whole
period (Cheshire, Devon, Dorset, Lancashire, Lincolnshire, Northamptonshire, Nottinghamshire, Shropshire, Somerset, Staffordshire, Worcestershire, and Yorkshire). These twelve counties, with the exception of
Yorkshire, led a placid political existence, firmly under the control of
peers or the country gentlemen; while Yorkshire only escaped a poll in
1784 at the last moment. In the thirteen counties which had 5,000 or
more electors, there were ten contests; in the 27 counties which had
electorates of less than 5,000, there were 40. The bigger the county
electorate the less chance there was of a contest.

The number of contests at particular general elections seems to
have been quite unaffected by political circumstances: there were
five contests in 1754, four in 1761, eight in 1768, eleven in 1774,
two in 1780, and seven in 1784. The election of 1780, when
political feeling ran high, produced the smallest number of county
contests; that of 1774, when there was no political issue at stake, the
highest. Of much more significance was the extent to which political
factors began to influence county elections towards the end of the period.
In 1754 only one county election, Oxfordshire, was fought on political
lines, over issues which meant little to the rest of the country. During
the next twenty years political questions hardly came into county elections,
except for the matter of general warrants, which was raised in Norfolk
and Somerset in 1768 but was in neither county a decisive factor. In
1774 America was rarely mentioned, and in 1780, when party had come
to mean a good deal in the House of Commons, only Surrey was fought
on party lines. But in 1784 every one of the seven county contests was
a struggle between followers of Pitt and Fox, and the issues of the East
India bill and of Pitt's minority Administration came up in them all.
Moreover, in at least three counties which did not go to the poll (Dorset,
Norfolk, and Yorkshire), these issues were decisive. The counties had
long claimed to be the barometer of political feeling in the nation; by
1784 that feeling was developing along party lines.

THE ENGLISH BOROUGHS

The 203 English boroughs returned 405 Members of Parliament. 196
boroughs returned two Members each; two boroughs (London and the

united boroughs of Weymouth and Melcombe Regis) returned four
Members each; and five boroughs returned one Member each (Abingdon,
Banbury, Bewdley, Higham Ferrers, and Monmouth). From the point of
view of the franchise, the English boroughs can be divided into six
groups: householder boroughs; freeman boroughs; scot and lot boroughs;
corporation boroughs; burgage boroughs; and freeholder boroughs.

The householder or 'potwalloper' boroughs had the widest borough
franchise in England, for in them the right of voting was in all inhabitant
householders who were not receiving alms or poor relief. In 1754 there
were eleven of these boroughs: another was added in 1768 when the
House of Commons decided that the right of election at Preston was not
in the freemen, as had hitherto been assumed, but in the inhabitant householders. In size of electorate they ranged from 1,000 at Northampton to
20 at St. Germans, and, whether large or small, were in general very
difficult constituencies to manage; their electorates included a large
proportion of the labouring classes; and contests were frequent. Nearly
all of them had a number of venal voters, which meant that elections were
always expensive and very often riotous. Two men were killed in the riots
following the by-election at Taunton in December 1754, and it was said
that the trade of the town suffered for years from the dissipation of this
election. The famous 'contest of the three Earls' at Northampton in 1768
ruined Lord Halifax, forced Lord Northampton to live abroad, and
seriously embarrassed Lord Spencer, one of the richest men in England.
In 1774, in the same constituency, when Northampton and Spencer
refused to treat the electors, they broke the windows of the inn where
the candidates had their headquarters. At Preston in 1768 bands of miners
from Lord Derby's collieries terrorized the town, and John Burgoyne,
Derby's candidate, went to the poll with a guard of soldiers and a loaded
pistol in his hand. The householder boroughs illustrate the worst side
of electioneering in this period: inadequate policing, too plentiful supply
of drink, and voters as yet hardly conscious of political issues.

Broadly speaking they fall into two types: venal boroughs, and
boroughs under some degree of patronage; though characteristics of both
types are to be found in them all. Ilchester, Aylesbury, Hindon, and
Honiton were pre-eminently venal. The electors at Ilchester were described
in 1756 as 'poor and corrupt, without honour, morals or attachment to any
man or party', yet for most of this period the borough was under the

patronage of the Lockyer family. At Aylesbury, Welbore Ellis, returned unopposed in 1761, paid £5 to each voter (the electorate numbered about 500); on his re-election in 1762 he gave a further £3; and in 1765, when he expected to be given office, £3 to each voter was again demanded as the price of his re-election. And he was told that if he made any difficulties, the electors would 'bring in someone gratis rather than lower their rate'. Ellis refused to pay and in 1768 found himself another constituency. Still, things were done comparatively decently at Aylesbury, and towards the end of this period the borough led a more respectable existence under the patronage of the Marquess of Buckingham. At Hindon, where the population did not exceed 700, there were about 200 voters, and between 1768 and 1784 eight contests were carried to the poll. In the early part of the period the Beckford and Calthorpe families had run the borough, but after William Beckford's death in 1770 and the decline of the Calthorpe interest the electors began to form themselves into groups, the better to sell their votes. One such group was led by the Rev. John Nairne, vicar of Portwood, near Hindon, who promised to bring them a candidate, 'of great extent of fortune', who was prepared to go up to £3,000 and would not boggle at a few hundreds more. Nicknamed 'General Gold' by the expectant electors, he materialized in the person of Richard Smith, an East Indian with a large fortune, who had already made several attempts to obtain a seat. In February 1773 he paid his supporters at Hindon five guineas a man; at Easter 1774 a further ten guineas; and at the general election in October, fifteen guineas. Conditioned perhaps by the looser conventions of Indian life, Smith lacked all discretion and made no attempt to hide the bribery: his campaign succeeded but he was unseated by the House of Commons and sent to prison for six months. The borough narrowly escaped being reformed; the grosser aspects of its electoral existence disappeared when it was taken in hand by Lord Chancellor Thurlow, acting on behalf of young William Beckford, who was a ward in Chancery.

Honiton had an electorate of about 700, most of whom were labourers, artisans, or small shopkeepers, and for whom the rewards received at election time formed a substantial addition to their incomes. Candidates were sought out and even advertised for, and between 1754 and 1784 there were seven contests. As at Hindon, voters banded themselves into groups in order to get better terms. The Yonge family, whose estates gave them a natural interest in the borough, paid dearly for the privilege of representing Honiton. Sir George Yonge, who sat for the borough 1754–61 and 1763–96 and had six contested elections between 1754 and 1790, is reported to have said that he inherited £80,000 from his father, his wife brought him a like amount, and Government paid him £80,000, and yet Honiton swallowed it all. While this cannot be accepted as literally accurate, it gives some indication of the expense of cultivating an interest in a potwalloper borough with a fairly large electorate.

Northampton (1,000 voters), Cirencester (800) and Minehead (300) were all to some extent under patronage. At Northampton, aristocratic families, prevented by custom and tradition from representing the county, contended for supremacy. Lord Spencer, who got his candidate elected in 1768, lost the seat in 1784, and vowed that henceforth he would have nothing to do with Northampton. Cirencester, although it had three contests during this period, was a comparatively well-behaved constituency. The Bathurst family held one seat throughout and neighbouring country gentlemen the other. At Minehead, the Luttrell family of Dunster Castle generally held one seat, and after 1774 both, one of which they were able to sell to Government. But their hold on the borough was never secure: there was a fairly large venal vote, which in 1761 spirited up a third candidate in order to create expense.

St. Germans, the smallest householder borough, with an electorate of about 20, was a complete pocket borough of the Eliot family, the only one in this type of constituency. Tregony and Wendover, with electorates of about 150, were in 1754 counted as complete pocket boroughs also: Tregony of Lord Falmouth and the Trevanion family, and Wendover of Lord Verney. But the reality was far different from the appearance: both were very expensive constituencies and both were to prove unfaithful to their patrons. Thomas Jones, Lord Edgcumbe's electoral agent, wrote about Tregony in 1760: 'There are always a large number of votes . . . ready to receive any adventurer whatever who will bring them money'; and John Robinson, secretary to the Treasury, in 1774: 'The voters are a very venal set.' At the general election of 1784 Falmouth was attacked at Tregony by Sir Francis Basset, and although his candidates proved successful he found it advisable in 1788 to sell the borough to Basset. At Wendover, Lord Verney's tenants are said to have lived rent free on condition that they voted for his lordship's candidates. But he lost one seat, largely through his own neglect, in 1768; and in 1784, when bankrupt and presumably compelled to exact his rents, he had the mortification of seeing the borough turn against him and return two strangers who paid £3,000 each for their seats.

Preston is an interesting example of a borough which came under patronage as a result of having its franchise enlarged. Until 1768 the right of election was assumed to be in the freemen, the borough was controlled by the corporation, and neighbouring country gentlemen were usually returned. In 1768 Lord Strange, eldest son of Lord Derby, obtained from the House of Commons a determination that the right of election was in the inhabitant householders. Since many of them were tenants of Lord Derby, Strange was able to build up an interest in the borough, and from 1768 to 1790 one seat was held by his brother-in-law, General John Burgoyne of Saratoga fame. Preston had a large Dissenting population, and Strange allied himself with Sir Henry Hoghton, leader of the Lancashire Dissenters, who was seated with Burgoyne in 1768. The corporation did not easily surrender their control of the borough and there were further contests in 1780 and 1784; but the alliance of the Stanley family with the Dissenters was too strong for them.

At Taunton there was also a large Dissenting population, at odds with the Anglican dominated corporation. In 1754 Lord Egremont aspired to become patron of the borough, but with an electorate of about 500 and a householder franchise it was too large to be controlled without exorbitant expense, as Egremont found at the by-election of 1754. At that election Egremont's candidate, Robert Maxwell, supported by the Dissenters and subsidized by the Treasury to the tune of over £3,500, after a six months' campaign defeated a Tory country gentleman. The citizens of Taunton, appalled at the amount of money poured out on drink for the lower classes, with the consequent rioting and dissipation, resolved that if money was to be spent on an election it should serve some useful purpose. A group of 'sensible and public spirited tradesmen', most probably Dissenters, formed themselves into the Market House Society with the object of ensuring that money hitherto spent on treating the populace should be devoted to public works, to begin with the rebuilding of the old market area. This had a sweetening effect on Taunton politics, and at the general election of 1768 the Market House Society carried both candidates without a poll. The Society were not allowed to have it all their own way and further contests followed in 1774 and 1782, but some sense of civic responsibility had entered into Taunton politics and there was no repetition of the orgy of December 1754.

To what extent did political issues influence elections in these, the most democratic of English boroughs? At Aylesbury in 1780 an Opposition candidate stood against two supporters of the Government and was overwhelmingly defeated; and there was a political flavour to the election of 1784 at Northampton and the by-election of 1789 at Aylesbury. These are the only instances that have been noted of political issues influencing elections in this type of constituency. The householder franchise gave the vote to a class for whom public affairs meant little, and who saw elections as a source of material benefits. The influence of a neighbouring landowner of large property, or of the Dissenters, who tended to see politics as a matter of principle, raised the tone of such boroughs as Cirencester and Taunton; but where these moderating influences were absent, bribery and treating prevailed in the elections for the householder boroughs.

The 92 boroughs where the right of voting belonged to the freemen (the freeman boroughs) formed the largest group of the English constituencies. London had a unique franchise, with the right of voting in the livery (a more select body than the freemen), but it is more conveniently placed in the freeman group than in any other and it behaved pretty much as a freeman borough. In many of the other boroughs the freeman franchise was subject to restrictions and extensions as a result of decisions by the House of Commons. The chief distinction was between boroughs where the right of voting was in resident freemen only, and those where honorary and non-resident freemen also were entitled to vote. In addition, there were boroughs where the franchise was in the freemen and freeholders; in the freemen paying scot and lot; in the freemen and inhabitant householders; and in combinations of these. Lichfield had a very complicated franchise: in freeholders, burgage holders, and freemen paying scot and lot. The permutations on the freeman franchise were many; and because of conflicting decisions by the House of Commons and ambiguities in borough charters, were a rich field for litigation. But common to all these boroughs was the fact that the majority of the voters had to be duly enrolled as freemen before they could vote.

The qualifications for freemen varied widely from borough to borough and are more a matter of municipal than parliamentary history. Generally the freedom was obtained by birth, apprenticeship, redemption, or marriage to the daughter of a freeman. In all these boroughs the influence of the corporation over the creation of freemen was considerable, and control of the corporation was an important electoral asset. The corporation's influence tended to vary inversely to the size of the electorate: in small electorates, where the creation of only a dozen freemen might turn an election, control of the corporation was essential. At Bewdley, where there were less than 40 voters, the borough was disputed between the Lyttelton and Winnington families, and an election was often decided not on polling day but at the previous Michaelmas, when the mayor was elected and new freemen created. In the very large freeman boroughs control of the corporation, though still important in elections, was rarely the decisive factor.

The largest electorate in this group of boroughs was London, with 7,000 voters; the smallest was Camelford, with about 20. They may be arranged in three sub-groups: 28 larger boroughs, with electorates of 1,000 or above; 30 medium boroughs, with electorates of at least 200 but below 1,000; and 34 smaller boroughs, with electorates of less than 200.

The larger freeman boroughs had electorates comparable in size to those of the English counties, but were much more frequently contested. Each of the 28 boroughs with an electorate of 1,000 or above went to the poll at least once during this period. London had nine contests (every general election and three by-elections); Maidstone had eight; Colchester and Coventry seven; and Bristol, Canterbury, and Norwich had six. These contests were almost as expensive as those for counties: William Thornton's expenses at York in 1758 came to £12,000; Alexander Fordyce, barely defeated at Colchester in 1768, spent over £14,000; and the expenses at the by-election at Gloucester in 1789 came to over £30,000. The electorates were too large for the wholesale bribery of individuals (though Worcester had a large venal vote), and probably most of the money went on providing food and drink for the voters. At York in 1774 'the vulgar' were 'rather discontented for want of drink', and Charles Turner became very unpopular when he preferred to give his money towards some public cause. At Bedford and at Hull it was the custom to issue voter's tickets, which could be exchanged with the publicans for drink. 'So established is this species of corruption', wrote Oldfield about Hull, 'that the voters regard it as a sort of birthright.' Still, the comparative frequency of elections and the existence of bribery and treating, indicate that these constituencies were unfettered in the choice of their representatives.

Local landowners, of course, had potentially a great deal of influence, but it was rarely so commanding as in the counties. The Duke of Bedford, for example, held one seat for Bedfordshire throughout this period, but his influence in Bedford borough was lost in 1771 and never regained. Many of the urban freemen possessed no landed property, and could not be influenced by the same means as the freeholders in the counties. The influence of the larger landowners and gentry in the freeman boroughs was fitful and intermittent, depending often upon personality or the chapter of accidents, and exercised indirectly through control of the corporation. The first Lord Hardwicke, the great lord chancellor, who was a Dover man, was able to recommend one Member for Dover, but after his death in 1764 the family influence waned and ten years later it was extinct. Oxford was a very independent borough in 1754 and returned two Tories, but in 1768, when the corporation wanted the candidates to pay off the city's debts, the Duke of Marlborough managed to get his foot in and his family held one seat for the remainder of this period. Carlisle was fought over by the Earl of Carlisle, the Duke of Portland, and Sir James Lowther, and the Members were usually clients of one or the other of these patrons. There was, however, a strong independent interest, dormant so long as the patrons were rivals and bidding against each other, but active, as in 1774, when they had composed their differences and had agreed to divide the representation of the borough between them. Again, at Maidstone, Lord Aylesford and Lord Romney had considerable influence, but there were eight contests during this period. The Hotham family had a strong natural interest at Beverley, which was the reason Sir Charles Hotham's opponents gave for voting against him in 1774. They told me, wrote Hotham, 'their opposition was not owing to any disregard to me personally . . . but that unless they united against me . . . they never should have any chance for a third man'.

At Durham one Member was always a Tempest and the other a Lambton, and together they defied the Earl of Darlington, backed by the corporation. Apart from these examples, only Bridgnorth and Chester of the larger freeman boroughs could be said to be under the influence of a patron; both were in the west of England where feudal ties were strongest, and even so the candidates had to be of the patron's own family. Each had only one contest during this period—at the general election of 1784. The record of the Grosvenor family at Chester is almost unique in English parliamentary history: between 1715 and 1874 they held one seat without a break, and from 1754 to 1790 they had effective control over the second seat as well. The position of the Whitmore family at Bridgnorth was by no means so strong; they held one seat throughout this period, but at the contest of 1784 Thomas Whitmore was second on the poll. By then more than two-thirds of the electorate were non-resident, which had weakened the Whitmore hold on the seat.

Lord Rockingham's influence at York was of a different nature from that of the Grosvenors at Chester or the Whitmores at Bridgnorth. It stemmed not from his being a great landowner, but from his position as the leader of the Whigs in Yorkshire; and it was strengthened by his careful handling of the constituency. When in 1754 Rockingham was first asked to recommend a Member at York, one seat was accorded to the Whigs and the other to the Tory-dominated corporation. Rockingham, pressed by his more enthusiastic friends to try for both seats, refused and contented himself with one; but in 1758 successfully resisted the attempt of the Tories to win a second seat. By 1768 Whigs and Tories had become practically extinct at York (as at most other places), and when the corporation was unable to find a suitable candidate, Rockingham was able to recommend a second Member. When his control was challenged in 1774, he had the majority of the corporation on his side— a tribute to his delicate handling of a populous and difficult constituency.

The politics of the larger freeman boroughs often turned on the conflict between the corporation party and an independent party opposed to the corporation. This was preeminently the case in eight constituencies during this period: Colchester, Coventry, Exeter, Leicester, Liverpool, Norwich, Nottingham, and Worcester. At Exeter, Leicester, Liverpool, and Norwich the corporation was Anglican, while the independent party was based on a nucleus of Dissenters; but at Nottingham the Dissenters had control of the corporation. This religious division embittered politics and frequently led to rioting and disorders (as at Coventry in 1780 when the returning officers were forced to close the poll), yet it was possibly as much social as religious in its origin. Both at Liverpool and at Worcester there was something of a class basis to these divisions, the more well-to-do citizens going with the corporation, and the poorer ones with the independent party. And when the Duke of Portland intervened at Carlisle in 1764 against Sir James Lowther and the corporation, he was advised to cultivate the 'lower sort of freemen'.

The power of the corporation lay in its right to create freemen; in its control, through the Members, of local patronage; and in the influence it possessed through its distribution of charities and power to license inns. At Durham in December 1761 the corporation created over 200 honorary freemen, and its candidate, Ralph Gowland, defeated John Lambton by three votes on a poll of over 1,500. This led the House of Commons to introduce a bill preventing honorary freemen from voting in elections unless they had held their freedom for at least twelve months. In spite of the 'Durham Act', the making of honorary freemen continued to be relied upon by unscrupulous candidates, but they took care that the freedom was conferred at least twelve months before the expected date of the election. There was a mass creation of freemen at Leicester following the corporation's defeat at the general election of 1768, and the same weapon was used by Lord Lonsdale (the former Sir James Lowther) in the 1780s in his efforts to secure control of Lancaster and Carlisle. But it was never a very reliable electoral weapon, for the House scrutinized carefully elections carried by the votes of honorary freemen. The 1,400 honorary freemen Lonsdale created at Carlisle between September 1784 and February 1785, 'nearly the whole of whom were entirely unconnected with and unknown in the city', did him no good in the end, for though Lonsdale's candidates were successful at the by-elections of April and November 1786, they were both unseated on petition.

The non-resident freemen were genuine freemen who had left the constituency to reside elsewhere. They were a source of trouble and expense to candidates and election managers, for they had to be brought from all parts of the kingdom, free of expense to themselves, to record their votes. At Evesham in 1780 Charles William Boughton Rouse 'was so hard run as to send into the neighbourhood of London a post chaise and four horses to bring down a single vote'. For despite their large electorates, every vote counted in these boroughs. The Colchester election of 1788, when 1,280 voted, ended in a tie; there was a majority of only one at Gloucester in 1789 on a poll of 1,673; and of nine at Nottingham in 1754. When a handful of votes could turn the scale, it is no wonder that foul play was sometimes used. Dickens's story of how Tony Weller was hired to tip a coach-load of voters into the canal is matched by an incident in the Coventry by-election of 1768. An officer of marines at Portsmouth, a friend of the Duke of Portland, learning that a number of his men, freemen of Coventry, had been given furlough in order to go there and vote for the Government candidate, hastily got them on board a ship bound for the coast of Guinea. Proud of his astuteness, he wrote to Portland that the Government candidate would find them in Guinea ten months hence if he wanted them—that some of the poor fellows would probably never come back did not appear to trouble him. Chase Price, M.P. for Leominster and Radnorshire 1759–77, a master of electioneering, once said that 'every advantage is reckoned fair at an election'; and at Coventry in particular no holds were barred.

When political issues arose on which men felt deeply, as in 1780 over the American war, and in 1784 when Pitt versus Fox was a matter of widespread public concern, elections in these constituencies depended at least as much on the politics of the candidates as on their electoral manœuvres. This was the case in 1780 at Bristol, Evesham, Gloucester, London, Nottingham, Worcester, and York; and in 1784 at Bedford, Bristol, Hull, Leicester, London, Newcastle-upon-Tyne, Norwich, Oxford, Worcester, and York. These towns could claim to be the political barometer of urban opinion just as the counties were of rural opinion. And in these towns there is to be seen what was probably the most important political development of this period: the rise of urban radicalism.

It is sometimes assumed that the idea of political equality came into British politics as a result of the French Revolution, and that the growth of a working-class political movement was a consequence of the industrial revolution. But the beginnings of both these developments can be seen in the larger freeman boroughs ten years before the French Revolution and when industrial changes were as yet hardly under way.

Urban radicalism arose first in the metropolitan area following the Middlesex election of 1768 and the refusal of the House of Commons to allow John Wilkes to take his seat. Wilkes's case had a catalytic effect in metropolitan politics: it provoked reactions which might not otherwise have occurred, and converted a mass of deeply-felt but inarticulate discontent into an organized political movement. There was economic hardship amongst the labouring classes which resulted in rioting. The London mob shouted for 'Wilkes and liberty', but also 'that bread and beer were too dear and that it was as well to be hanged as starved'. Nevertheless, urban radicalism was primarily a lower middle class movement, which appealed to the smaller merchants, shopkeepers, and professional men. It demanded shorter Parliaments, place and pension bills, and tried to ensure that Members of Parliament would be more responsive to the wishes of their constituents. It went much further than previous political movements in demanding parliamentary reform and the abolition of rotten boroughs; and struck not merely at the rights of the Crown but at the privileges of the landed class. Yet it was not a revolutionary movement: it did not set out to re-model the state in accordance with a doctrine of social equality, but aimed to reform abuses and restore what was regarded as the original and purer form of the constitution. In its beginnings, at least, urban radicalism saw itself as a conservative movement.

By the end of 1769 radicalism had permeated the metropolitan constituencies of London, Westminster, Middlesex, and Southwark. The first constituency outside the London area to be affected was Bristol, the largest provincial borough. In March 1769 a public meeting drew up instructions to the Bristol Members demanding shorter Parliaments and the reduction of the number of placemen in the House; shortly afterwards a radical club was formed; and at the general election of 1774 the radicals succeeded in getting their candidate returned head of the poll. At Worcester radicalism seems to have begun about 1773, and Sir Watkin Lewes, a follower of Wilkes, contested the constituency four times between 1775 and 1780, on each occasion being defeated. The other large freeman boroughs where the radical movement made ground were Newcastle-upon-Tyne, Bedford, and Nottingham. In boroughs dominated by feuds between the corporation and the anti-corporation party, such as Norwich, Liverpool, Coventry, and Leicester, radicalism played little part in elections; and in other than freeman boroughs it often appears as an attempt to extend the franchise.

During the American war the stream of radicalism became swollen with other currents and was to some extent diverted from its original path. The radicals opposed the American war, and in this they had the support of the Protestant Dissenters and of the aristocratic Whigs who followed Lord Rockingham. An agent of Lord Sandwich, first lord of the Admiralty, wrote about Nottingham in 1777:

This town is without any exception the most disloyal in the kingdom, owing in a great measure to the whole corporation ... being Dissenters, and of so bitter a sort that they have done and continue to do all in their power to hinder the service by preventing as much as possible the enlistment of soldiers.

At Portsmouth, a freeman borough with an electorate of only about 100 and where the Admiralty had considerable influence, an agent of Sandwich warned him in 1775 not to try to procure an address in favour of Government: 'We should meet with great opposition, if not a defeat. We are beset with Presbyterians and Dissenters of every kind.' Indeed, throughout the American war the word 'Presbyterian' was used almost as a term of abuse for those who disapproved of the policy of coercion against the colonists.

Another movement which arose during the American war was that of rural radicalism, a revolt of the squirearchy against both Governmental and aristocratical interference in elections. Its aims fitted in with those of urban radicalism: a reduction of Government expenditure and influence, and parliamentary reform. But whereas in the counties landed property was an essential qualification for a voter, in the larger freeman boroughs the majority of voters had no property. Here was the essential difference between rural and urban radicalism. Robert Nugent, who had represented Bristol from 1754 to 1774, wrote to Edmund Burke on 18 September 1780, shortly after Burke's defeat at Bristol:

I believe with you that the Whigs have a superior weight of property, but however that may operate uniformly upon counties, where every voter must have property, and may sometimes prevail in great towns, where the majority of the electors have no property . . . other indefinable causes, when they coincide, will render a shoemaker presiding over a club an overmatch for a rich alderman who licenses the alehouse where they meet and enables them by employment to pay their reckoning.

In London throughout this period there were two parties, corresponding to class distinctions: a party of the larger merchants and financiers, who had strong ties with Government; and a party of the smaller merchants, shopkeepers, and artisans. In some of the large provincial boroughs there can also be seen the beginnings of a party based on the urban proletariat. At Worcester in 1773 William Kelly's supporters described themselves as 'labouring freemen of this city, who, though poor, are determined to vote for no man but what shall act independent, and use his utmost interest to obtain a triennial Parliament'. When Andrew Robinson Bowes contested Newcastle-upon-Tyne in 1777, his supporters took their stand on the rights of the freemen against the gentry—'O break the *closet-combinations* of the magistrates and gentry, whose glory it seems to be to treat their inferiors as slaves.' The journeymen of Bristol organized themselves in support of Henry Cruger, the radical candidate, at the by-election of 1781, and passed resolutions directed against the monopoly of the city's representation by the middle-class political clubs. They declared it to be 'a high infringement of the privileges of the freemen . . . for any club or combination of men to declare who shall or who shall not become candidates to represent us in Parliament', and urged journeymen to withhold their labour from employers who attempted 'to oblige any man to vote contrary to his conscience'. And in 1780 a sub-committee of the Westminster Association demanded adult manhood suffrage. 'A portion of the soil, a portion of its produce, may be wanting to many; but every man has an interest in his life, his liberty, his kindred, and his country.'

Even at the end of this period urban radicalism was confined to only a few of the larger constituencies, and as yet its aims were purely political. It was not a socialist movement; it did not seek to improve the economic conditions of the labouring class or to make fundamental changes in the social structure of the nation. Nor did it call for any basic changes in the balance of power between the three branches of the legislature. Finally, it was not supported by any large-scale agitation from the unenfranchised towns. But in the light of the industrial changes that were taking place, and of the challenge shortly to be faced from the French Revolution, its long-range significance can hardly be underestimated.

The 30 medium-sized freeman boroughs, with electorates above 200 but below 1,000, were a heterogenous lot. Among them were a number of open constituencies, relatively free from influence or corruption, which generally chose their representatives from local families: Berwick-upon-Tweed, Hertford, Ipswich, Maldon, Shrewsbury, and Southampton. Each of these was contested at least twice during this period. Lord Palmerston, M.P. for Southampton, wrote about the borough in 1767 with reference to the forthcoming general election:

The number of persons at Southampton who are not to be bought with money is very great, and whenever they unite, which happily they do in the present case, the lower sort, though they make a noise for a time, neither can nor dare resist them.

At Hertford, Maldon, and Ipswich there was a large Dissenting population, and at Berwick-upon-Tweed the Government had some influence. At Ipswich there were two parties, the Blues and the Yellows, but it is difficult to say what each party stood for. At the general elections of 1780 and 1784 political issues were important at Ipswich, and also at Hertford in 1784; but otherwise elections in these boroughs were conducted without much reference to national politics.

Barnstaple, St. Albans, and Sudbury were also fairly open constituencies; but in each there was a large venal vote. At Barnstaple in 1767
there was an association of two hundred voters, 'all out of the lower class',
who 'publicly hawked' the borough about. Sudbury had an electorate of
about 800 and went to the poll at each general election during this period.
It was, wrote John Robinson, the Government election expert, in 1783,
'as open as the day and night too'; and very expensive.

The nature of its franchise and the number of voters determined to some
extent the political life of a borough, but social and economic factors
were also of great importance. Hertford and St. Albans are less than
fifteen miles apart; and during this period each had the same type of
franchise and about the same number of voters. Yet the two boroughs
were very different in their political behaviour. Hertford was an independent constituency, with a large Dissenting population, particularly of
Quakers, and since the number of honorary freemen was limited by charter
to three it was not amenable to control by the corporation. Its representatives were always substantial local gentlemen, no one family overshadow-
ing the others, and it was free from corruption. At St. Albans Lord Spencer
and Lord Grimston aspired to become patrons of the borough, but even
when their interests were joined they could not completely control it.
During the earlier part of this period James West, recorder of St. Albans
and its Member from 1741 to 1768, had considerable influence, and in
1780 Lord Salisbury began to cultivate an interest there. There was also
a large number of venal voters who welcomed opposition to the established
interests. These two boroughs, so similar in outward appearance, had
only their outward appearance in common.

The remaining medium-sized freeman boroughs were all to some extent
under patronage. In six of them there was no contest during this period:
Grantham, Huntingdon, Ludlow, Monmouth, New Woodstock, and
Wenlock. Influence over these boroughs depended less on property than
on tradition supplemented by services to the corporation and freemen.
Thus Oldfield wrote about Huntingdon in the 1792 edition of his *History
of the Boroughs*:

The interest of the Earl of Sandwich is so powerful as always to return two
Members; and this he effects not by weight of property, for his lordship has but one
house in the whole town, but by his popularity, and the obligations he was enabled
to confer upon some of his principal friends during his connexion with Lord North's
Administration.

Sandwich used his official positions and his interest in the East India Company to find places for Huntingdon freemen and their relatives; his interest at Huntingdon was based on the long-standing connexion his family had had with the borough and was buttressed by Government patronage. In a similar way the Townshend and Walpole families controlled Great Yarmouth. But Yarmouth had an electorate of about 800, and a strong party, led by the Dissenters, opposed to the corporation; and in 1784 the Townshend-Walpole interest was overthrown by a combination of anti-corporation feeling and support for Pitt's Administration. Access to Government patronage, though useful, was by no means essential to control a freeman borough. The Duke of Devonshire held one seat at Derby throughout this period, though for most of the time his family were in opposition. The Martin and Dowdeswell families held Tewkesbury without Government patronage; nor did it save Sir John Turner at King's Lynn from the challenge of Crisp Molineux, a friend of Wilkes and admirer of Chatham.

The Admiralty effectively controlled two of these constituencies, Plymouth and Sandwich; and maintained a precarious hold over one seat at Rochester. At Plymouth, where the electorate numbered about 200, Admiralty control was achieved through the corporation. There was no opposition until 1780, when there began a movement to extend the franchise to the freeholders; and the Admiralty lost one seat at the general election of 1784. At Sandwich (about 700 voters) the Admiralty increased its influence from one seat in 1754 to both in 1784. The credit for this remarkable feat (for in general Government influence in boroughs was declining during this period) belongs to Philip Stephens, secretary to the Admiralty 1763–95, and M.P. for Sandwich 1768–1806. 'The inhabitants of this place', Oldfield wrote about Sandwich in 1792, 'are bound to this gentleman by every tie of gratitude, as there is scarcely a single family some part of which has not been provided for by him in the Admiralty, navy, or marines.' Rochester had about the same number of voters as Sandwich, but there was a strong independent party among the artisans and small shopkeepers, and there were eight contests during this period. In 1765, when Grey Cooper, candidate of the newly-appointed Rockingham Administration, was opposed by John Calcraft, the Government went so far as to send three members of the Admiralty Board to Rochester to canvass the borough and 'do any Admiralty favour that could procure a vote'. The old Duke of Newcastle was scandalized at this open avowal of Government influence in the borough. 'Sure it was very imprudent in our friends to hold ... an Admiralty Board at Rochester', he wrote to Rockingham. 'The same thing might have [been] done without the éclat. Sir Robert [Walpole] dared not do that.' Yet it seems to have been necessary, for Cooper had a majority of only 33 on a poll of over 500.

In fact these freeman boroughs could be a source of great trouble and expense to a would-be patron. Lord Gower allowed his tenants at Newcastle-under-Lyme to live rent-free, yet in 1774 nearly one-third of the electorate voted for a candidate in opposition to his interest. Gower and Lord Anson jointly controlled Lichfield but only after a long-drawn out struggle against a powerful independent party. There were five contests there between 1747 and 1761; and in 1761 the independent candidate received 313 votes out of a poll of nearly 700. At Wells, where the Tudway family had influence, there were five contests between 1754 and 1782, and in 1768 there was a large creation of honorary freemen to maintain the Tudway interest. And at Okehampton, as is described below (p. 70), both patrons in 1784 were anxious to end their connexion with a borough which had become both troublesome and unsafe.

The 34 smaller freeman boroughs, with electorates below 200, were mostly under patronage (in eighteenth-century parlance closed) by 1754. In 16 of them there was no contest during this period; while six boroughs went to the poll at one election only. Bishop's Castle, Cambridge, and Winchelsea, relatively open in 1754, had become closed by 1790. By then only five of these constituencies could be described as open boroughs.

The easiest way to control a freeman borough was to keep the electorate as small as possible. 'I am not fond of numbers', wrote Edward Milward, Government manager at Hastings, in 1761, 'for I have reduced ours from near 60 to 30 within eight years past.' Sometimes this process was taken so far that the freedom was restricted to members of the corporation, and the borough ceased to be a freeman borough in everything but name. An alternative way to control a freeman borough was to confer the freedom on none but trusted relatives or dependants of the patron. It was by this means that John Mortlock converted Cambridge into a pocket borough in the 1780s. If a Government department controlled the borough, as the Treasury did Hastings, a judicious distribution of Government places would secure the electorate, provided care was taken to choose men who could not afford to lose their offices. In the last resort, the freemen had to be bribed. Edward Wortley Montagu maintained his influence at Bossiney by lending money to the freemen 'on mortgage bonds and notes without any interest', and by paying the salary of the schoolmaster: a not unusual combination of private and public benefactions. His successor, Lord Bute, found it necessary to make a direct payment at each election.

Yet even in the tiniest freeman borough the electors could sometimes show a surprising degree of independence, or at least make a show of it to frighten the patron and exact from him higher terms. 'Although these people are never to be had without the perquisite', wrote Lord Edgcumbe's agent in 1769 about the electors of Bossiney, 'they are sometimes so obstinate as not to be had with it.' It cost John Offley £942 to be returned unopposed for East Retford in 1768, of which over £700 was spent on treating the 150 electors. Sir Jacob Garrard Downing controlled Dunwich by restricting the number of freemen to thirteen and allowing them to live rent-free, and to make assurance doubly sure obliged each man to sign a bond as a guarantee of loyalty. On Downing's death in 1764 his widow hoped to succeed to his interest; but the freemen of Dunwich, regardless of their debts and their bonds, offered themselves in a body to Miles Barne. A similar change of electoral allegiance occurred at Grampound on the death of Lord Edgcumbe in 1758: the freemen, determined 'to have no further connexions with the [Edgcumbe] family', put the borough into the hands of Edward Eliot and William Trevanion.

At Lyme Regis, where the number of voters did not exceed 50, there was after 1777 a strong movement to free the borough from the control of the Earl of Westmorland; and it was only by the creation of seventeen honorary freemen that Westmorland maintained his interest. During the minority of the 5th Earl of Carlisle, his family's hold on Morpeth was seriously shaken. According to a legal brief, drawn up in 1762:

For a long series of years the family of Carlisle had been accustomed to name the Members of Parliament . . . From this almost uninterrupted possession they began gradually to regard it as part of their private property and . . . having previous to the late elections treated the freemen *de haut en bas* and in such manner as they judged tyrannical and an insult upon their liberties, the whole corporation and those who wished well to it were in an uproar . . . To such a height had this political contest inflamed the minds of the freemen, that any opponent of the family of Carlisle would have been received in Morpeth with open arms.

Note the use of the word 'political': for the freemen of Morpeth this was a real political issue, involving the very existence of their rights and liberties. A group calling themselves 'the friends of liberty' issued a declaration of independence, and began to fight the Carlisle family both in the law courts and at parliamentary elections. The phraseology and the slogans used by the opponents of Lord Carlisle are curiously like those later used by the Americans during the revolutionary war; and both the Americans and the freemen of Morpeth were fighting to maintain their independence of a patron too insistent upon his rights. But while the 'sons of liberty' in America threw off their yoke, the 'friends of liberty' at Morpeth ran out of money and had to surrender to Lord Carlisle.

The five boroughs still relatively open in 1790 were Hedon, Hythe, Poole, Totnes, and Wigan. Of these, three (Hedon, Totnes, and Wigan) were open only in the sense that in each constituency there were a number of would-be patrons struggling for control and the freemen had room to manœuvre. Hythe is a rare example of a borough which was closed in 1754 and open in 1790, reversing the trend in most constituencies. In 1754 the Duke of Dorset, lord warden of the Cinque Ports, controlled both seats. On Dorset's death in 1765 his successor as lord warden, Lord Holdernesse, claimed the patronage of the borough; while Dorset's son, Lord George Sackville, contended that his father's interest was a personal, not an official, one. The issue was decided at the general election of 1768 when Holdernesse's candidates won, largely because they had the support of Government. But in fact Hythe managed to throw off both the Sackville family and the lord warden. Poole, though it had only about 100 voters, was a very independent constituency, and was contested at four elections during this period. The corporation was controlled by a group of substantial merchants, and no one succeeded in building up a lasting interest there.

The third main group of English borough constituencies consisted of 37 boroughs where the right of voting was in inhabitants paying scot and lot, that is in inhabitant householders who paid the poor rate. In size of electorate these constituencies varied enormously, from 12,000 at Westminster, the largest urban constituency in Great Britain, to only two at Gatton, where no one lived within the bounds of the parliamentary borough and voters were put in specially at election times. The scot and lot franchise excluded the lowest and poorest element of the population, but included also many uneducated and needy voters. All but six of these boroughs were contested at least once during this period. Seaford, Shaftesbury, and Southwark were contested seven times; Great Marlow and Reading, six; Bridgwater, Penryn, and Westminster, five times. Scot and lot boroughs were most contentious places, and from the point of view of a patron very difficult to control.

Yet the six constituencies where there was no contest, together with Steyning (where the one contest in 1761 was a farce), were virtually pocket boroughs. In each, control over the representation was achieved through the ownership of property in the borough. One of the Duke of Newcastle's Sussex agents wrote to him in 1767 about Steyning:

The state of the borough is this. There are 102 in number who claim a right of voting, but not more than 90 whose claim will bear a scrutiny. Out of this number Sir John Honywood has 40 tenants who at present are all disposed to stand by him, and about six or seven others who are full as closely attached to him as any of his tenants. This gives him nearly or quite a majority of the 90 real votes. The rest are all a rope of sand and may be had by anybody.

And in 1784 Thomas Cooke, mayor of Stamford and its returning officer, wrote about his borough (which had an electorate of about 500):

The interest of Lord Exeter ... is so great, arising from three causes, viz. his property, his employment of tradesmen, and his visiting and entertaining the gentry, that no one ever opposes those who are honoured with his recommendation, and the business of elections in this town for many years has been conducted from the beginning to the end in a mere formal, civil method between the agents of Lord Exeter, the candidates, and the mayor.

Aldborough (50 voters) was largely the property of the Duke of Newcastle, Amersham (70 voters) of the Drake family of Shardeloes; and in these constituencies the patron's control was almost as complete as if they had been burgage boroughs. At Corfe Castle (100 voters) two local families shared the representation, and Eye (200) was under the patronage of Lord Cornwallis, whose seat of Brome Hall was just outside the town: both boroughs required care and attention and in neither was the patron's hold beyond challenge: Gatton, often quoted as a typical rotten borough, was in fact an absolutely unique constituency.

Three scot and lot boroughs had electorates of 1,000 or above: Westminster (12,000), Southwark (2,000), and Newark (1,000). At

Newark the Duke of Rutland and the Duke of Newcastle each recommended to one seat, but it was by agreement and compromise with other
interests in the borough; and there were three contests during this period.
Westminster and Southwark were part of the metropolitan area, and
were strongly influenced by political movements emanating from London.
From 1768 onwards London radicalism was the strongest force in these
constituencies and at all elections political issues were dominant.
Westminster was a prestige constituency, the seat of the court and of
Parliament, and Government candidates were heavily subsidized by the
Treasury—often with little result. The Members for Westminster were
always of high social standing, and none but sons of peers or baronets
were chosen during this period. Southwark, on the other hand, was a
commercial constituency, and its representatives were always local
businessmen or City merchants.

The remaining 27 scot and lot boroughs may be broadly divided into
two types: the venal boroughs and the boroughs under some degree
of patronage. These categories must not be taken as exclusive: many of
these 27 boroughs exhibit characteristics of both types, and two
(Milborne Port and Penryn) were both venal and under patronage to
such an extent that to put them into either category would be misleading.
The ten venal boroughs were Arundel, Callington, Great Marlow,
Mitchell, New Shoreham, Reading, St. Ives, Shaftesbury, Stockbridge,
and Wootton Bassett. None, except Reading, had an electorate of more
than 300; and a remark made about Callington in 1768 applied to all
of them: money 'really was the constitution of the borough'. In 1754 the
electors of Mitchell were described as 'low, indigent people', who would
support any patron 'from whom they have reason to expect most money
and favours'. At Shaftesbury and St. Ives it was the custom to lend
money to the voters against their notes of hand, which were later
destroyed if they voted the right way—an indication not merely that
the electors were venal but that they could not be trusted. And here are
two examples to show the extent to which bribery could go in this type
of constituency: at Wootton Bassett in 1754 Lord Bolingbroke paid thirty
guineas a man, and his tavern expenses came to over £1,000; and at
Reading in 1754 forty guineas is said to have been offered for a single
vote—but then John Dodd, the defeated candidate, was beaten by a
majority of one vote only on a poll of over 600.

Worst among the venal boroughs were unquestionably Arundel and

New Shoreham, and both exhibit a form of organization common in venal boroughs—of voters banding themselves together into an association to sell their votes to the best advantage. A London newspaper, the *English Chronicle*, thus reported the general election of 1780 at Arundel:

It appeared that a majority of the electors had formed themselves into a society by the name of the Malt-house Club . . . and that the Honourable Mr. Wyndham . . . offered himself a candidate to this society to represent the borough in Parliament. The chairman of the club gave him to understand that as he was a gentleman of the neighbourhood and recommended by the Earl of Surrey they would give him the preference to any other candidate, provided he would speak so as for them to *understand him*. Mr. Wyndham told them he was an independent man and meant to remain so, that if they did him the honour to elect him their Member he would serve them faithfully and honestly to the best of his abilities. This was not the species of elocution adapted to the organs of the chairman, and he informed the honourable candidate that he might as well have said nothing. Sir Patrick Craufurd was then called in, and he, with a much keener perception of the peculiar style of oratory that would produce the best effect, told the Club that if they would honour him with their suffrages he would return the favour with a present of thirty guineas to each voter. Sir Patrick was given to understand that he spoke to the purpose, and the chairman pledged himself to the body to get another candidate . . . who would speak in a language equally intelligible and convincing.

This other candidate was Thomas Fitzherbert, a self-made business man, who was ready to give £3,000 and who apparently gave it more discreetly than Craufurd had done. On the poll, Craufurd received 167 votes, Fitzherbert 131, and Wyndham 69; but the House of Commons declared Craufurd's election void because of bribery.

At New Shoreham about 1760 a group of voters formed the Christian Society, originally a kind of friendly society, but which soon developed into an organization for selling the borough's parliamentary representation. 'Upon any vacancy in the representation of the borough', one of the electors testified before the House of Commons in 1770, 'the society always appointed a committee to treat with the candidates for the purchase of the seat, and . . . the committee were constantly instructed to get the most money . . . they could.' The society preferred candidates who could place orders for building ships—the town's main industry. The activities of the Christian Society having been revealed to the House of Commons, a bill was introduced disfranchising the corrupt electors and including within the borough the 40s. freeholders in the rape of Bramber. The number of electors was by this means increased to about 800, and henceforth New Shoreham became virtually a county constituency in miniature, noted for its respectability.

It was clearly a costly business to try to maintain an interest in this type of borough, and patrons changed quickly. In 1754 Henry Fox controlled Stockbridge; by 1774 he had lost the borough to the Luttrell family. Lord Ilchester and Lord Shaftesbury, who in 1754 shared the patronage of Shaftesbury, found it too expensive to fight the nabobs who invaded the borough after 1771, and sold out. Lady Orford, who controlled Callington in 1754, had practically lost the borough by 1784; and William Clayton sold his parliamentary interest at Great Marlow in 1787. The tendency on the part of patrons to abandon their boroughs (or to be driven out if they remained) increased towards the end of this period with the growing wealth of the country and the greater competition for seats in Parliament; and with the growth of party an element of political idealism was introduced into the larger of the venal boroughs. Thus at the by-election at Reading in February 1782 Richard Aldworth Neville was obliged to declare that if elected he would not vote for the continuation of the American war.

Of the scot and lot boroughs under patronage, Seaford is an interesting example of a constituency which was controlled by deliberately restricting the size of the electorate. In 1754 the borough was managed by the Duke of Newcastle on behalf of the Treasury; the number of voters never exceeded 50, and was often less; and the majority of the corporation held places under the Treasury. Care was taken to ensure that only those thought to be reliably inclined to Government should be rated to the poor, and consequently Seaford seemed to be a safe Government borough. But there was a section of the electorate, mostly labourers and fishermen, who were unsuitable for Government service; and it was to them that George Medley appealed when he stood in 1761 against the Treasury candidates. One of Newcastle's agents wrote to the Duke about a conversation he had had with an elector of Seaford:

I then asked him by what means it was possible that the lower class of Mr. Medley's voters could attach themselves so firmly to him (almost a stranger) in opposition to your Grace, who has been a continued patron to them for so many years. He answered it was through animosity for many grievances and injuries they imagine they have suffered, and also in the firm confidence they place in Mr. Medley's performing his promises whether he gains his point or not, such as erecting a free school at Seaford, procuring immediate admission into the hospitals (all expenses paid) for the poor people on any occasion, large donations every Christmas, &c.

Where the electors were poor but honest, schemes of social insurance instead of bribery were used to win them over. Similarly, at Fowey, which was a decaying port, Lord Edgcumbe and Jonathan Rashleigh in 1766 drew up plans for restoring full employment to the town: they were to fit out two ships to make a fishing voyage to Newfoundland and employ the electors of Fowey 'in their respective occupations'.

Medley's plan failed at Seaford because it did not appeal to the better-off class of electors who were capable of holding Government employments. Next, he won over the bailiff, and with his help began increasing the number of inhabitants rated to the poor. By now George Grenville was first lord of the Treasury, and was just as keen on maintaining the Treasury's interest as Newcastle had been; the Crown challenged the legality of the bailiff's actions in the courts, won its case, and thus for a time preserved its interest at Seaford. In 1774, when Stephen Sayre and John Chetwood stood against the Treasury candidates, their counsel stated before the House of Commons committee which tried the election petition:

It appeared that about fourteen of the voters for the sitting Members [the Treasury candidates] were custom house officers or boatmen, by which they got £30 a year. That exclusive of what they got in that way, several of them were in worse circumstances than several of the persons who were not rated [though entitled to be]. It seemed to be admitted that those who were not custom house boatmen were of sufficient substance to be rated.

The Treasury interest was weakened by the disfranchisement of the revenue officers in 1782, which opened the door to a host of candidates. The most persistent was Henry Flood, who in 1786 succeeded in getting his supporters at Seaford rated to the poor; and forced the Treasury to adopt new methods to retain its control over the borough.

The remaining non-venal scot and lot constituencies had electorates ranging from 250 to about 500, and are extremely difficult to classify. Wareham, which in the earlier part of the period was contested by the Drax and Pitt families, became almost a pocket borough in 1768 when John Calcraft acquired their property in the town. At Abingdon, Bridport,

Dorchester, Leominster, and Wallingford, it is difficult to trace any permanent interest, and political managers were rarely able to predict the result of elections in these boroughs. John Robinson described Bridport in 1780 as 'in a very dubious state', and in 1784 wrote that it was very uncertain who would be returned. At Leominster, several neighbouring families had an interest but the borough was very jealous of its independence, and it was said in 1767 that if two brothers were to stand at Leominster 'they must be clear of each other'. Yet political issues do not seem to have counted for much in these constituencies.

Seven of these boroughs had patrons: Bridgwater, Chichester, Lewes, New Windsor, Peterborough, Tamworth, and Warwick; yet none was a pocket borough, and each had at least two contests during this period. These boroughs had placed themselves voluntarily under patronage, usually that of a local magnate, because of the advantages which it brought them, yet in the last resort the patron was unable to enforce his commands. Local men were preferred to strangers, and it was generally understood that the patron would recommend to one seat only. At Chichester, John Page told the Duke of Richmond in 1760 that if he tried to recommend to both seats, he would finish by losing all his influence in the borough—a prediction which was very nearly fulfilled towards the end of this period. At Peterborough, where there were nearly 400 voters, most of them 'very necessitous people not influenced by anybody', Lord Rockingham warned his nephew, Lord Fitzwilliam, in 1775: 'The attempt to have two and keep two will, I should fear, be an endless trouble and expense to you, and perhaps it would be wisest to avoid the temptation.' In 1780 Lord Warwick provoked a revolt against his interest at Warwick by putting up two candidates. And even at Tamworth, where after 1768 the patrons, Lord Townshend and Lord Weymouth, had a very tight control over the borough, there was a large independent party.

The difficulties which could be encountered by the patron of one of these medium-sized scot and lot constituencies under some degree of patronage is well illustrated at Lewes which had an electorate of about 200. From 1754 to 1768 its patron was the Duke of Newcastle, but there was an undercurrent of hostility to Pelham family predominance, especially marked when from 1763 onwards Newcastle began recommending strangers. In January 1767 an agent reported to Newcastle a conversation he had had with a voter of Lewes:

He acknowledges that a spirit has arose among some of his All Saints neighbours not favourable to the election of strangers, and upon that account only . . . they would rather have chosen to be represented by some neighbouring gentleman, and in his own mind he could not but think that such a plan would be reasonable and proper, and he could wish to see it brought about at the next election.

At the general election of 1768 Newcastle lost a Member, largely because he withdrew his support from the candidate the town wanted. Deeply hurt by what he called 'the base and ungrateful behaviour of the town of Lewes', Newcastle resolved to punish the electors: he would give no plate for the races and provide no entertainments; announced his intention to withdraw the assizes from Lewes; and gave orders to evict his tenants and dismiss his tradesmen who had voted against his candidates. This was displeasing to Thomas Pelham, Newcastle's cousin and heir to his Sussex estates, who realized it would be the ruin of the Pelham interest at Lewes; and Newcastle's friend, the Duke of Richmond, also strongly advised against it:

It will be a handle for them to say that your friendship for Lewes was only for the sake of choosing the Members, that you looked upon them as slaves who were not only to obey your orders but to guess your will, that the moment they presumed to think of choosing one gentleman of the town to represent them they were directly to meet with your Grace's displeasure.

Newcastle relented, and declared that the tenants should remain, provided they would apologize. Most of them did; but the report of Newcastle's agent shows that some of them also remained obdurate. Thus, James Hutchins, a tailor, would 'say nothing as to future promises'; and Newcastle's agent wrote about another voter, Thomas Cripps, a cooper:

Is very unwilling to leave his house, but says he will never acknowledge his being sorry for his manner of voting, because he has declared to his acquaintance that he never would use that expression. Says he will make no absolute promises as to future times, except that he will never be ungrateful.

Here is an aspect of eighteenth-century electioneering often ignored: the ability of small men to defy a powerful patron. After Newcastle's death in November 1768 the Pelham influence declined, and for the remainder of this period one Member at least was always a townsman.

A large Dissenting population, such as there was at Lewes, always provided a leaven of independence in a constituency. Similarly, political issues, when they arose, could be an incentive to throw off what was felt as the yoke of patronage. For example, at Bridgwater in the earlier part of this period three interests contended for the borough, but by 1768 Lord Poulett appeared to have the upper hand. In 1780 a group of electors opposed to the American war invited Charles James Fox to stand on a joint interest with Benjamin Allen, one of the sitting Members. Fox did not appear at the election, nor if he had been elected is it likely that he would have chosen to represent Bridgwater: he stood as the candidate of the Opposition, and those who voted for him presumably did so on political grounds. He was badly defeated; and Allen, his partner, though second on the poll, was unseated in favour of a Government candidate. Nevertheless, what matters is that the patrons had been defied. At the general election of 1784 Fox's friends in the borough sponsored the candidature of Sir Gilbert Elliot, a prominent member of Fox's party; but again the effort failed, Elliot receiving only five votes. Distinguished names were not sufficient to carry an election when there was no burning political issue; and in any case much depended on good local leadership and organization.

At New Windsor, on the other hand, the methods of influence and interest were used to serve a political purpose. Windsor was in more senses than one a royal borough, but since the death of the Duke of Cumberland in 1765 royal influence had been in abeyance; and at the dissolution in 1780 both Members belonged to the Opposition. One of them, Admiral Augustus Keppel, was particularly obnoxious to Government, and his defeat would be a great blow to the Opposition. Lord North persuaded Peniston Portlock Powney, a Berkshire landowner, to stand, and promised him financial support; and the King personally canvassed his tradesmen on Powney's behalf. Keppel was defeated (but by only 16 votes), and George III became the effective patron of New Windsor. At the general election of 1784 candidates who supported Pitt's Administration were returned, and in 1787 a Government candidate who had no connexion at all with the borough.

The fourth group comprised the 27 corporation boroughs, those in which the right of voting was confined to the corporation (one of them, Banbury, being a single Member constituency) and in none did the electorate exceed 60. It might be supposed that a closed, self-recruiting corporation, composed for the most part of small tradesmen and professional men, would be peculiarly liable to the influence of a patron; and in fact fifteen were pocket boroughs (Banbury, Brackley, Buckingham, Calne, Christchurch, Droitwich, Harwich, Lostwithiel, Marlborough, New Romney, Newton, Thetford, Tiverton, Truro, and Wilton). In thirteen of these there was no contest during this period, and the patron was usually a neighbouring country gentleman or peer, seated within almost walking distance of the borough: Lord Guilford at Banbury, Lord Temple at Buckingham, Lord Shelburne at Calne, the Duke of Grafton at Thetford, &c. Harwich was a Treasury borough, the majority of the corporation being composed of revenue or post office officials; and even after the passing of Crewe's Act disfranchising the revenue officers in 1782 the Treasury remained in control.

The methods by which a patron maintained his interest in a corporation borough were many and various. Lord Pembroke packed the corporation of Wilton with his relatives and friends. Lord Shelburne owned extensive property in and around Calne and was lord of two adjoining manors. Lord Bruce (created in 1776 Earl of Ailesbury) employed the tradesmen of Marlborough, contributed to the relief of the poor, and gave prizes for the races (an important source of custom for the shopkeepers). His estate agent was a member of the corporation, and he secured an agreement that no new burgesses were to be created without his consent. To have access to Government patronage was, of course, an advantage but it was by no means essential; several patrons of corporation boroughs (e.g., Temple, Shelburne, Grafton, and Pembroke) were in opposition for long periods without effectively endangering their control.

The two pocket boroughs which were contested were Brackley and Truro. Without care and attention no corporation borough was safe; and local notables, often very much upon their dignity, had to be handled with tact and consideration. In 1754 Brackley seemed to be a complete pocket borough of the Duke of Bridgwater, but at the general election he lost one seat to a total stranger, Thomas Humberston, who bribed a majority of the corporation. Humberston's success was helped by the fact that the Duke was a minor and absent on the grand tour: minors and absentees were fair game for borough adventurers. Truro revolted against Lord Falmouth in 1780, complaining that his 'avarice, increasing with age, hath grossly abused a confidence as complete perhaps as unguarded, disinterested friendship ever placed in man'.

Something of the trouble involved in managing these small corporation boroughs can be seen at New Romney and Tiverton, neither of which went to the poll during this period. Sir Edward Dering at New Romney is said to have let out his property there to the electors of the borough at very easy rents; since he usually sold one of the seats to a Government candidate, he presumably recouped himself that way. His control of the borough had been won in the late 1750s against fierce competition from Rose Fuller, one of the sitting Members. The object of their attention at New Romney was an almost illiterate old woman named Mrs. Tookey, who had two sons and two nephews in the corporation. In an electorate which never exceeded 40 and was often much less, the change of allegiance of even four voters could be decisive. By outstripping Fuller in flattery and blandishments to Mrs. Tookey, and by encouraging her wishes for the social advancement of her family, Dering secured the support of her relatives and with it control over the corporation.

At Tiverton personal rivalries, the opposition between the Anglican-dominated corporation and the Dissenters, and economic troubles in the cloth-making industry, combined to present a very confusing electoral picture. The chief interest in 1754 was in Oliver Peard, the most considerable merchant in Tiverton and receiver of the land tax for Devon. Most of the corporation were clothiers, and by lending money to them and allowing arrears of tax to accumulate, Peard secured the controlling interest in the borough. On his death in 1764 the Baring brothers, rich Exeter merchants and bankers, aspired to his office and influence; and the corporation were divided among themselves. The more considerable merchants

did not approve electing any man into the corporation ... by whom they should be kept in as absolute a state of dependence as that from which they had lately been freed; and ... did not think it would be promotive of the trading interest of the town that any merchant should be receiver of the land tax, as it would give an individual the command of large sums of money, a private advantage often exercised heretofore to the injury of other merchants resident in the town, by its being employed to monopolize the trade.

The smaller merchants and the cloth workers, on the other hand, welcomed the Barings who would bring employment to the town; rioting followed their dissensions and troops had to be called in to preserve order. Nathaniel Ryder, M.P. for Tiverton since 1756, formed an alliance with the leading men in the borough; John Duntze, as Exeter clothier, was elected into the corporation; and the receiver's place was given to an ex-army officer, not engaged in trade. Henceforth Ryder and Duntze jointly controlled the borough, Duntze by bringing trade to the town, and Ryder by financing the cloth merchants when they were in need. Throughout this period the Dissenters agitated for the extension of the franchise to those paying scot and lot, but so long as there was full employment in the cloth-making industry their agitation was never formidable.

Eight corporation boroughs were disputed during this period: Andover, Bodmin, Bury St. Edmunds, Helston, Newport (Isle of Wight), Saltash, Scarborough, and Yarmouth (Isle of Wight). All were to some extent under patronage, yet none was completely closed. At Newport, Yarmouth, and Scarborough the Government had considerable influence, which was usually decisive. At Andover the Earl of Portsmouth recommended one Member, but on the understanding that he left the disposal of the second seat to the corporation. Bury St. Edmunds was disputed between three neighbouring families: the Earls of Bristol, the Dukes of Grafton, and the Davers family; and there were three contests during this period. Scarborough was similarly disputed and in addition had a reputation for venality. 'The voters of Scarborough are happy in the present situation of things', wrote a correspondent to the Duke of Rutland in 1787. 'Three interests, and a contest inevitable!' Yet in all fairness it should be said that Scarborough stuck to the Rutland family when they were in opposition from 1770 to 1782 and deprived of access to Government patronage. And even in a corporation borough, and a venal one at that, when there was a real political issue it had its weight in elections. At Scarborough in 1784 George Osbaldeston 'was obliged publicly to explain away' his support of Charles James Fox 'previously to his being elected'.

Four corporation boroughs—Malmesbury, Devizes, Salisbury, and Bath—each in its own way maintained some degree of independence, though independence is perhaps too strong a word to describe the political state of Malmesbury, where the families of Howard and Fox long contended for the supremacy. During most of this period the real power in the corporation was Edmund Wilkins, a Malmesbury apothecary, who used his influence first in favour of Lord Suffolk, then of Lord Holland, and finally on his own account. From 1774 Wilkins held the lucrative office of receiver of the land tax for North Wiltshire, and from 1779 to 1782 he had a subsidy from Government of £700 per annum.

He maintained his control by paying ten members of the corporation an annual retaining fee of £30 each and exacting from them a bond of £500 as a guarantee of their loyalty. And since he placed the representation of Malmesbury at the disposal of Government, it was naturally counted as a Government borough; and at the general election of 1784 John Robinson, the Government expert on elections, expected Wilkins to return two supporters of Pitt's Administration. But Wilkins jumped on the wrong band waggon and returned two supporters of the Opposition; however, he soon realized his mistake, and at the by-election of 1789 accepted a candidate recommended by Pitt.

Devizes, Salisbury, and Bath were genuinely open constituencies. Devizes was controlled by substantial clothiers and its representatives were always local men: its recorder or a merchant engaged in the cloth trade; and in 1761 and 1765 it defied the attempts of Sir Samuel Fludyer, probably the richest London clothier, to secure a seat for his brother. Money alone was not a sufficient recommendation at Devizes: indeed, there seems to have been some hostility among the smaller merchants to Fludyer, who, if he had succeeded in getting a foothold, might by his wealth and business connexions have come to dominate the corporation both economically and politically.

The corporation of Salisbury was composed of small gentry and substantial tradesmen; bribery was unknown; local men were always chosen; and it was considered a great honour to represent the city in Parliament. 'A seat for Salisbury', wrote Lord Herbert in 1789, 'is in my opinion a better thing than one in the House of Lords.' Bath, also, was a dignified and independent constituency, and took pride in having chosen William Pitt as one of its representatives. Sir John Sebright wrote to Pitt on 28 March 1761, shortly after his election:

Conscious of the dignity of their choice and the honour they derive from it, it has been with great difficulty that your electors are persuaded to accept of the customary treats. They think their present election cannot be too distinguishable from all others by rejecting every appearance of interest.

The Members for Bath during this period were either local men or national figures.

To sum up it may be said that in corporation boroughs everything depended on the economic standing of the men who composed the corporation. If they were small men, economically dependent upon a neighbouring peer or country gentleman, they tended to align themselves politically under his lead. If there was no family of sufficient wealth or standing in the vicinity, then the wealthiest man in the corporation would assume the lead, as Peard did at Tiverton or Wilkins at Malmesbury. Only when the members of the corporation were sufficiently well-to-do and imbued with corporate pride and dignity, as at Bath or Salisbury, was the corporation borough able to remain independent.

A burgage is defined in Beatson's *Parliamentary Register* as 'one undivided and indivisible tenement, neither created nor capable of being created within time of memory, which has immemorially given a right of voting'. In other words, the franchise in burgage boroughs was attached to property, not to persons, and could not be increased or diminished; and they were predestined to become pocket boroughs. For if one man owned a majority of the burgages, he was in a position to control the representation of the borough, no matter the size of the electorate; and a Member who could say that he sat by burgage tenure was understood to have an absolutely safe seat. It was the usual practice in burgage boroughs to keep the houses empty until shortly before an election, when the patron would convey them to friends or dependants who would return the conveyances to him after the election was over. Boroughs were handed down from father to son like family heirlooms, or bought and sold, like other kinds of landed property, with the parliamentary representation allowed for in the purchase price. Thus in 1779 Sir Robert Clayton sold his burgage houses at Bletchingley for £10,000, though their intrinsic worth was only about £100 per annum; they comprised, however, all the burgages in the borough and thus gave their owner complete control over its parliamentary representation.

Even so, there were factors which made burgage boroughs not quite as safe as they appeared to be. Occasional conveyances for the purposes of elections were frowned upon by the House of Commons, and were attended with all sorts of legal difficulties. In the larger boroughs particularly, not all the burgages were held by the patron, and where there were real voters in a borough their goodwill had to be won. There was no contest at Malton throughout this period, but Lord Rockingham, the patron of the borough, always made his Members attend their election. At Horsham, Lord Irwin owned a majority of the burgages, but the returning officers were chosen at the court leet of the lord of the manor, the Duke of Norfolk. At Newport (Cornwall) the right of election was in burgage holders paying scot and lot, which meant that the voters had to be resident; and at Newtown they had to be freemen. Even burgage boroughs, unless they had a very tiny electorate, required care and attention.

During this period there were 29 burgage boroughs in England, with electorates ranging from 300 at Malton to seven at Old Sarum. Eight were in Yorkshire (out of fourteen boroughs in that county) and six in Wiltshire; the remainder were spread over ten counties. (Cornwall, pre-eminently a county of small boroughs, contained only one burgage borough.) By 1754 thirteen of these boroughs had become completely closed and in these there were no contests throughout this period. In eight boroughs both seats were under the control of one patron (though the patrons changed through inheritance and sale of property): Bletching-ley, Boroughbridge, East Grinstead, Horsham, Malton, Old Sarum, Ripon, and Thirsk; in a further five the representation was shared between two patrons: Bere Alston (until 1780), Midhurst (until 1761), Northallerton, Richmond (until 1761), and Whitchurch (until 1774). No patron controlled more than one borough.

Four other boroughs were also to all intents and purposes closed, but because of peculiar circumstances there was a contest in each. At Petersfield in 1761 Edward Gibbon the historian challenged the hold of the Jolliffe family on the borough, in the belief that John Jolliffe, who had conveyed his burgages to his wife, could not legally re-convey them to dummy voters; but Gibbon did not proceed to the poll. In 1774 John Luttrell stood a poll, and on petition to the House of Commons unsuccessfully questioned Jolliffe's right to convey the burgages. At Knaresborough in 1784 Sir John Coghill and Bacon Frank opposed the Duke of Devonshire's candidates, contending that the right of election should be in the resident householders. An attempt was made at Heytesbury in 1754 to challenge the A'Court family's control of the borough, and though it was foredoomed to failure it caused the family considerable uneasiness.

These were pitfalls which might entrap any borough patron, and generally their only result was to tighten the patron's hold on the borough. The misfortune which befell Assheton Curzon at Clitheroe in 1780 was unique during this period: a deliberate attempt by one partner to cheat the other out of his share in the representation of the borough.

Curzon and Thomas Lister held jointly 53 out of the 102 burgages and recommended to one seat each. But in 1780 Lister refused to agree to the conveyance of the joint burgages, and, having a majority of the remainder, proceeded to recommend to both seats. He deprived Curzon 'of the natural advantages of his property' without in any way changing the nature of the borough—a trick hard to justify by eighteenth-century standards.

Of the remaining burgage boroughs, eight had contests: Appleby, Bramber, Cockermouth, Great Bedwyn, Newport (Cornwall), Newtown, Weobley, and Westbury; but by 1790 all were closed. At Westbury the Earl of Abingdon owned a majority of the burgages, but in 1754 his control of the borough was very insecure because the burgages were let on long leases. 'As most of the tenants were poor', wrote Abingdon's attorney, 'it afforded great scope for any adventurer to fight his Lordship with his own weapons.' In the 1760s the 4th Earl of Abingdon closed the borough by buying most of the independent burgages, packing the corporation with his own friends and dependants, and keeping the burgages unoccupied until shortly before an election.

Cockermouth and Appleby were both the objects of take-over operations by Sir James Lowther, whose electoral activities often resembled the business deals of a modern financial magnate. Cockermouth had about 280 burgages, and when Lowther began his campaign in September 1756 he held only 24, while his rival, Lord Egremont, had 80. Lowther's tactics were masterly: he began by accusing his rival of the very thing he intended to do himself, namely of trying to close the borough, and appealed to the proprietors to join their burgages 'into one common flock', the better to resist Egremont, offering £120 for each burgage. When the proprietors held back, hoping for a better price, Lowther's agents spread the rumour that he intended to buy only a limited number, and the poorer proprietors rushed to sell. Egremont's agent thereupon proposed to buy twenty burgages at £500 each, but only seven were now available at that price. With Egremont falling back in the race and the price having increased, the more well-to-do proprietors began to sell; obviously, once Lowther had a majority the price would drop, and those smaller proprietors who had hitherto supported the Egremont interest now hastened to offer their burgages to Lowther. In a little over a fortnight Lowther had bought 134 burgages, at a cost of over £58,000, and had gained complete control of the borough.

A similar attempt by Lowther to take over Lord Thanet's interest at Appleby was unsuccessful. At the beginning of 1754, when Lowther began to increase his burgage holding in the borough, Thanet retaliated, and purchased 65 burgages at a cost of over £18,000. He now held over 100, out of a total of 150, and could face the forthcoming general election with confidence. But he had paid dear to preserve his interest. 'All his pretended friends', wrote Lowther's agent, 'have obliged him to buy burgages at most exorbitant prices'; and Thanet himself admitted that he had been 'made a prey of by a parcel of designing, avaricious scoundrels' who had 'no other interest at heart than that of enriching themselves'. At the general election Thanet carried his candidates against Lowther's, and after protracted negotiations a compromise was reached whereby each patron agreed to nominate to one seat.

Ashburton was controlled for most of this period by Lady Orford and Robert Palk, but their joint interest was not overwhelming and there were contests in 1761 and 1784. Downton was contested five times between 1774 and 1784: if elections at Cockermouth and Appleby can be compared to deals on the stock exchange, those at Downton were more like the successive stages of a complicated lawsuit. The origin of the disputes at Downton can be traced to the will of Anthony Duncombe, Lord Feversham, who controlled the borough until his death in 1763. Feversham left his burgages partly to his distant cousin, Thomas Duncombe, and partly to his daughter Anne (who married Jacob Bouverie, 2nd Earl of Radnor); but the injunction that Anne's burgages should be sold, and Duncombe given the first refusal, was overruled in Chancery. Hence arose a struggle between Duncombe and Radnor for control of Downton, which was still undecided in 1790. A similar, but much shorter, dispute over the provisions of a will arose at Heytesbury. In 1768 Pierce A'Court Ashe, who controlled Heytesbury, was persuaded by his wife to alter his will and leave the burgages to her, instead of to his nephew. After A'Court Ashe's death, she sold the burgages to the Duke of Marlborough, who henceforth was able to nominate one Member.

The only burgage borough which could genuinely be described as open was Chippenham, where no single patron held sufficient burgages to reduce the smaller holders to insignificance. Moreover, these smaller holders were in the main substantial merchants and gentry, who banded together to keep the borough open. Though there was no contest during this period, elections cost money; and in 1790 the principal burgage owners signed an agreement with the corporation by which they were to make no new purchases and were to grant to their tenants leases of at least seven years.

Pontefract was a burgage borough until 1783, when the House of Commons determined that the right of election was in the inhabitant householders; and its story is an interesting example of the vicissitudes of borough owners if they insisted too strongly on the rights of property. Pontefract had about 325 burgages, and the patrons in 1754, George Morton Pitt and Lord Galway, had just about a majority between them. Most of the remainder were held in ones or twos by residents of the borough. Pitt and Galway worked closely together; and it was their custom at elections not to put in dummy voters but to canvass the electors, treat the inhabitants, and in general cultivate the goodwill of the independent burgage holders. It was expensive but it was worth it, for until 1768 no opposition was offered to the proprietary interest.

In 1766 Pitt's burgages in Pontefract were bought by John Walsh, a nabob and friend and relative of Clive. Imbued with something of the spirit of an Eastern tyrant, he determined to treat Pontefract with a masterly hand and persuaded Galway to fall in with his plans: there was to be an end of canvassing and treating, and faggot voters were to be put in shortly before the election. Pontefract was to have a master and Pontefract did not like it: Lord Rockingham, who knew something of the independent spirit of Yorkshiremen, could have told Walsh he was heading for trouble. The burgage holders and the voteless populace alike, deprived of their election perquisites, resented Walsh's behaviour; and at the general election of 1768 they persuaded Sir Rowland Winn, a local landowner, and his brother, to stand against the proprietary candidates. On election day the mob intervened, blocked up the entrance to the polling booth, kept out the faggot voters, and forced the mayor to return Galway (whom they acquitted of all offence) and Winn. The House of Commons declared the election void, and at a by-election in December 1768 the proprietary candidates were returned. But the fight went on, and in 1774 Charles James Fox and James Hare were persuaded to stand on the inhabitant householder franchise. Of course they lost, and the Commons confirmed the right of election to be in burgage holders. But in 1783 this decision was reversed and Pontefract ceased to be a burgage borough. By insisting too strongly on his proprietary rights, Walsh lost them altogether.

In brief, the position in the burgage boroughs was this: seventeen were closed by the time this period began and eight became so before it ended; three were to some extent open; and one had ceased to be a burgage borough by 1790. In none did an outsider without property in the borough stand any chance, unless he came with the recommendation of a patron; and in none did political issues count: these constituencies were impervious to public opinion, except as it affected the patron. Yet it should be remembered that both Charles James Fox and the younger Pitt first entered Parliament for a burgage borough; and Edmund Burke, after being rejected in 1780 by the electors of Bristol, found his way back to the House through the votes of the burgage holders of Malton. There was, after all, something to be said for the burgage boroughs.

The last group of English boroughs, the freeholder boroughs, comprised six constituencies: Cricklade, Haslemere, Ludgershall, Reigate, Tavistock, and the double constituency of Weymouth and Melcombe Regis (which returned four Members). None had electorates larger than 300, and they are best regarded as an appendage to the burgage boroughs. The right of voting lay with the freeholders, and if one person owned a sufficient number of freeholds he could control the borough with as much ease as if it were burgage tenure. Richard Rigby, thanking the Duke of Bedford for his election at Tavistock in 1754, wrote: 'There does not seem to be a single negative to your will in the whole town, nor would it be very safe in any one to offer it.' Ludgershall, Reigate, Tavistock, and Weymouth and Melcombe Regis were pocket boroughs, and in none of them was there a contest during this peroid. At Ludgershall there was some stirring of opposition, caused by the refusal of its patron, George Augustus Selwyn, to put himself to any trouble about the borough; but the storm did not break until the general election of 1790. At Weymouth and Melcombe Regis the Government had some influence, and the patrons habitually placed two seats at the Government's disposal. With these qualifications, these four boroughs may be regarded as private possessions of their respective patrons.

At Haslemere the property was divided between four families, and there was a contest at each general election between 1754 and 1774. Following the death of Thomas More Molyneux in 1776 his property at Haslemere was bought by a Guildford attorney named Chandler, who soon added to it the estate of Philip Carteret Webb, another of the would-be patrons of the borough. Chandler now held sufficient freeholds to give him complete control, but he was concerned more to make a profit on the deal than to build up a parliamentary interest, and in 1780 he sold the freeholds to Sir James Lowther. It was a smart piece of business on Chandler's part and effectively put a stop to contested elections at Haslemere, henceforth part of Lowther's electoral empire.

The one freeholder borough not closed during this period was Cricklade. Cricklade had a unique franchise, which included copyholders and lease-holders as well as freeholders. No one owned sufficient property to control the borough and there were eight contests during this period. The franchise reached down into the lower levels of the population, and Cricklade had a well-deserved reputation for venality. The size of the electorate—about 200 voters—tempted would-be patrons; and in about 1780 the borough became a haunt of nabobs.

The sad story of Samuel Petrie, who repeatedly contested Cricklade between 1775 and 1790, shows the difficulties facing a champion of pure elections in a corrupt constituency. Petrie, when he first stood for Cricklade in 1775, took his friend John Wilkes to help with the canvass. Wilkes, however, 'had not canvassed an hour ... before he discovered how the pulse of the voters beat'—'Sam', he is reported to have said to Petrie, 'Wilkes and liberty will not do here. I see it must be hard money.' And so it proved, for Petrie obtained only six votes. Nothing daunted, he stood again at the general election of 1780 against two wealthy East Indians, and this time got eleven votes. Not at all disappointed, for he had never really expected success, Petrie petitioned the House of Commons, and began actions for bribery against his opponents. This time he was successful beyond his expectations, for not only was one of the elected candidates unseated but Parliament passed a bill to enlarge the constituency by including in it the freeholders of the neighbouring hundreds. Cricklade thereupon ceased to be a small corrupt borough constituency; its electorate increased to about 1,000, and it became virtually a miniature county. Poor Petrie, who had ousted the nabobs, found their place taken by even more formidable competi-tors—independent country gentlemen. 'My complaint to the House of Commons ... having produced this Act', he wrote, 'I thought my claim upon the new class of electors irresistible, and that avowing myself a candidate was of itself sufficient to ensure me the certainty of their

franchise.' But at the by-election of 1782 he was forced to decline on
the second day of the poll, and at the general election of 1784 he
received so little support that he withdrew. To add to the irony of the
story, at these two elections most of his following came from the corrupt
electors of Cricklade, against whom his battle for pure elections had been
waged.

THE UNIVERSITIES

The franchise in the two universities was the same—in doctors and masters
of arts, and at each it appears that about 500 actually voted, but as
votes had to be cast in person it is probable that the number entitled to
vote was higher. In addition, in both constituencies the representatives
had to be members of the university. But apart from having the same kind
of electoral structure, the two universities were as different as could
be: Cambridge had a Whig tradition and Oxford a Tory, and these
differences continued even after these names had lost their party con-
notation.

At Cambridge the chancellor had considerable influence and Government candidates were welcomed. The Duke of Newcastle, chancellor
until his death in 1768, ran the university almost as if it were a Sussex
borough; his successor, the Duke of Grafton, also thought himself entitled
to recommend the representatives; and in 1784 William Pitt, first lord
of the Treasury, was elected Member for Cambridge University.
Oxford, however, was exceedingly jealous of its independence and
Government candidates were not welcomed: candidates were not allowed
to canvass, nor were they even admitted into the town while the
election was in progress. Lord North, who for ten years held the offices
of chancellor of the university and first lord of the Treasury, had never
the influence at Oxford that Newcastle, or even Grafton, had at
Cambridge. Cambridge returned prominent politicians such as Charles
Yorke, William de Grey, and William Pitt; dependants of the chancellor,
such as Edward Finch, and Richard Croftes; and heirs to dukedoms,
such as Lord Granby and Lord Euston; but every Member for Oxford
University during this period was a squire from the Midlands, of
little consequence in the House of Commons. Members for Oxford
University had to be warm defenders of the privileges of the Church of
England and independent of Administration; at Cambridge, especially

during the last ten years of this period, elections tended to be fought on party lines.

WALES

The twelve Welsh counties each returned one Member to Parliament and the franchise was the same as in the English counties. In size of electorate they ranged from Caernarvonshire, with about 500 voters, to Denbighshire and Pembrokeshire, with about 2,000. Four had electorates below 1,000 and six had between 1,000 and 1,500. Electorally, therefore, the Welsh counties were smaller than the English, but otherwise a good deal that has been said about the English counties applies also to the Welsh; and in both countries the county representation was dominated by the landed classes. Contests were not frequent. Anglesey had four during this period; Pembrokeshire three; Caernarvonshire and Radnorshire two; five counties had one; and three (Cardiganshire, Denbighshire, and Flintshire) none.

In one important respect English and Welsh counties differed. The rivalry between gentry and peerage families, which was so marked a feature of English county politics, was altogether absent in Wales. Many of the leading Welsh families, whose estates would have entitled them to a peerage, such as the Morgans of Tredegar, the Wynns of Wynnstay, or the Owens of Orielton, had remained commoners. Others, such as the Philippses of Picton Castle, the Vaughans of Crosswood, or the Bulkeleys of Baron Hill, had accepted Irish peerages, and were eligible to sit in the British House of Commons. Only one son of a British peer sat for a Welsh county during this period: James Brydges, Marquess of Carnarvon, who represented Radnorshire 1761–8; and he was an Englishman with but a peripheral interest in Wales.

The Welsh counties were exclusively the preserve of the country gentlemen and contests in them were struggles for local supremacy, fought with little reference to national politics. There does not seem to be a single Welsh county Member who owed his seat in any degree to the attitude he took at Westminster. Obviously the Welsh freeholders were much more amenable to their landlords than were the English, and the lesser gentry tended to follow the lead of the greater. The one occasion when a Welsh county Member was challenged for his political attitude was in 1784, when Sir Roger Mostyn, M.P. for Flintshire, was criticized for voting with the Fox-North party and against parliamentary reform. But Mostyn and his father had represented Flintshire unopposed since 1747, and no other candidate appeared at the general election of 1784. It is this absence of political content which makes Welsh county elections so lacking in savour—for no matter what a Welsh Member did at Westminster, it hardly affected his standing with his constituents. The Welsh county electors were far less politically conscious than the English, and the rural radicalism which began in England about 1780 found little support in Wales.

Four Welsh counties were entirely the preserves of one family: Breconshire, of the Morgans of Tredegar; Denbighshire, of the Wynns of Wynnstay; Flintshire, of the Mostyns of Mostyn; and Merioneth, of the Vaughans of Corsygedol. The only contests in these counties, in Breconshire in 1754 and in Merioneth in 1774, merely served to confirm the ruling family's supremacy. In Caernarvonshire the Wynns of Glynllivon lost their dominant position, largely through their own fault, when the Bulkeley interest was revived after Lord Bulkeley came of age in 1773. Montgomeryshire was fought over by the Wynns of Wynnstay and the Herberts of Powis Castle; and Pembrokeshire by the Owens of Orielton and the Philippses of Picton Castle. In the remaining five Welsh counties (Anglesey, Cardiganshire, Carmarthenshire, Glamorgan, and Radnorshire), electoral struggles were more complicated. There were in these counties three or four families all with an equal claim to the county representation, and the choice of a Member was often the result of a complicated series of negotiations, alliances, betrayals, and compromises.

The Welsh borough constituencies returned twelve Members of Parliament—one for each constituency. Five of them were single boroughs (Beaumaris, Brecon, Carmarthen, Montgomery, and Haverford-west); and the remaining seven were groups of boroughs united for electoral purposes. The group constituencies of Caernarvon, Denbigh, and Pembroke each contained three boroughs; while Cardigan contained four, Flint and New Radnor five, and Cardiff eight.

To deal first with the single boroughs. At Beaumaris the right of election was in the corporation; at Carmarthen and Montgomery, in the freemen; and at Brecon, in the resident freemen. The electorate in each of these four did not exceed 100. At Haverfordwest the right of election was in the freeholders, freemen, and inhabitants paying scot and lot; and the electorate numbered about 500. One thing was common to these constituencies: they were almost complete pocket boroughs of neighbouring families. Beaumaris, Brecon, and Montgomery were entirely so, and were not contested during this period. At Haverfordwest there were two interests: those of William Edwardes of Johnston and of the Philipps family of Picton Castle; and it was understood that Edwardes should represent the borough on condition that he gave his support to the Philipps candidate in Pembrokeshire. There was no contest at Haverfordwest during this period, but from 1784 to 1786 Edwardes temporarily lost the seat to Richard Philipps, Lord Milford, who had been defeated for the county. The only one of these five boroughs which went to the poll during this period was Carmarthen, and that only served to confirm the hold of its patron, Griffith Philipps.

In six of the seven groups of boroughs the franchise was in the freemen or resident freemen; in Flint Boroughs it was in inhabitants paying scot and lot. The number of voters in these constituencies is not easy to determine, since it varied even within a constituency owing to the practice of creating new freemen when an election was imminent. The lowest number who polled during this period was 820 at New Radnor in 1774; the highest, over 3,600 at Cardigan in 1769. It seems probable that none of these constituencies had an electorate of less than 500.

Yet contests were not frequent. There were none in the Cardiff, Denbigh, Pembroke, and Flint groups; one only in the Caernarvon group; two in the Cardigan group; and four in the New Radnor group. There was no essential difference between these constituencies and the single boroughs: patronage, not public opinion, governed their politics. But these, being groups of boroughs, were more difficult to control than the single boroughs. To give one example: the eight boroughs which comprised the Cardiff Boroughs constituency were controlled by four patrons, and it was by adjustment and compromises between them that the representation was decided. The four uncontested constituencies came near to being pocket boroughs; the contest for Caernarvon Boroughs in 1784 was provoked by a quarrel within the Wynn family, which had hitherto controlled it; while at both Cardigan and New Radnor there were a number of families with parliamentary aspirations.

With the exception of Beaumaris, all the Welsh constituencies had, by eighteenth-century standards, large electorates; yet, as in the counties, the parliamentary representation was confined to a few families who lived in or near the constituency. Strangers rarely represented Welsh constituencies, unless they came at the invitation of a patron. The urban middle class, like the independent freeholders in the counties, docilely followed their social superiors. There is not one case during this period of an attempt by the electors to free themselves from the control of a patron, and bribery seems to have been little practised.

The extent to which the leading Welsh families had succeeded in monopolizing parliamentary representation may be seen by the study of one county, Pembrokeshire. Pembrokeshire contained three constituencies: the county (about 2,000 voters), Haverfordwest, and Pembroke Boroughs (each with about 500 voters). These three seats were at the disposal of three families: Owen of Orielton, Philipps of Picton Castle, and Edwardes of Johnston. Pembroke Boroughs was under the influence of Owen, Haverfordwest of Edwardes, while the county was fought over between Owen and Philipps. Every representative for a Pembrokeshire constituency during this period belonged to one of these three families or was a relation by marriage, and no one outside these families ever contested a Pembrokeshire constituency. The social structure of Wales was much more feudal than that of England, and in political development Wales lagged behind: party was not an element in the Welsh electoral scene and radicalism was as yet unknown.

SCOTLAND

The Scottish representative system was adapted from that in use before 1707 in the Parliament of Scotland, and the franchise had remained unaltered. 27 of the 33 Scottish counties each sent one Member to the House of Commons. Six of the smaller counties were grouped together in pairs and one of each pair alternated with the other in electing Members, Parliament by Parliament: Buteshire and Caithness; Clackmannanshire and Kinross-shire; Nairnshire and Cromartyshire. Thus, of the 45 Members returned by Scottish constituencies, 30 came from the counties—a much higher proportion than in England. But in Scotland the difference in status between the Members for the counties and those for the burghs was by no means so pronounced as in England. Indeed, the representation of the Scottish counties was hardly comparable with that of the English.

Except in Sutherland, which had a unique franchise, the electoral qualification was the same in each county: it belonged to freeholders possessing land valued at 40s. 'of old extent', and to owners of land held of the Crown rated at £400 Scots (i.e. about £35 sterling). In Sutherland the right to vote extended also to those who held land of the Earl of Sutherland, so extensive were his estates in his county.

By a 40s. freehold 'of old extent' was meant a freehold so valued according to the ancient valuation in use during the middle ages, (though by eighteenth-century standards it was worth considerably more). The independent yeomen and smaller landholders were not enfranchised in Scotland, but only men of substantial property and those who held direct from the Crown. This immediate vassalage of the Crown was spoken of as superiority, and the conveying of property giving the right to vote was known as 'granting superiorities'. Moreover, the right to vote was attached to the superiority itself: if the property was mortgaged, the mortgagee (or wadsetter) could vote, and persons of large property could subdivide it, creating votes amongst their friends and relations which were known as life-rents.

The right of voting in Scottish county elections thus lay in the hands of a small number of substantial landowners, and in no county did the electorate exceed 200. In the majority of Scottish counties it did not exceed 100. All voters had to be entered on the roll of freeholders, which was made up annually at the Michaelmas head court of the county and immediately before an election. These head court meetings were frequently trials of strength between the contending interests, and it is not too much to say that a Scottish election began immediately after the last one had ended. The date of the election could itself be of critical importance, for a superiority, before it could give the right to vote, had to be held for at least a year and a day. In Dunbartonshire, at the general election of 1780, the sheriff, in the interest of the Duke of Argyll, arranged for the election to be held on 14 September, the day before the voters in the rival Elphinstone interest would be legally qualified. The Elphinstones, by filibustering and irrelevant speeches, prolonged the proceedings until after midnight, and then claimed that their newly-enrolled voters were duly qualified. The sheriff, on the other hand; argued that since the election had to be concluded in one day, he had to presume that the proceedings terminated on 14 September although they actually continued into the early hours of the next day, and accepted the old electoral roll minus the Elphinstone votes.

At the head court meeting the chair was first taken by the person who had last represented the county in Parliament (the commissioner). The court then proceeded to elect a chairman (the praeses) and a clerk. Since the praeses possessed a casting vote, his election was often decisive, as in Aberdeenshire in 1786, or in Stirlingshire at the general election of 1754 when James Campbell was elected by the casting vote of the praeses.

After electing the praeses, the meeting went on to consider the claims of those who had recently acquired the right to vote. The multiplication of votes is a notable feature in many of the Scottish counties during this period. In Ayrshire the electorate more than doubled between 1759 and 1788. In Sutherland it numbered about 10 in 1754; in 1757 the Earl of Sutherland created 23 new votes, and by 1788 there were 34 on the electoral roll. These votes were purely nominal, created by transferring property to reliable dependants. By resort to this device the large landowners were able to swamp the smaller men. In some counties, for example Linlithgowshire in 1784, more than half the number of votes on the roll were said to be fictitious. An Act of 1743 had attempted to curb the practice by compelling a voter, when challenged, to swear on oath that he was the real owner of the property for which he claimed the franchise and had not received it merely for electoral purposes (the trust oath). Though some landlords, like Sir James Grant of Grant in Inverness-shire in 1784 or John Ross Mackye in the Stewartry of Kirkcudbright in 1768, refused to make use of fictitious votes, the practice increased if anything during the period; and the imposition of the trust oath only disqualified the conscientious. At the Ayrshire election of 1774 five of David Kennedy's voters refused to take the oath; but all twenty of Sir Adam Fergusson's nominal voters, having been carefully coached, took the oath, and Fergusson won the election by a majority of thirteen. A decision of the House of Lords, following the Cromartyshire election of 1768, had given what appeared to be a legal sanction to the creation of nominal votes, and attempts to strengthen the law against them were unsuccessful.

The praeses's decision to admit or reject votes could be challenged in the court of session, from which there lay a right of appeal to the House of Lords. It has been said that if you wish to break the law, take care to be advised by a good solicitor; and certainly electioneering in Scotland during this period was a hazardous business without a lawyer at your elbow. Elections, in fact, were frequently decided in the courts. In the Fife by-election of 1776 James Townsend Oswald defeated John Henderson by one vote (61 to 60), the legality of which was upheld by Lord Auchinleck, James Boswell's father, in the court of session. Auchinleck, a supporter of Oswald, was accused by Henry Dundas of partiality, and Boswell was so incensed by the charge that he considered challenging Dundas to a duel. When it is remembered that many of the Scottish judges came from families with important electoral interests, the extent to which decisions of the courts of law could determine elections appears one of the most reprehensible features of the Scottish electoral system.

From all this it will be seen that county elections in Scotland in no way resembled those in England, but were more akin to the struggles in an English rotten borough. Public opinion could not express itself, and even property was denied its full weight. Influence in the Scottish counties, when it was not based on fictitious votes, was very largely a matter of the prestige derived from tradition and character. Gilbert Elliot, M.P. for Selkirkshire, wrote in 1760 about the influence of the Duke of Buccleuch in the county: 'The Buccleuch interest is not so much to be estimated by the votes it can at present command as by the credit . . . it bestows upon any candidate it adopts.' The great influence in Scottish elections of the Duke of Argyll at the beginning of this period and of Henry Dundas at the end, was not due to the extent of their property but to their intimate connexion with Government.

It is no wonder then that Scottish county elections should sometimes descend to the level of farce. At the Cromartyshire election of 1768 the rival candidates, Sir John Gordon and William Pulteney, had six votes each. Gordon as commissioner (he had sat for the county when it was last represented in the Parliament of 1754) took the chair at the election meeting, gave his casting vote to himself for praeses, and having been installed straightway struck off one of Pulteney's voters. At this stage the election degenerated into a brawl, and finally the meeting split up into two parties, each of which proceeded to elect its own candidate.

C

The sheriff, faced with two candidates both claiming to have won the election, returned Pulteney; but it was only after the House of Lords had confirmed a verdict of the court of session that Pulteney could be certain of his seat.

In the constituency of Orkney and Shetland, where there were only seven voters in 1759, the Shetland landowners had never applied for Scottish charters and therefore did not possess the vote. There were real economic grievances in Orkney, which had their effect on parliamentary elections, though these involved only the larger landowners. At the head court of 1760 only one freeholder turned up, who proceeded to enrol voters opposed to the interest of the Earl of Morton, the patron of the constituency. At the election meeting the following year, the Morton party attended in full force, elected one of their number as praeses, and struck off all the recently enrolled voters. In Linlithgowshire in 1768, when the Earl of Hopetoun's interest was attacked by the Dundases of Dundas, it was arranged to hold the election three days before one of the voters came of age. These examples are typical of the practices resorted to in Scottish county elections: weighty matters could indeed depend upon trifles.

Six of the Scottish counties were almost complete pocket constituencies, where the patron's interest was virtually unchallenged: Argyllshire (Duke of Argyll), Banffshire (Earl Fife), Buteshire (Earl of Bute), Dumfriesshire (Duke of Queensberry), Peeblesshire (Earl of March, succeeded in 1778 as 4th Duke of Queensberry), Sutherland (Earl of Sutherland). The largest of these counties, Banffshire, had 120 voters; no other had more than 50, and Buteshire had only 12. Buteshire, with eight of its twelve voters relatives or friends of the Earl of Bute, was more of a closed constituency than many of the English pocket boroughs. In English constituencies, such as Bath and Salisbury, where the right of voting was confined to the corporation, there was far more independence and political feeling than in any of these Scottish pocket constituencies. Nor does this list exhaust the number of Scottish county constituencies where one family was predominant: it only comprises those where a family interest was so powerful as to be almost beyond challenge. In Kinross-shire (about 25 voters) there was a contest for supremacy which ended in about 1778 with the Graham family of Kinross in command of the constituency. There were contested elections in Orkney and Shetland in 1761, 1780, and 1784; but the principal landowner in the constituency (Lord Morton until 1766, and afterwards the Dundases of Kerse) always succeeded in getting his nominee elected. In Kincardineshire and Selkirkshire no election went to the poll during this period. In Edinburghshire (Midlothian) the Dundas family of Arniston and the Duke of Buccleuch between them controlled the county.

In the remaining Scottish counties the electoral picture was uniform. There were in each constituency at least two families, but usually three or more, with claims to the representation, and elections were won by creating a broad-based combination of interests. Alliances and counter-alliances were made, broke down, and were reformed, like patterns in a kaleidoscope. At one election, A and B would join against C; next, A and C against B; or perhaps A, B, and C would all unite against an outsider D. Family connexions and traditional rivalries determined these combinations and overrode differences on national politics. Here are some examples. In Berwickshire, the Humes, Earls of Marchmont, and the Homes, Earls of Home, were deadly rivals, and almost everyone with any interest in the county was on one side or the other. In Ayrshire, there were three peers, the Earls of Loudoun, Eglintoun, and Cassillis, whose divisions were the stuff of Ayrshire politics for almost twenty years. In Elginshire, there were at least four families with parliamentary aspirations: the Grants, the Duffs, the Gordons, and the Brodies; and they quarrelled incessantly until a body of independent freeholders formed an association against them in 1783. In Wigtownshire, the Earl of Galloway, the Earl of Stair, and the McDowall family struggled for the representation of the county.

Since there were only fifteen burgh constituencies (including the city of Edinburgh) the opportunity for compromise between county and burgh did not exist in Scotland to the same degree as in England. Instead, the Scots worked out their own system for avoiding expensive contested elections where the interests of the candidates were nicely balanced. One example will explain the nature of these compromises. At the election for Berwickshire in 1780 there were three candidates: Sir John Paterson, standing on the interest of his father-in-law the Earl of Marchmont; Hugh Scott, Marchmont's grandson, standing in opposition to the Marchmont interest; and Alexander Renton. To ensure Paterson's defeat, Scott and Renton came to an agreement by which Scott was to stand, with Renton's full support, and if elected to vacate his seat after four sessions in favour of Renton. Similar electoral

compacts are to be found in Haddingtonshire, the Stewartry of Kirkcudbright, and Renfrewshire; while in Lanarkshire in 1768 Daniel Campbell
and John Lockhart Ross drew lots as to who should oppose the Duke of
Hamilton's candidate. The practice was strictly illegal, and if brought
to the notice of the House of Commons resulted in the election being
declared void. Following the Kirkcudbright election of 1780, when John
Gordon of Kenmure and Colonel Alexander Stewart had made a compact
of this nature, counsel for the third candidate, Peter Johnston, argued
before the House of Commons committee which tried the election petition:

If such a practice were allowed, it would soon run all over Scotland. The
English Members were indeed too apt to be dull and idle, and many of them
slept away seven whole years. But the Scotch Members were ... of an active and
bustling disposition and could do very pretty things in three or four years; so
that when a bargain was struck up between two persons, one had only to go to
Parliament for three years and get a snug thing, and then return to Scotland and
send his partner to come up to London and do the same thing.

This in effect is what happened at the Wigtownshire election of 1784,
when Andrew McDowall gave his interest to Keith Stewart, brother of the
Earl of Galloway, on condition that if Stewart was appointed to the office
of receiver-general of the land tax for Scotland (which would compel
him to vacate his seat in the House), the Galloway interest would be
given to a candidate nominated by McDowall. At the Kirkcudbright
election of 1784 three candidates agreed to an electoral compact by
which each was to hold the seat for two years, but because of unforeseen
circumstances the arrangement did not work out as planned.

    The electorates in the Scottish counties being so small, and almost
all the voters being of the educated classes (and therefore eligible for
Government appointments), the influence of Government in the Scottish
county elections was considerable. William Adam wrote about the
electors of Argyllshire in the survey of Scottish constituencies which
he drew up for the Opposition in 1788:

The greatest part of them have very near connexions in the army or navy. Many
of them are active, enterprising men, desirous of promotion, and the Duke
[of Argyll] it is thought would be in a very troublesome situation unless he was
acting with Administration.

'The weight of Administration is great in this county', wrote a prospective
candidate for Edinburghshire in 1764; and John Robinson wrote about

Kirkcudbright in his survey for the general election of 1774: 'It is thought whichever [candidate] has the support of Government, he will carry the election, as the numbers run very near.'

To the statement that Government had considerable influence in Scottish county elections must be added one qualification: before 1782 (and especially during the period of North's Administration) most Scottish Members voted regularly with Government as Government, irrespective of which group or party was in power; and at a contested election it was immaterial to Government which candidate was elected. The following extracts from Robinson's survey for the general election of 1780 give examples:

Berwickshire:	[After naming the candidates] : Whichever of these gentlemen come in will be a friend.
Haddingtonshire:	Whichever is returned will be a friend.
Kirkcudbright Stewartry:	The same to Government whoever succeeds.
Roxburghshire:	A contest. Issue uncertain, but whichever way a friend.

When a contest threatened and all the candidates were Government supporters, it was embarrassing to give the Government interest to one candidate at the expense of the others. Lord Suffolk wrote to the Duchess of Hamilton in 1774 about the contest for Lanarkshire: 'Administration for the most part does not choose to take an active and decided part in the contentions between great families ... equally well inclined to Government.' After 1782, as will be seen later, party reared its ugly head among the Scottish Members as among the English, and Government began to take a more decided part in Scottish elections.

Yet it must not be supposed that the Scottish county electors were all robots, moving automatically according to the whims of great landlords, or disposing of their votes for Government favours. There is plenty of evidence to show that the Scottish voters could be just as independently minded as the English, and that in Scotland, as in England, tradition and family allegiances, rather than the weight of property, governed the pattern of voting. The voters of Inverness-shire in 1761 elected as their Member Simon Fraser, son of the Jacobite leader Lord Lovat, in defiance of the wishes of the Duke of Argyll, the Government electoral manager for Scotland, and the Duke of Newcastle, first lord of the Treasury. And when a great landowner was too insistent on his rights, or had made himself unpopular, or combined with others to dominate the county, the freeholders were apt to remember that they were independent electors. When in 1774 the three most powerful peers in Ayrshire, Lords Loudoun, Eglintoun, and Cassillis, joined in support of the candidature of David Kennedy, a considerable opposition was provoked, and an alternative candidate, Sir Adam Fergusson, set up. An elector warned Loudoun: 'Such a county as Ayrshire will not allow any Member fixed upon in private by a few to be forced on them.' The triple alliance', Lord Auchinleck told Kennedy, would mean 'the annihilation of the gentlemen's interest'. The independent freeholders found support from the Duke of Buccleuch; copied the example of the 'triple alliance' by creating twenty nominal votes; and succeeded in getting their man elected.

The opposition to Lord Marchmont in Berwickshire in 1780 was provoked by his choosing an unpopular man as his candidate. When a contest threatened in Perthshire in 1760 between two members of the Duke of Atholl's family, Lord Breadalbane wrote to Lord Hardwicke: 'A great many gentlemen of consideration dislike them both, that is to say they want to get out of the hands of that family.' Most remarkable of all is the association formed in Elginshire in 1783 to campaign against the creation of nominal voters. They presented a petition to Parliament complaining that three-quarters of the electors on the Elginshire roll had no property in the county but were 'in servile dependence' upon a few 'overgrown proprietors and lords superior'. At the general election of 1784 the association sponsored a candidate against one put up by the 'overgrown proprietors', but were defeated. As will be seen in the section on the Scottish Members (p. 253), there were plenty of independent men in Scotland, but the electoral system did not permit them to exercise their full influence in the constituencies.

With the exception of Edinburgh, the Scottish burghs were combined in groups for the purpose of electing Members of Parliament: there were fourteen groups or districts, five of them having four burghs and nine having five burghs. The system of indirect election followed in them was unique in the eighteenth-century Parliament. At a parliamentary election every burgh council elected a delegate, and the delegates of each group then met together and elected the Member of Parliament. The elections to successive Parliaments were held at each burgh in the group in turn as the presiding or returning burgh for that general election and any by-elections which should occur. For convenience the fourteen constituencies (the groups or districts of burghs) are known in this *History* by the name of the burgh which was the returning burgh for the first Parliament after the Union.

In every group of burghs there were five votes (in groups of four burghs the returning burgh had a second vote which it could use in the case of a tie). Whoever, therefore, controlled three out of five burghs or two out of four (including the returning burgh), controlled the constituency. The burgh councils were small (none had more than 33 members and most not more than 20), and sensitive to the familiar pressures of influence and bribery, but the influencing and bribing had to be carried on in two or three burghs simultaneously. The prime object was to ensure that the councils elected suitable delegates; what followed afterwards, when the delegates met to elect the Member of Parliament, was usually no more than a formality. For this reason the Scottish burgh constituencies are omitted from our consideration of contested elections in the second section of this introductory survey. Some burghs, such as those in the constituencies of Anstruther Easter or Tain, were tiny places, little more than villages, whose political interests did not extend much beyond their own boundaries, and where the Parliament at Westminster seemed a very remote body indeed. Glasgow, already at the beginning of this period a populous trading and manufacturing city, was yoked for parliamentary purposes with four small burghs, who could out-vote it at election time.

In about half of these constituencies money counted for more than anything else in deciding elections, but the money was used rather to bribe the councils than to bribe individual voters. Thus in the Anstruther Easter group, where the by-election of 1766 was a contest between the Anstruther and the Erskine families, each of the burghs put itself up for auction with the object of paying off its municipal debts. Lord Kintore wrote about Elgin and Banff, in the constituency of Elgin Burghs: 'They depend on no particular person, but are determined sometimes one way, sometimes another, from different motives, and generally the candidate who gives the most money has the best chance of their votes'; and Andrew Mitchell, when elected in 1755, made a contribution of £300 to the Elgin burgh finances. 'These burghs', wrote Robinson about the Perth group in his survey for the general election of 1774, 'are very open, venal, and expensive, and few choose to engage in them'—a conclusion which would have been shared (at least as to the first part) by Thomas Leslie and George Dempster, the two Members who represented the constituency during this period. The constituencies of Dysart, Haddington, Linlithgow, and Stirling, all contained venal burghs; and Archibald Campbell, returned for Stirling Burghs after a hard contest in 1774, is said to have spent over £17,000 on his election.

A burgh found guilty of flagrant corruption could be temporarily disfranchised by order of the court of session, which would mean that there would be an election for a new burgh council and the burgh would not be allowed to send a delegate to the next general election. This occurred four times during our period: Inverkeithing (Stirling Burghs) was disfranchised in 1760; Pittenweem (Anstruther Easter Burghs) in 1767; Jedburgh (Haddington Burghs) in 1768; and Stirling (Stirling Burghs) in 1774. The disfranchisement of Jedburgh, which should have been the returning burgh at the general election of 1768, led to fierce disputes, for with the constituency of Haddington Burghs now reduced to four burghs, everything depended on which should be the returning burgh. Dunbar and Lauder both claimed it was their turn, and Haddington prudently nominated three delegates so as to be prepared for all eventualities. In the end, two elections were held, one at Dunbar and one at Jedburgh, and two returns made to the House of Commons, for the sheriff of Haddingtonshire accepted the return from Dunbar and the sheriff of Roxburghshire that from Jedburgh. On nine occasions during this period the election was decided by the casting vote of the returning burgh: Stirling Burghs and Wigtown Burghs in 1761; Anstruther Easter Burghs in 1766; Haddington Burghs and Inverness Burghs in 1768; Haddington Burghs in 1771; Wigtown Burghs in 1774; Dysart Burghs in 1780; and Glasgow Burghs in 1790. At the election for Inverness Burghs in 1768 Hector Munro and Sir Alexander Grant were the candidates; Munro was elected delegate for Fortrose, the returning burgh, and one can imagine with what pleasure he gave the casting vote for himself—a moment of exaltation which rarely falls to the lot of any candidate for Parliament. And one can imagine also the chagrin of Glasgow, which had been long accustomed to lord it over its four sister burghs, when at the by-election of February 1790 the delegate from Renfrew gave the casting vote against the candidate of the Glasgow council. So annoyed was the Glasgow council that it barely recognized the newly-elected Member John Crauford, and transacted its parliamentary business through

William McDowall, M.P. for Ayrshire. This may, however, have been something of a relief to Craufurd, for Glasgow had a great deal of parliamentary business and made heavy demands on its representative; Lord Frederick Campbell, who sat for Glasgow Burghs from 1761 to 1780, was glad in the end to move to the less exacting constituency of Argyllshire.

Six of the Scottish burgh constituencies can be described as under patronage, though the hold of their patrons was by no means unshakeable: patronage, in this case, merely meant that the constituency would give the patron the first preference provided he continued to look after the constituency to its satisfaction. The Duke of Argyll and the Earl of Bute between them controlled Ayr Burghs, but Ayr itself was a very independent burgh and in 1761 gave much trouble to both patrons: though prepared to yield, it would only do so after a prolonged courtship. In 1774 Argyll had serious doubts whether Bute's candidate, Sir George Macartney, would be well received in Ayr because he was not a Scotsman; but Bute convinced him that Macartney's having married Bute's daughter and possessing a small estate in Scotland would compensate for the deficiency of his having been born in Ireland.

Anstruther Easter Burghs was normally controlled by the Anstruther family, but they lost their hold over the constituency in 1754 and had a hard fight to get it back in 1766. Dumfries Burghs usually elected a Member nominated by the Duke of Queensberry, but his candidate was defeated in 1784. The Duke of Argyll had considerable influence in Glasgow Burghs, but through the neglect of his agents he lost the by-election of 1790. The Duke of Hamilton had considerable interest in Linlithgow Burghs, a very expensive and exacting constituency. The Earl of Galloway controlled two out of the four burghs in the Wigtown constituency, and when either Wigtown or Whithorn was the returning burgh could usually get his man elected. But the Earl of Stair had also a good interest, and in 1784 he won control of Whithorn and was thus enabled to defeat Galloway's candidate. In short, none of these constituencies was in the English sense a pocket borough, and Government had no influence except through the patrons.

While no Englishman ever represented a Scottish county during this period, six were returned for Scottish burgh constituencies. George Augustus Selwyn was returned by Lord Galloway for Wigtown Burghs in 1768, and on vacating his seat (he had also been elected for

Gloucester) was replaced by Chauncy Townsend, a Treasury nominee. In return the Government bought a seat at Ludgershall (Selwyn's pocket borough) for Lord Garlies, Galloway's son, who as the eldest son of a Scottish peer was ineligible to sit for a Scottish constituency. Both candidates for Wigtown Burghs in 1774 were Englishmen—a unique occurrence in this period: William Norton on the interest of the Earl of Stair, and Henry Watkin Dashwood, brother-in-law of the Earl of Galloway. Stair hoped that Norton, who had been recommended to him by Sir Lawrence Dundas, would if elected be able to find a seat in England for Lord Dalrymple, Stair's eldest son. But Norton, elected by the casting vote of New Galloway, was unseated on petition. The other two Englishmen returned for Scottish burgh constituencies were George Damer for Anstruther Easter Burghs in 1778 and Charles James Fox for Tain Burghs in 1784. Fox had also been elected for Westminster, but the returning officer's decision to hold a scrutiny would have kept him out of the House; his return for Tain Burghs was on the interest of his friend and political follower, Sir Thomas Dundas. In addition to these, George Augustus Selwyn was the unsuccessful candidate on the Duke of Queensberry's interest in Dumfries Burghs in 1784.

Finally there is Edinburgh, the capital of Scotland, the only single burgh constituency north of the Tweed. The contrast between the electoral state of Edinburgh and that of London exemplifies much of the difference between the Scottish and the English representative systems. London (though its franchise was not the widest possible) had about 7,000 electors; Edinburgh had 33—the city council, slightly augmented for electoral purposes. In London, elections were decided in the main by public opinion, while Edinburgh always had a patron: the Duke of Argyll until his death in 1761; the Earl of Bute 1761–7; Sir Lawrence Dundas 1767–81; and then Henry Dundas. And there was a radically different approach in the two capitals to political questions. At the election of 1774 one of the candidates for Edinburgh promised never, except on a point of principle, 'to clog the wheels of Government by voting against the Ministry'. A declaration of this nature by a candidate for London would have ensured his being bottom of the poll—if, after the reception his statement would have received, he had thought it worthwhile to go to the poll. The politics of Edinburgh turned largely on feuds in the council between the trades and the merchants, which were exploited by the politicians for their own advantage. Henry Dundas, who had long been trying to capture Edinburgh, wrote in 1781, shortly after the death of Sir Lawrence Dundas:

The party left by Sir Lawrence Dundas must be broke, and the town of Edinburgh brought under some respectable patronage on which Government can rely, for they must not be permitted to govern the town by a knot of themselves without the interposition of some such patron ... for if they do, the first good opportunity that offers some able individual who leads the rest will sell them to any rich man like Sir Lawrence.

The contempt for the electorate which is clearly expressed in this passage would hardly have been used by an English electoral manager for any but the most abject of rotten boroughs.

PARLIAMENTARY PATRONAGE

The word 'interest' has been used frequently in these pages; it will recur over and over again. What exactly was a parliamentary interest in the second half of the eighteenth century? On what basis was it founded and what was needed to cultivate and maintain it? Who were the great borough-mongers of the period, and what use did they make of their parliamentary interest?

An 'interest' in a constituency enables a patron or a Member of Parliament to influence the political conduct of the electors. Today it depends primarily on party feeling, and secondly on the personality of the Member and his relations with his constituency party. In the second half of the eighteenth century it resulted from a combination of three factors: the possession of landed property; services to the constituency; and the goodwill of the electors, which might be traditional or might be acquired.

Sir Francis Basset, the great Cornish borough-monger, in a pamphlet published in 1783 against parliamentary reform, argued that representation in the House of Commons was 'of property, not of numbers'. The same idea was expressed in a different form by Thomas de Grey in a debate on the Middlesex election, 31 January 1770: the people, he maintained, were not the mass of the population but the 'men of great property' with 'a great stake to lose'. In most constituencies the possession of landed property was an essential qualification for the franchise, and the large landowners seemed the natural representatives of an electorate of small landowners. Lord Rockingham in 1768 described a prospective parliamentary candidate as 'a very good sort of man ...with a thumping landed property', and obviously believed that this of itself entitled him to a seat in the House.

The possession of an estate in or near a constituency automatically gave some degree of parliamentary interest, depending on the size of the estate, and the nature of the constituency. Sir James Lowther boasted in 1783 that he was 'the owner of the land, fire, and water' at Whitehaven, and described it as a town which had grown up under the 'fostering care' of his family. Because of this he could rely upon the votes of the inhabitants of Whitehaven in elections for the county of Cumberland, and had Whitehaven sent Members to Parliament it would have been a pocket borough of the Lowther family. Robert, Earl Nugent told the House on 13 April 1780, during a debate on disfranchising the revenue officers, that his seat at St. Mawes was perfectly safe even without their votes. 'Five-sixths of the borough was his own property, his constituents were his tenants, and he was sure of his election.' Lord Clive built up his interest at Bishop's Castle by buying estates until the borough was surrounded by his property. Parliamentary interest acquired through the ownership of property was known in the eighteenth century as a 'natural' or 'family' interest.

Yet by itself property was rarely sufficient in any but a very small constituency or a burgage borough. It was a base on which to build a parliamentary interest, an essential foundation, but no more. Where there were real voters, they had to be wooed and cajoled; the patron had to show concern for their material welfare and respect their political and social prejudices. The interest derived from property had to be supplemented by services to the electorate. These could take several forms: the patron might become a benefactor to the town and procure Government appointments for its leading citizens, their relatives and friends. Access to Government patronage was a more important factor in the earlier part of the period than at the end, and it was perfectly possible to maintain a parliamentary interest without it. If the patron lived near the constituency he was expected to offer hospitality to the electors, to favour tradesmen with his custom, to help farmers in times of economic depression by reducing their rents, and even sometimes to lend them money. Cultivating a constituency was exacting work, and for a patron to take his interest for granted was the surest way to lose it.

Lord Shelburne wrote in his autobiography with reference to his experiences at the boroughs of Calne and Chipping Wycombe:

Family boroughs (by which I mean boroughs which lie naturally within the reach of cultivation of any house or property) are supposed to cost nothing: but I am sure from my own experience and observation that if examined into they will be found to cost as much as the purchase of any burgage tenure whatever, by means of what I call 'insensible perspiration'. Like public taxes, the amount is not perceived for a great while, and by some people not at all, because it consists in paying always a little and most commonly a great deal too much on every article, and in every transaction you are confined to a particular set of tradesmen, and often to their connections in town, and can never control their charges. The rents of houses and lands must be governed by the moderation of voters. You must be forthcoming on every occasion, not only of distress, but of fancy, to subscribe too largely to roads, as well as every other project which may be started by the idlest of the people; add to this, livings, favours of all sorts from Government, and stewardships, if there is an intriguing attorney in the town, who under the name of your agent will deprive you of all manner of free agency upon your own property, and sometimes of the property itself, if it is a small one; without mentioning the charge and domestic disorder attending a great deal of obscure hospitality, and a never ceasing management of men and things. And after all, when the crisis comes, you are liable to be outbid by any nabob or adventurer, and you must expect all that you have done to go for nothing, and the most you can look for is a preference.

Sir Charles Hotham, of a leading Yorkshire family, wrote in similar vein:

I cannot help offering it as my most serious and earnest advice to those who shall succeed me to suffer no consideration to induce them to be drawn in to become representatives of Beverley or Scarborough. They are both too near their places of residence, and will entail upon them a slavery and expense that will know no end. If they will be in Parliament . . . it should be much farther from home.

If the patron did not live near the constituency (and most patrons resided for part of the year in London), another set of problems confronted him. No constituency could be managed by remote control: an intimate and continuous acquaintance with its affairs was essential. To offer a five pound note to one man might secure his vote; to do the same to another might make an enemy for life. The patron had to know the ambitions and desires of the leading men in the borough, their friendships and enmities, the factions into which they were divided, and how much weight each carried in election affairs. Also, he had to have an agent in the borough, and the maintenance of his interest depended to a considerable degree on the agent's zeal and fidelity.

The patrons of Okehampton in 1754 were Thomas Pitt and the Duke of Bedford, and the management of the borough was in two branches of the Luxmoore family, local notables in Okehampton. The patrons worked closely together, but there was jealousy and rivalry between the agents and sometimes contempt for their masters. On the death of the 4th Duke of Bedford in 1771 Thomas Pitt junior renewed the agreement with the Duchess of Bedford by which each patron nominated to one seat, and confirmed the arrangements for the choice of mayor and the election of freemen. Pitt's agent, John Luxmoore of Fair Place, objected to the terms of this agreement; and Pitt wrote to him on 18 February 1771:

I received your letter of the 3rd instant ... I must tell you (and that very seriously) that I have not been used to receive a *dictatorial style* from any man; you will best judge whether it is a lesson I shall be inclined to learn from you. I am not to ask you whether you are *averse* or otherwise to any agreement I think fit to make for my *peace and happiness*; and as to anything further I may endeavour for the peace, quiet, and harmony of the borough, I shall not think myself obliged to consult your *pride*, whatever *character* and *figure* you may have chosen to assume to yourself in the corporation ... Assure yourself whatever interest I have I desire to have it my own, and not to hold it at the will and discretion of another, who is to give me the law as he thinks proper and fight me with the very weapons I have put into his hands.

Possibly it was dissatisfaction with his agent, and the difficulty of replacing him, that made Pitt sell his estate and parliamentary interest at Okehampton; it was purchased by Lord Clive, and after Clive's death was sold to Lord Spencer. Despite these changes of ownership, the two agents remained in effective control of Okehampton, and it required repeated coaxing and cajoling by their respective patrons to keep them in good humour and get them to work together. There was a contest in 1780, but the Bedford-Spencer candidates were returned. Then, at the general election of 1784, 'Esquire' Luxmoore, the Duke of Bedford's agent, set up himself and a friend in opposition to the patrons' candidates. He kept his intentions secret until almost the last moment, and, by persuading his brother the mayor to agree to the creation of thirty-five new freemen, carried both seats. The patrons were furious: they succeeded in having their candidates returned on petition, and after a series of lawsuits Luxmoore's creation of freemen was declared invalid. But what had hitherto been a safe and comparatively cheap borough was now become an exceedingly insecure and expensive one, and both Bedford and Spencer felt it was no longer worthwhile maintaining their interests at Okehampton. Humphrey Minchin, Spencer's Member for the borough, wrote to him on 7 November 1787:

I did understand that your Lordship for prudential and undoubtedly right reasons intended to dispose of your Devonshire estate . . . I saw great difficulty attending it, because when Okehampton was purchased from Lord Clive it was supposed to be a perfectly secure borough . . . but the contested elections, particularly the last, having proved the contrary, it appeared to me that few could be found to pay anything near what it had cost.

Spencer replied:

My [intentions] with respect to the borough of Okehampton were decidedly not to stand the expense and trouble of another general election there, and if between this time and that I could not find a purchaser for the estate, to take some convenient opportunity of informing the electors that I had no more to say to the borough interest in that place.

Spencer offered his estate to Bedford, who replied that he also intended to sell out. Eventually Spencer found a purchaser, but at a price 'entirely fixed from a valuation of the estate, without considering at all the borough interest'. That interest, he told his mother, 'I can consider . . . as only a dead weight upon it and a cause of constant expense instead of profit'. Indeed, towards the end of this period there are signs that more than one borough owner was beginning to think his parliamentary interest to be 'a cause of constant expense instead of profit'.

As well as being concerned for the welfare of the electors, the patron had also to respect the interests of other borough owners. He had to be prepared to compromise, to avoid what Chase Price called 'the improvident exertion of power', and not to stretch his claims too far. The electoral agreements which existed in Cornwall and Shropshire at the beginning of this period whereby the Whigs concerned themselves with the boroughs and left the Tories a free hand in the county, are typical of this kind of compromise. So also is the understanding by which a patron recommended to one seat and left the other to the free choice of the electors. 'When I recommended Major-General Griffin to my friends at Andover', wrote Lord Portsmouth to Newcastle in 1760, 'I promised them that I would not interfere farther in the election'—i.e., he would leave the corporation free to decide who should be the second Member.

For even in small boroughs consideration had to be paid to the wishes of the electors. James Buller, patron of West Looe (which had about 50 voters), refused Grenville's recommendation of John Bindley in 1765 because it was popularly believed in Cornwall that Bindley was the originator of the odious cider tax. And at Launceston in 1758 Humphry Morice refused to accept Lord Tylney, a relative of the Duke of Bedford, because Bedford was unpopular in the west of England. 'That is really not in my power, if it was ever so much my inclination', he told Tylney. 'I should lose my interest entirely by doing so.'

The 3rd Duke of Portland and the 2nd Duke of Newcastle, the leading magnates in Nottinghamshire, were on opposite sides politically for most of this period—Newcastle supported North's Administration and afterwards that of Pitt, while Portland was one of the leaders of the Rockingham party. Yet in electoral affairs this political difference did not count, and they had an understanding that each would support the other against any third interest. When in December 1774 Lord Edward Bentinck, Portland's brother, was threatened with an opposition in Nottinghamshire, Newcastle wrote to Portland:

The peace of the county, as well as every public and private consideration, makes me most *sincerely* congratulate your Grace and Lord Edward on Mr. Masters' declining ... Your Grace will ever find me most desirous and ambitious of cementing the strictest cordiality and friendship between our families.

On his side Portland refused an invitation from Newark in 1769 to set up a candidate against Newcastle's interest, or to heed a suggestion from William Burke in 1774 that Lord Edward Bentinck would prove a more popular candidate at East Retford than the one Newcastle had recommended. And here is the reason the Duke of Richmond gave Edmund Burke in 1774 for refusing to support Lord Verney in Buckinghamshire against Lord Temple's candidate:

Although I have no political connexion, I have some remains of old family acquaintance with Lord Temple, and should not choose to offend him so much as I myself should feel at any other person for an endeavour to oppose a family interest. There are few things I would not do to oblige you; but I confess that, not knowing Lord Verney, and having no other reason to wish him better than Lord Temple, except for his friendship for you, I do not think it would be right for me to interfere where I have so literally nothing to say.

Both Richmond and Verney followed the political lead of Lord Rockingham, but political considerations had to give way to electoral interests. As a rule, patrons respected the rights of property and did not interfere in constituencies where they had no concern.

A lasting electoral interest could rarely be built on a foundation of bribery alone. Bribing electors was like paying blackmail: the more was paid, the more was asked. Henry Drummond, the banker, when invited to contest Northampton in 1774 on the interest of his uncle, Lord Northampton, refused to give money to the electors. 'I ... told them', he wrote, 'I never should think a family interest worth preserving that was to be bought by money.' Boroughs where the electors were to be bought were never safe. John Page, who had represented Great Grimsby 1727–34, wrote about the borough in 1762:

I am very sure Lord Luxborough's personal interest is stronger there than any man's, because they have had more of his money than anybody's and he has always been punctual to all his engagements ... and yet, should a dashing gentleman go down and offer three or four thousand, Lord Luxborough and Mr. Gore together could not get their man chose for less than was offered by a stranger.

This was only to be expected: for when the patron's only recommendation was his money, there was no inducement to adhere to him if a candidate prepared to spend more money came along. The venal boroughs—Stockbridge, Hindon, Cricklade, New Shoreham—were boroughs without an established patron and in them elections were really free—corruption, wrote Gibbon in the *Decline and Fall*, was 'the most infallible symptom of constitutional liberty'. It flourished in boroughs where the electorate was for the most part poor and ill-educated, and where there was neither a patron nor a political issue to determine their voting.

Interest could rarely be measured quantitatively, and the simple statement that a patron commanded a certain number of seats in Parliament can only be accepted with qualifications. Consider, for example, the parliamentary interest of the Duke of Newcastle at the height of his power in about 1760. At Aldborough and Boroughbridge, which he used to call 'my own two boroughs', he could nominate the Members and there was no need for them to put in an appearance on election day. But one of the Members had to be Andrew Wilkinson, who managed the boroughs for Newcastle; he had some property of his own in the constituencies and could claim a seat almost in his own right. In Sussex, Newcastle claimed control over nine seats: one for the county, and two each at

Lewes, Rye, Hastings, and Seaford. But the county seat had to be filled from the senior branch of the Pelham family; both Lewes and Rye preferred to have Sussex men represent them and grew restive when Newcastle began recommending strangers; and at Hastings and Seaford Newcastle's influence lasted only so long as he was first lord of the Treasury—they were really Treasury boroughs, managed by him. In Nottinghamshire he could claim three seats: one for the county, one at Newark, and one at East Retford. The occupant of the county seat had to be a Nottinghamshire man, nor were strangers welcome at either Newark or East Retford. In short, only at his two pocket boroughs could Newcastle have safely recommended a stranger, and his 'command' extended to no more than three seats. Nor does this enumeration take into account the many compromises and adjustments Newcastle had to make with other patrons before his recommendations could be effective.

Cornwall, with its 21 boroughs, none of which had an electorate of more than 200, was pre-eminently the county of what might be called the professional borough-mongers. In 1754 twenty of its seats in Parliament were controlled by four men: Lord Edgcumbe and Lord Falmouth had six each, Edward Eliot and Humphry Morice had four each. The Cornish borough-mongers usually confined themselves to constituencies in which their families had an hereditary interest; rarely trespassed on each other's preserves (obviously for fear of reprisals); and usually sold to the Government any seats they did not want for their families or friends. It is doubtful if they made much profit out of their borough transactions; indeed, Edward Eliot told Pitt in 1797 that the money he received for the sale of seats was barely sufficient to cover his expenses. No patron made a fortune out of borough-mongering.

By 1789 a new and formidable rival to the old established interests had entered Cornish borough politics. Sir Francis Basset had filched two seats from Lord Edgcumbe (one at Mitchell and one at Penryn), and two seats from Lord Falmouth (one at Penryn and one at Tregony). Edgcumbe was left with four seats (two at Lostwithiel, one at Bossiney, and one at Fowey). Of these, Fowey had been attacked by Basset, and Bossiney was in a perilous state since the passing of Crewe's bill disfranchising the revenue officers. Falmouth's holding had sunk to three (two at Truro and one at Mitchell): he had lost two seats (Penryn and Tregony) to Basset, and had sold his interest at St. Mawes to Lord Buckingham. Eliot alone had increased his seats, to six in 1790 as against four in 1754, by acquiring both seats at Grampound in 1758. Morice had sold the boroughs of Launceston and Newport to the Duke of Northumberland in 1775. In a paper written for Lord North he explained why he had decided to part with his borough interest:

An estate of £1,200 per annum in a manner given up to the supporting the boroughs and £3,000 besides annually expended for that purpose and keeping up the house, etc.

The trouble of it, not to say anything of the expense, is more than Mr. Morice can bear with a constitution much impaired by the gout . . .

He lost a Member last year after all the trouble and expense he had been at, and notwithstanding the established interest he seems to have, he may be worse off next time.

In order to keep up his interest he has been obliged to let a steward, who naturally is not any economist, act without control. By this means occasional expenses have been sometimes enormous, and he has done what he pleased in regard of the rest of Mr. Morice's estates under his care, so that upon this account there is not any calculation to be made of the expense.

The biggest of the aristocratic borough-mongers in 1754 was the Duke of Newcastle, whose parliamentary interest had for fifty years been strengthened by the patronage of Government. On his death in 1768 his landed property passed to his heirs, but much of his parliamentary interest died with him: there was a personal element in borough-mongering which could not be transmitted to a successor. Aldborough, Boroughbridge, East Retford, and Newark passed to Henry, 2nd Duke of Newcastle; but whereas his uncle had controlled both seats at East Retford, he controlled only one. The Pelham estates in Sussex were inherited by the old Duke's cousin, Thomas, Lord Pelham, but all that was left of Newcastle's parliamentary interest was some influence at Lewes and in the county. Rye reverted to the Treasury, as had Hastings and Seaford before Newcastle's death.

The Duke of Northumberland, who had no borough interest in 1754, acquired control of three constituencies by purchase: Bere Alston, Launceston, and Newport. The Duke of Portland spent a fortune in electioneering, and achieved very little for it. At the general election of 1768 he led the anti-Lowther party in Cumberland and Carlisle, and won both seats in these constituencies, but by 1780 he had yielded his position to Lord Surrey; in 1768 he won control of Wigan, a very expensive borough, but by the end of the period had surrendered his interest to Sir Henry

Bridgeman; and his interventions at Callington and Coventry in 1768 were unsuccessful and never repeated. Even the vast resources of Lord Clive brought him but a meagre yield: he dabbled in some half a dozen constituencies yet Bishop's Castle was his only lasting acquisition. Finally, towards the end of this period, the Earl of Surrey, who had turned Protestant, began to exploit his natural interest, hitherto dormant because of his family's Catholicism. Surrey intervened in five constituencies: Arundel, Carlisle, Gloucester, Hereford, and Horsham; and by 1790 had succeeded in bringing three seats under his control.

The biggest borough-monger of all in this period was Sir James Lowther, and a study of his career throws light on the psychology of this form of political activity. Lowther set out to monopolize the parliamentary representation of Cumberland and Westmorland, and by 1784 controlled seven seats in these counties (one for Cumberland, one at Carlisle, two at Cockermouth, two for Westmorland, and one at Appleby). In addition he owned the pocket borough of Haslemere in Surrey, which he bought in 1780. Achieving this electoral empire cost him at least £100,000, and probably a good deal more. One of the richest men in England, he was a large landowner; developed the coal mines on his estates and engaged in coastal shipping; and supplied capital for the financial activities of Robert Mackreth, one of the great usurers of the age. In short, Lowther was a big business man, and his boroughs were a symbol of his success. Yet it was not simply the acquisition of a number of seats in Parliament that drove him on: had that been the case, he could have obtained a far larger electoral empire at a much smaller cost. In 1786 Lonsdale (as Lowther had then become) fought three elections within nine months: two at Carlisle and one at Lancaster. He spent over £50,000 in a vain attempt to acquire one seat at each of these constituencies, which even had he been successful would have been held on a precarious tenure (they were both open boroughs with large electorates). For less than half this sum he could have bought the borough of Gatton, which was then for sale, a complete pocket borough with no real voters. Between 1780 and 1784 he tried to buy Lord Egremont's Cumberland estate, which would have strengthened his interest in that county, offering £5,000 above the price agreed upon by arbitrators together with an option on the borough of Haslemere. In other words, he was ready to trade two seats in a perfectly safe borough for the doubtful chance of being able to return a second Member for Cumberland.

Lowther's electoral activities were not prompted solely by the desire to make a figure in politics through the acquisition of a following in the House of Commons. They resulted in large part from a passion for drive and domination, which he strove to satisfy by commanding the parliamentary representation of the counties where his estates lay. His Members (his 'ninepins' as they were called) surrendered their political independence as the price of their seats, and voted in a solid block the way Lowther dictated. But what did he achieve through his control of nine votes in the House of Commons? Though courted and flattered at moments of political crisis, he was neither esteemed nor respected; he never held office (though at least in the early part of his career his ambition looked in that direction); and his only gain for a lifetime's borough-mongering was an earldom.

In fact, the possession of borough interest led none of these borough-mongers to high political office. Edward Eliot never rose higher than the Board of Trade; Humphry Morice and Lord Edgcumbe held court or sinecure offices only; and the Boscawens were politically unambitious. The peers were politically important because of their rank, not because of their boroughs. Electoral interest had a local, not a national, significance. The Morgans of Tredegar, probably the leading political family in South Wales, commanded three seats in the House of Commons during this period. Five members of the family sat in Parliament between 1754 and 1790 for a combined total of 85 years. Only two of them are known to have spoken in the House: John Morgan in 1772, to ask why there had been a delay in issuing a writ for Monmouthshire; and Charles Morgan in 1780, when he presented the Breconshire petition for economical reform. They never held, nor apparently ever desired, political office. But when in 1770 Lord North conferred on Thomas Morgan the lord lieutenancies of Breconshire and Monmouthshire, in preference to the family's hereditary rival the Duke of Beaufort, the Morgans felt obliged to break off their contacts with Opposition and support North's Administration.

If borough interest by itself did not confer a claim to office, neither did the lack of it prevent men from reaching the top. Neither the elder Pitt and George Grenville in the 1760s, nor the younger Pitt and Charles James Fox twenty years later, had any borough interest. Henry Fox had none of his own, and Lord North's family controlled only one seat in the House. To lead the House of Commons required entirely different qualities of mind and character from those needed to maintain an electoral interest, and it seems highly unlikely that the disposition towards both these types of political activity could be found in the same man.

The one exception to the general rule linking interest to property was the interest of Government. Wherever there were voters who held office under Government or were aspirants to Government favours or were employed by a department of Government, there was a potential Government interest; it was built upon the support of placemen and would-be placemen, just as a family interest was built upon property. The Government interest extended to every constituency where there were real voters, but in the majority of them it counted for little. As a general rule its strength varied inversely with the number of voters in the constituency. There were exceptions—Hampshire among the counties, and Dover and Sandwich among the larger boroughs; but it is clear that a small group of placemen would have more influence in a small constituency than in a large one. Even in large constituencies the Government interest could be decisive in a close-fought election, but only in conjunction with a private interest.

It is not always easy to say which were or were not Government boroughs. Obviously constituencies such as Ludgershall or Weymouth and Melcombe Regis, where the patron habitually placed one or more seats at the disposal of Government, were not. More difficult to classify are those constituencies where the Government interest was interwoven with a natural or family interest, such as the three Isle of Wight boroughs. They were invariably classed as Government boroughs in 1754, yet by 1784 there was little trace of Government interest. East and West Looe were sometimes counted as Government boroughs in 1754 because Government candidates were accepted in them, but in fact they were both under the control of the Buller family. At Dover and Hythe the Government had considerable influence, and could usually return one Member in alliance with a neighbouring family. At the beginning of the period the majority of borough owners were on the Government side and could count on Government support in elections: it is therefore less easy to isolate the Government interest in 1754 than at the end of the period when there was a clear division in the House of Commons between Government and Opposition.

In 1754 thirteen boroughs were controlled by the Government

alone, yielding 25 seats in the House of Commons (at Sandwich the
Government controlled only one seat). Six of these boroughs were controlled by the Treasury (Harwich, Hastings, Orford, Rye, Seaford,
and Winchelsea); six by the Admiralty (Dartmouth, Plymouth, Portsmouth, Rochester, Saltash, and Sandwich); and one (Queenborough) by
the Admiralty and the Ordnance. Only Rochester (600 voters) and Sandwich (700 voters) had electorates larger than 200. All were corporation or
freeman boroughs, except Seaford, a scot and lot borough where the
electorate was deliberately restricted.

The Treasury boroughs were all ports, and Treasury control was
effected through the customs and excise officers. Harwich and Orford
were the safest Treasury boroughs: both had electorates below 50 and
in neither was there a contest during this period. But the Treasury surrendered its interest at Orford in 1766 to a private patron, Lord Hertford.
Of the other Treasury boroughs, only Hastings was under its control
throughout the period. Rye remained faithful to the Duke of Newcastle
after his resignation in 1762; reverted to the Treasury after his death
in 1768; but one seat was lost there in 1784. Seaford was lost in 1786,
when Henry Flood succeeded in getting the electorate increased; and
Winchelsea, where the Treasury interest was never very strong, was
lost altogether by 1784. At the end of the period the Treasury controlled
only five seats in these boroughs, whereas in 1754 it had controlled
twelve.

The Admiralty boroughs were naval centres or dockyard towns, where
the Admiralty was one of the chief employers of labour and Admiralty
contracts were competed for by local business men. None of these boroughs
was safe, and two—Dartmouth and Saltash—were lost during this period.
The Admiralty boroughs had larger electorates than those influenced
by the Treasury, and Admiralty control could never be as stringent. At
Plymouth and Portsmouth there was a strong independent party, and at
each borough in 1784 one seat was wrested from the Admiralty. At
Rochester there were eight contests during the period; at Queenborough
there were three; and Sandwich, with 700 voters, was described by
Robinson in 1784 as 'a borough of contests': there were in fact a number
of private interests besides that of the Admiralty. Thus the 13 seats
controlled by the Admiralty in 1754 had fallen by 1784 to seven.

Crewe's Act of 1782, which disfranchised the revenue officers, was
intended to reduce the Government's influence in elections. Its full effects

were not felt until after 1790 and how far it succeeded in achieving its object is not easy to say. It was one reason why the Treasury lost Seaford, and it played some part in the decline of the Government interest at Rye, Portsmouth, and Plymouth. No doubt, also, it helped to reduce the Government interest in other boroughs where that interest was only marginal. But Dartmouth was lost two years before Crewe's Act became law, and the disfranchisement of the revenue officers does not explain the loss of Saltash or Winchelsea. The Government interest was declining throughout this period, in correlation with the growth of party. And if Crewe's Act failed to achieve all the Opposition expected from it, it was probably because they greatly over-estimated the influence the Government exercised through the revenue officers.

Scarborough, for example, seemed a borough predestined to pass under Government control. It was a port, dependent to some extent on Admiralty orders for its shipping; and the franchise was in the corporation, a body of less than 50, about a quarter of whom were revenue officers. Yet, though Government had considerable influence, Scarborough never became a Government borough—indeed, Henry Pelham told the corporation in 1753 that it was 'not at all proper' for him to interfere in an election there. Lord Granby carried a Member at Scarborough in 1768 entirely through the influence of Administration, and yet from 1770 to 1782 when the Manners family were in opposition, they still held one seat at Scarborough. The corporation, wrote the Duke of Rutland in 1785, 'starved with me in opposition on the empty diet of promise and expectation'. Nor did the Rutland family have an estate near the borough; their interest, in the Duke's words, was 'an artificial one, nourished in the hotbed of Government favour'—yet it survived the cold winds of opposition.

Rye remained faithful to Newcastle after he had gone into opposition in 1762 and successfully defied the Treasury. Yet it had an electorate of less than 40, about half of whom held places under Government. Its fidelity to Newcastle was not dictated by political motives: there was an old feud between Rye and Winchelsea, and Edwin Wardroper, the Government manager at Winchelsea, was trying to extend his control over Rye. Fear of Wardroper, not dislike of Treasury control, made the freemen of Rye remain faithful to Newcastle. Rye was managed by an oligarchy of its leading citizens, and the only way the Treasury could have won back the borough would have been by a purge of the oligarchy and a new creation of freemen—a remedy worse than the disease. Rather than follow such a course the Treasury preferred to wait. By 1767, when the danger from Wardroper had considerably lessened, Rye was ready to accept again a Treasury recommendation; but at the general election of 1768 Newcastle's candidates were returned without Treasury interference. After Newcastle's death in November 1768 Rye became once more a Treasury borough. But in 1784 William Dickenson, who had represented the borough since 1777, was again returned, although he was in opposition to Pitt's Administration, together with a Government candidate.

The strength of the Government interest in any borough depended in a great degree upon the manager, and when the manager tried to misappropriate Government interest there was little the Government could do to stop him. The classic case during this period was at Dartmouth in 1780, when the Government manager, Arthur Holdsworth, having become sympathetic to the Opposition, refused to accept Government candidates and returned himself and Lord Howe. The Phillips family began as Government managers at Camelford, but by 1780 were in complete control of the borough; they still accepted a Government nominee for one seat, but as a favour not an obligation. Edmund Wilkins cultivated Malmesbury in the late 1770s with a Government subsidy of £720 a year, and the Treasury naturally counted Malmesbury as a Government borough. But in 1784 Wilkins returned two Members of the Opposition, much to the indignation of George Rose, Pitt's secretary to the Treasury. Harwich was managed from 1770 by John Robinson, secretary to the Treasury until 1782, which helps to explain why it was the safest Government borough; yet Oldfield, in the 1792 edition of his *History of the Boroughs*, described it as 'formerly a Treasury borough', now controlled by Robinson.

The same rule holds good for a Government borough as for one under private patronage: whatever the basis of an interest might be, whether in land or in Government favours, the constituency had to be nursed with care; and in the last resort the man on the spot had more sway with the electors than the more distant patron. It was as the result of assiduous courting of the electors that Philip Stephens, secretary to the Admiralty, increased the Government's hold over Sandwich from one to both seats; and by the same means George III converted New Windsor into a court borough. Despite the growth of party during this period, there was little change in the essential nature of the patronage system.

2. THE ELECTIONS

THE GENERAL ELECTION OF 1754

Henry Pelham, first lord of the Treasury and leader of the House of Commons since 1743, died on 6 March 1754, in the midst of preparations for the general election. The Duke of Newcastle, his brother and successor as head of the Treasury, upon whom now devolved the management of the election, had to be informed of all Pelham's plans. This was done by Pelham's election manager Lord Dupplin, his 'very faithful secretary' John Roberts, and the secretary to the Treasury James West. Between them they supplied Newcastle with a mass of papers, which provide an electoral survey more complete than is available for any of the three following general elections, and is only equalled by John Robinson's surveys for the elections of 1780 and 1784. Among them are some of Pelham's original lists (undated, but partly or wholly in his hand) of 'persons to be provided for', 'persons not settled', 'places and persons destined for them', etc., none of them complete or systematically arranged. There are lists drawn up for Newcastle's information, summarizing what Pelham's three assistants could recollect or extract from his surviving correspondence; and day by day memoranda dealing with the election campaign as it developed. Most comprehensive of all is a document entitled 'The Present State of Elections for England and Wales', undated but placed by internal evidence between 16 and 21 March 1754.

In this document the names of the candidates are given for each constituency, together with remarks about the state of the election. Sometimes these are very short: 'Lord Godolphin's interest', 'Mr. Gashry can best inform', 'a strong contest', etc.; but some also give a brief picture of the various interests in the constituency. At a superficial glance it would appear that the Treasury was concerned with almost every constituency in England and Wales, and had directed a nation-wide planting out of candidates. But many entries in the 'Remarks' column go far to correct this impression. Against many constituencies the only entry is the word 'Tories'—obviously a Whig election manager had nothing to do in such places. For Chester no candidates are named: 'Two Tories' is the remark under the heading—Newcastle either did not know or did not care who they were. And in many constituencies the electoral prospect is sufficiently indicated by the name of the patron. Where contests took place, it is not easy to see any common link between the constituencies or evidence of a nation-wide electoral campaign. Possibly the two bitterest contests of this general election were in Oxfordshire and at Appleby: Oxfordshire a contest between Whigs and Tories in a constituency of 4,000 electors; Appleby a fight between two Whig magnates for control of a pocket borough, with no real voters and no political issues involved. In Oxfordshire the Treasury could provide financial help for the Whig candidates, but could directly influence very few voters; at Appleby it did not interfere for it could do nothing. In fact, there was no Treasury directed country-wide campaign in 1754 and the role of the Treasury was confined to placing certain candidates in certain constituencies: with the majority of constituencies it had little, if anything, to do.

In which constituencies was the Treasury actively concerned? In the Newcastle manuscripts there is a document, dated 15 March 1754, which begins:

The Duke of Newcastle went through (with Lord Dupplin and Mr. Roberts only) the list of Members of the House of Commons for the general election, as produced by Mr. Roberts.

The following names of places and persons had been settled by Mr. Pelham with Lord Dupplin at Richmond in last January, and was copied by Mr. Roberts.

Then follows a list of 35 constituencies, with the names of 65 candidates selected for them (in five constituencies only one seat was available for Government candidates). Sixteen of these constituencies were in Cornwall and the names of the Cornish borough-mongers are prominent in the list: Lord Edgcumbe, Lord Falmouth, John Bullen, Edward Eliot, &c. Of the remainder, two were Admiralty boroughs (Dartmouth and Plymouth), one a Treasury borough (Orford), three seats had been sold to Government by Thomas Pitt (one at Okehampton, two at Old Sarum), two were controlled by Henry Fox (at Malmesbury) and two by George Bubb Dodington (at Weymouth and Melcombe Regis), &c. In all, 31 of these constituencies were controlled by private patrons, and only four by Government. But not all of the 65 candidates for these constituencies were Government nominees: at least 20 seats were filled by the patrons themselves, their relatives or friends, independently of Government.

This leaves 45 seats for Government candidates, and to this figure can be added about 25 more (not on the list) which the Government also had at its disposal (in other Government boroughs, the Isle of Wight boroughs, and seats sold to the Government by patrons). Thus, out of a total of 513 Members elected by English and Welsh constituencies, only about 70 were found their seats by the Government, almost all in pocket boroughs. And even this figure is too high if it is taken to mean the number of men personally chosen by Newcastle and on whose loyalty he could depend. The candidates had to be selected in co-operation with the patron and his wishes had to be taken into account: few patrons were prepared to give the Treasury *carte blanche* in respect of nomination to a borough. The Admiralty seats were filled by the first lord of the Admiralty, not by the Treasury, and naval officers or Admiralty officials had first claim upon them. Lastly, it must be remembered that most of the candidates with whom Newcastle was in some way concerned in 1754 had been nominated by Henry Pelham and their loyalty to their new chief had yet to be proved.

As well as acting as a sort of electoral clearing house (though on a small scale) for candidates and patrons—putting them in touch with each other and regulating the financial arrangements—the Treasury also partly financed candidates. This was done through the secret service account, or the King's private account to give it its better title—money for which the King was not accountable to Parliament. In round figures, almost £25,000 from this account was spent in 1754 on 22 English constituencies, of which £5,000 was spent in vain: John Dodd, who received £2,000 for his election campaign at Reading, was beaten by one vote; Robert Tracy, a candidate at Worcester, received £1,000, and when refused a further subsidy gave up the contest; and the defeated Government candidates at Wallingford took another £2,000. In addition, the Government paid £3,000 towards the expenses of the Whig candidates in Oxfordshire, who were seated only as the result of a party vote in the House. £1,800 was spent on aiding the two Government candidates at Westminster against an opposition that stood little chance of success—but then, Westminster was a prestige constituency and a very expensive one. The remaining £15,000 was spent on 17 constituencies: nearly £1,500 at Tregony; £1,000 each at Ilchester, Barnstaple, Steyning, Minehead, Bramber, New Shoreham, Evesham, and Newark; £800 at Chippenham; £700 at Camelford, Grampound, and Newport (Isle of

Wight); £500 at Honiton and Dunwich; £300 at Shaftesbury; and £200 at Totnes. In eleven of the 22 constituencies where the Treasury subsidized candidates there were contests, and at Worcester a contest was only averted at the last moment. In the remaining ten constituencies, the money was paid to borough patrons on behalf of candidates who considered they had a claim on Government for their election expenses and were able to bully the Treasury into admitting it.

£2,500—about one-tenth of the Government's expenses in the English constituencies—was spent on shoring up Newcastle's private electoral interest. At Newark, where Newcastle and the Duke of Rutland each recommended to one seat, there was an opposition sponsored by the vicar of Newark, who owned considerable property in the borough and was always making trouble for the patrons. Newcastle and Rutland were victorious, at the cost of about £1,700 of which £1,000 was paid from secret service money. And £1,500 was spent on buying off John Fuller, the leader of the malcontents in Newcastle's borough of Lewes; he was provided with a seat at Tregony and thus prevented from giving Newcastle any opposition at Lewes.

Besides the money spent on English constituencies, £1,800 was spent on Scotland. £1,000 went to the Duke of Argyll, who managed the general election for the Government in Scotland, to be spent at his discretion; and £800 was given to Thomas Leslie, an impecunious army officer, son of the Earl of Rothes, who was threatened with an opposition in Perth Burghs. Leslie pleaded so piteously for assistance that Newcastle must have been hard-hearted indeed (which he was not) not to have helped him. This was really a charitable donation, and at the next general election in 1761 Leslie was again pleading for financial help.

The total Government expenditure at the general election of 1754 was much less than was spent by the Whigs and Tories in Oxfordshire or by Lord Thanet and Sir James Lowther at Appleby. Nor would the Government's majority have been much smaller had it spent nothing at all: most of the subsidized candidates could have brought themselves into Parliament at their own expense but saw no reason to refuse Government aid if they could get it. Jobbery and charity, rather than any political purpose, dictated this expenditure. A typical case is that of Charles Whitworth, who first received £1,000 towards the expenses of his election at Minehead and then a pension of £400 a year to enable him to keep up his position as an M.P. The game of trying to live at the expense of Government was a favourite one with mid-eighteenth-century politicians, and in 1754 there was no strong political cause to lead them away from Government.

In the 1754 election 62 constituencies went to the poll, excluding the Scottish districts of burghs. The contests can be subdivided as follows:

5 contests in 40 English counties

17 in 32 English boroughs with an electorate of 1,000 or over (the large boroughs)

10 in 28 English boroughs with an electorate of at least 500 but below 1,000 (the medium boroughs)

24 in 143 English boroughs with an electorate below 500 (the small boroughs)

3 in 12 Welsh counties

1 in 12 Welsh borough constituencies

2 in 30 Scottish counties

What were these contests about and how far was there a common issue involved?

The five English counties which went to the poll were Herefordshire, Hertfordshire, Kent, Oxfordshire, and Rutland. Two of these were purely local contests, with national issues playing little part: in Hereford-shire an outsider tried to break the hold of two of the leading county families, the Cornewalls and the Harleys, on its representation; and the contest in Rutland was a fight between the three leading peers in the county. The other three county contests were between Whigs and Tories. Kent, represented in the Parliament of 1747 by two Tories, only one of whom stood again in 1754, was successfully contested by two Whigs; and in Hertfordshire a candidate backed by some of the leading Tory country gentlemen and an independent element in the county, stood against the two sitting Whig Members. Oxfordshire was the classic case of a Whig v. Tory contest, the one contest carried on in 1754 whole-heartedly in terms of an old cause and ancient loyalties; and the last. Nor was Oxfordshire again contested during the remainder of this period. In a few other counties opposition was mooted but not pressed to the poll, as in Cornwall, where an interesting and unusual manœuvre was attempted by Admiral Boscawen to break through the monopoly of a few inter-married Tory families by promoting the candidature of a third

Tory, but was soon abandoned; and in Dorset, where Lord Digby, a Whig, toyed with the idea of standing for the county against two Tories, but desisted because of the expense. In most counties the representation was settled by the county meeting.

Of the 17 contests in the large boroughs, eight turned on purely local issues, and three were fought in terms of corporation versus independent candidates. In only six were there contests based on matters of national interest: Bristol, London, Southwark, Evesham, Colchester, and Nottingham; and even in these the contests were fought in terms of traditional loyalties rather than of concrete political issues and programmes. At Bristol, the Tories broke the electoral compact with the Whigs and put up two candidates. But their successful candidate, Richard Beckford, was only a Tory by courtesy: a few years later his brother, Alderman William Beckford, who backed Richard's candidature at Bristol, was to boast that he had always been a Whig. William Beckford himself was returned for London, together with Sir John Barnard, as the candidates of the party of small merchants and tradesmen, defeating two Government supporters. At Southwark, Sir Crisp Gascoyne, who had Tory connexions, was defeated; Edward Rudge who, though voting with Government, received Tory support, was defeated at Evesham; and Charles Gray, a Tory, was successful at Colchester but unseated on petition. At Nottingham, where the Duke of Newcastle, leader of the Whigs, and Lord Middleton, leader of the local Tories, had concluded a compact by which each side was to return one Member, John Plumptre, a second Whig candidate, stood without Newcastle's support and was defeated. Among the large boroughs which did not go to the poll the only one where political issues seem to have played much part was Exeter, where the Anglican-dominated corporation refused to endorse the candidature of Humphry Sydenham, one of the sitting Members, because he had voted for the Jew bill.

Six of the ten contests in the 28 medium boroughs were of a purely local character. Of the remaining four, the contest at Berwick-upon-Tweed could hardly be said to involve a political issue, though Government was concerned in it: Newcastle gave Government support to John Wilkes against John Delaval, in retaliation for the Delaval family's interference at Newark; but all three candidates were Whigs. At Maldon, John Bullock, a Whig, but supported by the Essex Tories, defeated one of the Government candidates; here, local issues were far more important than national politics. Sudbury and Reading had straight political contests. At Sudbury, Richard Rigby, a Bedford Whig, failed against two Government candidates; and at Reading, John Dodd, who had received £2,000 from Government for this election, failed by one vote against a Tory and a Bedford Whig. 'The electors, principally of the court side, have been remarkably venal', wrote an observer. '. . . The electors on the Tory side are comparatively upright.' The Tory candidate came top of the poll; but money, rather than party feeling, decided the issue between the two Whigs.

In short, in 100 English constituencies (the counties and large and medium boroughs) in 1754 there were 32 contests, of which only 12 had any national significance. In Wales, only the election for Carmarthen was fought on party lines. In Scotland, Ross-shire was contested by Kenneth Mackenzie, son of an attainted Jacobite peer, and James Stuart Mackenzie, brother of Lord Bute and nephew of the Duke of Argyll; but there is no evidence that Kenneth Mackenzie's success was due to pro-Jacobite feeling.

Naturally, in the small boroughs almost all contests were fought without any reference to the candidates' political allegiances. There was the appearance of a political contest at Newport (Cornwall), where two Bedford Whigs were defeated by two Government supporters, but the real issue at stake was whether Humphry Morice or the Duke of Bedford was to control the borough. Similarly, Bedford tried to revive his interest at Camelford, where both seats had been placed at the disposal of Government, but did not press the issue to a poll. At Wallingford two Government candidates were defeated by Richard Neville Aldworth, a Bedford Whig, and John Hervey, a Government supporter. Hervey had been invited to contest Wallingford by a group in the corporation, about half of whom were for, and half against, the Administration; their purpose in inviting him was 'to recover the credit of the borough and get it out of the hands of the lower people'. Hervey told Aldworth that if elected he would continue to vote with Government, but refused to make any public declaration which he believed would have lost him some support. So there was, after all, a political flavour to the Wallingford election. Still, when Henry Pelham named two Government candidates to stand against Hervey and Aldworth, no political consequences followed. 'Hearken, Hervey', said Pelham, 'we'll fight it out in the country and be good friends in town.'

Hervey and Pelham were not the only ones to fight it out in the country and remain good friends in town. One of the most controversial contests of this general election was at Mitchell (Cornwall), where Robert Clive and John Stephenson stood against Simon Luttrell and William Hussey. The leading members of the Administration were deeply divided over this election, and for once Newcastle and Hardwicke were on opposite sides and Henry Fox and Hardwicke (who loathed each other) on the same side. Fox, Hardwicke, and Lord Sandwich, a Bedford Whig in opposition to Government, supported Clive and Stephenson, who were returned; and Newcastle used his majority in the House of Commons to have the defeated candidates, Luttrell and Hussey, seated on petition. The result, as far as Government was concerned, was the same either way, for all four candidates were disposed to support Newcastle's Administration. Here, as elsewhere, party politics and personal friendships cut across parliamentary allegiances, and there was no straightforward line-up on the Government or the Opposition side.

In 1754 the only organized group in opposition to Newcastle's Administration was the Bedford Whigs. The Tories, a body of about a hundred Members, were separated from Administration by a gulf of temperament, rather than of politics. They did not wish for office, and since on crucial questions they did not vote as a bloc they were not a force in politics. The general election of 1754 was not a contest between Government and Opposition, nor was it a device for testing public opinion on political issues (there were none in 1754, with the possible exception of the Jew bill). Its outcome was the resultant of a number of local forces, personal rivalries, struggles for local consequence and importance.

When the election was over the Duke of Newcastle, always anxious and needing to be reassured, deputed Lord Dupplin to draw up lists of the House of Commons and calculate the size of the Government's majority. Dupplin calculated that the Government had gained 33 seats and lost 22; and this was his forecast of political allegiances in the new Parliament (excluding five Members who had died since the elections and allowing for Members returned for more than one constituency):

Government	368
Tories	106
Opposition Whigs (i.e., the Bedford group)	42
Doubtful	26

The Government Members were divided into two groups: one classed on an occupational or professional basis, the other according to their known (or assumed) political affiliations and tendencies; and in some of the lists the two criteria of division intercross with confusing results. The 202 Members classed on an occupational basis comprise 87 country gentlemen, 45 placemen holding office at the pleasure of the Crown, 20 army officers, 20 merchants, 12 naval officers, ten placemen for life, and eight 'lawyers and placemen'. (It must be remembered that these groups are not complete, e.g., many army officers and merchants are classed according to their political affiliations, not their occupations.) Presumably Dupplin felt that these 202 Members classed on an occupational basis would look to the Duke of Newcastle alone as their political chief. The other 166 Government supporters were ranged by Dupplin under their several leaders as follows:

Prince of Wales	34
Henry Fox and the Duke of Cumberland	26
Duke of Argyll	15
Lord Powis	8
Duke of Rutland	6
Horace Walpole	6
Lord Hartington	6
Lord Rockingham	4
Lord Ravensworth	3

Finally, there is a residual group entitled 'For, of various connexions', which includes 58 names.

Reassured by Dupplin's lists, Newcastle wrote on 14 May:

The Parliament is good beyond my expectations, and I believe there are more Whigs in it, and generally well-disposed Whigs, than in any Parliament since the Revolution .... The great point will be to keep our friends together, and that they should do right when they are chose. For from the enemy we have nothing to fear.

But who were the enemy? and who were Newcastle's friends? Eighteen months later, when foreign policy became the burning question in the House of Commons, the Duke of Bedford's party had joined Newcastle's Administration and the Opposition was formed round a nucleus of the Prince of Wales's friends, whom Dupplin had counted in May 1754 as

Government supporters. Even the men on whose behalf Newcastle had particularly exerted himself at the general election of 1754 were not to be depended upon when a real·political issue came before the House. Among those who voted against Newcastle on the treaties with Russia and Hesse in November 1755 were Samuel Martin, whose election at Camelford had been partly financed by the Government; George Amyand, who had received £1,000 from the Treasury for his election at Barnstaple; and Richard Hussey, one of the candidates on whose behalf Newcastle had fought the election petition at Mitchell. And the leader of the Opposition in November 1755 was William Pitt, returned in 1754 for Newcastle's own borough of Aldborough.

When Newcastle was making his arrangements for the leadership of the House of Commons after Henry Pelham's death, Pitt had warned him:

Indeed, my dear Lord, the inside of the House must be considered in other respects besides merely numbers, or the reins of government will soon slip or be wrested out of any minister's hands.

It is a revealing comment upon Dupplin's calculations; and the Parliament of 1754 was to show that something more than a paper majority was necessary to lead the House of Commons.

THE GENERAL ELECTION OF 1761

The Parliament of 1754 ran its full course, and was dissolved on 20 March 1761. George III had then been five months on the throne, and, with the eagerness and naïvety of youth, was burning to rid himself of his grandfather's ministers and reverse the policy of the previous reign. To inaugurate a reign of virtue and purity, he gave orders that no money was to be issued from the Treasury for the general election. Newcastle wrung his hands and complained to his friends: how was he to manage the election with no money at the Treasury's disposal? It seemed to him a dire omen for the future. But in the event, it did not have the consequences which George III had hoped for and Newcastle had feared: it did not inaugurate a reign of virtue and purity and it made little difference to the composition of the new House of Commons.

This general election took place at a time when there was no organized Opposition in the House of Commons, and thus, to an even greater extent than in 1754, there was no political issue to divide the electorate and distinguish the candidates. The questions which were to lead to political divisions in this Parliament—the Peace of Paris, the expulsion of Wilkes and the question of general warrants, the taxation of America, the regulation of the East India Company—were as yet in the future, and in 1761 politicians harped on the prospects of unanimity under a new King rather than of party conflict. The nation was in the midst of a successful war, and with the accession of Bute, the King's favourite, to the Pitt-Newcastle Cabinet, all the front-rank politicians were comprehended within the Government fold. There were strains and stresses between the three principal members of the Administration, and Bute's favour with the King threatened both Newcastle's control of patronage and Pitt's conduct of the war, but in March 1761 no issue had yet arisen which could lead to a breach in this uneasy coalition.

In 1754 there was only one market where borough owners could sell their seats, and it was to Newcastle, as head of the Treasury, that candidates went in search of constituencies. But in 1761 Newcastle was the aged minister of a dead monarch. Pitt disliked election business and would not meddle with it: he never took the trouble to cultivate a constituency himself nor to win the friendship of borough owners. He owed his following in the House of Commons to his successful conduct of the war, not to his electoral interest; and, provided his close friends were accommodated with seats, he was indifferent as to who ran the general election. Those who were ambitious or thought they could forecast political trends, who considered themselves disobliged by Newcastle or had old scores to pay off, hastened to pay their court to Bute, the favourite of the young King, the man of the future. George Bubb Dodington, who had been excluded from the Pitt-Newcastle coalition, and who, though approaching seventy, still fancied his chances in the new reign, offered two seats at Weymouth and Melcombe Regis to Bute. But Bute had no taste for electioneering, nor had he the knowledge and experience to do the work. Even had he wished to do so, he would have had to use the Treasury machine; and Bute, who wanted Newcastle as an ally against Pitt, did not care as yet to antagonize the Duke. Lord Shelburne encouraged Bute to inform himself of the state of the constituencies, but judging from the list Shelburne prepared for Bute's information, there was a lot Shelburne himself had to learn. In fact in 1761 there was only one person capable of managing the general election. 'The new Parliament', said Bute, 'would be the King's, let who will choose it'; and it was better to leave it to Newcastle, the old and experienced hand, than to venture himself, untried and ill-informed. Newcastle's fear of Bute's interference in the conduct of the general election, like so many trifles that harassed his mind, was a neurotic symptom, not a calm assessment of political probability.

When, after many delays and postponements, Bute submitted to Newcastle the list of those whom the King wished to see brought into Parliament on the Government interest, it contained only three names: Lord Parker, to whose election for Oxfordshire in 1754 the Treasury had contributed, and who was returned in 1761 on the Government interest at Rochester; Thomas Worsley, a close friend of Bute who had taught the King to ride, and whom Newcastle placed in the Treasury borough of Orford; and William Breton, the King's privy purse bearer, for whom Newcastle failed to provide and who never sat in the Parliament of 1761. In addition, by the King's command Newcastle arranged a seat at Harwich for Charles Townshend, his great-nephew, who under the Pitt-Newcastle coalition had been kept in minor court office far below his pretensions, and who now swore allegiance to Bute ('for a time only', as Bute with foresight expressed it). Other friends of Bute, such as Samuel Martin or Sir Edward Turner, were also brought in by Government as they had been in the Parliament of 1754; but the majority of Bute's friends were returned by private patrons (John Richmond Webb at Bossiney, Charles Jenkinson at Cockermouth) or on their own interest (John Morton at Abingdon, Sir John Cust at Grantham).

Newcastle's apprehension that Bute would interfere in the Treasury's conduct of the general election arose from disputes in constituencies where Bute was not directly concerned, and which indeed caused him considerable embarrassment. These were the results of old feuds in which former followers of Leicester House, the Prince of Wales's party, worsted under George II, now tried to obtain their revenge in the more favourable circumstances of the new reign. Henry Bilson Legge, the chancellor of the Exchequer, had insisted on contesting Hampshire at a by-election in 1759, and had forced Simeon Stuart, the candidate favoured by Bute and the Prince of Wales, to withdraw. Legge had been closely allied with Bute and Pitt in 1756–7, and George III, resenting his behaviour in Hampshire, had conceived a strong aversion to him. In 1761 Legge and Stuart were again the candidates in Hampshire, and the King gave orders that the Government voters (numerous in this county) should be allowed to vote as they pleased. It was a petty act of resentment and also a gesture in favour of virtue and purity, but since Legge and Stuart were unopposed, had no consequences. Still, it provoked Newcastle, who protested to Fox:

The Duke of Bedford hates or despises Legge, and the Duke of Devonshire and Mr. Pitt hates or despises Legge, and Lord Bute hates or despises Legge, and I don't care a farthing for Legge . . . but whilst he is chancellor of the Exchequer ought he not to have the Government interest?

Before the election came on, however, Legge was dismissed, which at least put an end to one of Newcastle's worries.

The dispute in Hampshire in 1759 was really a squabble between two local magnates, the Duke of Bolton backing Legge, and Lord Carnarvon, son of the Duke of Chandos, backing Stuart, each of whom tried to find protection at court. Carnarvon, a headstrong and touchy young man, also had political ambitions in Radnorshire, and at the general election of 1761 tried to enlist Bute's help against the old established interests there who looked for support to Newcastle. Carnarvon set out to deprive Howell Gwynne of his seat for Radnorshire and of the lord lieutenancy of the county, ostentatiously obtained the King's permission to stand at the general election, and then demanded Treasury support. Newcastle shuffled as he always did on such occasions, made promises to both sides, and then found he could not keep his engagements. Carnarvon asked Newcastle to secure for him the support of Thomas Lewis, the sitting Member for New Radnor Boroughs, and to make sure of Lewis's compliance raised an opposition to him in his constituency. All this Newcastle regarded as a challenge to what he called 'the Whig interest' (which he identified primarily with himself and his friends), and he complained of the 'little weight he had in the Closet' and that 'the Whigs were given up in many parts of England'. In the end Carnarvon secured Radnorshire and Government found a seat for Gwynne at Old Sarum; Carnarvon was unable to stop the contest in New Radnor Boroughs and Thomas Lewis's long supremacy there was ended. The election of 1761 had great significance in Radnorshire, but it was fought in terms of local interests and was not a struggle between Whigs and Tories or between Newcastle and Bute.

In 1761 there were 53 contested elections, as against 62 at the general election of 1754:

\# 4 contests in 40 English counties
 15 in 32 large boroughs
  6 in 28 medium boroughs
20 in 143 small boroughs
  1 in 12 Welsh counties
  1 in 12 Welsh boroughs
  5 in 30 Scottish counties
  1 Scottish burgh (Edinburgh)

Of these only a few are worth singling out for comment as distinguished by anything more than local interest.

The county of Durham went to the poll for the second time within six months—a most unusual proceeding for an English county. One seat was normally conceded to the Earl of Darlington, while the other was left to the choice of the country gentlemen. Rejecting the advice of the bishop of Durham, who had considerable weight in elections, 'to follow, not to force, the bent of the county', Darlington at the by-election of 1760 had put up a candidate for the seat hitherto held by a country gentleman; and, with the bishop's reluctant support, had succeeded. Newcastle, to whom Darlington appealed for the Government interest, was very embarrassed, for Darlington's candidate Robert Shafto came of a Tory family while Sir Thomas Clavering, the candidate of the country gentlemen, was unimpeachably Whig. At the general election the contest was repeated with the same candidates, and again Darlington was successful. In the city of Durham also, Darlington, with the support of the corporation, attempted to break the Lambton-Tempest control of the borough; his candidate was defeated, was returned at a by-election in December 1761 by three votes on a poll of over 1,500, but was unseated on petition.

The Hertfordshire election of 1761 well illustrates the confused and unpredictable nature of county politics. In 1754 two Whigs, standing on a joint interest, had defeated a Tory; and in 1761 Jacob Houblon, a Tory who had represented Hertfordshire 1741–1747, came forward against Charles Gore, one of the sitting Members, and Thomas Plumer Byde, another Whig. Byde had the support of some prominent City men with estates in the county and also of the Dissenters, who were very numerous in Hertfordshire, and came out top of the poll. Gore and Houblon, the one Whig, the other Tory, were supported by most of the county's aristocratic families and also by some leading Tories. Houblon won the second seat, defeating Gore by nearly 300 votes. Gore's vote slumped from 1,727 in 1754 to 1,244 in 1761; and while in 1754 he had a majority of nearly 500, in 1761 he lost his seat by nearly 300. A result such as this, not uncommon in an independent county like Hertfordshire, where there was no dominant aristocratic interest, can hardly be explained in terms of party or national politics.

The Gloucester borough election of 1761 was the last to be fought in this constituency in terms of the old Whig-Tory alignment, but the issues were confused, an indication that that alignment no longer corresponded to the facts of political life. In 1754 each side had returned one Member, George Augustus Selwyn, a Whig, and Charles Barrow, a Tory. The Tories had wanted to try for both seats and Powell Snell had declared his candidature on the Tory interest, but Selwyn and Barrow stood as joint candidates and Snell had been forced to withdraw. In 1761 Snell stood again, and Barrow the Tory again preferred to join with a Whig rather than with another Tory, which would have brought down on the Tory candidates the resentment of those voters who disliked the prospect of one party gaining control of both seats. Barrow came out top of the poll and Selwyn just behind him, with a majority of nearly 400 over Snell. To illustrate the confusion between party names and realities, here are the subsequent records of the two successful candidates: Barrow, the Tory in 1761, became a devoted member of Lord Rockingham's self-styled Whig party and ended his life a follower of Charles James Fox; Selwyn, the Whig in 1761, supported Lord North throughout the American war and subsequently the younger Pitt.

At Exeter in 1761 there was an unsuccessful attempt by two Whigs, sponsored by the Government and supported by the Dissenters and 'those who were termed the low church', against two candidates named by the Anglican-dominated corporation. At Lichfield, the Tories made their last stand against the Whigs, whose strength had been increasing in recent years; and a study of this election throws some light on what the words Whig and Tory meant in Staffordshire. Lichfield had an electorate of about 700, with a wide franchise which included 40s. freeholders, burgage holders, and freemen paying scot and lot. The Whigs were the followers and dependants of Lord Anson and Lord Gower, who were trying jointly to close the borough; and the Tories were the independent party, headed by a few local country gentlemen, who were trying to keep the borough open. There were five contests between 1747 and 1761, and the defeat of the Tory in 1761 (he was returned through the partiality of the returning officer but unseated on petition) marked the end of the independent interest. Lord Gower and the Anson family returned one Member each for the remainder of this period; and even after 1784, when they differed in politics, they continued to co-operate at Lichfield.

At Canterbury, another open borough with about 1,500 voters, Bute and Newcastle together were unable to secure the return of their candidates. Newcastle backed Sir James Creed, one of the sitting Members, a London merchant and director of the East India Company, and Bute William Mayne, a Scottish merchant who appears to have had no connexion with Canterbury. Their opponents, Richard Milles and Thomas Best, were local country gentlemen, and received support from both Whigs and Tories. 'No Scotch, no foreigner', was the cry at Canterbury; and the success of Milles and Best shows how little Administration could do, even when both parts of it were united, against strong local feeling.

One contest at this general election, almost unnoticed by the politicians at court and in Adminstration alike, was a portent for the future. In Westmorland Sir James Lowther took a further step towards monopolizing the parliamentary representation of the north-western counties. Lowther himself was returned head of the poll, and his follower John Upton won the second seat, but only 26 votes on a poll of 2,000 separated Upton from the candidate of the independent freeholders. It was the first sign of popular opposition to Lowther, and a foretaste of the bitter contests that were to rend Cumberland and Westmorland at the next general election.

THE GENERAL ELECTION OF 1768

The Parliament of 1761 was dissolved on 11 March 1768: the last Parliament before the first Reform Bill to live the full seven years of its allotted life. The three statesmen who had dominated the political scene seven years earlier were no longer on the stage. Bute had retired from office in 1763, unable to cope with the strains and stresses of political life, his ideals and visions having vanished at the first touch of reality; and after 1766 he played no part in politics. Newcastle was an old and ailing man with only a few months to live and was of little consequence even in his own party. Chatham, as Pitt had now become, had formed his Administration in July 1766 with the avowed object of abolishing party distinctions; within six months his plans had been thwarted by his impracticable and arrogant temper, and since March 1767, a sick man mentally and physically, he had been absent from court and cabinet. The leading men in 1768 had been of very small account seven years earlier: the Duke of Grafton, first lord of the Treasury, the effective head of Administration since Chatham's withdrawal; his leader in the House of Commons, Lord North; and the leaders of the two Opposition parties, Lord Rockingham and George Grenville.

The general election of 1768 took place at a curious time in politics: there was a lull between two periods of intense political conflict over important issues of policy and principle. The debate about American policy which arose over the repeal of the Stamp Act had gradually died down during 1767, and the colonies' reaction to the recently imposed Townshend duties had not yet made sufficient impact in Britain to revive it. The two Opposition parties, those of Grenville and Rockingham, owed their origins to a time when their leaders were in office, and had carried with them into opposition the policy with regard to America which they had followed in office. Grenville was a stern and relentless defender of the rights of Great Britain over the American colonies; Rockingham, while he did not deny that Britain was sovereign in America, advocated moderation and caution. Chatham's Cabinet contained men who had belonged to both leaders and followed no clear line: Grafton and Henry Seymour Conway were survivors from Rockingham's Administration and had taken the lead in the repeal of the Stamp Act; Lord Hillsborough, in January 1768 appointed colonial secretary, and North followed Grenville on American affairs; while Shelburne and Camden were adherents of Chatham who, differing from both Grenville and Rockingham, denied the right of Great Britain to tax the colonies. With the Cabinet such a jumble of different opinions, no clear lead was given to the nation; nor was the American issue so urgent as to impinge on the political consciousness of the electors. 'It is from the next Parliament', wrote Newcastle on 12 November 1767, 'that this country must be saved, and the cause of those who wish it best be supported.' There were indeed grave issues at stake in 1768, but they were rarely presented to the voters at the general election and they occupied little of the thoughts of politicians.

Little material exists for a study of the Treasury's activities at this election. There is almost nothing in Grafton's papers, and the papers of Thomas Bradshaw, Grafton's secretary to the Treasury and his chief assistant in the management of the election, have not been found. Nor are there any secret service accounts for the period of the Chatham-Grafton Administration. It is probable that in 1768 the Treasury's activities were much less than at any other general election during this period. Grafton was a disciple of Chatham, and Chatham not only disliked electioneering himself but deprecated Treasury interference in elections. In 1766 he had given his consent to the transfer of the Treasury borough of Orford to Lord Hertford, and had gone out of his way to antagonize Lord Edgcumbe, who commanded five seats in Devon and Cornwall. (1768 was the only general election of this period at which Edgcumbe did not accept Government candidates for his boroughs.) And here is another example of Chatham's dislike of the Treasury's interference in elections. In the autumn of 1766 Grafton had received a memorandum from Chase Price, M.P. for Leominster, who probably knew better than any man the electoral situation in Radnorshire and New Radnor Boroughs. The stewardship of the King's manors in Radnorshire was about to become vacant, and Price pointed out the tremendous electoral advantages this office gave in both constituencies. He urged Grafton, as first lord of the Treasury, to assume it himself, which Grafton was inclined to do until told by Chatham that it would be improper for the head of the Treasury to hold an office which conferred electoral advantages. When, therefore, the stewardship fell vacant in 1768 Grafton gave it to Lord Oxford, who henceforth had the strongest interest in Radnorshire.

Chatham's reluctance to see the first lord of the Treasury interfere in elections reinforced Grafton's disinclination to take the trouble upon himself: negligent of his duties and fond of his pleasures, he had no taste for the difficult and tiresome work of electioneering. It was Lord Holdernesse, lord warden of the Cinque Ports, not Grafton, who drove Lord George Sackville out of Hythe; and it may be presumed that Grafton left much of the detail of the general election to Bradshaw. Still, Grafton did take care of his personal friends and men to whom he had obligations, on one occasion with little regard for the feelings of the constituency concerned. He nominated Lord Villiers for Dover, where the Treasury had some influence, and thus provoked an opposition, for the borough wanted a local man and disliked carpet-baggers sent down from the Treasury. Like other election managers of the period, Grafton used the influence of his office to buttress his personal interest. Sir Charles Davers, who was opposing him at Bury St. Edmunds, was bought off with one of the Treasury seats at Weymouth and Melcombe Regis, though Davers was in opposition to the Administration of which Grafton was the head. On the other hand, John Bindley and Samuel Touchet, the two men who had assisted Charles Townshend, late chancellor of the Exchequer, in his revenue plans, were left to fend for themselves without Government assistance. Bindley contested Reading and Touchet Shaftesbury, expensive and venal constituencies, and both were defeated.

Nothing illustrates better Grafton's inertness than his failure to drive Newcastle out of those constituencies which more properly belonged to the Treasury. Newcastle had built up his interest at Rye and Seaford with Treasury support, and his hold on both boroughs now depended on the personal loyalty of their managers. Firm and resolute action by Grafton could have won them back for the Treasury. But despite Newcastle's fears of Treasury intervention, there was none, and he was allowed once more to nominate the candidates as he had done in the days of his power.

It would have been embarrassing for Grafton to have opposed men with whom he had been allied in opposition to Bute and Grenville and with whom he had served in the Rockingham Administration. Ministries changed swiftly during the first ten years of George III's reign and political principles rarely governed their composition. In 1766 Grafton had served alongside Newcastle and Rockingham in the Cabinet which repealed the Stamp Act, and one of the leaders of the opposition to that measure had been the Duke of Bedford; two years later, Bedford's friends formed a majority of Grafton's Cabinet, and Newcastle and Rockingham were the leaders of the Opposition. The enemies of yesterday were the colleagues of today, and none could tell who would be the colleagues of tomorrow. And so Grafton ignored Bradshaw's suggestion about finding a candidate to oppose Admiral Keppel at Windsor, and let Newcastle know that he would not oppose him at Lewes. Only when party differences became acute, as they did some ten years later, did political factors count for more than personal in determining the approach to elections.

Yet in 1768, 83 constituencies went to the poll, 30 more than in 1761, a figure only surpassed during this period at the general election of 1774.

An analysis according to the different types of constituencies, as has been done for the general elections of 1754 and 1761, gives the following figures:

8 contests in 40 English counties
1 in 2 universities (Oxford)
14 in 32 large boroughs
8 in 28 medium boroughs
38 in 143 small boroughs
3 in 12 Welsh counties
2 in 12 Welsh boroughs
9 in 30 Scottish counties

In the large and medium English boroughs there were 22 contests as against 21 in 1761 and 27 in 1754; in the small boroughs, 38 as against 20 and 24. In the combined English, Welsh and Scottish counties there were 20 contests in 1768, compared with 10 in each of the two previous general elections. It is difficult to find an explanation for these differences. Had political feeling been high, it would have been manifested in the larger boroughs as well as in the counties. The increased number of contests in the small boroughs is the first indication of what was to become towards the end of this period a definite trend: the increasing difficulty of managing small boroughs and defending them against the attacks of outsiders.

The county elections in Berkshire and Derbyshire were purely local contests. So too was the election in Huntingdonshire, where the Earl of Sandwich and the Duke of Manchester, though politically opposed to each other, joined their interests to maintain their monopoly of the county representation. The contests in Cumberland and Westmorland, arising from the attempt of Sir James Lowther to dominate the parliamentary representation of those two counties, were also local though not exclusively so. The independent freeholders opposed to Lowther found a leader in the Duke of Portland; and since Portland was one of the magnates of the Rockingham group and Lowther voted with Administration, the struggle between the two took on a political complexion. This was increased by the Treasury's action in granting Lowther a lease of part of Portland's Cumberland estate, held by Portland on a Crown grant which Lowther maintained was invalid. One can sympathize with Portland's indignation, and the struggle of the freeholders of Cumberland and Westmorland against an overbearing tyranny. But the leaders of the

Rockingham party elevated this local dispute to the dignity of a political
conflict and invested it with issues which it did not possess. Lowther's
success in gaining Treasury support was taken as evidence of the influence
of Bute behind the scenes (Lowther was Bute's son-in-law), and Portland's
eventual success as a victory for what Rockingham and Newcastle liked
to call 'the cause'. But Lowther came of as good a Whig family as
Portland, and both were to take the same line in opposition to the American
war. Moreover, after Lowther had secured his return for Cumberland
through the partiality of the returning officer, the Treasury could not
or would not save him from being unseated by the House of Commons.
In the end, he lost both seats for Cumberland, both for Carlisle, and
one for Westmorland: a convincing proof of the strength of the
independent freeholders when united against even such a powerful magnate
as Lowther, but not a victory for a political principle or cause.

Essex was contested by Whigs and Tories, to use Burke's words,
'on the business of a century ago'. Political attitudes and allegiances, once
based upon principle, had hardened in this county until they had become
fossilized. At the by-election of 1759 the Essex Whigs, unable to find a
suitable candidate of their own complexion, had been driven to adopt a
Tory and call him a Whig. To this extent had the old party names become
meaningless, and their further remoteness from reality was illustrated at
the by-election of 1763. John Conyers was supported by the erstwhile
Tories and John Luther by the erstwhile Whigs, but both candidates
applied for the interest of prominent members of the Grenville
Administration and declared themselves its supporters. In 1768 Sir
William Maynard, the former Tory, a supporter of the Grafton
Administration, and John Luther, the Whig, an opponent, stood on a
joint interest, and carried it by a large majority against two candidates
put forward by a group of Old Tories. This provincial rivalry, based
upon long standing family connexions and traditions, still counted for more
in Essex politics than the opposition between the two sides at
Westminster.

The extent of Essex's political immaturity can be seen from a comparison
with its neighbouring county Middlesex: the difference was between the
politics of an almost purely agricultural county and a highly urbanized
one. The Middlesex election of 1768 was the surprise event of that general
election, and the issues arising from it were to dominate politics for the
next two years. The sitting Members at the dissolution, George Cooke and

Sir William Beauchamp Proctor, both Government supporters, had held their seats unopposed since before 1754 and confidently expected re-election. Two days before the election was due John Wilkes, a returned outlaw awaiting sentence for blasphemy and libel, who had been defeated on the preceding day in the city of London, declared his candidature for Middlesex. Wilkes had no programme and no time to canvass the county, he was supported by none of the leading peers or gentlemen, and yet he won by a majority of more than 400 over both his opponents on a poll of about 2,000. Here was a political sensation and a portent for the future. Wilkes's success in the most urbanized county in England was due mainly to the support of the smaller shopkeepers, tradesmen, and craftsmen. This was the first election during this period where the voting followed class lines, and marks the rise of a new political factor: urban radicalism. A class of electors whose aspirations and interests had hitherto met with little consideration, now chose Wilkes for their representative in the Commons. The measures subsequently taken by Grafton's Administration against Wilkes, his repeated expulsions from the House of Commons, and finally the seating of his defeated rival as M.P. for Middlesex, only strengthened the movement he had begun, and accelerated the spread of radicalism from the metropolitan area into the provinces.

But in 1768 there was as yet little sign of this outside Middlesex. The electors, where they were politically conscious, seemed occupied by past issues. In the bitterly contested election for Norfolk, one pair of candidates was attached to Lord Rockingham and the other pair to George Grenville. Yet the election was not fought on the issue of American policy, so recent and still unresolved, which sharply divided Rockingham and Grenville, but on the dead issue of the legality or otherwise of arrest by general warrant in case of seditious libel. Local issues also counted for a good deal in determining the result of this election, and general warrants appeared more as a shibboleth to distinguish the two sides. The only other county constituency in which general warrants appears as an issue at this election was Somerset, which did not go the poll. And even here it was mixed up with the far more relevant and locally comprehensible topic of Dashwood's cider tax of 1763. One of the candidates, Sir Charles Kemys Tynte, felt obliged to publish an advertisement denying that he had voted for the cider tax: on the contrary, he said, he had gone down to the House of Commons, wrapped in flannel and suffering from the gout, to vote for the repeal of 'that odious and detestable tax'. The canvassing returns gave Tynte and his colleague a large majority, and John Trevelyan declined the poll.

Among the boroughs there were four very expensive and riotous contests at Carlisle, Colchester, Northampton, and Preston. Carlisle was a straight fight between two candidates on the Lowther interest, and two candidates of the independent freemen, sponsored by the Duke of Portland: of the 694 freemen who voted at this election, only five split their votes between the two sets of candidates. At Colchester, a borough with 1,500 voters, many of them venal, a body of electors had been searching since November 1767 for a 'third man' to oppose the sitting Members. He eventually materialized in the person of Alexander Fordyce, the banker, and was defeated by only 24 votes, after having spent, it is said, £14,000. The Northampton election was the famous 'contest of the three earls', in which Lords Halifax, Northampton, and Spencer (all, incidentally, supporters of Grafton's Administration) fought for control of the borough at an almost ruinous expense to themselves. The Preston election, one of the fiercest of the century, was an attempt by Lord Strange, son of Lord Derby, to wrest control of the borough from the corporation.

At Leicester and at Coventry there were contests between candidates on the corporation interest and candidates of the independent party. At Coventry the corporation party, who called themselves Whigs, put forward Henry Seymour Conway, son of Lord Hertford, a prominent courtier, and Andrew Archer, who was attached to the Rockingham group; the political sympathies of the unsuccessful candidate, Walter Waring, are unknown at this time and certainly played little part in his defeat. At Leicester the Whig magnates intervened in the election and gave it something of a political colouring. Here the corporation was Tory, and the independent party turned to the Duke of Portland to find them candidates. Portland recommended Booth Grey, his relation by marriage, and Eyre Coote, a soldier who had made his reputation in India and was anxious to return there. To judge from Portland's correspondence this was a straight fight between two Whigs and two Tories. But, as at Coventry, the opposing sets of candidates did not line up on a party basis: John Darker and Edward Palmer, the corporation candidates, were very independent men, not likely to attach themselves to any party; Grey was a Rockingham Whig; and Coote, who returned to India shortly after his election, was a Government supporter. The electorate did not vote on party or political lines and the corporation itself was divided, a substantial minority voting for the independent candidates. In short, what appears at first sight to have been a straightforward contest resolves itself on examination into something of a free-for-all; which is what one might expect in a large urban constituency where the voters were not accustomed to think in terms of national parties.

At King's Lynn, where the electorate numbered about 300, Crisp Molineux, a friend of Wilkes and Chatham, raised the issue of general warrants, and directed his attack particularly against Sir John Turner, standing for re-election, who had been a member of Grenville's Treasury Board. But whether general warrants was an important issue in this election, or whether it was raised simply because Molineux felt intensely about political matters, is hard to say. In any case, in the context of 1768, it was irrelevant.

This general election marks the beginning of a great change in British politics. Neither in 1754 nor in 1761 was there an Opposition, aspiring to office, to contest the election on party lines; nor was there the essential prerequisite, a deep division in the electorate on political questions. In 1754 and 1761 the old allegiance of Whig and Tory still meant something in the constituencies, though that meaning was increasingly unrelated to divisions in the House of Commons. But by 1768 the names of Whig and Tory were hardly used at all. Elections were still decided primarily upon local issues, and the hardening of party lines at Westminster, as yet scarcely begun, was not reflected in the constituencies. In Middlesex there had been a new development and a new issue raised; a new force was to play its part in the large urbanized electorates. But in 1768 this was only just emerging: radicalism had scarcely touched the metropolitan constituencies of Westminster, Southwark, and Surrey; and in the provinces it was still submerged. The historian with his hindsight can see developments which were invisible to contemporaries.

THE GENERAL ELECTION OF 1774

Grafton resigned in January 1770, sick of an office he had never desired, the duties and responsibilities of which he found distasteful; and was succeeded by Lord North. North could hardly have taken office at a more critical moment: the re-emergence in 1769 of Chatham into active politics and his announcement that he would oppose the action taken by the Government over the Middlesex election had been followed by the withdrawal from the Cabinet of two of his followers, Lord Camden, lord chancellor, and Lord Granby, commander-in-chief. Neither had been replaced by the time North assumed the post of first minister. The Rockingham party had increased in strength during the first session of the new Parliament, and was now about to unite with Chatham against what seemed to be a tottering and discredited Administration.

North brought to his task qualities of courage and coolness few had suspected him to possess, and his position as a Member of the House of Commons gave him an advantage denied to his two predecessors. By the end of 1771 his Administration was secure, and the two wings of the opposition, Chatham's and Rockingham's, at odds with each other, were in confusion. Enjoying the confidence of both the Crown and the House of Commons, North was in a stronger position than any minister since Bute. In 1773 he successfully tackled the problem of regulating the government of the East India Company's territories. Then in 1774 came the greatest challenge to his statesmanship, when news reached England of the attack on the East India Company's ships in Boston harbour ('the Boston tea party'). The problem of relations with the American colonies, dormant since 1770, now had to be faced. In the spring of 1774 North introduced into the House of Commons a series of measures to restore British authority in America: bills to close the port of Boston, to regulate the government of Massachusetts Bay, and to ensure the administration of justice in the colony. In May he introduced the Quebec bill, to fix the boundaries of Canada and give a political and ecclesiastical constitution to the colony. On 22 June 1774 this busy and momentous session, one of the most fateful in the history of the British Parliament, came to an end.

The decision to dissolve Parliament, nine months before a general election was due, seems to have been taken very shortly after the end of the session. It is mentioned in a letter from North to the King of 6 July, and at that time was probably known only by the Cabinet and the secretaries of the Treasury. Grafton, who had resumed office in 1771 as lord privy seal but not as a member of the Cabinet, did not know of the decision to dissolve as late as 6 September, when he returned Lord Petersham for Thetford. The Opposition, though they knew that Parliament must be dissolved no later than the spring of 1775 and should therefore have spent the summer in completing their plans, were taken completely by surprise. 'This manœuvre of the ministry has taken me very much unaware', wrote Rockingham to Portland on 1 October, 'and I am not a little perplexed with it.'

What were the reasons for North's decision to dissolve prematurely? In a letter to the King of 27 September he wrote:

As a premature dissolution of Parliament renders the necessary preparation almost impossible, Government cannot expect to be so strong in the next House of Commons as if we were at the natural end of the Parliament. Lord North hopes that his Majesty will not think him to blame if some important elections succeed contrary to his wishes. Many good consequences will result from a sudden dissolution, but some seats in the House of Commons will probably be lost by it.

Some reaction was to be expected from America to North's punitive legislation but the British Government was resolved to make a decisive stand. 'The die is now cast', wrote the King on 11 September. 'The colonies must either submit or triumph. I do not wish to come to severer measures, but we must not retreat; by coolness and an unremitted pursuit of the measures that have been adopted, I trust they will come to submit.' Obviously, it was better for the Government to face the next stage of the American dispute with a new Parliament, rather than be caught by it in the middle of preparations for a general election. But there is nothing to suggest that North dissolved in order to obtain a vote of confidence from the electorate or to strengthen his majority; and indeed such ideas were alien to the political practice of his day.

The morale of the Opposition on the eve of the general election was as low as it could possibly be. Chatham, after his brief appearance, had virtually retired from politics; and his lieutenant Shelburne, with only a handful of followers, seems to have been negotiating with the court. Rockingham was now approximating to the position of a modern leader of the Opposition: he was the only politician in either House with a following sufficiently large to be called a party. Yet his following was sadly depleted since the struggle over the Middlesex election in 1769–70, when the Opposition had numbered between 150 and 200. North's punitive legislation had hardly been challenged in the House of Commons: the Boston port bill had been unopposed; Rose Fuller's motion to repeal the tea duty, when Burke made his celebrated speech on American taxation, had been defeated by 182 votes to 49; and in two divisions on the bills regarding Massachusetts Bay the Opposition had numbered only 24 and 64 respectively. Some of the most able opponents of the Government over the Middlesex election, men such as Lord George Germain, Charles Wolfran Cornwall, and Constantine John Phipps, had now crossed the floor of the House or were about to do so. William Dowdeswell, leader of the Rockingham Whigs in the House of Commons, was seriously ill with tuberculosis and not expected to recover: ordered abroad by his doctors, he died the following year. Charles James Fox, who was to become Dowdeswell's successor, had not yet made the decisive break with Government. To add to Rockingham's misfortunes, his trusted friend Sir George Savile, M.P. for Yorkshire, was reluctant to stand again at the general election. 'I confess indeed', wrote Rockingham to Portland on 1 October 1774, 'that I think that *all politics* are now in so low a state and so little likely to revive, that I should feel a hesitation in giving encouragement to an expectation that we can continue long to drudge on in such unsatisfactory and so unthanked a laborious occupation.'

There was another reason for the Opposition's poor morale. However sympathetic they were to the American cause, few of them were prepared to defend the Boston rioters or to deny the Government's contention that if punitive action were not taken against the colony, Great Britain would virtually have renounced her sovereignty in America. The Opposition did not contest the principle of North's punitive legislation: they merely contended that the measures proposed against Massachusetts Bay were excessively severe and that they should be accompanied by some attempt at conciliation. This is the reason why the Boston port bill was unopposed and the numbers against the other bills so small. Only one division list has been preserved for this period, that of 6 May on the third reading of the bill to regulate the administration of justice in Massachusetts Bay. Most of the 24 who voted against the bill that day were radicals or independent Members: not half a dozen were followers of Rockingham. Neither of the Burkes voted, nor their close friend Lord Verney; none of the Cavendishes appear in the list; nor Savile, nor the Members particularly connected with Portland and Richmond. William Baker's story that the Opposition had gone that day to Newmarket might account for the absence of Fox but not for that of Burke or Savile.

The truth is that neither Government nor Opposition had the faintest notion of the deep and widespread resentment felt in America against

North's legislation, nor of the impetus it would give to American nationalism. It was only in the following year, when it was seen that North's policy had driven America to take up arms and led to the imminent outbreak of civil war, that an opposition to that policy arose. It was not North's rigorous policy that roused the Opposition, but the attempt to enforce that policy by war.

At this election America was mentioned as an issue in not more than ten constituencies, and then always as part of an attack by Opposition candidates against the Government. It was not made an issue by Government candidates and the Government did not ask the electors to endorse their policy. The only county election in which American policy appeared in the candidates' programme was Middlesex, where the Government were unable to find anyone to oppose John Wilkes and John Glynn. Here, discontent in America was merely one in a catalogue of grievances for which the candidates pledged themselves to obtain redress, and there is no evidence that it occupied a prominent place in the minds of electors. In three large urban constituencies, Bristol, London, and Westminster, America figured on the programme of the Opposition candidates, and at Bristol, where Edmund Burke was one of the candidates, it received particular mention. Burke dealt with the Government's American policy in his speech on the hustings, but judging from broadsheets issued during the election campaign the Quebec bill was singled out by the opponents of Government as a more reprehensible measure than the Boston port bill or the legislation against Massachusetts Bay. Radicalism had been growing rapidly in Bristol since 1769, and the Quebec bill was particularly obnoxious because it gave toleration to Roman Catholics (eighteenth-century radicalism was fiercely anti-Catholic). At Worcester, Southwark, Newcastle-upon-Tyne, and Great Yarmouth, American policy may have been discussed by the Opposition candidates, but in each constituency it could only have been a minor issue.

Also, in two of the small boroughs the American question figured prominently in the speeches of Opposition candidates. At Cambridge, where the electorate numbered about 150, there had been a party, led by the Dissenters, opposed to Government influence in the borough. At a meeting in the guildhall they drew up a statement binding the candidates, if elected, to oppose the Government's American policy, and press for increased toleration for Dissenters and a more equal representation in

Parliament. The statement was signed by the Opposition candidates Thomas Plumer Byde and Samuel Meeke; the Government candidates of course would not subscribe to it. About three-fifths of the electorate voted for the Government candidates and about two-fifths for the Opposition; but to what extent political motives dictated their voting is hard to say.

At Milborne Port, with an electorate of about 120, there was a fierce contest for control between Thomas Hutchings Medlycott and Edward Walter. They were the two largest property owners in the borough and until 1772, by an amicable arrangement had held one seat each. Then they had quarrelled, and now each was bent on driving the other out of the borough. One would hardly expect a struggle for power in a corrupt borough to be fought on political issues, but political issues were certainly brought in. One of Medlycott's candidates was Temple Luttrell, brother of the famous Colonel Henry Lawes Luttrell, the instrument by which the Government had ousted Wilkes from Middlesex in 1769. Temple Luttrell, however, was an out-and-out pro-American, of great enthusiasm and energy, but naïve, intemperate, and reckless. His colleague, Charles Wolseley, professed the same political sentiments, though his real inclination seems to have been to go with Government (he was apparently hard up and anxious for a job). Medlycott and Wolseley attacked the Government's American policy which they asserted would bring on a civil war in America, and denounced the Quebec Act as 'shocking to the feelings of humanity' because (so they alleged) it 'empowered the Catholics to persecute'. How far this mixture of sense and nonsense had any effect on the electors of Milborne Port can be seen from the course of the election. Owing to the complexities of the borough's constitution there were four possible returning officers and three polls were taken: two of these polls were won by Medlycott's candidates and the third by Walter's. It was left to a committee of the House of Commons to straighten out the tangle and declare Medlycott's candidates duly elected. And one can hardly avoid the suspicion that they would have been elected whoever they were, and that nobody at Milborne Port in 1774 would have bothered his head about America had not one of the candidates been Temple Luttrell.

The second feature of the 1774 election was the spread of radicalism from Middlesex throughout the metropolitan area and into some large provincial cities. North was doubtful at first whether the Government could hold a single seat in the three Middlesex constituencies. In the county itself no candidate could be found to stand on the Government interest. The best the Government could hope for in London was that the more extreme radicals would be defeated. But radicals filled three out of the four seats, and the fourth went to Richard Oliver, who regularly voted with the Opposition but had broken with Wilkes. Among the defeated candidates were John Roberts, a Government supporter, and William Baker, a follower of Rockingham. At Westminster Wilkes early set up two candidates, and Lord North had a great deal of trouble to persuade the Duke of Newcastle to allow his son to stand as joint Government candidate with Lord Percy. Eventually Newcastle agreed, and the Government won a great victory: Percy and Pelham Clinton were returned with majorities of more than 2,000 over the Wilkites. Still, Wilkes and his followers had won five out of the eight seats for the county of Middlesex: an extraordinary achievement for a man who seven years before had been a political outcast.

In the metropolitan constituencies of Surrey, radicalism had spread more slowly. Nathaniel Polhill, a Wilkite, headed the poll for Southwark, but the second seat went to Henry Thrale, a Government supporter. In the Surrey county election a curious situation arose. Sir Joseph Mawbey, a Southwark distiller, a strong opponent of Government and a parliamentary reformer, had been canvassing the county for some time. Mawbey had about him the air of the *nouveau riche* and was very much disliked by the upper crust of the county. A number of would-be candidates appeared against him, some supporters of Government, some of the Opposition. George Onslow, who had represented Surrey since 1761 but had now grown so unpopular that he stood little chance of being re-elected, persuaded the county meeting, irrespective of their political feelings, to rally behind the candidature of Sir Francis Vincent and James Scawen as the only way to keep out Mawbey. Onslow was a leading spokesman for the Government in the Commons and a member of North's Treasury Board, while the two candidates he sponsored both voted with the Opposition. The manœuvre came off and Mawbey was defeated, only to be triumphantly returned at a by-election a year later.

Radical candidates also contested five provincial cities, all large open constituencies. At Bristol radicalism had been growing steadily since 1769, and Henry Cruger, born in America and settled in Bristol as a merchant, had long been adopted as the radical candidate. He came head of the poll, and the second votes of his supporters helped to return Edmund Burke, although Burke made it quite clear that he had little sympathy with radicalism. Here was a great triumph for the Opposition, or it would have been had the two candidates and their party organizations been able to work together. But events in the next few years were to show that radicalism was as distasteful to Whigs like Rockingham and Burke as it was to the court; and the triumph of 1774 was never repeated. At Worcester, Sir Watkin Lewes, a Wilkite, who had twice been defeated at by-elections within the last twelve months, was again defeated; but the figures on the poll showed that there was a substantial volume of support for radicalism in Worcester. At Newcastle-upon-Tyne, Constantine John Phipps and Thomas Delaval, supported by the radicals, made a poor showing against the sitting Members. Neither Phipps nor Delaval was a radical, nor was the issue fought solely on political lines: there was a dispute about the corporation's right to let out the town moor for cultivation which figures far more prominently in election propaganda than national issues. At Bedford, Sir William Wake, a Northamptonshire country gentleman, was elected with the support of the radicals; and John Trevanion, a friend of Wilkes, was returned unopposed for Dover.

For the general election of 1774, as for that of 1768, there is little material for a study of the Treasury's campaign. There are a few letters from North to the King, but almost nothing in North's private papers, and no secret service accounts for this period have been found. This was the first election managed by John Robinson, who became secretary to the Treasury shortly after North took office and remained with him until 1782. Robinson was taken ill in the middle of the election and his duties were assumed by William Eden. According to North, writing in 1782, the election cost the Government 'near £50,000', which was about double the Government's expenses in the general election of 1754. This increased expense, however, does not necessarily represent an increase in governmental activity in elections, but probably merely reflects the inflation which affected elections as well as everything else. The average price demanded by a patron for a safe seat in 1754 was £1,500; in 1774 it had risen to about £3,000. The amount which had to be laid out on a contested election had presumably increased in the same proportion.

Judging by the number of contests, there was a greater desire to enter Parliament in 1774 than at any other general election in this period. The 95 contests were distributed among the constituencies as follows:

11 contests in 40 English counties
20 in 32 large boroughs
14 in 28 medium boroughs
35 in 143 small boroughs
 4 in 12 Welsh counties
 2 in 12 Welsh boroughs
 8 in 30 Scottish counties
 1 Scottish burgh (Edinburgh)

The figure of 11 county contests is astonishingly high, and it is hard to say why there should have been so many. The contests in Cumberland and Westmorland were the aftermath of the great struggle of 1768. Lowther and Portland had reached a compromise which they hoped would bring about an electoral settlement; but in each county there was a party which opposed the dictates of the two principal magnates. Hence the contests of 1774, both rather forlorn attempts. Six other county contests were of purely local interest: those in Cornwall, Herefordshire, Hertfordshire, Northumberland, Sussex, and Warwickshire. To say that these were of local interest does not imply that they were of no significance politically, but rather that their significance was not immediately reflected at Westminster. The contest in Northumberland was a great determinant in county politics. The Duke of Northumberland had hitherto been content with the recommendation of one Member for the county and had left the other to the choice of the country gentlemen. At this general election he made a bid for both seats, and the result confirmed the unwritten compromise of one Member for the Duke and one for the country gentlemen. The contest in Sussex, on the other hand, was a struggle amongst the country gentlemen themselves; the seat of Lord George Lennox, brother of the Duke of Richmond, was not in dispute. The contest in Warwickshire, though entirely local, was of great political significance, for it established the right of the industrial area round Birmingham to have one of the county Members specially devoted to its interests.

The contest for Surrey has already been discussed in connexion with the growth of radicalism. Those for Bedfordshire and Essex, though primarily local, had overtones derived from national politics. In Bedfordshire, Lord Upper Ossory, as yet still attached to the court, and Robert Ongley, also a follower of North, were challenged by Thomas Hampden, who had the backing of a number of Opposition leaders, including Burke and the Duke of Portland, as well as supporters of the Administration, such as Sir George Osborn, who were opposed to the influence of the Duke of Bedford in Bedfordshire politics. The contest for Essex, another forlorn attempt, arose out of that for Maldon. Lord Waltham had been persuaded to contest Maldon by his father-in-law John Coe, a leading Dissenter, and his brother-in-law, John Luttrell (brother of Temple Luttrell, who contested Milborne Port). Waltham had been defeated and had then, at the last moment, decided to contest Essex, to be defeated even more decisively than he had been at Maldon.

The numbers of contests in the large and medium boroughs also show substantial increases on the figures for 1768. There was no influx of new men to contest these constituencies nor any indication of unusual political excitement. Perhaps the very absence of political questions stimulated contests: where a serious political issue was at stake, men were prepared to compromise rather than let in an opponent. But when the issue was primarily local or personal, the disposition to compromise was less.

In present-day politics local government elections rarely arouse as much excitement as parliamentary elections, and the question as to who shall govern the nation appears to the electors more momentous than who shall govern their county or their borough. In the second half of the eighteenth century this attitude was reversed, for the central government did not make as much impact as the local authority on the lives of the masses of the people. Hence it was that in large freeman boroughs, politics frequently turned on the conflict between the corporation party and the independents, a conflict spiced by religious differences. Coventry was a typical borough of this kind, and a study of its politics shows that local issues could be as engrossing and as momentous for the lives of its citizens as any question of national politics. Local politics were not necessarily personal or sordid in their nature or lacking an idealistic element. At the Coventry election of 1774 the corporation candidate was badly defeated; and an address to the freemen, printed in the poll book, read:

Permit me to congratulate you on the noble stand you have made in support of the liberty, freedom, and independency of this great city. Your children's children—nay, lasting posterity, will from this great example learn to know that no *body corporate* has a right to exert *undue* power, or trample with impunity on the privileges, franchises, and freedom of the people.

Though expressed in hyperbolical language, this declaration was sincere.

York provides a typical example of an election in a large urban constituency untroubled by political issues on the eve of the American war. In this city, conscious of its dignity as the capital of the largest English county and the seat of an archbishop, the feud between the corporation and the anti-corporation party was not strong. There had been no contest since 1758, and during that time Lord Rockingham, leader of the largest Opposition party at Westminster, had built up his interest in York to the point where he could influence the choice of both Members. This he had done through the Rockingham Club, a group of York trades-men, civic and ecclesiastical leaders, and neighbouring country gentlemen, devoted to his interests at York but not all of whom sympathized with the line his party took in national politics. In 1774 the sitting Members, Lord John Cavendish and Charles Turner, both prominent members of the Opposition, stood for re-election; and were opposed by Martin Bladen Hawke, of an old Yorkshire family and son of Admiral Sir Edward Hawke. At the previous general election, when his father had been first lord of the Admiralty in the Chatham Administration, Hawke had been returned for the Admiralty borough of Saltash. But after his father's resignation in 1771 Hawke had wavered in his support of Administration, and by the dissolution was no longer reckoned by Government as on their side. There was thus no clear-cut political division between the candidates and neither political nor local issues were prominent. As a result the election degenerated into an orgy of eating and drinking; there was rioting in the town; and Turner was insulted because he objected to treating. Yet York was not a corrupt constituency, and at the next two general elections was the scene of real political conflicts. There was little political difference between the candidates in 1774, but that has never yet prevented election contests.

In the remaining English constituencies two trends are noticeable at this general election: the increasing number of attacks on Government boroughs, and the intrusion of the nabobs into the venal constituencies.

At Rochester and Sandwich, two medium-sized constituencies, the Government candidates met with differing fates. At Rochester Robert

Gregory, a friend of Rockingham, defeated one of the Government candidates, Admiral Thomas Pye, who seems to have made himself peculiarly unpopular in the town; while at Sandwich two Admiralty nominees easily routed Lord Conyngham, a Government supporter who claimed a personal interest in the borough. The independent party at Portsmouth very nearly succeeded in carrying one seat against the Government; but at Queenborough Sir Piercy Brett, who had been returned as Government candidate in 1768 and now voted with the opposition, was well beaten.

The nabobs, retired East Indians 'gorged with the spoils of the East', and anxious for a seat in Parliament either as a symbol of their newly acquired wealth or a safeguard against investigation into the means by which they had obtained it, made their first appearance in the two venal constituencies of Shaftesbury and Hindon. At Shaftesbury, Thomas Rumbold and Francis Sykes are said to have paid twenty guineas a man, and though returned were unseated on petition. Hans Winthrop Mortimer, their defeated opponent, prosecuted Sykes for bribery and secured £11,000 damages. And at Hindon also, Richard Smith won a seat by bribery only to lose it on petition.

THE GENERAL ELECTION OF 1780

The Parliament elected in 1774 was dissolved on 1 September 1780, more than a year before a general election was due under the Septennial Act. By 1780 the war against America, or, as the British Government regarded it, the rebellion in the American colonies, had been in progress for five years. Divided purposes had from the beginning marked its conduct: the British Government was never quite certain whether its aim was to wage war, ruthlessly and destructively, or to induce deluded and misguided subjects to return to the comforting care of the mother country. Coercion and conciliation had gone hand in hand, and both had been pursued half-heartedly. France and Spain, seeing in Britain's difficulties the opportunity to avenge their losses in the seven years' war, had come to the aid of independent America; and by 1780 North's Administration was conducting a world-wide war. British power was attacked at its focal points: on the seas, in India, and in the Mediterranean; and an attempt to invade the homeland had been foiled less by the alertness of the Government than by the incompetence of the enemy. By 1780 it

was generally acknowledged in Government circles that even if the
rebellion should eventually be suppressed, the object which the British
Government had originally in mind, the raising of a revenue in America,
was unattainable. Yet, short of complete subjugation, the war could only
be ended by Great Britain acknowledging the independence of the United
States—a price which a section of the Opposition was prepared to pay,
but which was not yet acceptable to the mass of the nation. And so
North continued a policy in which he had no faith, while the King hailed
each victory in America as evidence that the tide of rebellion was
slackening—'Have you realized', asks the American in Bernard Shaw's
play, 'that though you may occupy towns and win battles, you cannot
conquer a nation?' Like a man caught in a traffic jam, the British Government could neither move forward nor get out, but had to sit and wait.

   Little of this was reflected directly in the House of Commons. On
the continuance of the American war, North had a comfortable majority;
and even on motions criticizing its conduct, the Opposition had so far
failed to make much impression on the House. But since 1779 there had
been a movement, both in Parliament and in the constituencies,
ostensibly not directed against the war policy of the Administration,
and supported by friends and enemies of Government alike. Its aim was
the reduction of unnecessary Government expenditure, the abolition
of sinecures, and the curtailment of political pensions, by means of
which, according to the Opposition, Administration maintained a
corrupt majority. It took concrete parliamentary shape in February 1780,
when Burke introduced his economical reform bill. On a motion for an
account of pensions, 21 February, and on the clause of Burke's bill
which abolished the Board of Trade, 13 March, the Government was
defeated; Jennings Clerke's bill to prevent Government contractors
sitting in the House passed the Commons without a division; and though
Burke's bill was eventually withdrawn because emasculated of what its
author considered its essential provisions, on 6 April 1780 the
Government suffered its most serious defeat of the session when a
resolution proposed by John Dunning, Lord Shelburne's friend, 'that
the influence of the Crown has increased, is increasing, and ought to be
diminished' was carried by a majority of 18 votes. Dunning's motion
summarized in one pithy sentence the stock grievances of all Opposition
parties against all Governments throughout the century, and indeed of
independent men in general. But when on 24 April Dunning introduced

a further resolution, that Parliament should not be prorogued until measures had been taken to reduce the influence of the Crown, the Government had a majority of 51. The House was content to make an abstract enunciation of grievances but not to take practical steps towards their redress, as if to symbolize both its dissatisfaction with North's Administration and its lack of confidence in the Opposition.

Harassed in Parliament, waging war against a coalition of three nations, with Europe unfriendly and Ireland in political turmoil, the Government received yet another shock when in June the Gordon riots terrorized London. At the end of June, North took two decisions: he opened negotiations with Rockingham for a coalition Administration, and he placed before the Cabinet the question of an early dissolution of Parliament.

The negotiations with Rockingham failed because there was no basis for a coalition. Rockingham demanded an end to the American war, even at the price of acknowledging the independence of the United States; a programme of economical reform; and a majority in the Cabinet. For there was in 1780 a real difference of policy between Government and Opposition, and no possibility of an adjustment between them. During the summer, as favourable news was received of General Clinton's campaign in the southern colonies, opinion in the Cabinet hardened in favour of an early dissolution. In July John Robinson began to draw up a survey of the constituencies, in preparation for the general election. It was at the same time a state of opinion in Parliament and a forecast of what the politics of a future Parliament might be. And since there was still no absolutely clear-cut division between the two sides, as is shown by the existence of a large body of Members who supported North on the American war yet were sympathetic to the Opposition's programme of economical reform, Robinson's attempt both to survey the politics of the House and to forecast its future politics could only be conjectural.

Robinson reckoned 290 Members to be supporters of Government and 233 of the Opposition; 19 more he classed as 'hopeful' and 16 as 'doubtful'. About the new Parliament he could not have the same degree of certainty and the number of 'hopefuls' and 'doubtfuls' in his calculations increased. His figures were: Government 252; Opposition 189; 'hopeful' 47; 'doubtful' 70. He then went into a further analysis of the 'hopefuls' and 'doubtfuls' and produced the figures of 343 for the Government and 215 for the Opposition. Robinson thus expected the

Government to increase its majority at the general election, which was presumably the reason why he himself favoured a dissolution. But in February 1781, when he came to analyse the new House, he reckoned the Government's strength at 260 and the Opposition's at 254. Mr. I. R. Christie, who has made an exhaustive study of this general election in his book *The End of North's Ministry, 1780–1782*, considers that Robinson's calculations before the election were 'far wide of the mark' and that the Government 'were greatly deceived in their expectations'. It is important to understand exactly why and how.

In the first place, the Government was losing ground in the boroughs under patronage. Before the general election two leading borough-owners, Sir James Lowther and Sir Lawrence Dundas, had gone over to the Opposition, and in consequence the Government lost some fifteen votes in the House of Commons. In this type of constituency there were in 1780 only about 55 seats available for Government candidates, 24 in Government boroughs and 31 belonging to private patrons, as compared with 70 in 1754. Most of the borough owners with seats to dispose of continued to accept Government nominees with the significant exception of Edward Eliot, who had resigned from the Board of Trade on the outbreak of the American war and now offered his surplus seats to the Opposition leaders. Rockingham recommended both Members at Grampound and one at St. Germans, and Shelburne recommended one Member at Liskeard, each candidate paying £3,000 for his seat. Among the Government supporters who lost their seats as a result of Eliot's defection to the Opposition were his relation Edward Gibbon, the historian, and his close friend Benjamin Langlois. Another striking defection at this election, partly forecast by Robinson, was that of the Government manager at Dartmouth, Arthur Holdsworth, who returned himself and Lord Howe, both now supporters of the Opposition.

Secondly, there was a movement of opinion against Government in the open constituencies, the extent of which was insufficiently appreciated by the Government's election manager. Robinson had a unique knowledge of the boroughs under patronage, and could forecast with tolerable accuracy the politics of the men who would represent them (but not how their politics would change under the stress of circumstances). But in the counties and the larger boroughs, where in any case it was difficult to forecast election results, Robinson was handicapped by his failure to perceive the larger trends in politics. He was what we should call today a back-room boy or a Central Office man: preoccupied with details of patronage, he rarely spoke in the House or visited the constituencies. He was completely out of touch with opinion in the nation at large, which indeed for him hardly existed. Precise, methodical, an indefatigable worker, he thought of politics in terms of administration and method rather than of policy and ideas. Opposition to the King's Government seemed to him factious, and those who led it to be weak or wicked men intent on their own self-advancement. That Rockingham or Charles Fox might be sincerely opposed to the policy of war in America or that there might be a case for economical reform, seems never to have occurred to him. There is hardly a line in his correspondence to suggest that he realized that there might be genuine differences of opinion on political questions or that men might go into opposition through honest conviction. He looked at politics from the point of view of a patronage secretary and seriously under-estimated the strength of popular feeling against Government.

A few examples taken from the counties will illustrate Robinson's failure to appreciate the state of public opinion. In Bedfordshire he expected Lord Upper Ossory, a friend of Fox, and Lord Ongley, a Government supporter, to be returned again. 'I put Lord Ongley down for [the Government]', wrote Robinson in his survey, 'because he generally is so except in some of the questions of economy, and I think he may be mostly depended upon if attended to and humoured a little.' But Ongley, as a result of his support of the Government, lost the backing of the Bedford interest, managed during the minority of the 5th Duke by Ossory and the Duchess of Bedford, which was given to St. Andrew St. John, another friend of Fox. Ongley canvassed the county, decided he had no chance, and withdrew.

In Hampshire, Kent, and Yorkshire Robinson tried to induce Government supporters to stand, professing to believe that only a little spirit (and plenty of money) was needed to ensure success. His friend Charles Jenkinson wrote to him from Winchester about the Hampshire election: 'Anyone may be chosen for this county that Government pleases without either trouble or expense. The Opposition has had a meeting and say they will not put up a second candidate.' Probably no single sentence could illustrate better the shortsightedness of the Government election managers. In December 1779 Sir Richard Worsley, financed by £2,000 from secret service funds, had contested Hampshire as a Government candidate and had been soundly beaten. Now Robinson and Jenkinson proposed to put him up again and expected him to be returned 'without either trouble or expense'. In the event, Jervoise Clarke Jervoise and Robert Thistlethwayte, both inclined to the Opposition, were returned unopposed. In Kent, also, Robinson was sure that a Government candidate could be returned: 'Kent I find every day would do, was there but a good man. But we have no ardour amongst our friends.' It was no light matter to undertake a contest for Kent, with its 8,000 voters, when the sense of the county was strongly in favour of economical reform. In his survey Robinson had hoped that Lewis Thomas Watson, son of Lord Sondes, might be persuaded to stand, but the best that Robinson could say of him was that he was 'not very averse to Government' and 'in time may not be averse'. Charles Marsham and Filmer Honywood, both determined opponents of North's Administration, were returned unopposed.

It is in his estimate of the situation in Yorkshire that Robinson showed most clearly of all his neglect of the factor of public opinion. He recognized indeed that Sir George Savile, Rockingham's close friend and one of the leaders of the movement for economical reform, was certain of being re-elected. Savile's colleague, Edwin Lascelles, had voted with the Rockingham party until the outbreak of the American war, had then gone over to Government (apparently through honest conviction), but in the divisions on economical reform in the spring of 1780 had again voted with Opposition. Robinson wrote in his survey:

Mr. Lascelles is threatened with an opposition for his conduct, which though he voted with Opposition has been imputed to be with a view to his election, not from principle, and by his management he has not pleased the other side. The Patriots despise him, the friends of Government in Yorkshire are disgusted with him for his trimming. However no one had yet publicly stood forth, and an opposition for the county of York is so very serious a matter in point of expense, for the person attacking as well as the person attacked ... and Mr. Lascelles having ready money to fight with and a fortune not easily hurt, it is probable that weight may deter the part from an attempt against him.

One would hardly guess from this that Yorkshire was the centre of the movement for economical reform, and that the Yorkshire Association, formed to secure that reform, was a powerful factor in the county's politics. In fact, a more ludicrous summing up of Yorkshire politics on the eve of the election could hardly be imagined: Lascelles, despite his having antagonized both sides, would probably not be opposed because he had ready money and 'a fortune not easily hurt'. Had not others too? When Henry Duncombe, an out-and-out opponent of Administration, announced his candidature, and secured the support of both Rockingham and the Yorkshire Association, an election fund of over £12,000 was subscribed in support of him and Savile. Lascelles wisely decided not to contest the election, and retired to his pocket borough of Northallerton.

Since November 1777 the King had been putting aside £1,000 a month from his privy purse to form a fund for election purposes; and at the general election of 1780 the Government spent about £62,000. This compares with the sum of £27,000 spent on the general election of 1754, the last election for which figures are available. Altogether the Government disbursed about £103,000 in 1780, but of this sum £31,000 was recouped from Members on whose behalf seats had been bought. The King's election fund was too small to meet all the claims upon it, and in December 1780 North had to borrow £30,000 from Drummond's bank.

As in 1754, so in 1780, a large part of the Government's money was spent in vain: over £8,000 in trying to keep Charles Fox out of Westminster; £4,000 in Surrey, where Admiral Keppel was one of the Opposition candidates (the only English county on which the Government spent any money at this election); and over £4,000 in London. Here, at least, the Government got some value for their money, for although their candidate Richard Clarke came bottom of the poll, Government intervention led to the displacement of John Sawbridge, an extreme radical, by Nathaniel Newnham, a more moderate man whom Robinson hoped might be induced 'to be more friendly'. But Newnham was bitterly opposed to the American war and consistently voted against Administration; while Sawbridge, whose exclusion was particularly desired, returned to Parliament as M.P. for London at a by-election in November 1780. In all, over £16,000 was spent on the three metropolitan constituencies of London, Westminster, and Surrey, and the only Government Member returned was Admiral Sir George Rodney, who would probably have been elected anyway and who spent most of the next two years at sea.

Besides this sum, almost £10,000 was spent in other open constituencies without any return to Government in the form of votes in the House of Commons. In the turbulent and populous constituency of Gloucester,

George Augustus Selwyn's interest had been decaying for years and in 1780 the chances of his re-election were doubtful. Yet Robinson not merely pressed him to stand but found a partner for him, and £2,600 was spent from the Government's election fund in a vain attempt to gain both seats. Besides over-estimating the degree of support for Government at Gloucester, Robinson had seriously misjudged his man: Selwyn had not the stomach for a hard-fought contest, and he and his colleague abandoned the struggle the night before the poll. The Government also spent £1,500 at Stafford, where two Opposition candidates were returned after a contest; and £2,900 was given to Henry Dundas, who vainly attempted to oppose the interest of Sir Lawrence Dundas (a recent convert to Opposition) in Edinburgh and Orkney and Shetland. John Clevland received £1,500 for Barnstaple, and £650 was spent at Penryn to buttress the Government interest there; yet in neither constituency were Opposition candidates concerned: these were fratricidal contests between Government supporters. To sum up: about £25,000, out of the Government's total expenditure of £62,000, brought returns wholly incommensurate with the outlay.

About £14,000 was spent in helping to finance the expenses of eleven candidates who had some claims on Government (North, like Newcastle before him, could be cajoled into spending money against his better judgement); £4,000 was spent on buying a seat at Tamworth for John Courtenay; and nearly £4,000 was paid to Thomas Hutchings Medlycott to help him gain control over both seats at Milborne Port (which were, of course, placed at the disposal of Government). Anthony Bacon and Thomas Orde, who contested the venal borough of Aylesbury, received £1,600; £2,900 was spent at Taunton, where North was recorder and was hoping to establish an interest; and over £4,000 was spent in trying to keep out of Parliament two members of the Opposition who had made themselves especially objectionable to Government, Temple Luttrell at Reading and Admiral Augustus Keppel at New Windsor. Both were defeated; but Keppel was immediately nominated a candidate for Surrey and was returned with a comfortable majority. Thomas Onslow, the defeated Government candidate, received £4,000 from the Treasury. When Peniston Portlock Powney first undertook to oppose Keppel at New Windsor, he had asked for only £1,000 from Government; but before the general election was over North had spent above £6,000 in trying to keep Keppel out of the House (£2,000 at

Windsor and £4,000 in Surrey), the only result being that Keppel had exchanged a shaky seat at Windsor for a perfectly safe one for Surrey. In truth, there was not much planning or even purpose behind the Government expenditure at this election, and on more than one occasion (Windsor is the obvious example) North incurred far greater expenses than he had ever intended. Of all Government subventions at this general election, that at Bristol brought the greatest results. At the cost of only £1,000 to the Treasury, Edmund Burke and Henry Cruger were defeated and both seats at Bristol gained for Government supporters. It is true that Burke and Cruger contributed to this result by quarrelling between themselves, but tribute must also be paid to the excellent organization built up since the débâcle of 1774 by the Government supporters in Bristol. Where there was good local organization, as at Bristol, Government money was well spent; where it was absent, as at Gloucester, the money was thrown away.

The decision to dissolve prematurely again took the Opposition leaders by surprise as it had done in 1774. 'I am exceedingly vexed at the sudden dissolution of Parliament', wrote Rockingham on hearing the news. 'I think it a *wicked* measure in the *advisers*.' ('Unprepared' would have been a good motto for Rockingham.) Yet he and the other leaders of Opposition managed their elections very well. Rockingham in particular faced a delicate situation in Yorkshire, for he was confronted with the Yorkshire Association, a challenge to his own authority in the county and an advocate for a much more radical system of reform than he cared to see. In addition, his great friend Sir George Savile, the source of much of his strength in the county, had declared his support of the Association's programme. In Henry Duncombe, Rockingham found a candidate for Yorkshire acceptable both to himself and the Association; but in York city his influence was directly challenged.

The Association tried to obtain a pledge from Rockingham's candidates at York, Charles Turner and Lord John Cavendish, that if elected they would support measures for parliamentary reform and shortening the duration of Parliaments. Turner, who advocated these measures, was prepared to give such a pledge, but Cavendish refused and the Association threatened to run a candidate against him. With Cavendish wishing to back out and Turner prepared to go over to the Association, Rockingham's interest in York was seriously threatened; but he kept his head, got his candidates started off on their canvass, and gave Cavendish some very sensible advice. 'I have particularly desired Lord John', Rockingham wrote to his wife, 'to state that he looks to the *approbation and support of the citizens of York* and that he shall not submit to be *catechized* by *persons* who are not under that description.' In the end the Association's threat did not materialize and Rockingham's candidates were returned unopposed.

In the five metropolitan constituencies, returning twelve Members to Parliament, the Opposition carried eleven seats, the only Government success being Rodney's election at Westminster. Middlesex returned Wilkes and George Byng, a Rockingham Whig, unopposed; London, three professed radicals and Newnham, an independent Opposition candidate; while in Southwark Dr. Johnson's friend Henry Thrale was beaten by two radicals. Mawbey and Keppel in Surrey, and Fox at Westminister, complete the tally of Opposition Members returned for the London constituencies—almost a clean sweep. Rather surprisingly, radicalism seems to have lost ground in the provinces. Radicals were defeated at Worcester and at Bristol; none appeared at Newcastle-upon-Tyne; and at Nottingham, where opposition to the American war was strong, John Cartwright, standing on a programme of parliamentary reform, was decisively beaten.

In 1780 there were 76 contests taken to the poll, a reduction of 19 from the very high figure for 1774:

    2 contests in 40 English counties
    1 in 2 universities (Cambridge)
   19 in 32 large boroughs
   13 in 28 medium boroughs
   32 in 143 small boroughs
    1 in 12 Welsh counties
    1 in 12 Welsh boroughs
    6 in 30 Scottish counties
    1 Scottish burgh (Edinburgh)

By no means all of these contests, even in the open constituencies, were straight fights between Government and Opposition or concerned political issues. The contest for Cambridgeshire, for example, was a very confused one, with three candidates each standing separately on their family interest. In that respect Sir Sampson Gideon, the defeated candidate, was much weaker than his opponents, Lord Robert Manners and Philip Yorke, scions of the two principal aristocratic houses in the county; but an additional reason for Gideon's defeat was that he had been a too-faithful supporter of North's Administration and had not voted for any measure of economical reform. In other large constituencies, such as Norwich and Coventry, local issues were probably more important than national; while the vast majority of the small boroughs, the Welsh constituencies, and the Scottish were contested along familiar lines, with little reference to national politics.

Still, when all allowances have been made for local issues in large constituencies and the weight of property and long established interests in small constituencies, it remains true that this was the first general election during the period to have important political questions at stake on which two parties held diametrically opposite opinions. It has been said that no Government in the eighteenth century ever lost a general election, which is really meaningless, for under eighteenth-century conditions a general election was not a contest between Government and Opposition. But North's ministry in 1780 certainly suffered a moral defeat. The following table is based on the voting records in the new Parliament of Members returned for the English open constituencies:

Type of constituency	Government supporters	Opposition supporters
Metropolitan area (London, Westminster, Middlesex, Surrey, Southwark)	1	11
English counties outside metropolitan area	15	61
Provincial boroughs, with over 1,000 voters	19	39
	35	111

It was in the medium and small boroughs and in Scotland that the Government found its majority. But many of the representatives of the smaller boroughs sat on their own interest and were independent alike of Government and Opposition. If they were to lose confidence in North, his Administration would be doomed.

THE GENERAL ELECTION OF 1784

The general election of 1784 was the last act in a political drama which had begun in December 1781 when the news reached England of Lord Cornwallis's surrender at Yorktown. Whatever hopes North's

Administration had of regaining the revolted provinces had to be abandoned, and North was compelled to assure the House of Commons that it was no longer intended to prosecute offensive warfare in America. Yorktown broke the morale of the North Administration; on 27 February 1782 the Opposition carried a motion for abandoning the attempt to reduce the colonies by force, and the policy pursued by North since 1775 was in ruins. He himself recognized that the end had come at last, but it took some little time to convince the King; and it was not until 20 March that George III faced the fact that a motion for North's dismissal would certainly pass the House and agreed to accept his minister's resignation.

The struggle for power which began on North's resignation and was terminated only by the general election of 1784 was really a search for a minister who could command the confidence of both the Crown and Parliament. This was the recurring problem in eighteenth-century politics. It had been raised in 1754 by the death of Henry Pelham, and was only settled when Newcastle joined Pitt in July 1757. The death of the King was always followed by a crisis in the ministry, for in a period when the sovereign was an active partner in government he could not be expected to take over automatically his predecessor's ministers. The crisis was unusually prolonged at the accession of George III and it was not until 1770 that a minister was found who could command the confidence of both Crown and Commons. The crisis which began in March 1782 was rendered more serious by differences of political principles as well as by conflicting personal ambitions, and by the fact that Charles James Fox, the man who seemed most to possess the confidence of the Commons, was peculiarly disliked by the King. After Fox and North had in February 1783 joined their forces to bring about the defeat of Lord Shelburne on the issue of the peace treaties, the King, though sorely against his wishes, was compelled to accept the Coalition. Only in December 1783 did he find in the younger Pitt a minister prepared to stand against Fox in the House of Commons.

Even today, the details of the negotiations which led to Pitt's assumption of office are by no means completely known, yet it seems clear that Pitt must have agreed to take office even before Fox's East India bill was defeated in the Lords on 17 December. That defeat was followed the next day by the dismissal of Fox and North and the appointment of Pitt as first lord of the Treasury. When Fox had taken office in April he had enjoyed the confidence of the Commons, and it should have been his task (which he hardly even attempted) to secure the confidence of the Crown. Pitt, on taking office in December, had the full backing of the Crown, and within three months was well on the way to winning the support of the Commons. On 12 January 1784, when Parliament reassembled after the Christmas recess, Fox had a majority of 54, but on 8 March he carried a resolution against the continuance of Pitt's Administration by one vote only.

Parliamentary conflicts, when they are fought on a two party basis, resemble the operations of war: superior strategy and better morale will often succeed against numerically larger forces. When Rommel took over command of the German army in France at the end of 1943, he realized that the only way to stop the expected invasion of Europe was to defeat the allied forces on the beaches: if once they effected a lodgement and penetrated inland, the Germans were doomed. A similar situation faced Fox in the House of Commons in 1784. If he could drive Pitt out of office within the first few days after Parliament reassembled, the King would have to take back the Coalition, and Fox's position would be even stronger than in April 1783. But if Pitt survived the first few days of the parliamentary assault and showed no signs of yielding, the morale of Fox's troops would fall and their numbers gradually decrease. This, in the event, is what happened, in spite of Fox's efforts to rally his troops, and of the active encouragement of the Prince of Wales, who several times watched debates from the gallery. By 10 February, when the *Morning Post* published a list of Members who had left Fox, the result of the battle was hardly any longer in doubt. Fox's failure to sweep away Pitt in the January offensive led to frustration and dejection among his followers, and it was henceforth through their abstaining or being absent from the House, rather than from positive desertions, that Fox's majority decreased. Motions of no confidence in the Administration were ignored by Pitt, and Fox could not be sure that his followers would go with him if he pressed the drastic measure of refusing supplies. That was the last step of all, only to be contemplated if supported by strong and vocal public opinion outside the House, the declaration, in fact, of a revolutionary situation. His decision not to oppose the passage of the mutiny bill on 9 March was Fox's admission of defeat.

It may be asked why, since Pitt knew on taking office that he would be in a minority, he did not advise an immediate dissolution. Several reasons can be given. There was no precedent for a dissolution by a ministry on taking office, though the Rockinghams had contemplated it in July 1765, and Dowdeswell had advised Rockingham in July 1767 that if he succeeded in forming an Administration he should proceed to the election of a new Parliament. But Pitt could not, in any case, dissolve immediately: the Treasury needed time to make arrangements with candidates and borough owners, and above all, to learn which Members of Parliament were friendly to the new Administration and which were not. Moreover, had Pitt dissolved without meeting Parliament or after his first defeat in the House, he would have triumphed only by the use of the King's prerogative. It was essential to weaken Fox's position in the House itself, to beat him with his own weapons. And, in deference to a substantial body of independent opinion which was pressing for a union between Fox and Pitt, it was desirable to show that such a union was impossible except by admitting Fox's charge that Pitt's Administration was unconstitutional. Finally, it would have been difficult to dissolve Parliament until the supplies had been voted.

On the East India bill, the Fox-North coalition had a majority of about 100; according to the list published by Stockdale on 19 March 1784, Fox shortly before the dissolution had a majority of 13; and Pitt's majority after the general election was about 120. Had Pitt held on a little longer before dissolving, Fox's majority might have vanished altogether. The general election of 1784 was the 'crowning mercy', the rout of an already beaten army. In that case, why was it necessary to dissolve at all? Would not Fox's followers have gradually melted away until Pitt had a safe majority? They probably would, but even so Fox would have been left with a formidable following. For many of North's friends, returned in 1780 when North was in power, held seats under Government control or sat for boroughs where the patron was now disposed to support Pitt's Administration. It was clearly undesirable, for example, to allow George Augustus North to continue to represent the Treasury borough of Harwich, or to allow the seats placed at the disposal of the Opposition by Edward Eliot in 1780 to continue to be held by men who now followed Fox. A general election would be an opportunity to drive those followers of North, who still remained faithful to him, from the constituencies which he had found for them in 1780. In this rout North's men would suffer more than Fox's, for Fox's friends had been returned by patrons the majority of whom still remained faithful to him. The Members who lost their seats at the general election of 1784 were nicknamed by contemporaries 'Fox's martyrs', but most of them were really followers of North.

The decision to dissolve was taken on wider grounds than those of electoral mechanics. Ever since Pitt's assumption of office, addresses had been coming in from the constituencies, expressing approval of the change of Administration and condemning Fox's East India bill. It was clear that there was a large volume of support for Pitt in the nation, and obviously it was wise to take advantage of that support while feeling against Fox was running high. The general election of 1784 was unique in this period as being an appeal to the nation at large upon a political issue. It was not so much an appeal by one party against another, as are general elections today, but rather an appeal by the executive branch of government against the legislature. Ever since the revolution of 1688 harmony between these two branches had been essential, and, in the absence of anything like the party system, that harmony was often disturbed. Thus, in 1784, while the King, the head of the executive, wished to have Pitt as his first minister, one branch of the legislature (the House of Commons) preferred Fox. The only way this deadlock could be overcome was by an appeal to the nation at large, the supreme arbiter in political disputes.

There were thus two aspects to the general election of 1784. On the one hand, it was a new Administration clearing out the followers of the old ministry from the constituencies under its command; on the other hand, it was an appeal to public opinion. The interpretation of this election has long been a matter of dispute between historians: some have seen Pitt's victory as the result of John Robinson's skilful manipulation of the old engines of influence and patronage; to others, it was a triumph of public opinion. It was, of course, both these things at the same time. In constituencies under patronage, public opinion had little chance to express itself; and in constituencies where political feeling was strong, no amount of influence was of any avail.

Two qualifications have to be made to the view that the election was managed by Robinson, using the methods he had long practised under North, and that, because it was so much a matter of influence and patronage, he was able to forecast the result of the election with almost mathematical precision. Firstly, the election was not managed by Robinson, but by George Rose, Pitt's secretary to the Treasury; and secondly, Robinson, far from making a correct forecast of the result of the election, seriously overestimated the majority Pitt would receive and was wrong in most of his forecasts of election results. It has been shown that at the general election of 1780 Robinson completely neglected the influence of public opinion; in 1784 he did so again, with even more disastrous results as far as his election forecasts were concerned, for in 1784 public opinion played a much larger part than it did in 1780. And, what was even worse, in his appraisal of the political conduct of Members, he made insufficient allowance for the degree of party connexion and feeling.

Robinson had left the Treasury with North in 1782, but during the period of the Shelburne Administration he was frequently consulted on the state of parties in the House of Commons. In March 1783, for example, after Shelburne's defeat on the peace preliminaries, Robinson drew up, probably with the assistance of Henry Dundas, a survey of political allegiances in the House. He had tried in vain to dissuade North from joining with Fox, and early in December 1783 was asked to prepare a survey of the House and of the constituencies, together with a forecast of the composition of the House after a general election. He placed his unique experience and knowledge of constituencies at the service of Pitt's Administration, but the management of the election, the work of interviewing patrons and candidates, bringing them together and regulating their financial arrangements, was done by George Rose. Robinson looked after Harwich, which he had managed for the Treasury under North, and intervened in the election at Ipswich (only a few miles from his house at Harwich); but it is clear that Rose had the main responsibility for the conduct of the election. Robinson's part was mainly that of supplying information and advice, which the inexperienced Rose was greatly in need of. (Rose's first estimates of the number of seats available to Government and of the amount of money required, were so inaccurate as to be almost useless.)

Robinson's survey of December 1783 considered the constituencies under the following headings: English counties; English boroughs, open; English boroughs, close (i.e., under patronage); Wales; Scotland. The Members of the existing House were classified according to their attitude towards Pitt, as 'pro' (viewed from Robinson's angle, i.e., opponents of the Coalition), 'hopeful', 'doubtful', and 'contra' (i.e., supporters of the Coalition). There are notes on the patronage or influence in each constituency, together with an estimate of which way the constituency might go at the general election; and finally a forecast of how the newly-elected Members might be expected to behave towards Pitt's Administration after a general election. Robinson was thus trying to make two forecasts: of the Members who might be returned at a general election, and of the way they would react towards Pitt's Administration. Here are the results of his survey of the existing Parliament and of a future Parliament:

	Existing Parliament				Future Parliament			
	Pitt	Hopeful	Doubtful	Fox	Pitt	Hopeful	Doubtful	Fox
English counties	18	19	12	31	22	18	11	29
English boroughs, open	70	40	30	92	84	54	36	58
English boroughs, close	49	34	18	76	99	32	15	31
Wales	5	4	4	11	8	10	2	4
Scotland	7	7	10	21	40	2	2	1
Totals	149	104	74	231	253	116	66	123

Thus, in the new Parliament there were expected to be 182 Members (nearly a third of the House) about whose political allegiance Robinson could not be sure. If, however, we add the 'hopefuls' to Pitt's total and the 'doubtfuls' to Fox's, Pitt's following becomes 369 and Fox's 189—a majority of 180 for Pitt.

Before proceeding to analyse Robinson's forecasts in the light of the results, it is well to be clear as to what the general election was about. The two sides were personified, almost as at a modern general election, in their respective leaders: it was Pitt and the King versus Fox and (to a much lesser extent) North. The propriety of Fox joining with his old enemy North in an 'unnatural coalition' was hardly an issue in any constituency, but much rather a brickbat to hurl at Fox when all other weapons had been exhausted. It was generally recognized that with three parties in the House, a coalition of two of them against the third was almost inevitable. Nor was parliamentary reform a serious issue in most constituencies. Much more important was Fox's East India bill. Fox could rightly complain that Pitt had come to power by doubtful means, through a backstairs intrigue and the King's intervention against the East India bill in the House of Lords. Such action would today be regarded as highly unconstitutional. Yet it did not make anything like the impression on the electorate which Fox's East India bill did. To the eighteenth century it was the India bill, not the King's intervention against it, which was unconstitutional. Its merits or defects as a plan to reform the government of India were hardly discussed at all, but it was denounced as an attempt by Fox to arrogate to himself the patronage of the East India Company. And here, without doubt, the popular image of Fox as a confirmed gambler, ruined and desperate for money, did him infinite harm. 'God forbid the patronage of India should go to the Crown', said Lord Fauconberg at the Yorkshire meeting of 25 March 1784, 'but shall it go to Charles Fox? Is he a man of such virtue?' And here are a few examples from the reports of Lord Fitzwilliam's agents of the state of feeling against Fox in Yorkshire: '[The merchants of Wakefield] are so hot at present and angry with Charles Fox upon his India bill that many of them are not to be talked to' (11 February); 'The people have no idea but that Mr. Fox wants to get the better of the King and be the lord protector' (8 March); 'The received notion amongst the inferiors in many parts is that Mr. Fox was attempting to dethrone the King and make himself an Oliver Cromwell' (26 April). The comparison of Fox with Cromwell (and it was not intended to be complimentary to either) was particularly common. Those voters who saw the election on political lines thought of it not so much as a contest between Fox and Pitt as between Fox and the King. Fox, always insensitive to public opinion, had not realized that enthusiasm for reducing the influence of the Crown was waning, and that a reaction had begun in favour of the Crown. Pitt, on the other hand, was defending prerogatives of the sovereign, which the majority of subjects believed the sovereign should possess.

To return to Robinson's survey of December 1783. In the English counties, he forecast a majority for Fox of 29 against 22, with 18 hopeful for Pitt and 11 doubtful. In no case did he assume that Pitt would win a seat as the result of a contest. In fact, in 38 counties he thought the same Members would be returned, and in only two (Cumberland and Monmouthshire) did he suggest that there might be a change. In the case of Cumberland he was wrong, in that of Monmouthshire substantially right. Robinson thought Pitt would gain six seats through their present occupants changing their political allegiance, and in only two of these was he correct.

But, above all, what he did not forecast was the substantial swing of opinion towards Pitt in the counties. If we count the 'hopefuls' with Pitt and the 'doubtfuls' with Fox (which will be done henceforth for the other groups of constituencies), it will be seen that Robinson expected each side to win 40 county seats. In fact Pitt won 48 seats, Fox 29, and three Members were classed as doubtful. Pitt made 12 gains in the English counties: two in Berkshire and Buckinghamshire, and one in Dorset, Hertfordshire, Middlesex, Norfolk, Staffordshire, Surrey, Suffolk, and Yorkshire. None of these was forecast by Robinson. Humphry Sturt, a friend of Rockingham, whom Robinson expected to be again returned for Dorset, was refused nomination by the county meeting because he had supported the Coalition. Thomas William Coke of Holkham, whose seat for Norfolk Robinson believed to be impregnable, was met at the county meeting with the cry 'No Fox! No Coalition! Pitt and the King for ever!'; spent three days canvassing the county, and received so little support that he declined the poll. Probably the most surprising result of all was the election in the neighbouring county of Suffolk, where Robinson expected Sir Thomas Charles Bunbury, another friend of Fox, to be again returned. Bunbury was first elected for Suffolk in 1761 when under age, and with the single exception of the Parliament of 1784, represented the county until 1812. At this general election he was defeated by a man of little standing in the county, Joshua Grigby, who only became a candidate shortly before the election. When Bunbury declined the poll at the end of the first day he had received only 739 votes, as against 1,283 for Grigby and 1,652 for Sir John Rous, both supporters of Pitt.

It seems that in East Anglia the run against Fox was very great. But it may also have been that Norfolk and Suffolk, both independent counties, resented their Members taking so decided a political line, instead of trying to maintain the attitude of independence and detachment from parties which was supposed to be the hall mark of the county Member. In the election for Yorkshire there was a mixture of local and national issues. The Yorkshire Association, strongly pro-Pitt and for parliamentary reform, backed Henry Duncombe and William Wilberforce, against the candidates of Lord Fitzwilliam and the Fox-North party.

Some of the animus against Fitzwilliam was due to his attempting to assume, as a matter of property and hereditary right, the lead in county affairs which had been slowly and laboriously acquired by his uncle Rockingham; but the defeat of Fitzwilliam's candidates (they retired the evening before the poll) was also a great triumph for Pitt.

In the open boroughs, Robinson forecast 138 seats for Pitt and 94 for Fox. He had hoped to gain 28 seats in this type of constituency but had to be content with 15: the result worked out at 125 for Pitt, 96 for Fox, and 11 doubtful. He expected to lose six seats: two at Barnstaple, and one at Wallingford, Truro, Pontefract, and Bishop's Castle. This forecast was 100% wrong. Pitt did not lose a seat at Wallingford or Truro; at both Pontefract and Barnstaple he gained, instead of losing, one; and the forecast at Bishop's Castle was based on the assumption that Henry Strachey and William Clive were supporters of Pitt: in fact they were supporters of Fox and remained so after the general election.

There were 25 Members sitting for the open boroughs whom Robinson expected to be returned to the new Parliament but to change their political allegiance: 11 were to become supporters of Pitt and 14 were to be reckoned as 'hopeful'. Of the 11 Members who were expected to swing over to Pitt, only two, Lord Lincoln and Sir Charles Farnaby, did in fact do so, while Sir Henry Clinton remained attached to Fox but was replaced at the general election by a supporter of Pitt. The other eight followers of Fox who were expected to change remained with Fox and retained their seats.

Robinson also hoped to gain nine seats in seven constituencies by turning out followers of Fox. In nearly all of these constituencies Government had considerable influence—indeed, it is difficult to understand why the Treasury boroughs of Harwich, Hastings, and Rye were included in this section of Robinson's survey, since they could hardly be described as open constituencies. One might, therefore, expect these forecasts to have been reasonably near the mark. In fact, Robinson made only five gains where he had expected nine: two at Hastings, and one each at Hedon, Harwich, and Sandwich. At Plymouth, the Admiralty lost one seat to the independent party; and at Rye the Treasury manager revolted against his masters: he accepted the Treasury's nomination of Charles Wolfran Cornwall, the Speaker, for one seat, but returned a Foxite for the other. 'Measures were taken for Winchelsea', wrote Rose to Robinson on 31 March, 'but were defeated by the people there deserting their own cause.' The Treasury interest in this borough was, in fact, practically extinct, and two followers of Fox were returned.

Even in the two groups of constituencies where public opinion played little part and where the results of the elections could most easily be forecast—the English boroughs under patronage and the Welsh constituencies—Robinson was unduly optimistic. In the English close boroughs, he expected Pitt to gain 131 seats (including the 'hopefuls') and Fox 46 (counting the 'doubtfuls'). The actual figures were 109 for Pitt, 61 for Fox, and 7 doubtful. In Wales, Robinson's forecast was: Pitt 18, Fox 6; and the result: Pitt 9, Fox 12, and 3 doubtful. The Government's defeat in Wales was due mainly to the fact that some influential Welsh families, including the Morgans of Tredegar and the Vaughans of Crosswood, remained loyal to Fox and did not, as Robinson expected, swing over in support of the Administration.

In England, Robinson underestimated the force of public opinion; in Scotland, where public opinion could hardly express itself in elections, he underestimated the strength of party connexion among the Scottish Members. One can almost reconstruct the reasoning behind his forecast of the situation in Scotland. The Scottish Members had as a rule supported every Administration since the death of Henry Pelham. There had been one exception—the first Rockingham ministry (but in this case there had been special circumstances to account for the opposition of the Scots); and the Scots had also been divided in their attitude towards Shelburne's Administration and the Fox-North coalition. But that had been a time of intense party conflict, and Robinson obviously expected that when the general election of 1784 had established Pitt's majority, party feeling amongst the Scottish Members would die down. No doubt Henry Dundas gave assurances that he could take care of the Scots. During North's Administration the Scottish Members had voted almost in a block for Government, and Robinson and Dundas confidently expected the return of those halcyon days. And so Robinson in his survey counted 40 Scottish Members as attached to Pitt, two hopeful, two doubtful, and one only (the Member for Orkney and Shetland, a constituency controlled by Sir Thomas Dundas) as a downright opponent of Pitt. In fact, the Scottish Members divided in pretty much the same proportions as the English: 24 went with Administration, 15 with the Opposition, and 6 were classed as doubtful. The element of party had come to stay, in Scotland as well as in England.

Robinson knew more than any man of the political allegiances within the House of Commons and of the Members' relations with their constituencies, and if his forecast of the state of parties in the new House was inaccurate, it was because the task he had been given was impossible. Within less than two years there had been four Administrations, and in a period of confusion and instability no one could accurately forecast the political inclinations of a House of Commons, most of whose Members owed their seats neither to the Crown nor to a patron. It must be remembered that the survey was drawn up before Pitt had taken office and before the first manifestations of political feeling in the constituencies had begun. No one in December 1783, for example, could be expected to foresee the whirlwind which blew Bunbury out of his seat for Suffolk or caused Coke to abandon Norfolk. Even in our own time, when the science (or art) of testing public opinion has been refined to a high degree and when there is a mass electorate thinking largely along party lines, the result of the general election of 1945 took politicians of all parties by surprise. Robinson had no devices at his disposal for testing public opinion, and the extent of its manifestations at this general election was new in his experience. His inclinations and temperament led him to undervalue the strength of party feeling and overrate the attractive pull of Government. If in these observations on the general election of 1784 his reputation as a political manager has suffered, it is largely because historians have exaggerated his ability to influence the results of that election and forecast the politics of the Members who would be returned.

Of course Pitt had in 1784 all the resources and advantages of the Treasury at his disposal and he made full use of them. The Treasury boroughs were not as safe as they had been before the passing of Crewe's Act disfranchising the revenue officers, but that measure had hardly affected the boroughs under private patronage. Edward Eliot still commanded six seats in Cornwall, and all six were disposed of to supporters of Pitt's Administration. Sir James Lowther's nine Members were counted on the Government side (and with the Opposition in 1788 when Lowther was persuaded to desert Pitt on the Regency bill). Lords Falmouth and Edgcumbe, the Cornish professional borough-mongers *par excellence*, returned candidates friendly to Government. Sir Francis Basset, alone of the great Cornish borough-mongers, went with the Opposition. Richard Rigby said in the House on 4 February 1784, with reference to the Government's plans for an early election:

That House had seen four peerages within the last month, and he understood there was a promise of thirteen or fourteen more. It was not a little extraordinary that three out of four were bestowed on gentlemen from Cornwall, a county that was ever remarkable for more of what was called rotten boroughs than any other county in the kingdom. It was extraordinary that they should happen to be created just then.

It was a little late in the day for Rigby, who for fourteen years had held the office of paymaster-general under North, the most lucrative office in the gift of the Government, and had used the vast balances of money entrusted to his care to enrich himself, to complain of Government for favouring borough owners. But in fact, of the four peerage creations mentioned by Rigby, only two were given to borough owners: Thomas Pitt, William Pitt's cousin, who controlled both seats at Old Sarum, and Edward Eliot, who had in any case applied for a peerage while Shelburne was minister. Still, the idea was current that Pitt intended to strengthen his electoral prospects by ennobling those who could return Members of Parliament. In May, after the results of the election were known, there was a batch of peerage creations which included Lord Bulkeley, already a peer of Ireland, who controlled two seats in Wales; Charles Cocks, who had placed his seat at Reigate at Pitt's command; and Sir James Lowther. In addition, Lord Paget, who had wrested control of Anglesey from Bulkeley, was created Earl of Uxbridge. The remaining five creations were of men who had no electoral interest. A further batch of four creations in July was also unconnected with the general election. All Administrations used the peerage to reward men who had supported the Government in the constituencies, and Pitt was no more lavish in this respect than his predecessors.

The Government's expenses in 1784 were very much smaller than North's in 1780 and, in spite of the fall in the value of money and the increased price of seats, were not much more than Newcastle spent in 1754. Pitt spent nearly £32,000 (this does not include the amount used to subsidize newspapers), and most of it, as was usual with Government money at election time, was spent in vain. The enormous sum of £9,200 was expended in trying to keep Fox out of Westminster, and a further £2,000 in an attempt (which however, very nearly succeeded) to oust the obnoxious Sawbridge from his seat for London. Stafford took £400 and returned two friends of Fox; £2,500 was spent in Berkshire and £1,000 at New Windsor, constituencies where the

King felt his personal prestige involved, but where the Opposition candidates stood little chance anyway. At Colchester, where the Government spent £2,500, its candidate was only returned after a petition. These constituencies accounted for £17,000, and it could hardly be claimed that Government received value for its money. Elsewhere, over £6,000 was spent on five open constituencies where there were contests between supporters of the Government and the Opposition (Great Yarmouth, Middlesex, Rochester, Southwark, and Surrey), and in each the Government candidates won. It is surely a supreme stroke of irony that John Wilkes, for so long a thorn in the flesh of Government, an avowed enemy of every form of corruption and secret influence, should have retained his seat for Middlesex only by the skin of his teeth and with the help of £1,000 from the King's election account. £1,000 was spent on Hastings, where the Government interest was in jeopardy and where for the first time during this period there was a contest: this was a borough which had cost little before the disfranchisement of the revenue officers. Also, five Government candidates (at Lostwithiel, Great Bedwyn, Bossiney, Lymington, and Chipping Wycombe) received help towards the purchase of their seats in pocket boroughs: a total of over £6,000.

Pitt appears to have gained about 85 seats at this election, and Fox about 17. Pitt's gains were in the following types of constituency: 12 in the English counties; 2 in the reformed and enlarged quasi-county constituency of Cricklade; 21 in open boroughs with electorates of at least 500 voters; 7 in smaller open constituencies; 14 in Government-influenced boroughs; 6 in Scotland; 11 as the result of purchasing borough seats from patrons; and 12 in closed boroughs, where the patrons replaced friends of Fox by friends of Pitt. Of Fox's 17 gains, 10 were in English pocket boroughs, 3 in Scotland, and only 4 in open English constituencies. The only English county where a Foxite replaced a follower of Pitt was Derbyshire. The three large open boroughs where the same change took place were Hereford, where Fox's friend, Lord Surrey, had considerable influence; Bedford, where William MacDowall Colhoun, a very shady character, stood as a Pittite and immediately after his election joined Fox; and Maldon.

Another way of showing Pitt's triumph in the open constituencies is by means of a table (shown overleaf), similar to that drawn up for the general election of 1780.

It is clear from this table that the swing against Fox was much greater in the London area than in the provinces. The two Foxites returned in the metropolis were Fox himself at Westminster, where he had a strong body of supporters but even so had to fight the longest and one of the hardest contests of the period; and John Sawbridge, who came fourth on the poll for London, with a majority of only nine over a follower of Pitt and more than 1,400 votes behind the next successful candidate.

Type of constituency	Supporters of Pitt	Supporters of Fox	Doubtful
Metropolitan area (London, Westminster, Middlesex, Surrey, Southwark)	10	2	0
English counties outside metropolitan area	44	29	3
Provincial boroughs, with over 1,000 voters	36	22	0
	90	53	3

There seem to be two reasons why Fox did so much worse in London than in the rest of the country. Parliamentary reform was much more an issue in London than elsewhere, and Pitt was its champion while Fox, by his alliance with North, had seemed to betray the cause of reform. Secondly, there were no patrons in the metropolitan constituencies and the middle and lower classes had a much greater chance of making their opinions felt in elections. In many of the provincial counties and boroughs there was no contest and the issue of Pitt v. Fox was never presented to the electorate. In Sussex, for example, the county representation was divided between the two greatest landowners in the county, as it had been in 1780: one seat went to Lord George Lennox, brother of the Duke of Richmond, and the other to Thomas Pelham, son of Lord Pelham. The fact that Lennox happened to be a follower of Pitt and Pelham of Fox was incidental; had both been either Pittites or Foxites the result would have been the same. Similarly, the Duke of Portland, the titular head of Fox's party, divided the representation of Cumberland with Sir James Lowther and of Nottinghamshire with the Duke of Newcastle, with the result, as far as the House of Commons was concerned, that both parties gained one Member for each of these two counties. The electoral pattern was reproduced as it had been on former occasions, irrespective of party politics, and both elections were unopposed: there was far more excitement in Cumberland in 1768, when no political issue was at stake, than there was in 1784. Many of the large towns too were under the influence of patrons, and it seems probable that the results in London are a more accurate indication of urban opinion than those in the provinces.

Here is a table of contests for comparison with previous elections:

  7 contests in 40 English counties
  1 in 2 universities (Cambridge)
18 in 32 large boroughs
12 in 28 medium boroughs
35 in 143 small boroughs
  1 in 12 Welsh counties
  1 in 12 Welsh boroughs
  8 in 30 Scottish counties

It will be seen that there were 75 contests in England and Wales at the general election of 1784, and eight in the Scottish counties— more than in 1780 but less than the record figures for 1774.

3. THE MEMBERS

AGE AND PARLIAMENTARY EXPERIENCE

Between the dissolution in 1754 and the dissolution in 1790, the number of men elected as Members of the House of Commons was 1,964. This includes John Kirkman, returned for London at the general election of 1780, who died six hours before the conclusion of the poll: technically, however, he was a Member of Parliament, because a writ had to be issued for a by-election. The exact dates of birth or baptism of most of these Members have been ascertained, but in some cases an approximate date of birth, correct to one or two years, has been derived from school and university registers, age at date of death, age at entry into the army or navy, and so on. The following table shows the age composition of each Parliament immediately after the general election. Members returned for more than one constituency are included only once.

| General election | Age on election | | | | | | | Age not known | Returned for more than 1 constituency |
	Under 30	30–39	40–49	50–59	60–69	70–79	Over 80		
1754	87	141	144	105	43	13	1	19	5
1761	81	154	127	109	51	14	2	13	7
1768	99	143	159	96	32	7	2	9	11
1774	86	128	157	110	39	8	1	11	18
1780	95	133	125	114	43	12	6	17	13
1784	98	155	122	108	39	11	—	19	6

The general age distribution is very similar from Parliament to Parliament, as might be expected in a period which did not see any violent social changes affecting the upper classes. The majority of Members, ranging from 398 in 1768 to 372 in 1780, were between the ages of 30 and 59 at the time of the general election. At each election, about 15% of the House was below 30, which again might be expected in a time when men assumed full adult responsibilities earlier than they do today. The Parliament elected in 1784 was somewhat younger than the average (253 Members were under 40) and the Parliament of 1774 somewhat older (214 Members under 40).

At each general election (except those of 1754 and 1784) there was a handful of Members returned under the age of 21: one in 1761; four in 1768; six in 1774; and two in 1780. Legally, these Members were not allowed to speak or vote in the House and their elections were automatically null and void; but no action was ever taken against any of them during this period. There was an opposition to Robert Lowther's election for Westmorland in 1759 and threats that a petition would be brought against him because he was under age, but nothing was done. Still, in 1780 Lord Compton, who was under age, withdrew his candidature at Northampton at almost the last moment because of 'rumours in the town', although there was no opposition. And Lord Ailesbury in 1780 preferred to return a stop-gap at Great Bedwyn rather than his eldest son, who would not be of age until March 1783. Most of the Members returned under age sat for pocket boroughs, but two were elected for counties (Robert Lowther for Westmorland in 1759 and Thomas Charles Bunbury for Suffolk in 1761), and one for a large borough (Henry Seymour Conway for Coventry in 1766).

The average age of the Parliament elected in 1754 was 43.6 years, and the figures for the succeeding Parliaments do not vary from this by more than 2%. The average age on first entering the House, taken throughout the period, was 32.6 years. Naturally, there were wide divergences from this figure in different social classes: sons of Peers or members of families with an old-established electoral interest entered the House at a much earlier age than merchants, who had first to make their way in the world and who only developed parliamentary ambitions somewhat late in life. The average tenure of a seat of the Members returned at the general election of 1754 was 22 years 7 months, and of Members returned at by-elections between 1754 and 1761, 15 years 3 months.

The numbers of new Members returned at each general election are shown in the table overleaf.

The continuity of membership from Parliament to Parliament was considerable: at each general election except that of 1768 about 400 Members of the preceding Parliament were again elected, with around 130 new Members who had no parliamentary experience and a score or so of former Members who had not been in Parliament at the preceding dissolution. The number of new, inexperienced Members was higher in 1768 than in any other Parliament of the period, and though with this single exception it would be true to say that in general the proportion of new Members to old remained fairly constant, the tendency of the time was for the number of new Members to show a slight increase. The figures are as follows:

	General Elections					
	1754	1761	1768	1774	1780	1784
New Members (i.e. returned for the first time)	123	127	149	122	130	132
Former Members (i.e. with parliamentary experience) who had not been in the previous Parliament	26	21	11	20	20	22
New and former Members elected but unseated on petition	3	1	8	12	9	8
New and former Members returned on petition or *vice* Members returned for more than one constituency	4	5	6	12	7	1
Totals	156	154	174	166	166	163

The percentage of young men was greater among the newly-elected Members than in the House as a whole, as is shown by the following table.

General Election	% of House under 30	% of new Members under 30
1754	15%	33%
1761	14%	33%
1768	17%	39%
1774	15%	31%
1780	17%	34%
1784	17%	28%

SOCIAL STANDING

A statistical analysis of the Members of the House of Commons according to their social standing would be an almost impossible undertaking and would be unlikely to yield results commensurate with the labour involved. The very term 'social standing' is ambiguous; it is also misleading because it implies that English society in the second half of the eighteenth century was arranged in a rigid, hierarchical pattern. In fact social classes were remarkably fluid and their boundaries ill-defined; a family could rise or fall in social standing within a generation, and a man's social position in the last resort depended on his own estimate. Still, it may be objected, there were ranks in society: men were either peers, baronets, knights, or commoners; and Members of Parliament could be classed according to their rank or that of their fathers. But even so such a classification would be highly misleading, if presented in statistical form without qualifications.

Throughout this period about one-fifth of the Members of the House of Commons were sons of peers or were themselves Irish peers. But the difference between British, Scottish, and Irish peerages is crucial, for these honours were not regarded as being on the same level. A British peerage, which automatically conferred upon its holder (with certain exceptions) a seat in the Upper House, and was usually granted only with remainder in direct male descent, seemed to many Members the natural conclusion of a successful career in the House of Commons, made all the more covetable by the difficulties which faced them in attaining the prize. A landed estate was an essential qualification, and previously to have had a peerage in the family was a strong recommendation. Service in the House of Commons or in office did not in itself qualify for a peerage: there were too many Members whose claims on that score would have had to be admitted, and neither George II nor George III was fond of making peers. And it was only by constantly importuning the King and his ministers that peerages were obtained. In histories of families which had remained commoners, published in the nineteenth century, one frequently meets with the story that an ancestor had been offered a peerage by the elder Pitt or Lord North and had declined it, but while dozens of examples can be given of Members who applied unsuccessfully for peerages, there is not one case of any Member being offered a peerage and declining it. All such stories must be treated very sceptically, as will be seen from an examination of one or two specimens of the peerage-hunting species.

George Pitt, M.P. 1742–74, was a distant cousin of the elder Pitt, and under George II counted as a Tory. Soon after the accession of George III he was appointed groom of the bedchamber and envoy to Turin, and began applying for a peerage. He adhered to each successive Administration in turn, and to each he asserted that he had been promised a peerage by the King. In 1770 he refused the appointment of ambassador to Madrid because the peerage had been denied him, and in letters to Lord North he wrote of the 'unparalleled hardships' he had undergone in pursuit of his aim and the 'state of anxiety and suspense' in which he had been 'unmercifully tossed during the long space of twelve years'. Finally, in 1776, after fifteen years' solicitation, the King put an end to his sufferings and created him Baron Rivers.

Thomas Brand, M.P. 1741–70, was closely connected with the Duke of Bedford, whose political lead he followed in Parliament. During the years when the Bedfords were in office Brand pressed his claims to a peerage and in 1763 Bedford obtained a promise that he should be included in the next creation. In December 1766, when Bedford was negotiating to join Chatham's Administration, a peerage for Brand was one of his conditions, and was definitely promised by Grafton when the Bedfords took office in December 1767. In March 1769, when nothing had been done for Brand, Bedford took the matter up with Grafton, who threatened to resign rather than agree to an immediate creation. Brand died the following year, without his peerage.

George III's habit of promising applicants for peerages that they would be included in the next creation—a way of putting them off until the Greek kalends—recoiled on his own head, for when there had to be a creation of peers he was swamped by applicants, all of whom claimed to have the King's promise. Thus in 1776 ten peerages were created, seven of which were the result of past promises to Members of Parliament. One of them, that bestowed on Thomas Foley, M.P. for Herefordshire, throws an interesting light on the practice of peerage creations in the later eighteenth century, for Foley belonged to the Opposition and in his 28 years in the House of Commons is not known to have voted for any Administration. His claim to a peerage was based on the fact that he had inherited the estates of his cousin, the Lord Foley of the last creation; it was a mark of rank to which his estates naturally entitled him, not a reward for political services.

The Brudenell family were courtiers *par excellence* and were special favourites of George III, George Brudenell, 4th Earl of Cardigan, was created Duke of Montagu in 1766, and a younger brother Thomas, who had inherited from his maternal uncle the title of Lord Bruce, was created Earl of Ailesbury in 1776. Ailesbury controlled the boroughs of Great Bedwyn and Marlborough, and made a particular point of always returning Members whose fidelity to Government was absolutely dependable. Another brother, Robert, M.P. 1756–68, entered the army and (though apparently he never saw active service), at his death in 1768 was colonel of the 16th Foot, vice-chamberlain to the Queen, and lieutenant-governor of Windsor Castle. The second brother, James, heir to the earldom of Cardigan, also held court office, but had to depend for a seat in Parliament on his younger brother, Lord Ailesbury, who patronized him with considerable hauteur. In 1780 James, revolting against his treatment as 'a poor younger brother of no consequence whatever', applied to North for a peerage; and North commented to the King:

The principle objection appears to be that he has no estate at present, and that he seeks for this dignity purely to avoid the trouble and fatigue of attending the House of Commons. On the other hand, Mr. Brudenell is a man of a very noble family, very polite manners, much respected, and generally beloved. His elder and his younger brethren are both peers. He will probably not have any progeny, and he will certainly succeed to a peerage, so that this creation will add to the House of Lords for a very short time.

A month later James Brudenell became a peer.

The scramble for peerages extended further in Scotland than in England, since until 1782, by a doubtful interpretation of the Act of Union, peers of Scotland could not be created peers of Great Britain. To get round this, eldest sons of Scottish peers were created peers of Great Britain in their father's life-time. In 1766 John Campbell, Marquess of Lorne, M.P. for Dover, deserted the Bedford party (who had tried in vain to obtain for him a British peerage) and by appealing direct to Chatham obtained the honour he desired. One could hardly blame him, since his father the Duke of Argyll was over seventy and could not be expected to live much longer. Another of Bedford's Scottish followers, John Stewart, Viscount Garlies, M.P. for Ludgershall, was in a similar situation, and believing that 'being in a constant opposition' would weaken his chances of getting a peerage, also deserted Bedford for Chatham. But Garlies was not so fortunate as Lorne, and had to wait until 1796 for what he called his 'omnium', the only thing in life he wished for.

Irish peers were of two types during this period: genuine Irishmen, who sat in the Irish House of Lords; and Englishmen, who more often than not sat in the British House of Commons and hoped one day to sit in the British House of Lords. Irish peerages were given to Members of Parliament whose estates and standing did not qualify them for the British peerage and yet who had made such a nuisance of themselves that they had to be given some honour; to Members engaged in trade; and to men who had distinguished themselves in the service of their country— though distinguished service only slowly became a recommendation for entry into the House of Lords. The great Robert Clive, on his return from India after Plassey, was created an Irish peer, and henceforth it was the ambition of his life to obtain a British peerage—by virtue of the estates which he had purchased with his Indian wealth. William Eden, after having served as secretary to the conciliation commission in America, envoy to France to negotiate a commercial treaty, and ambassador to Spain, was created an Irish peer in 1789 and four years later a British peer. It was only towards the end of the century that men of merit were created British peers without having passed the intermediate stage of the Irish peerage: Rodney, victor of the battle of the Saints, in 1782; Charles Jenkinson, after nearly thirty years in the service of the state, created Baron Hawkesbury in 1786; and James Harris, perhaps the foremost diplomat of his day, created Baron Malmesbury in 1788. In the earlier part of the period, peerages were much harder to get, even by men apparently entitled to them by their offices: Dudley Ryder was lord chief justice of the King's bench from 1754 to his death in 1756 without a peerage; and Robert Henley, appointed lord keeper in 1757, did not become a peer until March 1760 (and only then to enable him to officiate as lord high steward at the trial of Earl Ferrers for murder). Charles Yorke, when offered by Chatham the place of lord chief justice of the common pleas in 1766, claimed that the office entitled its holder to a peerage; which George III denied. Yet the King was forced to concede a similar claim made by Wedderburn in 1780, because Wedderburn was an important political figure and it would have been injudicious at that time to offend him.

Eight out of the eighteen Irish peers created in 1776 and four out of the nine created in 1783 were Members of the British House of

Commons, and of these only two were Irishmen. Richard Philipps, Thomas Wynn, and William Edwardes were Welsh squires; William Mayne was a Scot, who had been engaged in the Portugal trade; Richard Pennant, the son of a Jamaica planter; and the remainder were English country gentlemen. The Irish peerage was useful in that it conferred social prestige on such Members of Parliament as required it, and did not materially increase the numbers of the Irish House of Lords, since the majority of English M.P.s with Irish titles rarely participated in the proceedings of the Irish Parliament. Promotion to the Irish peerage was often the last resource of a minister who did not know how else to meet a Member's importunities. John Pennington, who bought himself a seat in Parliament at Milborne Port in 1781, had an old claim on the Duke of Grafton for services rendered by Pennington's father when the Duke was first lord of the Treasury. When Grafton returned to office in March 1782 he tried to find a place for Pennington, but demand far exceeded supply, and in the end Pennington was fobbed off with an Irish peerage.

When Henry Fox was created Baron Holland in 1763 it was virtually the end of his political career: although he had been a front bench man in the House of Commons for nearly twenty years, he took no part in the debates in the Lords. The peerage was the sign of his retirement. But in 1766 the elder Pitt was created an earl to signalize his acceptance of the place of first minister: for him the peerage was not a refuge from the hurly-burly of the House of Commons, but a lofty pinnacle from which he could survey the battle and possibly direct the course of events. Few contemporaries seem to have understood the political consequences of leaving the House of Commons for the Lords. Yet while William Pitt had been a great power in politics, as Earl of Chatham he was virtually impotent. The eighteenth-century House of Commons could only be led from the House of Commons, and the longest and most stable Administrations of this period were those of commoners. The Duke of Newcastle, with a majority of 200 in the House, had to resign in 1756 because he could not find a leader to put at the head of his troops; and it seems very doubtful if Shelburne would have been beaten in February 1783 had he been a commoner. The golden age of the House of Lords as a political institution (if there ever had been one) was over before this period began, and the attraction of the Upper House for M.P.s during the eighteenth century was purely social and implied a weakening of their political ambitions. The politically important peers whose names are stamped on the history of the time—Newcastle, Bute, Rockingham, Portland, and Shelburne—were like the battleships during the second world war: possessing immense fire power, they were yet useless without the air cover supplied by the aircraft carriers in the Commons. And to reach the top in the House of Commons, debating skill, the ability to attune oneself to the moods of the House and to understand its business and procedure, were of far greater importance than social standing. On the floor of the House it was every man for himself, and the devil take his pedigree and his connexions. James Harris wrote about a debate in the House on a private bill, 29 March 1762:

A bill had come to us from the Lords about certain trust lands at Tavistock, relating to the Duke of Bedford's affairs, and which he had brought in. There was a clause in it to declare that those lands were to convey no right of voting in that borough. This got among the Commons as a breach of their privileges, and the bill had certainly been flung out had not Alderman Dickinson moved that it be withdrawn. He was mistaken in the manner of doing this, by beginning that *he had authority from a noble duke*, etc. *We* want no authority from noble dukes, nor from those greater than dukes, to empower us to do our acts.

As compared with the Crown and the Lords, the Commons had only comparatively recently become an essential element in government; and, as is shown by the case of the printers prosecuted in 1771 for publishing reports of debates, the House was sometimes excessively concerned for its dignity and its privileges.

The rank of baronet was not highly valued in the eighteenth century. It was merely the first rung of the social ladder; almost any M.P. with landed property could obtain a baronetcy, unless he were in declared opposition to Government. The Order of the Garter was almost exclusively the preserve of peers: the only Member of the House of Commons to hold it during our period was Lord North. The situation is not very different today: at the time of writing Sir Winston Churchill is the only Member of the House of Commons with the Garter. The Order of the Bath was usually reserved for men who had served the state: diplomats, soldiers, or sailors, whether or not they were Members of the House of Commons. When in 1759 Newcastle asked George II to confer the Order of the Bath on George Warren, whose only claims to the honour were that he was rich, a Member of Parliament, and had served four years as a subaltern in the Guards, the King 'flew into a passion'. 'What!' he burst out to Newcastle, 'do you think I dote? Pray don't come to me with such proposals as these.' Warren obtained the honour in the new reign by timely application to Bute, but that was in the days when George III refused Bute nothing.

A plain knighthood was much beneath the dignity of a Member of Parliament. Aldermen, recorders, and bearers of complimentary addresses were knighted, but not M.P.s. The attorney- and solicitor-general were not invariably knighted during the eighteenth century, nor were the judges. The honour, not being hereditary, was little sought after.

There were men in the House of Commons whose wealth and the extent of whose estates were on a level with those of any in the House of Lords; and at various times during this period the much-coveted distinction of being 'the richest commoner in England' was ascribed to some half-dozen M.P.s. Three were country gentlemen, whose wealth came mostly from agricultural rents: Charles Anderson Pelham of Brocklesby, Lincolnshire; John Tempest of Brancepeth Castle, Durham; and John Jolliffe Tufnell of Langleys, Essex. Anderson Pelham, alone of these three, is known to have applied for a peerage, which he eventually received when he went over to Pitt in 1794. Common estimates of what men were worth in the eighteenth century are notoriously suspect (as indeed they are today), but at least they give some idea of what was considered to be wealth. Tufnell, at his death in 1794, was estimated to have a rental of £18,000 per annum, and to have left £150,000 in cash or in the funds. Robert Child, the banker (the only 'richest commoner' engaged in trade) was reported to have had an income of £15,000 per annum from land and £30,000 from the profits of the bank. Probably the man who best deserved the title of the richest commoner in England was Sir James Lowther, in whose person was concentrated the wealth of three branches of the Lowther family: from his father he inherited estates in Westmorland and plantations in the West Indies; from his great-uncle Henry, 3rd Viscount Lonsdale, further property in Westmorland; and from his cousin Sir James Lowther, 4th Bt., the Whitehaven estates of his family and a sum estimated at £2,000,000.

There were other men in the House whose claims to be the richest commoner must be seriously considered: Robert Clive, who made his fortune in India; William Beckford, whose wealth was based on his West Indian plantations; and Samuel Fludyer, probably the biggest clothier in England, who died in 1768 'reputed worth £900,000'.

There were, in addition, men in the House who had risen from very humble beginnings, and from whose lives could be compiled a hand-book on how to rise in eighteenth-century society.

Here, to begin with, are some examples of self-made men who sat in Parliament during this period. Robert Darling was born of humble parentage and as a boy is said to have been employed to look after cows. He then became apprenticed to a lapidary, and 'by great diligence and other means acquired a large fortune.' He became a merchant in London, served as sheriff in 1766 and was knighted, and in 1768 entered Parliament for Wendover. He died in 1770, leaving property in London, the home counties, and Cumberland. Of his short parliamentary career little is known: to most of these self-made men, membership of the House was coveted as a symbol of success, not as the basis of a political career. James Dickson, a native of Stitchell in Roxburghshire, of whose parentage and antecedents nothing has been discovered, made his fortune as a merchant in London and returned to Scotland to buy estates, develop local industries, and enter Parliament in 1771 as M.P. for Linlithgow Burghs. George Gipps, a younger son of a staymaker of Ashford, Kent, became an apothecary in Canterbury, but did not prosper. He left medicine for trade, became 'an extensive and fortunate speculator in the hop trade', and subsequently a banker; and in 1780 was returned head of the poll in a contested election for Canterbury. Of William James, M.P. for West Looe 1774–83, Wraxall wrote in his *Memoirs*: 'His origin was so obscure as almost to baffle inquiry, and he had derived no advantage from education, but he possessed strong natural abilities, aided by a knowledge of mankind.' He was apparently the son of a miller of Haverfordwest in Pembrokeshire. He entered the naval service of the East India Company; returned to England in 1759 with a fortune; and subsequently became a director of the Company, a Member of Parliament, and a baronet. James was politically connected with Lord Sandwich, as was also another self-made man, Thomas Fitzherbert, M.P. for Arundel 1780–90. In a long notice of Fitzherbert, soon after his election to Parliament, the *English Chronicle* wrote:

Had any person seen Mr. Fitzherbert twenty years ago, with his coat out the elbows, or even beheld him at the shorter interval of twelve years, measuring coals to the labourers in the dockyard at Portsmouth at thirteen pence a bushel, and told him that he would be a Member of Parliament, he would certainly have concurred in the mirth of the ridicule or have expressed resentment for so insulting a prediction.

According to this newspaper, Fitzherbert first attracted Sandwich's attention by the support he gave to the Admiralty candidate at the by-election for Portsmouth in March 1774, and through Sandwich's influence obtained a contract for supplying the army with horses. Further Government contracts followed, and at the general election of 1780 Fitzherbert purchased a seat in Parliament for the corrupt borough of Arundel.

Probably the most remarkable self-made man to sit in the House during this period was Robert Mackreth, M.P. for Castle Rising 1774–84 and for Ashburton 1784–1802. Mackreth began as a waiter at White's Club, married the daughter and heiress of its owner, became himself the owner of the club, and then set up as a usurer, lending money on the security of landed estates. Ruthless, shrewd, and ego-centric, Mackreth was a hard man at a business deal and relentless in the pursuit of his own interests. He was closely connected in business with Richard Rigby, paymaster general 1768–82, and Government money held by Rigby was put out on loan through Mackreth. Mackreth was returned to Parliament by Lord Orford, as contemporaries believed because Orford was in debt to him. His election was regarded at first as a joke on Orford's part, but Mackreth was soon accepted in the House. His great ambition, according to Jeremy Bentham, 'was to be considered a gentleman and to be admitted among the quality'—which was presumably the reason for his wishing to be in Parliament.'

A study of the Members of Parliament in our period reveals five ways by which a man could rise from humble origins to the 'quality': by means of a fortunate marriage; through the law; through trade, especially if Government contracts were obtained; by participation in the profits of war; and by making a fortune in India. The last will be considered in a later section; and here only a few examples can be given of men who made their way by these different roads to wealth and a seat in the House of Commons.

In an age when mercenary considerations entered into most marriages, it is not surprising to find men who prospered in this way. Brass Crosby, M.P. for Honiton 1768–74 and lord mayor of London 1770–1, was apprenticed to an attorney in Sunderland but moved to London and set up in practice himself. His first wife is described as a 'rich widow'; his second, the widow of a 'collar-maker to the Ordnance'; his third, the widow of a wine merchant, had a jointure of £1,000 per annum, £25,000 in Government stock, and the manor of Chelsfield, Kent. George Hayley, a London merchant and M.P. for London 1774–81, married the sister of the famous John Wilkes and was closely associated in politics with his brother-in-law. The *English Chronicle* wrote about him in 1780:

He was originally a clerk to the house in which he is now the principal, and by a fortunate marriage with his present amiable consort, with whom he received a dower of £15,000, and by the exertions of honest industry, has so increased his fortune as to be deemed at this time one of the wealthiest merchants in the City.

Of Andrew Robinson Bowes, M.P. for Newcastle-upon-Tyne 1780–84, more will be said in a later section. Here it is sufficient to notice that his first wife had a fortune of over £20,000, and that after her death Bowes retained her property. His second wife was the daughter and heiress of the immensely wealthy George Bowes, M.P. for Durham County 1727–60, and widow of the 7th Earl of Strathmore, and it was on the security of her fortune that Bowes based his candidature for Newcastle.

No survey of the matrimonial adventurers of this period would be complete without mention of Robert Nugent. Nugent came of an old established Irish Roman Catholic family, and in Horace Walpole's words made Protestantism and rich widows the means of his success in life. He became a tutor in the family of the Earl of Fingall and married the Earl's daughter. His second wife, though fat and ugly, brought him a country estate in Essex and control over one seat at St. Mawes. His third wife was the widow of the 4th Earl of Berkeley. But here Nugent had over-reached himself: the lady was notorious for her infidelities, Nugent refused to acknowledge paternity of her second daughter, and the marriage ended in a separation. There was a dangerous side to marrying for money.

The law was the hard way to social preferment: it required abilities, constant application, and a measure of good luck. But success at the bar made a man's name known and pointed the way to a seat in the House, and it was a line of life where hard work could overcome the disadvantages of humble origins. Thomas Clarke was born the son of a carpenter in Holborn, and ended as a privy councillor and master of the rolls. The great John Dunning, one of the foremost advocates of his day, was the son of a west country attorney; he started his legal career in his father's office, and died a peer of the realm. James Hewitt, later lord chancellor of Ireland, was the son of a Coventry draper; and Thomas Sewell, later master of the rolls, of a West Ham attorney. The father of John Scott, the famous lord chancellor Eldon, was a Newcastle merchant of modest means. Scott's rise, wrote Wraxall, 'resulted from a combination of talent, labour, and character. Neither noble birth, nor favour, nor alliances produced it.' The same might have been written about most of the M.P.s who made their way to the top through the legal profession.

Long before the eighteenth century, participation in trade and commerce was a recognized way of rising in the world, and during this period the opportunities were many. The business of a merchant easily expanded into that of a banker, and to the big men Government contracts and a share in Government loans brought fat profits. The career of Benjamin Hammet, M.P. for Taunton 1782–1800, might have been taken as a model by an eighteenth-century Samuel Smiles. Hammet is variously stated to have been the son of a Taunton serge-maker and of a Taunton barber, to have been educated at a charity school, and to have started life as a porter in a London bookshop. He became a banker in London and Taunton, acquired considerable property in his native town, and it was largely through his efforts that the centre of Taunton was cleared of slums and re-built. His election to Parliament for Taunton in 1782 put the final seal on the classic story of the local boy who made good. Thomas Hallifax, son of a clockmaker of Barnsley and originally apprenticed to a Barnsley grocer, became a clerk in Martin's bank and left to become one of the co-founders of the bank known today as Glyn's. He was elected lord mayor of London in 1776, and sat for Coventry 1780–1 and for Aylesbury from 1784 till his death in 1789. Samuel Whitbread, founder of the brewery which bears his name, was the son of a Bedfordshire yeoman, and became a large landowner in Bedfordshire and the head of the largest brewery in the country. He represented Bedford, a large and open constituency, for over twenty years, and his 'great pride', wrote the *English Chronicle* in 1781, was 'in being deemed an independent country gentleman'.

The opportunities given by war to men of ambition and energy are obvious enough and were well recognized in the eighteenth century—Edmund Burke noticed on the eve of the American conflict that the 'haut goût of lucrative war' was turning the merchants of London towards the Government's policy. The men who did the actual fighting did not have such opportunities for making their fortunes as the men responsible for victualling and paying the armies and providing the sinews of war, though there are examples in this period of men who grew rich through success in the field or at sea: Lord Albemarle, who commanded the expedition which captured Havana in 1762 is said to have received £120,000 as his share of the prize money; and Samuel Cornish, who began his career in the navy as an able seaman, grew rich through his share in the plunder of the Philippine Islands, bought himself a seat in Parliament, and obtained a baronetcy. The seven years' war, when a British army fought in Germany and British money subsidized continental princes, was more lucrative to the commissaries and contractors than the American war. No full study of their activities yet exists, and it is by no means easy to say in individual cases whether fortunes were or were not made at the public expense. But here are some examples of men who, emerging from the war with increased fortunes and enhanced social standing, found for themselves seats in the House of Commons.

Lawrence Dundas came from an impoverished younger branch of an old Scottish family, and began his career selling stockings in his father's shop in Edinburgh. During the '45 he was commissary for supplying the Duke of Cumberland's army in Scotland and afterwards a contractor for the British army in Flanders. He was already a rich man when the seven years' war broke out, and he further increased his wealth as contractor for bread and forage to the allied armies in Germany. Nicknamed 'the nabob of the north', he was created a baronet in 1762, and was brought into Parliament by Lord Gower for Newcastle-under-Lyme. During the next few years his electoral interest increased considerably: he secured control of the borough of Richmond and of the constituency of Orkney and Shetland; was returned himself for three successive Parliaments for Edinburgh; and had influence in Clackmannanshire, Dunbartonshire, and Stirlingshire. His ambition was a peerage, which he would undoubtedly have achieved had he lived to see his friends the Rockinghams come to power in 1782. The honour was granted to his son in 1794 when he went over with the Duke of Portland to Pitt.

During the eighteenth century anyone appointed to an office which involved holding balances of Government money was in a position to use that money to his own advantage. Henry Fox and Richard Rigby, who each held the office of paymaster general of the forces for long periods, invested the money entrusted to them and pocketed the interest; and it was not until 1782 that Burke's bill for regulating the pay office prevented this practice. By then the House had come to disapprove of office holders enriching themselves with Government money, and Rigby, instead of being allowed to retain his balances after he had left office, as had hitherto been the custom, was called upon to pay them in. In Henry Fox's case it seems likely that he also had a rake-off from the various deputy paymasters who served under him with the armies in the field. Two of these men, George Durant and Peter Taylor, rose to affluence through opportunities given them by Fox during the seven years' war, and both set the seal on their success by entering the House of Commons.

In 1761 George Durant was a clerk in the pay office at a salary of £250 per annum. In 1762 he went as deputy paymaster on the expedition to Havana and returned a rich man. How he obtained this sudden accession of wealth is by no means clear: men who have made money by dubious means seldom leave evidence behind them in the records of Government departments. Over £300,000 of public money passed through his hands, and in addition Durant had a share of the enormous prize money. In 1764 he purchased from the Duke of Kingston the estate of Tong in Shropshire and re-built the sixteenth-century castle. In 1765 he unsuccessfully contested Southwark, and in 1768 was returned to Parliament for Evesham, paying the expenses of the other candidate, John Rushout, as a *quid pro quo* for receiving the support of the Rushout interest. He made no mark in Parliament, never spoke in the House, and was badly defeated at Evesham in 1774.

Peter Taylor, the son of a Wells grocer, was left an orphan at the age of thirteen. 'I was turned into the wide world without a friend', he wrote subsequently, 'without learning, with a small fortune to begin with.' By 'honest industry and perseverance' he made a success of his career as a silversmith and won the friendship of Henry Fox. In 1757 Fox sent him to Germany as deputy paymaster; and in the course of four years Taylor amassed a fortune estimated at £400,000, apparently by arranging the exchanges to his own advantage and by paying the army in light coin. Back in England in 1763, he bought an estate near Wells, began to build an 'elegant mansion' on another estate near Portsmouth, and determined to enter Parliament for his native city. He stood at the by-election of 1765, but his newly-acquired wealth had brought grossness and insensitivity in its train, and he quarrelled with his old patron because Fox (now Lord Holland) would not support him. Taylor won the election through the favour of the returning officer, was unseated on petition two months later, and was defeated for Wells at the general election of 1768. He re-entered Parliament on the Admiralty interest at Portsmouth in 1774, and died in 1777.

There were a few men in this period who began as election managers on behalf of others and ended in Parliament themselves. Among them were Arthur Holdsworth, Government manager at Dartmouth and its M.P. 1780–87; William Masterman, election agent for Lord Edgcumbe and M.P. for Bodmin 1780–4; and John Robinson, North's secretary to the Treasury, who began his career as an attorney and election agent for Sir James Lowther. Most remarkable in this class was John Mortlock, the son of a Cambridge woollen draper, who became a banker in his native town. Mortlock set out to secure control of Cambridge by re-modelling the corporation and packing it with his friends; be became a sort of Tammany Hall boss, with the representation of Cambridge completely in his hands and the borough revenues used to buttress his interest. He was returned for Cambridge at the general election of 1784, but in 1788 vacated his seat in favour of a candidate nominated by the Duke of Rutland in exchange for the place of receiver-general of the Post Office.

These success stories have their counterpart in the Members who fell from affluence to poverty and who ended by clinging to their parliamentary seats as the last refuge from their creditors. Sir Charles Frederick, after over thirty years' service as an Ordnance official, begged to be allowed to retain his seat for Queenborough in 1782: 'he was so poor he was afraid of the Fleet or King's Bench prison'. Sir Alexander Gilmour, M.P. for Edinburghshire 1761–74, who had been an officer in the Guards and had held court employment for fourteen years, ended his life at Boulogne, piteously begging for a pension. General John Irwin, M.P. for East Grinstead 1762–83, was a great favourite of George III and the very model of a fine gentlemen. But he did not have the income to sustain the part, and in 1783 had to decamp to the

Continent; when he died in Italy in 1788, the King sent £500 to his widow to enable her and her children to come home. John Jeffreys represented the Government borough of Dartmouth 1747–66 and for most of this period had to be kept by Government. These are examples of men who ruined themselves through their general extravagance or disregard of Mr. Micawber's maxim; but in addition there were three distinct ways in which a man could ruin himself during this period. 'Wine, women, and song' are said to be the surest paths to moral and financial degradation; in the eighteenth century speculation, building, and women led to the same end.

Sir George Colebrooke, M.P. for Arundel 1754–74, was a leading London merchant and banker, for many years a director of the East India Company and its chairman in 1769, 1770 and 1772. He engaged in speculative activities of various kinds: in West India land, in Scottish estates, and in East India stock; but it was his attempt to corner the supply of certain raw materials (principally alum, flax, hemp, and logwood) which brought about his downfall. The financial crisis of 1772 entangled him in hopeless difficulties, his bank stopped payment, his property (including his parliamentary interest at Gatton) had to be sold, and in 1777 he was declared bankrupt. The former chairman of the East India Company had to retire to Boulogne on a pension of £200 a year granted by the Company and was grateful for the loan of £500 from Rockingham to enable him to send his son to India. His friend Sir James Cockburn, M.P. for Linlithgow Burghs 1772–84, who had been a commissary in Germany and a director of the East India Company, ruined himself through lending money to Indian princes and went bankrupt in 1781. Lord North helped him by giving Cockburn's wife a secret service pension of £800 a year, which was continued by succeeding Administrations. 'In the extremest distress', Cockburn lost his seat in Parliament at the general election of 1784; but subsequently, largely through the efforts of his sons, overcame his financial difficulties.

Building and collecting (the two activities are psychologically connected) were the downfall of a number of M.P.s. Probably the most prominent were Joseph Gulston, M.P. 1765–8 and 1780–4, and Lord Verney, M.P. 1753–84 and 1790–91. Gulston's father had been a merchant, but Gulston abandoned the business, built himself an Italian villa at Ealing, and began to amass the finest collection of prints in England. According to Horace Walpole, in his eagerness to build up his collection he paid extravagant prices and forced other collectors to do the same. By 1784 he was ruined; he was defeated at Poole at the general election, and was compelled to sell his collection. Over 60,000 prints were sold, but they brought only £7,000.

Lord Verney began life with the fairest prospects: he was one of the largest landowners in Buckinghamshire, controlled the borough of Wendover and had a considerable interest at Great Bedwyn, and was liked and respected by his neighbours. He set out determined to rival in magnificence and display the Grenvilles of Stowe, the leading family in the county; spent profusely on building, on pictures and works of art; and is thus described in Lipscomb's *History of Buckinghamshire*:

Lavish in his personal expenses and fond of show, he was one of the last of the English nobility who, to the splendour of a gorgeous equipage attached musicians constantly attendant upon him, not only on state occasions but in his journeys and visits: a brace of tall negroes with silver French horns behind his coach and six, perpetually making a noise.

To these extravagances he added others of an even more dangerous character: in 1766 he began speculating in East India stock, but the slump of 1769 left him with large liabilities and debts which he could not collect. Verney's political friends the Rockinghams did nothing for him when they returned to power in 1782; and, defeated for Buckinghamshire in 1784 he had to go to France to escape arrest for debt. 'Your situation is awful and lamented by all honest men', wrote one of his friends, and it improved little during the remainder of his life though he regained his seat for Buckinghamshire in 1790.

John Norris, M.P. for Rye 1762–74, like his father was a faithful follower of the Duke of Newcastle, but as he did not enter Parliament until shortly before the Duke's fall the connexion was of little financial benefit to him. He was also 'a great dupe to the sex', with 'such attachment to women of no character as is extraordinary'. His first wife was the famous Kitty Fisher, Sir Joshua Reynolds's model, a high-class society prostitute; his second wife was divorced on his account, for which he had to pay £3,000 damages. Norris sold his estates, and the loss of his seat in Parliament in 1774 forced him to flee to the Continent. He returned in 1795 to plead unsuccessfully with Newcastle's old friend, the Duke of Portland, for a place under Government.

John Proby, 1st Baron Carysfort, M.P. 1747–68, was another who ruined himself by what Mrs. Elizabeth Montagu called 'an enormous expense in kept women'. 'His credit has been so bad for a long time', continued Mrs. Montagu, 'that the butcher in the country would not trust him for a joint of meat nor bakers for a loaf of bread.' On the whole, elections were a far less expensive way of diverting oneself. Only one man in this period is known to have ruined himself through elections— Hans Winthrop Mortimer, who spent a considerable fortune in cultivating an interest in the venal borough of Shaftesbury, and ended his life a prisoner for debt in the Fleet. Gambling, surprisingly enough, ruined few Members; and at least two Members lived largely by gambling: John Scott of Balconie, M.P. 1754–75, who is said to have amassed a fortune of £500,000; and Richard Vernon, M.P. 1754–90, who by betting and horse breeding is stated to have converted 'a slender patrimony of £3,000 into a fortune of £100,000'.

The conventional impression of the eighteenth-century social scene hovers between two extremes. On the one hand, there is a picture of silk-stockinged gentlemen and elaborately coiffured ladies dancing minuets to the tune of 'Here's to the maiden of bashful fifteen'; on the other hand, there are the scenes of drunkenness and debauchery depicted in Hogarth's election cartoons. But between these two extremes there was a multitude of social gradations, faithfully reflected in the membership of the House of Commons; and no statistical analysis or selection of examples can do justice to the diversity of human life on display in the biographies accompanying this survey. The House contained Members drawn from all classes of the population, and since there were no nation-wide parties and fundamental political divisions to divide them, drew them together into a homogeneous whole.

EDUCATION

The educational system of this period (in so far as there was anything which could be called a system at all) was not hierarchical as in popular estimation it is today, nor was education considered to be an essential requisite in the life of every child: it was a commodity, to be bought and sold like other commodities, and of which there were both cheap and expensive varieties. The eighteenth century did not know the difference between public schools and other kinds of school: a public school education was an education at school as opposed to an education at home by private tutors. Oxford and Cambridge were not the 'older universities': they were the only universities in England; and the Scottish universities and Trinity College Dublin drew their students mainly from their own regions.

Eton and Westminster were the only large boarding schools drawing their pupils from all parts of the kingdom; and at least one-fifth of the Members in each Parliament during this period had been educated at one or the other of these schools. At the beginning of the period Westminster was supplying the larger number of Members to the House; at the end, it was Eton. In many cases boys went to Eton or Westminster for one, two, or three years only: the formal part of their education they received at home, and they were sent to school mainly for the experience of living with other boys. The popularity of Winchester as a school for children of the upper classes is difficult to ascertain because of its defective school list. Harrow, until the last years of the period, was little more than a preparatory school for Eton. Rugby, Shrewsbury, and Felsted attracted boys only from their immediate neighbourhood; and Charter-house was not yet a school for children of the upper classes.

About a half to three-fifths of the Members in each Parliament were either educated entirely at home or went to an old-established grammar school or a school known only by the name of its founder or proprietor. There were a number of these schools in the eighteenth century, kept by clergymen of the Church of England or by Dissenting ministers, and since few of them survived we have little information about their size or curricula. No doubt they varied in quality, but the best of them were good enough to be patronized by aristocratic parents. One of the most remarkable schools of this description was Dr. Newcome's academy at Hackney. Newcome was a Dissenting minister and a Whig of the old stamp. Crisp Molineux, M.P., one of his former pupils, wrote about him in 1771: 'Old Newcome so strongly rivetted the Whig principles in his boys that, the black Duke of Grafton excepted, none of us have ever deviated from them.' Molineux was a partisan of Wilkes, which explains his reference to the Duke of Grafton; but though several eminent Whig families sent their children to Newcome's school, it is difficult to see any common pattern in the political behaviour of those who subsequently became Members of Parliament. During our period there were in the House of Commons 26 Members who had attended the Hackney school. The first, Matthew Wyldbore, went there about 1731; the last, Lord Charles Fitzroy, about 1779. This suggests that the school lasted for at least two generations of the Newcome family. Four sons of Lord Chancellor Hardwicke attended in the late 1730s; Lord John Cavendish, son of the 3rd Duke of Devonshire, went to the school in 1747, and twenty years later was followed by two of his nephews, sons of the 4th Duke; Lord Euston (Crisp Molineux's 'black Duke of Grafton') went in 1750, and one of his younger sons in 1779. Within a period of fifteen years the school educated a future lord chancellor (Charles Yorke), a future chancellor of the Exchequer (Lord John Cavendish), and a future prime minister (Lord Euston).

There were in this period, as there are today, certain families who by tradition or preference favoured certain schools. Most of the Leveson Gower family who sat in Parliament had been educated at Westminster. Of the ten members of the Manners family who sat during this period, five went to Eton, one to Westminster, one (who became a soldier) to the military academy at Caen in France; and for three no school has been ascertained. The educational records of the Members sent to the House by two other ducal families, those of Devonshire and Grafton, show no preference for any particular school. Of the three sons of the 3rd Duke of Devonshire, one went to Hackney school, one to a school at Chesterfield, and the third (who entered the army) appears never to have attended school; the two sons of the 4th Duke both went to Hackney; and two members of collateral branches of the family went to Eton. Lord Euston, subsequently 3rd Duke of Grafton, was at Hackney school; and his brother (subsequently Lord Southampton) entered the army at the age of fifteen apparently without having been to school. Of Grafton's two sons, the first went to Harrow, the second to Hackney; while Lord Southampton's eldest son went to Eton. Charles Fitzroy Scudamore, an illegitimate son of the 2nd Duke of Grafton, went to Westminster.

Approximately two-fifths of the Members returned to each Parliament had received a university education. Oxford sent more Members to the House than Cambridge. At the beginning of the period, a majority of the Tories had been to Oxford and a majority of the Whigs to Cambridge; but as these distinctions died out it is hardly possible to see any preference for either university except on grounds of family tradition or propinquity. Oxford was traditionally the Tory university, but the leaders of those who in 1784 called themselves the Whig party had been educated at Oxford; while Pitt's following, later to be dubbed by historians the Tories, had a nucleus of Cambridge men. Though Oxford remained throughout the period what would in the nineteenth century have been called High Church, while Cambridge was inclined more towards latitudinarianism, it is not clear that either university imprinted a definite religio-political pattern upon its alumni.

Trinity College Dublin catered almost exclusively for Irishmen. The Scottish universities admitted students at a much younger age than the English: fourteen or fifteen was the usual age of matriculation, while at Oxford or Cambridge it was two or three years later. Many Scottish M.P.s, especially from aristocratic families, having attended a Scottish university, passed on to Oxford or Cambridge, while only a handful of English Members ever went to a Scottish university. No clear picture of the quality of education given at the universities has emerged from our study of the Members. Oxford, no doubt largely owing to Gibbon's reminiscences, has acquired a reputation for slackness, but it is apparent from the correspondence of Lord Fitzmaurice, the son of Shelburne, that at Christ Church in the 1780s undergraduates were both taught and examined regularly. Doubtless the amount and quality of teaching varied from college to college, and with the inclinations of both teachers and pupils.

About 70 Members during this period, nearly half of them Scots, were educated at foreign universities or educational institutions. The most popular was the University of Leyden, attended by 33 Members, 19 of them Scots. At Leyden in about 1745 there was a remarkable group of British students, each one of them destined to become prominent later in the House of Commons: George Colebrooke, subsequently chairman of the East India Company; William Dowdeswell, leader of the Rockingham Whigs in the House; Gilbert Elliot, a close friend and adviser of Bute and one of the best debaters in the House in the early 60s; John Glynn, Wilkes's counsel and fellow Member for Middlesex; William Gordon, a diplomat; James Johnstone, an independent and respected Member in the Parliament of 1784; Charles Townshend, chancellor of the Exchequer, for ever associated with the Townshend duties; and the celebrated John Wilkes. But it is difficult to find any common element in the lives of these Members resulting from their having been educated at the same foreign university. Leyden in the eighteenth century was a centre for legal and medical studies, but none of these Members took up medicine and only two (one Scot and one Englishman) became lawyers. Elliot, Gordon, and Johnstone, the three Scots, belonged to the Presbyterian Church of Scotland; Glynn and Wilkes were Dissenters (and therefore excluded from the English universities); while Dowdeswell certainly, and Colebrooke probably, were members of the Church of England.

Next to Leyden came Geneva, where seven Members were educated, including John Baring, who was of foreign ancestry, Lord Barrington, a Dissenter who later conformed to the Church of England, and Lord Mahon, whose father had also been educated at Geneva. The only Scot among them was Archibald Montgomerie, M.P. for Ayrshire 1761–8, whose education was of a most varied nature. He attended Irvine and Haddington grammar schools; went to Eton for three years and then moved to Winchester, which he left after only six months; and finished off his schooling in Berwick and London.

Three Members attended the University of Utrecht, one of whom was the elder Pitt. Robert Dundas of Arniston, M.P. for Edinburghshire and lord advocate 1754–60, who belonged to a family of distinguished lawyers and like his father became lord president of the court of session, studied at four universities—Edinburgh, Utrecht, Frankfurt, and Paris. Only two Members went to Göttingen University in Hanover, which had been founded by George II: John Murray of Strowan, whose father was 'out' in both the '15 and the '45 and who was particularly anxious to prove his loyalty to the reigning dynasty; and Thomas Hay, who became an army officer. Other continental universities attended by Members of Parliament were Paris, Halle, Lausanne, Tübingen, and Leipzig. A handful of Members who made the army their career attended foreign military academies: Caen, Turin, and Strasbourg; and two Members, born in America, were educated at American universities: Henry Cruger at King's College, New York (now Columbia University), and Staats Long Morris at Yale. Four Members who were brought up as Roman Catholics were educated in France: Lord Surrey, Lord Fortrose, Sir John Edward Swinburne, and Lord Molyneux (Molyneux apparently at the Jesuit academy at St. Omer); and three Members (all Scots), whose fathers were exiled for Jacobitism, were educated abroad: Lord Panmure, Sir James Steuart Denham, and James Murray of Strowan. There were probably others as well. These lists cannot be treated as exhaustive: information about the education of Members (except those who attended schools and universities which have published their registers) is not easy to obtain and often depends on the chance survival of private papers.

For the same reason it is impossible to give the precise number of Members who made the grand tour. The impression exists, largely because of the correspondence of Horace Walpole and the journals of Gibbon, that the grand tour was an integral part of eighteenth-century education. But neither Walpole nor Gibbon was representative of the upper-class young men of their day: one was passionately interested in antiquities, and the other in scholarship, and neither had the tastes or adopted the pursuits of the typical country gentleman or man about town. As far as can be ascertained, only about 10 per cent of the Members returned during this period had made the grand tour, and the majority of these were eldest sons of peers or landed families. The grand tour was an expensive undertaking even for a wealthy family, and was an indulgence rarely granted to younger sons. And few young men destined to make a career in business or a profession ever made the grand tour. Moreover, the grand tour was at the height of its popularity in the 1730s and 1740s; twenty years later it was by no means as fashionable. Lord North and Lord Granby, to give two examples, both made the grand tour, but their sons, who grew to manhood during the period of the American war, did not. Even in aristocratic families it was by no means customary: none of the Finches or the Townshends or the Brudenells, to mention three families who each had a number of representatives in the House during this period, ever made the grand tour.

The grand tour almost invariably included long sojourns in France and Italy, and sometimes also in Austria or Germany. The northern countries were rarely visited and Vienna usually marked the eastern limit of the young Englishman's journey. The tour undertaken by Lord Herbert between 1775 and 1780, in which he visited practically every European country including Russia, was exceptional—the whim of an eccentric father. Lord Lansdowne was another father who sent his son on a prolonged grand tour which, with intervals in England, lasted eight years, and included a long visit to Canada and the United States. But most fathers were content if their sons came back able to speak French correctly and with an interest in painting and *objets d'art*—the mark of the man who had made the grand tour.

RELIGIOUS AFFILIATIONS

When Denys Rolle, M.P. for Barnstaple, set out in 1764 to settle 200 colonists in the newly-acquired province of East Florida, one of the aims of his settlement was 'the cultivation of Christianity free from enthusiasm'. No one would describe the latter half of the eighteenth century as an age of religious zeal or bigotry: the ruling class valued religion as a restraining and civilizing force in social life rather than as a revelation of man's nature and destiny, and 'Christianity free from enthusiasm' conferred the maximum of social benefits and demanded the minimum of inconvenient obligations. Yet the age witnessed two of the most significant developments in modern religious life: the spread of Methodism, and the rise of Evangelicalism. How far were these developments reflected in the membership of the House of Commons, and what can we learn from the biographies of Members of the religious life of the period?

Information about the religious persuasions of Members is not always easy to find, and it is presumed, unless there is evidence to the contrary, that English Members belonged to the Church of England, Scottish Members to the Church of Scotland, and Irish Members to the Church of Ireland. Conformity to the established religion was a social virtue and was rewarded with social advantages. Of the religious minorities, the largest was the English Dissenters, a group which includes Baptists, Congregationalists, and Presbyterians. Contemporaries used the word 'Dissenter' carelessly, and often it is not easy to tell to which denomination a Member belonged.

There is plenty of evidence that the Dissenters formed a considerable proportion of the voters in the English boroughs and counties, and that in certain constituencies their support was almost essential. When Thomas Sewell, a barrister, was importuning Newcastle for a seat in 1758, Lord Kinnoull wrote to the Duke: 'If your Grace thinks proper to choose him, it may be very agreeable to ... the Dissenters, by whom Mr. Sewell is said to be much employed in law matters'; and when Sewell stood for Exeter at the general election of 1761, it was 'in the interest chiefly of the Low Church party'. And Sir John Trevelyan, M.P. for Somerset, a county where religious divisions were acute, wrote on 1 March 1787:

I hear that the Presbyterians intend to propose in the House of Commons the repeal of the Test Act, with the object of distressing Ministry: the Opposition will adopt it to a man as a party question; and many Members are returned by a majority of such interest who will not dare to oppose it.

The Dissenters had their particular grievances and opinions which candidates and Members could not afford to ignore. Naturally, their first grievance was against the Test and Corporation Acts. John Halliday, M.P. for Taunton, wrote to John Robinson in December 1781:

It must be observed that all the principal manufacturers of Taunton are Dissenters, and much at enmity with the corporation, who will not admit any person of that description to become a magistrate of the town.

In freeman boroughs, as is shown in the first section of this introductory survey, the conflict between an Anglican-dominated corporation and an independent party led by Dissenters was endemic; and may well represent a class division between the two parties.

On general political issues, no specific Dissenting point of view is clearly discernible before the outbreak of the American war. The Dissenters as a body were strongly opposed to the policy of coercion and seem even to have sympathized with the demands of their 'brethren across the seas'; and during the war they came out in favour of parliamentary reform. An agent of Lord Sandwich wrote to him about Nottingham on 21 November 1777:

This town is without any exception the most disloyal in the kingdom, owing in a great measure to the whole corporation . . . being Dissenters [a rare exception], and of so bitter a sort that they have done and continue to do all in their power to hinder the service by preventing as much as possible the enlistment of soldiers.

When Sir Henry Peyton stood for Cambridgeshire at the by-election of 1782, he was pressed by the Dissenters to declare his support for parliamentary reform, was reluctant to do so, but finally agreed to move an address in its favour. At the county meeting on 8 June,

Mr. Hollick junior [a leading Cambridgeshire Dissenter] acquainted the freeholders that since their last meeting he with some others had conferred with Sir Henry on the subject of their former differences, that now he with his friends were perfectly satisfied with Sir Henry's political principles, and therefore . . . would decline any further opposition.

Peyton was returned unopposed, but the suggestion is clear that he would not have been had he not come out in favour of the policy advocated by the Dissenters. Burke subsequently claimed that at the general election of 1784 the Dissenters strongly favoured Pitt, which may well have been so, though it is difficult to prove: in 1784 Pitt was pre-eminently the champion of parliamentary reform, while it had been one of the tacit conditions of Fox's alliance with North that parliamentary reform was to be dropped.

On the other hand, there does not appear to have been any specific Anglican attitude towards the American war or any other aspect of policy. The bishops generally voted with the Government in the House of Lords, whichever party was in power; in certain cathedral cities (e.g., Exeter, Canterbury, and Wells) the chapter was a factor in local politics, without however being identified with the opinions of any group at Westminster; but no clear-cut attitude emerges among the lower clergy. Some of the radical leaders of this period were clergymen: Horne Tooke in London and Christopher Wyvill in Yorkshire; and it seems probable that the clergy in general were attuned politically to their neighbours the country gentlemen. Only when the special position and privileges of the Church of England were threatened, did the Church show any signs of acting as a pressure group in politics. In 1787, when John George Philipps, M.P. for Carmarthen, voted for the repeal of the Test and Corporation Acts, the bishop of St. David's called on the Anglican clergy in the town to oppose him at the next general election. It is uncertain, to say the least, whether the clergy approved of their bishop's attitude; in any case, Philipps retained his seat.

Nineteen Members who are known to have been Dissenters sat in the House during this period. Two Members (John Lee and James Martin) are included though it is not absolutely certain that they were Dissenters—they attended the Unitarian meeting house in Essex Street, but may have remained nominally members of the Church of England. In addition, there were eight Members who had left Dissent for the Church of England (including John Wilkes, who had best be described as a sceptic). This is a very tiny proportion indeed of the number who sat in Parliament during this period, and the question immediately arises why was not the numerical strength of the Dissenters more adequately represented in the House. No Dissenter sat for Nottingham, where they were in control of the corporation; or for Taunton, where they formed a considerable proportion of the voters and acted as a body in elections. The Dissenters were without parliamentary ambitions: they were artisans, small freeholders, or merchants, and could not spare the time or money for a parliamentary life. If they rose socially and acquired parliamentary ambitions, they joined the Church of England. Here is one example of a Dissenter who made the change: Samuel Fludyer, M.P. for Chippenham 1754–68, the son of a Somerset clothier who had married the daughter of a Huguenot refugee. Fludyer's father migrated to London and Fludyer so developed the business that he became the leading cloth merchant in the kingdom. Of the parentage and antecedents of his first wife nothing is known, but she may also have been a Dissenter. After Fludyer had become an M.P. and one of the richest men in England, he married, secondly, a niece of the 3rd Earl of Cardigan; and a little later was created a baronet and joined the Church of England. Conformity to the established church was part and parcel of his rise in the social scale.

Only four of the Dissenter Members belonged to old-established landed families: Sir Henry Hoghton, M.P. for Preston 1768–95; Sir William Middleton, 3rd Bt. and his nephew Sir William, 5th Bt., who both represented Northumberland; and John White, M.P. for East Retford 1733–68. To these might be added Thomas Brand Hollis, M.P. for Hindon 1774–75, who belonged to the younger branch of a Hertfordshire landed family. Families, whether they were Protestant Dissenters or Roman Catholics, who had resolutely refused to conform to the established church despite the advantages conformity would have brought, were proud of their religion and regarded their nonconformity as an honoured part of their family heritage. Nor was there any longer a strong pressure towards conformity: the Hanoverian dynasty was firmly established on the throne, and nonconformity was regarded rather as a tolerable eccentricity than as a danger to the state.

The remaining fourteen Dissenters who sat in Parliament were engaged in trade or the professions. Three were barristers (James Adair, John Glynn, and John Lee); four were bankers (Richard Fuller, James Martin, Thomas Rogers, and Jacob Wilkinson); five were merchants (Frederick Bull, Thomas Lockyer, Nathaniel Newnham, William Smith, and Samuel Touchet); and two were sons of merchants, though not apparently themselves in trade (Joseph Tolson Lockyer and Richard Slater Milnes). With the exception of Martin, all these men came from families without parliamentary ancestry. Three (Adair, Bull, and Glynn) were strong radicals, and all who were in the House during the American war opposed the Government. Radicalism had a strong Nonconformist core, which may account for the radicals' vehement opposition to any relaxation of the penal laws in favour of Roman Catholics.

Methodism was still a movement within the Church of England during this period, though towards the end it was beginning to break away. No Methodist sat in the House, unless Richard Hill, M.P. for Shropshire 1780–1806, may be classed as one. Hill wrote a pamphlet in 1768 in defence of six students expelled from Oxford as Calvinistic Methodists, and patronized Methodism. He was well known in the House for introducing into his speeches references to and quotations from the Bible and also for spoiling their effect with a rather outré and buffoon style of humour. Hill was an opponent of the American war and a supporter of parliamentary reform, an enemy of luxury and corruption, and a friend of the poor.

The Evangelical movement developed late in the eighteenth century, and the six Evangelical Members who sat in the House during this period were first returned after 1774: Walter Spencer Stanhope in 1775, William Wilberforce in 1780, Henry Thornton in 1782, Sir Charles Middleton and Samuel Thornton in 1784, and Robert Thornton in 1785. These Members were closely associated both in religion and politics, and they were all parliamentary reformers and supporters of Pitt. Middleton was a naval officer and a Scot; Stanhope came of a Yorkshire landed family and Wilberforce was the son of a Hull merchant; and the three Thorntons were the sons of John Thornton, the biggest English merchant trading to Russia. There was a middle-class business background to the early Evangelicals which formed a striking contrast to the atmosphere of Methodism, the poor man's religion. The influence of the early Evangelicals was out of all proportion to their numbers in the House, mainly because their attitude to the problems of government merged into that of the general mood of the House after 1784. The Evangelicals stood for the reformation of manners: they were opposed to nepotism and corruption in Government appointments and adopted a moral attitude towards politics. Probably it was Wilberforce's conviction that there was a case to answer against Hastings which determined Pitt to vote for the impeachment; and Wilberforce's advocacy of the abolition of the slave trade crystallized the Evangelical attitude towards politics. In one other respect also, the influence of the Evangelicals was important. Their attempt to consider political questions in the light of morality and religion was incompatible with a strict party allegiance; and it was on this ground that Wilberforce welcomed Pitt's plan of parliamentary reform:

It would tend . . . to diminish the progress of party . . . from which . . . our greatest misfortunes arose. There were men and parties in this country which derive most of their power and influence from these burgage tenures, against which the operations of this bill were to be directed. By destroying them the freedom of opinion would be restored, and party connexions in a great measure vanish . . . He wished to see the time when he could come into the House and give his vote, divested of any sentiments of attachments which should induce him to approve of measures from his connexion with men.

Members of the Church of England were Protestant Dissenters in Scotland. Three are known to have sat in the House during this period: Alexander and David Murray, who between them represented Peeblesshire 1783–90, sons of a Church of England clergyman and educated in England; and William McDowall, who sat for Renfrewshire 1768–74. It seems probable that many Scots M.P.s, especially those educated at English universities, came under Anglican influence, but that in Scotland they remained staunch Presbyterians.

Quakers, Roman Catholics, and Jews could not sit in the House of Commons without abjuring their religion. Five Members of Quaker families sat in the House during this period: Henry Beaufoy, Nathaniel Brassey, John Cator, Thomas Dimsdale, and Richard Penn. Beaufoy, who joined the Church of England in order to enter the House, was the son of a vinegar distiller; Brassey was a banker; and Cator, a friend of Dr. Johnson, was a timber merchant. Brassey represented Hertford 1734–61, a town with a large Quaker population, and his son-in-law Dimsdale also sat for the borough 1780–90. Dimsdale was a surgeon, who inoculated Catherine of Russia and her son against smallpox and was created a baron of the Russian Empire. Richard Penn was a grandson of the founder of Pennsylvania, and had lived in the colony before the outbreak of the American war.

There were seven Members who had abjured Roman Catholicism for the Church of England: Charles Dillon; Sir Thomas Gascoigne; Charles Howard, Earl of Surrey; Charles William Molyneux, Viscount Molyneux; Kenneth Mackenzie; Robert Nugent; and Sir John Edward Swinburne. Dillon and Nugent were Irish, and Mackenzie the son of a Scottish peer attainted for his part in the '15. The remainder came from old English Catholic families.

Only one Jew sat in the House during this period: Sampson Gideon, the son of a great Jewish financier who during George II's reign had been one of the Government's principal financial advisers. Gideon was baptized into the Church of England, and while a boy at Eton was created a baronet. He inherited considerable property in Cambridgeshire, and in 1770, in the absence of a suitable candidate from the two leading families, the Yorkes and the Manners, was elected M.P. for the county. In 1780 the Duke of Rutland and Lord Hardwicke each had a candidate and joined their interests against Gideon. Gideon spent heavily, but was unpopular because of his constant support of North's Government and also because he was a Jew. Philip Yorke, Hardwicke's candidate, wrote on 30 April 1780:

It is rather remarkable to see how violently the common freeholders are prejudiced against Sir Sampson Gideon. I went to pay my compliments to a room full of them ... and they all declared they would choose their countrymen for their Members, and not a Jew.

Gideon withdrew at the end of the first day's poll, having obtained 1,038 votes as against 1,455 for Yorke and 1,741 for Lord Robert Manners. He was provided with a seat by North at Midhurst, and in 1784, having gone over to Pitt, successfully contested Coventry. In 1786 Pitt recommended him to the Duke of Rutland, lord lieutenant of Ireland, for an Irish peerage—he was 'as good and generous a Christian as any' and Pitt was 'extremely anxious to gratify him.' Rutland objected, apparently on racial grounds. 'I am afraid', wrote Thomas Orde, his secretary, 'that Judaism will not be admitted an obstacle to his success, for Mr. Pitt observed that *he* had never been a Jew, and that he *had been* a Member for a county, and of course a good candidate for the peerage'; and on 24 September 1789 Gideon was created Baron Eardley.

Deism, so fashionable in French intellectual circles during the eighteenth century, was not taken up on any large scale in England; and while there were undoubtedly men in the House who would be described today as agnostics (Gibbon and Wilkes are obvious examples), a decent respect for the outward forms of religion was expected from Members and freely accorded. Unitarianism was strong in English intellectual circles; and there was a movement within the Church of England itself against a too rigid application of the authority of the Church in matters of doctrine. On 6 February 1772 a petition was presented to the House from a body of the Anglican clergy, praying to be relieved from the onus of subscribing to the Thirty-Nine Articles, and was rejected by 217 votes to 71. The argument of the petitioners was summarized by Sir George Savile, M.P. for Yorkshire:

I distinguish between the Church of God and Christ and the Church of England, and whenever the Church of England differs from the Church of Christ I give the preference to the latter. The point in question is whether we shall lay aside subscription to the Articles and adopt the Scriptures in their room. The Scriptures are the only rule of the Church of Christ, and adhering to the Scriptures in opposition to human inventions and corruptions is the first principle of Protestantism.

This was an argument very similar to that of Bishop Hoadly in the earlier part of the century. The minority on the division were mostly drawn from the Opposition, but the question did not divide the House on strict party lines; and Edmund Burke was not the only Opposition Member who objected to this attempt to diminish the authority of the Church.

PLACEMEN AND PENSIONERS

There were three kinds of placemen in the House during this period: those who held political office, or 'offices of business' as the eighteenth century described them; those who held court office; and those who held sinecure office. These did not form separate classes, and the line of division between office holders and independent Members did not necessarily correspond to that between Administration and Opposition. Moreover, some sinecures were for life, which rendered their holders independent of Administrations; while others had such a small salary attached to them as to be valued for prestige rather than financial reward.

The number of Members who held political office varied between 40 and 50 throughout the period. This number included holders of important political offices and heads of Government departments, who were appointed, as they are today, because of their standing in the House: the first lord of the Treasury (if a commoner), the chancellor of the Exchequer, almost invariably one of the secretaries of state, the secretary at war, etc. Some heads of Government departments (e.g., the Treasury, the Admiralty, the Board of Trade) could be either peers or commoners; others (e.g., the law officers or officials who held balances of Government money—the paymaster general, the treasurer of the navy) were almost invariably Members of the House of Commons. Every Administration tried to achieve a balance in the distribution of offices between Lords and Commons, and it was particularly important to ensure that the Government had first-rate debaters in the House of Commons to present its case. The

Cabinet usually contained only one or two Members of the House of Commons, but the key position in the Cabinet was that of the leader of the House. This might go to the first lord of the Treasury (who, if a commoner, always combined the office with that of chancellor of the Exchequer) or a secretary of state, or the holder of some other Government office: Henry Fox, as paymaster general of the forces, from October 1762 to April 1763, and Lord North, as chancellor of the Exchequer, from January 1768 to January 1770.

To assist the minister in the House of Commons (as the leader of the House was usually styled during this period) there had to be a deputy leader, though that name was never used. Until 1780 this duty usually fell to the attorney-general, whose political standing was very much higher than it is today. In the House the attorney-general did not confine himself to the work of his own department but intervened in debates on all subjects, a logical consequence of the fact that much of the business of the House was quasi-legal in character. This can be seen particularly during the debates on Wilkes and general warrants in 1763–4 or on the Middlesex election in 1769–70; but even the Government's policy towards America, a political issue if ever there was one, was presented in legal as much as in political terms. North's principal assistants in the House during the American war were the successive attorney-generals, Edward Thurlow and Alexander Wedderburn; and after the departure of Wedderburn for the Lords and the appointment of a non-political attorney-general, it was Henry Dundas, the lord advocate, who became in effect deputy leader of the Commons for the remainder of North's Administration, and he regained the post under the younger Pitt. By then Dundas had abandoned his legal business and had become a politician pure and simple, with special responsibility for the conduct of Indian and Scottish affairs. On 5 February 1784 he defended his conduct against Fox's charge that by accepting office in a minority Administration he was flouting the dignity of the House:

Those who know what I was, and what I am, will never think that I, of all men, could ever entertain a design to lessen the dignity of this House; for whatever little consequence and distinction I have, if I have any, I derive entirely from this House; and I know that if the House of Commons was to cease to be what it is now, a branch of the legislature and a check and control upon the executive power, I must again return to the obscurity of a dull and laborious profession.

There were a number of secondary offices, occupied mainly with routine administration, which were usually held by Members of the House of Commons: the boards of Treasury, Admiralty, Trade (abolished in 1782), and Ordnance; and the deputy headships of Government departments. These were usually filled by friends or clients of ministers, and one or two places at the Admiralty Board were always held by serving naval officers. It was rare for any but Members of the House of Commons to be appointed to the boards, but it by no means followed that because a Member lost his seat in the House he would lose his office. William Sloper remained at the Board of Trade for nearly five years after resigning his seat for Great Bedwyn in 1756; and George Onslow was a lord of the Treasury for two years without a seat in Parliament. Nor was there any strict rule about Members resigning their places if they disagreed with the policy of the Government. Practice was extremely lax and a good deal of latitude was allowed to Members; which accorded with contemporary political theory, that an M.P. ought to give his vote independent of Crown or party.

Here are a few examples. Welbore Ellis, treasurer of the navy, a consistent advocate of coercive measures against the American colonies, opposed North's conciliatory measure of February 1775. 'Mr. Ellis', wrote North to the King, 'who differed from us upon a real conviction that our measure was wrong, spoke against us in the most friendly terms.' Robert Nugent, who throughout the American war held the lucrative sinecure of joint vice-treasurer of Ireland, had at first supported North's American policy but by 1780 had become convinced that the colonies were lost and that it was useless to prosecute the war against them any further. During the last two years of North's Administration, though he voted with Government on motions of confidence, he spoke in favour of peace with the colonies.

Jeremiah Dyson, a member of the Board of Trade in the first Rockingham Administration, voted against the repeal of the Stamp Act, the Government's principal measure, and opposed its commercial and financial policy. Summoned by Rockingham to account for his conduct, Dyson thus reported the interview to a friend:

[Rockingham] readily acquitted me of any professions or other engagements than what must be understood to be implied by a man's continuance in office. This I admitted as amounting to an obligation not to go into opposition without notice, but that whatever was expected beyond that must depend upon the measures and the degree in which they were communicated.

Dyson did not admit that voting against the Government was equivalent to going into opposition, and the King refused Rockingham's request to dismiss him. An argument similar to Dyson's was used by Henry Seymour Conway in November 1763 to excuse his voting against the Grenville Administration on Wilkes's case, but when Conway also voted against the Government on general warrants in February 1764 George III insisted that he should be dismissed. The case of Richard Sutton, under-secretary of state to Lord Rochford 1766–72, is extraordinary only in the length to which Sutton carried his opposition to Government. Horace Walpole described him as a young man 'of a very singular turn, often, though in office, speaking against the court, and never speaking for them when he voted for them (but too necessary to be dismissed)'. Sutton voted with the Opposition on the Middlesex election and even on the royal marriage bill of 1772, a measure introduced at the King's express command. Lord Rochford, alarmed by his subordinate's conduct, advised the King to dismiss him, though he did not believe that Sutton was 'designedly connected with Opposition'. In September 1772 Sutton succeeded his brother in the family property and resigned his place: he was given a pension of £500 per annum and was created a baronet— an almost unique case of a Member who profited despite his having opposed the Administration to which he belonged. The even more extraordinary case of Henry Seymour Conway and Charles Townshend, the two leading Members of the House of Commons in the Chatham Cabinet, who in May 1767 voted against the Government's East India policy, may be explained by the chaos into which the Administration fell after Chatham's illness. Still, it further illustrates one of the basic conventions of eighteenth-century politics: that every Member of Parliament, whether or not he held office, was entitled to vote as his opinion dictated.

By the end of the period, when party lines had hardened, this convention was beginning to break down. Pitt did not take action against placemen who voted against his plan of parliamentary reform or the Ordnance's plan to build fortifications at Plymouth and Portsmouth; but in 1788 when the King became insane and a regency bill was introduced, no back-sliding was excused. The restrictions on the authority of the Regent imposed by the bill gave rise to genuine controversy, but it was assumed by Pitt and his friends that Government supporters voting against it did so in order to curry favour with Fox, who was expected to succeed Pitt when the Prince of Wales became Regent. Sir John Aubrey, a member of Pitt's Treasury Board, spoke against the bill; and his arguments met with derision from those Members who had remained faithful to Pitt. One of them, Sir William Young, wrote to Lord Buckingham:

Our rats ... all showed their tails on last night's motion ... Sir John Aubrey, rat-major, receiving his emoluments of the Treasury for five years and declaring himself unconnected with any, afforded a subject of a general laugh.

Aubrey denied that he had any connexion with the Opposition and maintained that he had voted against Pitt on conscientious grounds, but he lost his place at the Treasury. Forty years earlier things had been different: in 1755 George Bubb Dodington had accepted office from Newcastle on the express understanding that he was free to vote against the subsidy treaties, the main plank of Newcastle's foreign policy.

There were also a number of placemen who held their offices on a quasi-civil service tenure: chief among them under-secretaries of state, secretaries to Government departments, and diplomats. The dividing line between politicians and civil servants was unknown in an age when the term 'the King's servants' was used to describe all office holders from the first lord of the Treasury downwards. The secretary of the Treasury nearly always sat in Parliament (the exceptions were in the two short Administrations of Lord Rockingham), and indeed could hardly perform his functions effectively without a seat in the House. In addition, he always retired with his principal. However much he might try to avoid it, he insensibly became a politician. In contrast, the secretary of the Admiralty, a Member of Parliament throughout this period, held his office independent of Administration and was a true civil servant in the modern sense, the permanent head of a Government department. John Clevland began his career as a clerk in the navy office, and when he was appointed secretary of the Admiralty in 1751 had had nearly thirty years' experience of naval administration. He sat in Parliament for the Admiralty boroughs of Sandwich and Saltash, and managed the Government interest in both boroughs. When Pitt took office in 1756, the first lord of the Admiralty, Lord Anson, was dismissed as allegedly responsible for the loss of Minorca, but Clevland retained his place. In 1762 Lord Halifax did not accept the Admiralty until he was assured that Clevland would remain secretary at least for the duration of the war. On Clevland's death in 1763 he was succeeded by his deputy Philip Stephens, Member in turn for Liskeard and Sandwich, who held the secretaryship under successive Administrations until in 1795 he was promoted to the Admiralty Board. Stephen's career at the Admiralty lasted over sixty years: he began as a clerk at the Victualling Board before Anson had made his voyage round the world, and he resigned from the Admiralty Board at the age of 83, the year after Trafalgar. He was a senior Admiralty official before Nelson was born, and he was still at the Admiralty when Nelson died. And for the greater part of this period, from 1759 to 1806, he was a Member of the House of Commons, though apparently never speaking in the House.

It was almost a rule of Government service that the man made the job, not the other way round: the status and authority of any office depended as much on the occupant at any particular time as on the powers theoretically conferred upon him. Consider, for example, the men who held the office of private secretary to the first lord of the Treasury, which was not strictly an official position since the holder enjoyed no salary and had to be provided for with sinecures. Newcastle's private secretary, Hugh Valence Jones, a nephew of the Duke's great friend Lord Hardwicke, was a mere amanuensis: he copied Newcastle's letters, arranged his papers, kept the secret accounts, but took no part in politics or in the framing of Government measures. He sat in Parliament for Dover 1756–59, not at the recommendation of Newcastle but as the choice of the townspeople themselves, who were tired of having strangers sent down to them by the Treasury (Lord Hardwicke was a native of Dover). In every other respect, he was a nonentity.

Bute's private secretary was Charles Jenkinson, who was already a Member of Parliament when he became connected with Bute and had served his apprenticeship as under-secretary of state. For Jenkinson this appointment with Bute was a stage on the ladder of his official career, which culminated thirty years later in his becoming a Cabinet minister and an earl. Jenkinson had the mind and outlook of a permanent official, but in an age when the civil service was not yet divorced from Parliament he had to be to some extent a politician. His successor Charles Lloyd, George Grenville's private secretary, was never more than a clerk, did not sit in the House of Commons, and after his principal's dismissal from office remained attached to him in a private capacity.

Lord Rockingham, who succeeded Grenville as first lord of the Treasury in July 1765, took as his secretary a man completely unknown to him except by recommendation: Edmund Burke. Six months later Burke entered the House of Commons, not through the influence of the Treasury but on the interest of his friend, Lord Verney; and soon made his mark as a debater and as a man of business. Unlike Jenkinson, he thought of himself as a politician not as a servant of the Crown, and followed Rockingham out of office and into opposition. Richard Stonehewer, Grafton's private secretary, was a personal dependant, as was also North's private secretary, William Brummell (father of the famous Beau Brummell); and neither Stonehewer nor Brummell sat in the House of Commons. William Bellingham, Pitt's private secretary, represented Reigate 1784–89, but was not important either in the House or in Government service.

Four of these seven private secretaries sat in the House, but only one (Jenkinson) was a Member of Parliament when he was appointed. Jenkinson and Burke became two of the foremost politicians of their day, but the rest remained in humble, dependent situations. An examination of the careers of the men who filled the office of under-secretary of state would reveal the same differences. Only one of them, William Eden, became a prominent politician, and most of them did not sit in the House.

The diplomatic service had not yet become professionalized during this period: appointment was by favour and no special qualifications, beyond a knowledge of French, were necessary. In the majority of diplomatic posts the work was not onerous and the responsibilities were light, and it was generally believed that it was cheaper to live abroad than in England. Hence diplomatic posts were much sought after by impecunious Members of Parliament. When James Hare, a friend of Charles James Fox, was able no longer to keep his head above water by gambling, his friends could think of no better provision for him than a diplomatic appointment at Warsaw or Munich; and Gibbon in 1783 applied for the secretaryship to the Paris embassy because he could no longer afford to live in England after losing his place at the Board of Trade. For those who aspired to a diplomatic post a seat in the House of Commons was an added qualification, and once the post had been obtained the seat was valued because of the consequence it gave to its occupant. Sir Andrew Mitchell, envoy to Berlin, resented attempts to dispossess him of his seat for Elgin Burghs in 1768, and secured Government support for his candidature. Sir Joseph Yorke, ambassador at The Hague, wanted a seat in Parliament purely for its prestige value—if he were not in Parliament, he wrote, 'the foreign circle I live in might imagine I was in disgrace'. In 1774 he paid £2,500 for a seat at Grampound, negotiated for him by the Treasury, and apparently never attended that Parliament. In 1780, when war with Holland seemed imminent, he wrote to his brother Lord Hardwicke about a seat in the next Parliament: 'If I continue in a public character, there is a kind of decency in being decorated with such a distinction.' But if war broke out and he had to return to England, he did not wish to remain in Parliament: he felt himself to be too old and too out of touch with English affairs to begin a career in the House of Commons.

Court appointments were well paid and attracted those who were flattered by access to the Royal family. The ceremony attendant upon court life was enjoyed by some and found fatiguing by others. Philip Goldsworthy, M.P. for Wilton and equerry to the King, complained ironically to Fanny Burney:

After all one's labours, riding and walking, and standing and bowing, what a life it is? Well! it's honour! that's one comfort; it's all honour! Royal honour! One has the honour to stand till one has not a foot left, and to ride till one's stiff, and to walk till one's ready to drop—and then one makes one's lowest bow, d'ye see, and blesses oneself with joy for the honour.

But James Harris, M.P. for Christchurch, a cultured and scholarly man, thoroughly enjoyed the opportunities his post as secretary to the Queen gave him to participate in court ceremonies. After attending the christening of the King's sixth son on 24 March 1774, when the Queen inquired after his gout, he replied in the style of a born courtier 'such a sight was enough to cure any complaint'.

The highest court offices were reserved for peers; but the dozen or so grooms of the bedchamber (£500 per annum), the eight clerks of the Green Cloth (£1,000 per annum), the various administrative or financial offices at court (groom porter, treasurer of the chamber, treasurer and comptroller of the Household, etc.) were nearly all held by Members of the House of Commons. Their number was considerably reduced by Burke's establishment bill of 1782, which attempted to reform the medieval system of administration at court as well as to reduce the number of places available for Members of Parliament. In addition, there were places about the Queen, the Princess Dowager, the Prince of Wales, and the royal Dukes. These, not being offices under the Crown, had the additional advantage that they did not involve a Member in the trouble-some and expensive necessity of applying for re-election on his appointment. But they did compel the Member to follow the politics of his royal master. When the Duke of York, the King's brother, went into opposition to the Chatham Administration in 1767, he took with him Charles Sloane Cadogan, M.P., his treasurer, and Henry St. John, M.P., one of the lords of his bedchamber. And the Prince of Wales had sufficient patronage at his disposal to provide the nucleus of an opposition party.

Burke in his speech on economical reform in 1780 recognized the value of sinecures in the political system of his day: they provided a comfortable retirement for those who had served the state well. Though George III and Burke would no doubt have disagreed about who had served the state well, neither wished to abolish sinecures altogether. The sinecures in the Exchequer, probably the most profitable of all (the tellerships were worth over £10,000 per annum during the American war), were out of reach of all except the most favoured Members of Parliament; but down the line there were posts which either involved no work or could be performed by deputy, and which provided decent retirement pensions for Members. Alexander Wedderburn wrote about John Dickson, M.P. for Peeblesshire, in 1761: 'His fortune is so narrow that he will not refuse a moderate place, and after serving two Parliaments he really has some sort of right to retire upon a decent provision.' And the Duke of Rutland thus appealed to Pitt in 1786 on behalf of one of his poor relations, George Manners Sutton: 'I think you might give him a pension of about £300, which would make him comfortable. A decayed gentleman, and particularly if a *Member of Parliament*, is surely a proper object for such a provision.'

But it was not as easy for Pitt to provide for 'decayed gentlemen' as it had been for Newcastle thirty years earlier. The reform legislation of 1782 and the need to reduce expenditure after the war, had diminished the number of places available. 'The source of pensions is absolutely stopped', wrote Gibbon, himself a solicitor for a retirement pension, in 1783, and a double list of candidates is impatient and clamorous for half the number of desirable places.' And the House of Commons now looked doubtfully upon the practice of providing for Members of Parliament at the public expense. The pensions granted to Shelburne's friends, Barré and Dunning, in 1782, though they could be defended on Burke's principles as a means of honourable provision for men who had served the state well, were severely criticized in the House. Daniel

Pulteney, a client of the Duke of Rutland, who had entered Parliament in 1784 only because he was practically bankrupt and whose sole aim in Parliament was to provide for himself, recognized the change of mood which had passed over the House. Gone were the days when the profits of a ministry were divided 'in their several proportions down to the lowest of their adherents'. Instead—

If Mr. Pitt can long persuade a House of Commons that they are to spend their time and fortunes *independently* to support an independent minister ... it will certainly be better for the country and more honourable to themselves. . .

When no places were available, the last resource of the needy Member of Parliament was a secret service pension, or a private pension as it was sometimes called. The secret service money was entirely at the King's disposal and he was not accountable to Parliament for its expenditure; consequently no one, except the persons immediately concerned, knew how it was spent. A proportion of it was used for genuine secret service purposes—to procure intelligence or to bribe foreign politicians; but it was also used to provide pensions for deserving objects of charity— 'decayed' peers and men of good family, Members of Parliament, servants of the royal family, men of letters and scholarship, etc., and in the early part of the period to finance elections. The money was disbursed by the secretary to the Treasury under the supervision of the first lord, and the accounts, when made up, were usually returned to the King and apparently destroyed by him.

Some of the accounts have survived: for the period when Newcastle was head of the Treasury (March 1754–November 1756 and July 1757– May 1762); for Rockingham's first Administration (July 1765–July 1766); and for the last three years of the North Ministry (1779–82). There are also extant fragments of Grenville's secret service accounts and the accounts for the general election of 1784. In addition, there is a list of secret service pensions, compiled for Shelburne in August 1782; and one or two other lists of a similar kind. Although, therefore it is not possible to make a complete list of Members of Parliament who received secret service pensions during this period, the surviving material is sufficient to enable us to discern the nature of these pensions and the type of Member who received them.

In 1762 sixteen Members were in receipt of secret service pensions, and in 1780 ten. It does not seem likely that these numbers were exceeded at any time during this period, and by August 1782 only three Members were left on the secret service list (one receiving the pension in the name of his wife). The value of these pensions was usually between £500 and £1,000 per annum; they were not paid automatically, the recipients having to apply each quarter to the first lord of the Treasury; and they were not subject to deductions for the land tax, as were other pensions. It was exceptional for a Member to be allowed to retain his pension after he had left the House, and it was understood that he would cease to apply for it if he went into opposition.

When Newcastle was at the Treasury, a secret service pension was the favourite expedient to satisfy a Member who could not be accommodated with office or had lost his office through no fault of his own. Of the 34 pensions granted during Newcastle's time, eighteen were of that nature. During North's period, it was more usual to reward Members who had been of service to Government: John Mayor, M.P. for Abingdon, who assisted in framing the paper duty, was given a pension of £1,000 per annum; George Augustus Selwyn, who regularly returned Government candidates at Ludgershall, had £1,500 per annum; and James Macpherson, who wrote pamphlets on behalf of the Government, had £300. The chairman of the committee of ways and means, who was not provided with a salary, always had a secret service pension of £500 per annum. A third class of Members who received pensions were those who were financially embarrassed, or who had left their families in distress. The widow of Thomas Bradshaw, M.P., Grafton's secretary to the Treasury, was granted a pension of £500 per annum in consideration of her poverty and her husband's services, and three of his children were also given pensions of £100 per annum each. The wife of Sir James Cockburn, M.P., was granted a pension of £800 per annum when her husband went bankrupt in 1780, which gave Cockburn an income which could not be seized to pay his debts.

It was a constant cry throughout this period that places, pensions, and contracts were used by the Government to bribe Members of Parliament; and it was part of the programme of Opposition, whether Whig or Tory, to reduce the influence of Government over the House. The Tories tried to do this in 1760 by strengthening the law which imposed a property qualification on Members. Men without independent means were excluded from the House, because it was feared they would be susceptible to bribery by Government; but in practice the law never worked and was widely evaded. Daniel Pulteney, elected for Bramber in 1784 without having the necessary qualification, estimated that one-third of the House was in the same plight. The Whigs, when they returned to office in 1782, abolished a number of sinecures and other offices deemed to be unnecessary, but it is doubtful whether this measure fulfilled its authors' expectations.

The premise upon which the Opposition acted—that the Government owed its majority to the patronage it could distribute among Members—is disproved by the evidence of division lists, by a study of the lives of Members, and by simple common sense. Division lists show that the majority of Members voting with Government held no office and did so through honest (though possibly mistaken) conviction; while common observation of humanity tells us that Members were given office because they voted with Government, not that they voted with Government in order to obtain office. The situation in this respect was not very different from what it is today, allowing for the fact that today Members owe their seats to their party while in the eighteenth century most of them had no party and brought themselves into Parliament. There was a great deal of jobbing, as there must always be when offices are distributed through favour, but little evidence of corruption.

Government patronage, both in the House and in the constituencies, was important but never decisive; it could not save North's ministry in 1782, when North's policy no longer commended itself to the House, nor a weak ministry, like that of Shelburne in 1783. In quiet times, when no political issues were at stake, placemen could be relied upon to vote with Government; but on questions of principle or conscience they would follow their own convictions even if these directed them into the Opposition lobby. The point was well put by William Jolliffe, himself a placeman, in the debate on North's conciliatory propositions, 23 February 1778:

In questions of small importance, if every man was to follow his own caprice no Government could last a day, the business of this empire would be anarchy and confusion; but when the fate of thousands is at stake, when millions may be wasted, and an empire lost, he ill deserves to sit here who can from any motive sacrifice his opinion. It is not in the power of the Crown to bribe a man of property on such occasions.

G

LAWYERS AND PROFESSIONAL MEN

The eighteenth century knew only four professions: the law, the church, the army, and the navy. Though medicine was sometimes referred to as 'the profession', presumably because it involved a degree of specialized knowledge as well as a code of conduct, it was not yet organized nor was it on the same social level as the older professions. Sons of aristocratic or landed families could become barristers or clergymen or accept commissions in the army or navy or even enter trade, but they did not as yet practise medicine. Army and naval officers will be considered in later sections, while this section will deal mainly with the lawyers who sat in the House of Commons.

Of the three branches of the legal profession—barristers, attorneys and solicitors, and civil lawyers—the bar supplied most members to Parliament. It is impossible to give precise figures because of the difficulty of deciding who were or who were not barristers. The fact of having been entered at an inn of court is not evidence that a Member studied law there, nor is the fact of his having been called to the bar evidence that he ever practised. Then there were other Members, such as George Grenville or Charles Townshend, who abandoned their legal careers after having entered the House of Commons. In the figures given below Members have been counted as practising barristers only if they are known to be such from contemporary references or correspondence, from their having held judicial office, or from their having become a bencher of an inn of court or retained chambers there.

At each general election about thirty practising barristers were returned to the House, and altogether about 120 sat in Parliament during this period. Most of them came from the landed or commercial classes and only a handful from peerage families. Some were of very humble parentage. The division between King's Counsel and junior barristers was not of great professional concern during this period. A King's Counsel, strictly speaking, held an office of profit under the Crown, which was granted by favour and, if to a Member of Parliament, involved re-election to Parliament. Many barristers who reached the top ranks of their profession did not bother to take silk, while others reaped its advantages and avoided the nuisance of having to be re-elected by accepting a patent of precedence from the Crown.

About half the number of barristers who sat in the House went on to hold legal office. Six became lord chancellor (Robert Henley, Charles Pratt, John Scott, Edward Thurlow, Alexander Wedderburn, and Charles Yorke), and one (James Hewitt) became lord chancellor of Ireland after having been a judge of the King's bench. A further eight became judges of the courts in Westminster Hall (King's bench, common pleas, and Exchequer). In all, 15 Members were appointed to judicial offices which vacated their seats in the House of Commons.

When in March 1763 Henry Fox was asked to sketch the plan of a new Administration to be formed on the resignation of Bute, he suggested that the lord chancellor should be compelled to appoint judges 'with a view to parliamentary interest where they are equally fit'. 'If Mr. Fox is minister,' commented the King, 'I plainly see the very judges must be filled by wretches that are unfit to decide the properties of free men, because they can be the means of acquiring a vote in Parliament.' It was not the practice during this period to appoint judges because of their parliamentary interest, and in fact the majority of men who were raised to the bench never sat in the House of Commons. The eleven Members of Parliament who were appointed to judicial office not tenable with a seat in the House (excluding those appointed lord chancellor without having previously sat on the bench) had all achieved distinction in their profession and were well qualified by their experience and characters for the judicial office. They were William Blackstone, author of the *Commentaries on English Law*; William de Grey, a former attorney-general; James Hewitt, subsequently lord chancellor of Ireland; Beaumont Hotham; Lloyd Kenyon, formerly attorney-general and subsequently lord chief justice of the King's bench; William Murray, one of the greatest lawyers ever to preside over the King's bench; George Nares; William Noel; Charles Pratt, formerly attorney-general and subsequently lord chancellor; Alexander Wedderburn, who was also destined to hold the Great Seal; and Edward Willes, who had been solicitor-general. In only one of these appointments was there any suspicion of jobbery, and that, ironically enough, was in the case of Beaumont Hotham, who in the House was a leading member of the Opposition.

Hotham was legal adviser to the Dukes of Portland and Devonshire, and was returned to Parliament in 1768 on Portland's interest at Wigan. In 1775, when the place of a baron of the court of Exchequer seemed likely to become vacant, Portland did a deal on Hotham's behalf with Government. Hotham was to become a judge, and in return for this favour

to his friend, Portland was to return at Wigan John Morton, a
Government supporter who had lost his seat at the general election of
1774. 'I thoroughly approve of the arrangement', wrote the King to
North. '. . . Mr. Hotham's character qualifies for this promotion,
and Mr. Morton will prove a more agreeable attender in his room.' The
implication plainly is that had Hotham not been considered suitable,
he would not have received the office; but the transaction struck outside
observers as curious to say the least. It is the only example during the
period of a Member in opposition being promoted to the judicial bench.

In 1754 Sir John Strange, master of the rolls, wished to retire from
the House of Commons, but Newcastle informed him that the King
thought it 'extremely for his service that the master of the rolls should
be in Parliament'. Strange's successor, Sir Thomas Clarke, was provided
with a seat at Lostwithiel in 1754, the Government paying all expenses
except £500. In 1761 he refused to stand when he found the seat was
to cost him £2,000, and never returned to the House. Clarke's successor
as master of the rolls, Thomas Sewell, was already an M.P. when
appointed in 1764; he was defeated at Winchelsea in 1768, and although
he retained his office until his death in 1784 he never re-entered
Parliament. George III did not find it as necessary to his service to have
the master of the rolls in the House of Commons as George II had done.

There were also other legal appointments tenable with a seat in the
House. Eleven Members became Welsh judges; seven were solicitor- or
attorney-general; a further seven held similar appointments in the service
of other members of the royal family (the Queen or the Prince of Wales);
five were masters in chancery; and four were commissioners of bankruptcy.
Three Members were counsel to Government departments (the Boards of
Ordnance and Admiralty), and one was judge advocate general. Two
Members had held legal office in the colonies: William Hey as chief
justice of Quebec; and John Stanley, solicitor- and attorney-general of
the Leeward Islands.

The same difficulties attend the compiling of a list of Members who
practised at the Scottish bar as were found in listing the English barristers,
and again no precise figures can be given. About twenty practising
advocates sat in the Commons during this period, and the average number
returned to each Parliament was six. This total excludes two Members—
William Adam and Sir John Anstruther—who left the Scottish bar for
the English.

Fewer places were available for advocates than for barristers, and it seems that in Scotland, even more than in England, parliamentary considerations were not the decisive factors in determining legal appointments. The solicitor-general for Scotland, for example, rarely sat in the House of Commons: Alexander Murray was the only one who did so during this period, and he had been solicitor-general for five years before he entered the House. The lord advocate, however, if not a Member when appointed, was brought into the House as soon as practicable. In the appointment of judges of the court of session, as in the appointment of English judges, parliamentary considerations played some part but were by no means predominant. Of the 28 lords of session appointed between 1754 and 1790, six sat in the House of Commons: Ilay Campbell, Robert Dundas, William Grant, Thomas Miller, Alexander Murray, and James Veitch. Campbell and Dundas were both promoted to be lord president of the court of session after having held the office of lord advocate. But the lord advocate had no automatic lien on the lord president's place, as is shown by the appointment of Thomas Miller, an ordinary lord of session, in 1787. Five Members were appointed to be barons of the Scottish court of Exchequer, three from the Scottish bar (Cosmo Gordon, James Montgomery, and William Mure), and two from the English (Robert Ord and Fletcher Norton junior).

The distinction between an attorney (practising in the courts of common law) and a solicitor (practising in Chancery) was a real one in the eighteenth century, but in contemporary correspondence it was often ignored and the word 'attorney' used to describe both professions. Johnson's remark—'he did not speak ill of any man behind his back, but he believed the gentleman was an attorney'—is often quoted to illustrate the low social standing of the profession in his day. Probably their social position varied a good deal, but none of the ten who sat in the House during this period came of a peerage or landed family. Five of them sat in Parliament on the interest of great landowners, to whom they acted in a professional capacity: Marshe Dickinson, John Baynes Garforth, Francis Gregg, John Paterson, and John Sharpe. For them a seat in the House represented an extension of their professional duties. There were others. Francis Eyre was a London attorney who was invited to contest Morpeth in 1774 by a group of freemen opposed to Lord Carlisle's interest and to undertake (at his own expense) the legal disputes pending with Carlisle. Jarrit Smith was a Bristol attorney, much concerned with its politics, who represented the city 1756–68; and John Pitt a Gloucester attorney, and the candidate of the independent party at Gloucester against the Duke of Norfolk's interest in the great contest of 1789. William Masterman, who sat for Bodmin 1780–4, was a west country attorney, much concerned in Cornish election affairs and at one time an agent of Lord Edgcumbe. John Smith, solicitor to the East India Company, was a mere stop-gap at New Romney in 1784, and held the seat for only three months. Dickinson and Paterson were successively (from 1761 to 1768) chairmen of the committee of ways and means, and Sharpe was solicitor to the Treasury from 1742 until his death in 1756, but otherwise none of these men rose to any consequence in the House. They were good men of business, but neither debaters nor politicians.

Only one writer to the signet sat in the House during this period: Andrew Stuart, M.P. for Lanarkshire 1774–84. Stuart had succeeded his father as legal agent to the Duke of Hamilton, and managed the legal proceedings involved in the Duke's claim to the Douglas estates (the famous Douglas cause). He was brought into Parliament on the Hamilton interest and through their influence was provided with sinecures, apparently as a reward for his professional services; but he was dropped in 1784 (when the Hamiltons followed Pitt) and remained loyal to Fox.

The third branch of the legal profession comprised the advocates at Doctors' Commons who practised in the ecclesiastical and Admiralty courts. There were eight in the House during this period. James Adams and Scrope Bernard entered the House in 1784 and 1789 respectively, when they were both young men just on the threshold of their profession. William Burrell, who specialized in Admiralty cases, retired from Parliament and his profession in 1774 with a commissionership of the Excise. Philip Champion Crespigny was of little account in his profession and seems to have owed his office of King's proctor to parliamentary considerations: he was brother-in-law of Thomas Fonnereau, patron of the borough of Aldeburgh, and succeeded to the Fonnereau interest there in 1779. Crespigny remained with North after his junction with Fox, and in 1784 lost his place of King's proctor.

The remaining four advocates who sat in the House—George Hay, Sir George Lee, Sir James Marriott, and Edward Simpson—filled the highest offices in their profession. Members of Parliament had a preferential claim on these offices, because there were usually only two or three advocates in the House; but professional experience and knowing the right people counted for nearly as much as voting with the Government. In 1756 Edward Simpson was the senior practising advocate and although not in the House was appointed King's advocate by Newcastle, only to lose his post to a Member of Parliament when the Pitt-Devonshire ministry was formed a few months later. In 1758 Simpson was appointed dean of the arches (an office in the gift of the archbishop of Canterbury) at Newcastle's recommendation, and in 1759 the Duke brought him into Parliament for Dover. He remained with Newcastle in opposition, and on his death in 1764 was succeeded as dean of the arches by George Hay, M.P. for Sandwich. Hay had been appointed King's advocate by Newcastle in 1755 but had deserted him for Pitt and afterwards had deserted Pitt for Bute and Grenville. Yet when Simpson died in 1764 Newcastle recommended Hay to the archbishop for dean of the arches, for which he was strongly criticized by his friends in opposition. Hay was also a member of the Admiralty Board, from which he was dismissed in July 1765 by the Rockingham ministry; and the Rockingham and Chatham Administrations are the only ones he is known to have opposed. He was defeated for Oxford University at the general election of 1768, but returned in November by Lord Gower at Newcastle-under-Lyme; and henceforth steadily supported Government, becoming in 1773 judge of the court of Admiralty. Hay was unquestionably an able man both in the House and in the courts—Newcastle in 1761 seriously considered him for the Chair; but he was quite unscrupulous in the pursuit of his own interests and had no political loyalties. 'He had no opinion of any cause', a friend wrote of him after his death, 'but considered them all as the pretences under which men carry on their selfish schemes.'

Hay's career as a time-server is matched by that of another ecclesiastical lawyer, Sir James Marriott, M.P. for Sudbury 1781–84; but Marriott's success came through servility and fawning to ministers, and he did not enter the House until he had reached the pinnacle of his career as a lawyer. He began as Newcastle's 'most devoted dependant', and in return for cataloguing Newcastle's library bullied the Duke into getting him elected a fellow of Trinity Hall, Cambridge. He deserted Newcastle for Bute in 1762 but when informed that the Duke intended to bring him into Parliament, apologized humbly for his conduct and returned to his former allegiance; only to leave Newcastle again in 1764 when he obtained through Lord Sandwich's influence the mastership of Trinity Hall. In 1778 he became judge of the Admiralty, but no Administration

would bring him into Parliament and it was not until 1781 that he came
in at Sudbury on his own interest. He was a devoted follower of North,
and afterwards of the Shelburne, Fox-North, and Pitt Administrations;
and retired from Parliament in 1784, professedly because of his health
and age. Twelve years later, when presumably his health had improved
and he no longer felt his age, he re-entered the House but received no
further preferment.

There were two other Members during this period who might be
described as professional men. Robert Adam, the architect, M.P. for
Kinross-shire 1768–74, found his seat very useful for the furtherance
of his speculative building projects in London and for winding them up
after they had failed. Thomas Dimsdale, M.P. for Hertford 1780–90,
was the doctor who had inoculated the Empress Catherine of Russia,
but it seems probable that he had given up his practice long before he
entered the House. Another ex-doctor in the House was Lauchlin
Macleane, M.P. for Arundel 1768–71, who had practised at
Philadelphia and been an army surgeon during the seven years' war, but
he gave up his profession in favour of the more lucrative trade of a
speculator in East India stock and came to an untimely end.

Finally, two ordained clergymen of the Church of England sat in
Parliament during this period. The first was Robert Palk, who took
deacon's orders and became a chaplain in the service of the East India
Company. Soon after his arrival in India in 1749 he turned to administrative duties, became governor of Madras in 1763, and in 1767 returned
to England with a fortune. He was a native of Ashburton in Devon,
where he had a strong parliamentary interest, and was returned for the
borough at a by-election in December 1767. Legally Palk remained a
clergyman, since at that time there was no provision for the renunciation
of orders, but his career was predominantly lay. The second, Edward
Rushworth, was ordained deacon in 1780 and became a curate in the
parish of Newport in the Isle of Wight. There he met the daughter of
the Rev. Leonard Troughear Holmes, whose family had a considerable
parliamentary interest in the Isle of Wight boroughs of Newport and
Yarmouth. In August 1780 Rushworth married Holmes's daughter, and
at the general election a few days later his father-in-law sprung a surprise
on the Administration. In order to force Lord North to provide for
Rushworth, presumably in the Church, he returned him for Yarmouth
instead of one of the Government candidates. North was highly indignant

but the scheme worked in so far as a few months later Rushworth vacated his seat in favour of a rich nabob, presumably for a financial consideration. Whether he continued to exercise his ecclesiastical functions is not certain. At the general election of 1784 he was elected for Newport after a contest, and his defeated opponent petitioned against him on the ground that since Rushworth was in holy orders his election was invalid. But a committee of the House of Commons decided in Rushworth's favour, and Rushworth had by then become sufficiently interested in politics to vote with Fox throughout the Parliament.

MERCHANTS

The word 'merchant' had a wide meaning in the eighteenth century, including at one extreme small shopkeepers and at the other, wholesalers, exporters, bankers, and financiers. The merchants who sat in the House of Commons can best be described as business men; most of them were engaged in large-scale dealings, and their business brought them into close connexion with Government and could be vitally affected by changes in Government policy. They entered the House at a higher average age than that of the House as a whole, were not prone to form strong political attachments, and were not intent on attaining office. Membership of the House marked a stage in their business careers: it was not a duty enjoined upon them, as it was for the country gentlemen, nor did it imply strong political convictions and an urge to take part in the game of politics. Socially, the merchants ranged from self-made men of humble parentage to sons of the aristocracy, but the majority of them came from middle-class families and pursued a family calling. The average number returned at each general election was about 60, slightly lower in the earlier part of the period and slightly higher at the end. No list could be compiled of merchants in the House which would not be subject to the vagaries of individual judgement, for they were not a distinct group, clearly marked off from the professional or landed classes.

In the coal-producing areas of the north-east and south Wales it was not uncommon for country gentlemen, as they began to exploit their estates, to become business men and even industrialists without ever losing the character or distinctive outlook of a country gentleman. George Bowes, M.P. for Durham county 1727–60, was one of the largest coal owners in the north-east and left a fortune estimated at £600,000. With the Wortleys and the Liddells, two other leading county families, he

founded a cartel which dominated the north country coal trade throughout the century. Yet he remained a typical county Member, standing
aloof from close connexions with Government and thoroughly independent
in his political outlook. Matthew Ridley of Blagdon, Northumberland,
M.P. for Newcastle-upon-Tyne 1747–74, was another country gentleman
who exploited the coal seams on his estates. Coal naturally led him
to the industries which used it, and he became the owner of a glass works
and a brewery, mayor of Newcastle, governor of the Company of
Merchant Adventurers, and a leader of the Newcastle business community.
George Warren, who represented Lancaster for 26 years during this
period, was another country gentleman who engaged in industry: he
tried to develop the coal mines on his Cheshire estates and promoted a
scheme for a canal to link the rivers Weaver and Mersey. This clashed
with another plan for a canal put forward by the Duke of Bridgwater, and
Warren's estates remained comparatively undeveloped during his lifetime.
He also engaged in cotton manufacturing and tried to enclose common
lands for building factories.

Capel Hanbury and his son John belonged to one of the leading landed
families in south Wales and between them represented Monmouthshire
from 1747 to 1784. The family had owned iron works at Pontypool since
the sixteenth century and these they considerably extended in the eighteenth
century. The Mackworths of Gnoll in Glamorgan were another leading
south Wales family with a strong parliamentary interest based on the
ownership of land—father and son held the seat for Cardiff Boroughs
from 1739 to 1790. They owned coal mines and also the Gnoll copper
works at Neath, developed a local bank, and had a business address in
the city of London. It would be the extreme of pedantry to try to
decide whether men like these should be classified as country gentlemen
or industrialists for they were in fact both—the ownership of mineral-
producing land leading them by a natural and almost insensible process
into becoming business men.

There was also a movement the other way, of men who had grown
rich in business abandoning their trade and becoming country gentlemen.
Joseph Mawbey at the age of seventeen became a partner in his uncle's
vinegar distillery at Vauxhall, and by the time he was twenty-four was
sole owner. In 1761 he entered Parliament for Southwark, a constituency
which always returned local business men; but in 1774, having sold
his distillery and turned country gentleman, he aspired to represent the

county of Surrey and did so 1775–90. George Medley, after having made a fortune as a wine merchant in Portugal, settled as a country gentleman in Sussex and gave Newcastle a lot of trouble by challenging the Duke's interest at Seaford. At last, in 1768, Newcastle returned him for Seaford, which he represented until 1780. He, too, had a typical country gentleman's attitude in politics: he once said in the House that 'he never would either ask or accept of any favour from the Crown', and as far as is known he kept his word. John Strutt, M.P. for Maldon 1774–90, was the son of a miller and had been apprenticed to his uncle, another miller. Strutt, after succeeding to his uncle's estates, became a country gentleman in Essex and applied to agriculture the lessons of thrift and good management he had learnt in commerce. In politics he belonged to the Essex Tories, and he remained a Tory in outlook and principle long after the Tories had ceased to exist as a coherent group in Parliament.

Numerous examples can be given of Members who grew rich in business, bought landed estates, and became country gentlemen without abandoning their business. Here is one good example. John Major of Bridlington, Yorkshire, began life as the owner of a ship which he himself commanded. He left the sea and went into the iron trade, at the same time remaining financially interested in shipping. He was returned to Parliament for Scarborough in 1761 at the age of sixty-two, and in 1765, when his son-in-law John Henniker, M.P., applied for a baronetcy on Major's behalf, owned estates in seven English counties with a rental of about £5,000 per annum. Though Major's estates were larger than those of many country gentlemen who sat in the House, business remained his predominant interest and no one would have classed him as anything but a merchant.

In 1754 banking was hardly as yet a separate branch of commerce. There were a number of great houses wholly devoted to the business of banking—Child's, Drummond's, and Martin's are notable examples; and representatives of these families duly found their place in the House of Commons. But a good many merchants were also bankers: the transition from granting credit to their customers to the business of banking was not a very difficult one. To give one example: Sir George Colebrooke, M.P. for Arundel 1754–74, was a banker, a merchant trading to America, a director of the East India Company, and a speculator in land and raw materials. Country banks were often started by groups of landed gentlemen, probably as much for their neighbours' convenience as for their own profit. The founders of the Cornish bank in 1771 included Edward

Eliot, Humphrey Mackworth Praed, William Lemon, and Sir John Molesworth, all at some time Members of Parliament for Cornwall during this period and none of them could be described as a merchant. The career of Thomas Hill, M.P. for Shrewsbury 1749–68, is a remarkable example of large scale finance carried on by a former merchant who had settled down as a country gentleman.

From a study of the Members of Parliament in this period it would appear that capitalism had developed most in three industries: clothing, brewing, and mining. The clothiers who sat in Parliament came mostly from the west country, and, having settled in London, acted as financiers and agents for the smaller manufacturers. The brewers and distillers, for example Sir William Calvert, Henry Thrale, and Samuel Whitbread, were all established in London. Those engaged in the mining industry were country gentlemen such as George Bowes, Sir James Lowther, or Sir Francis Basset, who exploited the natural wealth of their estates. But the typical English business man of this period engaged in all kinds of ventures where a profit was to be made, though he often ended by concentrating upon one. Anthony Bacon and Chauncy Townsend were two Members who did so.

Bacon, M.P. for Aylesbury 1764–84, was a Manxman who began his business career by keeping a store in Maryland. About 1740 he began trading between England and the southern colonies as master of his own ship, and in 1748 settled as a merchant in London. He dealt in tobacco, coal, Senegal gum, slaves, and a wide range of other commodities; engaged in shipbuilding; and obtained Government contracts for victualling troops in West Africa and the West Indies, for supplying coal, slaves, and ships. In 1765 he took out a lease of land around Merthyr Tydfil, set up furnaces and forges, and became a gun founder. He was one of the first industrialists to use Wilkinson's invention of boring cannon from the solid, and one of the largest suppliers of guns during the American war. He also held contracts for victualling troops in America and for supplying coal, but by 1782, when he retired, gun-making seems to have been the largest part of his business. Our second example, Townsend, M.P. for Westbury 1748–68 and for Wigtown Burghs 1768–70, was apprenticed to his uncle, a linen-draper. He began working coal mines around Swansea, engaged in mining and working copper and lead, and held contracts for provisioning troops in America. But by the time of his death his mining ventures overshadowed all his other concerns.

The majority of merchants who sat in the House during this period were in business in London. At the general election of 1754 only five provincial merchants were returned to the House (including one from Scotland); in the Parliaments of 1780 and 1784 there were nine. Only the biggest merchants aspired to a seat in the House (the smaller ones were far too occupied with their businesses), and the biggest merchants naturally gravitated to London. The five provincial merchants returned in 1754 were William Alexander of Edinburgh, Samuel Dicker of Bristol, John Hardman of Liverpool, Jonathan Rashleigh of Fowey (where the Rashleigh family controlled one seat), and Matthew Ridley of Newcastle-upon-Tyne. All, except Dicker, sat for constituencies where they carried on their business, as did the majority of provincial merchants returned to Parliament during this period. Bristol sent four merchants to the House between 1754 and 1790; Liverpool sent three; Edinburgh and Exeter two; and no other provincial town more than one. Towards the end of the period there was a tendency for smaller provincial towns to return local merchants to Parliament. George Gipps, a hop merchant, sat for Canterbury 1780–1800; Thomas Kemp, a wool stapler and an important figure in local politics, for Lewes 1780–1802 and 1806–11; and John Mortlock, founder of the first bank in Cambridge, for Cambridge 1784–8. These were genuine local merchants, men of substance and standing in their native towns, of a type rarely found in the earlier part of this period.

'I see many solid advantages accruing to my family from a seat in Parliament', wrote Abel Smith, the Nottingham banker, shortly before the general election of 1774, 'the best of which, the article of franking, will save a very considerable expense in so very extensive a business as that I am engaged in.' The right to frank letters gratis (which Members extended to include letters sent out by their firms as well as by their friends) was a valuable perquisite in an age when postage rates were heavy. But once in the House, Smith found that there were other perquisites to which a Member of Parliament might lay claim. His first speech, on 25 February 1782, was to attack Lord North for alleged partiality in the allotment of subscriptions to the Government loan; his second, 25 April 1783, was to complain of Lord John Cavendish, North's successor as chancellor of the Exchequer, for the same offence. Smith's firm had been left out of both loans, and presumably he felt that as a Government supporter and an eminent banker, he had a right to a share.

Edward Lewis, M.P. for New Radnor, held a Government contract for supplying ships for the packet service to the West Indies. In 1773 the Post Office, dissatisfied with the terms of the contract, proposed to discontinue it; and Lewis appealed to Lord North. North wrote to the postmasters general on 29 January 1774:

Mr. Lewis is a very honest, worthy man, and an excellent Member of Parliament. Nobody has more zealously and uniformly supported his Majesty's Government, from which he receives no advantage whatsoever except the contract which he holds with the Post Office ... I do assure you that I think the King's affairs in Parliament may suffer unless such good and steady friends as Mr. Lewis have from Government all the countenance and favour that justice and the public service will permit.

Something had to suffer, either the King's affairs in Parliament or those of the Post Office, and Lewis was shown rather more favour than the public service permitted. Lord le Despenser, joint postmaster general, in his reply to North described Lewis's contract as detrimental to the public; still, realizing that it was necessary 'to show complaisance and favour to those who are steady to Government', he left the matter to be decided by North at his discretion. Lewis retained his contract until North left office.

It was against jobbery of this kind in the allotment of Government contracts that the Opposition complained, and the contractors bill, introduced by Sir Philip Jennings Clerke in 1778, excluded them from the House unless they held their contracts as the result of a public auction. 'Members of Parliament would not be contractors', said Jennings Clerke on introducing his bill, 'if extraordinary and improper advantages were not given them ... giving these contracts to Members was an arrant job, and did create a dangerous influence in that House which must operate much to the injury of the nation.' The bill, repeatedly rejected by the Commons or the Lords, finally became law after the Rockinghams came to power in 1782. There were then twelve Government contractors sitting in the House, all of whom chose to retain their seats and surrender their contracts.

Thus it is not easy to say whether Jennings Clerke's allegations were correct, or the similar allegations made by George Byng and Sir George Savile in 1781 against partiality in the allotment of Government loans. Certainly Edward Lewis's contract appears to have been an arrant job, and throughout the period merchants voting with the Government stood to gain contracts and those voting with the Opposition stood to lose them. But before the charges of wholesale jobbery and corruption could be justified, there would have to be a thorough examination of the terms of the contracts, the prices of provisions, shipping freights, commissions taken on the remittance of money, &c. If contracts were the places of merchants, as Sir Lewis Namier has said, it would be reasonable to expect a good deal of jobbery in their distribution but little downright corruption. Merchants received contracts because they voted with the Government; it is by no means certain, and would be difficult to prove, that they voted with the Government because they received contracts.

How many merchant M.P.s held Government contracts? Again, the figures cannot be exact: too much depends on the definition given to the word merchant and exactly what is meant by a contract. Sir Lewis Namier found thirty-seven Members returned to Parliament in 1761 who 'had extensive business dealings with the Government' (which includes also the principal subscribers to Government loans). Mr. Christie calculates that there were fifteen Government contractors elected to Parliament in 1780. My own figures for the number of contractors returned at each general election are as follows: 17 in 1754, 27 in 1761, 14 in 1768, 14 in 1774, and 17 in 1780. The principal Government contracts were for the pay, clothing, and provisioning of troops abroad; for the equipment of the army and navy; and for remitting money to foreign states. Naturally there were more and bigger contracts in time of war than in time of peace, and one would also expect the number of contractors in Parliament to be larger during the seven years' war than during the American war. During the seven years' war Great Britain had an army in Europe and paid large subsidies to her European allies, but during the American war there were no continental campaigns and no allies.

A list of the principal Government contractors who sat in the House during this period appears on p. 200.

There were other Members who held contracts of a miscellaneous nature. Christopher Atkinson supplied wheat and malt to the Victualling Board during the American war; Anthony Bacon, among other contracts, held one for victualling and paying the troops in West Africa during the seven years' war and during the American war supplied cannon to the Board of Ordnance; Sir Lawrence Dundas and Nicholas Linwood were the chief contractors for horses for Prince Ferdinand's army in

Germany; Brice Fisher supplied clothing to the army during the seven years' war; John Sargent and Richard Stratton contracted for mail boats to the West Indies; and Thomas Fitzherbert held a number of contracts during the American war—for waggons, horses, arms and ammunition. Nor are these lists exhaustive: a close scrutiny of the records of the Admiralty, the Ordnance, the Victualling Office, &c., would probably provide evidence of other contracts held by Members of Parliament; but the results would not be commensurate to the work involved.

For remitting Continental subsidies, provisioning and paying troops in Germany [Seven years' war only]	For provisioning and paying troops in America	For provisioning and paying troops in Gibraltar and Minorca
George Amyand	John Amyand	George Amyand
Peregrine Cust	Richard Atkinson	Richard Atkinson
John Gore	Sir William Baker	John Bristow
Joseph Mellish	Sir George Colebrooke	Merrick Burrell
Samuel Touchet	James Colebrooke	Peter Burrell I
Thomas Walpole	Laurence Cox	Peregrine Cust
	William Devaynes	Thomas Fonnereau
	Adam Drummond	Z. P. Fonnereau
	Henry Drummond	Robert Jones
	John Drummond	Thomas Walpole
	Samuel Fludyer	George Wombwell
	Thomas Harley	
	John Henniker	
	Edward Lewis	
	John Major	
	Robert Mayne	
	John Nesbitt	
	Arnold Nesbitt	
	Christopher Potter	
	Abel Smith	
	John Stephenson	
	Chauncy Townsend	
	George Wombwell	

The Government contractors who sat in the House were the leaders of the business community of their day, and most of them were merchants and bankers, exporters and importers, rather than industrialists. They had access to large amounts of capital, and were, together with the three great joint-stock companies, the principal subscribers to Government loans. But when the Government wanted money it was compelled to go to the men who had it to lend, irrespective of whether they were in Parliament or not, and to borrow on the most favourable terms. Other things being equal, Members of Parliament who supported the Government would receive priority; but there is little evidence that the Government favoured Members of Parliament at the expense of making a bad bargain for the nation. One of the most considerable subscribers to Government loans during the seven years' war was Anthony Chamier, a broker and leading City financier, who did not enter the House until 1778, by which time he had retired from business. Robert Ladbroke, M.P., a big London banker, was a large subscriber to Government loans during the American war although he voted regularly with the Opposition. As with Government contracts, there was jobbery in the allotment of loans, but the idea that they were used by Government as an instrument to preserve its majority in the House does not bear examination.

The three great joint stock companies, incorporated by royal charter, were the Bank of England, the South Sea Company, and the East India Company. The affairs of the East India Company were the subject of prolonged political controversy during this period, and the Members of Parliament concerned in them are dealt with in a later section. The Bank of England and the South Sea Company were the chief sources of credit in the City of London and their relations with Government were necessarily close. Throughout this period there was always a number of directors of each company in the House.

Ten directors of the Bank of England sat in the Commons between 1754 and 1790, including three who held the post of governor of the Bank while they were in the House. Merrick Burrell (governor 1758–60), Bartholomew Burton (governor 1760–2), and Martyn Fonnereau, were London merchants principally engaged in the American trade. Burrell and Burton were two of Newcastle's financial advisers while he was at the Treasury; and Burton had been brought into Parliament by the Treasury in 1759 at a time of acute financial crisis when Newcastle wanted a leading City man in the House. The other Bank directors in Parliament were William Ewer (governor 1782–3), wholesale grocer and Turkey merchant; Samuel Fludyer, clothier; Benjamin Hopkins, underwriter and a leading Government supporter in City politics; John Sargent, draper and American merchant, and a close friend of Benjamin Franklin; Richard Stratton, Turkey merchant; Samuel Thornton, Russia merchant; and

Brook Watson, underwriter and member of Lloyds. Five of these men—Burrell, Burton, Fludyer, Sargent, and Stratton—held Government contracts for some part of their time in Parliament; and with the exception of Sargent, who remained loyal to Grenville after his dismissal in 1765, none was in declared opposition for more than a few months.

Sixteen directors of the South Sea Company sat in the House during this period, including three who held the office of sub-governor (the King was the governor). The number of directors in the House decreased as the period advanced, possibly a reflection of the diminishing importance of the Company. Nine were returned at the general election of 1754, seven in 1761, four in 1768, three in 1774, two in 1780, and one in 1784. Nor was the direction wholly mercantile, as was that of the Bank of England. Nine of these sixteen directors were merchants (John Bristow, Peter Burrell, Brice Fisher, John Gore, Joseph Gulston, Abraham Hume, Thomas Lucas, John Major, and Nathaniel Newnham). Three (Bristow, Burrell, and Gulston) were principally in the Portuguese trade; and six (Bristow, Burrell, Fisher, Gore, Hume, and Major) held Government contracts while they were in the House. Three of the remaining directors were barristers: Thomas Coventry (who became sub-governor in 1769), Samuel Salt, and Benjamin Way. William Burrell, a son of Peter Burrell, was an advocate at Doctors' Commons; Francis Gashry and John Phillipson were Government officials; and Thomas Edwards Freeman was a country gentleman.

The aldermen of London claimed to represent the business interests of the City. Of the 31 aldermen who sat in the House during this period, 26 were merchants or bankers, two (Richard and William Beckford) were Jamaican planters, and one (Marshe Dickinson) was a City attorney. Only John Wilkes and James Townsend, leaders of the City radicals, were unconnected with the business world. The number of aldermen returned at each general election is as follows: 9 in 1754, 8 in 1761, 8 in 1768, 6 in 1774, 8 in 1780, and 13 in 1784. Twenty of the aldermen who sat in the House became lord mayor of London, and fifteen represented the City in Parliament (every Member for the City during this period was an alderman). In addition, Sir William Calvert, who had represented London since 1742 and been defeated at the general election in 1754, was returned by the Treasury for Old Sarum; John Wilkes, defeated for London in 1768, was returned for Middlesex; while Paul le Mesurier and Sir Barnard Turner represented Southwark.

The City of London, in eighteenth-century parlance, had both a political and commercial implication, and from a study of the voting records of the aldermen who were returned to Parliament it seems that they were representative of political rather than of commercial opinion in the City. In the Parliament of 1780, six of them voted with the Opposition and only two with the Government; in that of 1784, ten with Pitt and three with Fox. Most big business men preferred to come into Parliament for a pocket borough rather than engage in the hurly-burly of City politics, at the best an uncertain way of getting into the House and one involving the expenditure of considerable time and effort.

The period 1754 to 1790 witnessed technical changes in industry which were to affect profoundly the nation's economic life. These changes are not visible in the composition of the House of Commons: no Lancashire cotton spinner, no Yorkshire woollen manufacturer, no Black Country industrialist sat in Parliament during this period. The first generation of families who made their fortunes as a result of the Industrial Revolution were too occupied with their businesses to think of entering the House of Commons. For the merchant and business man, membership of the House was a status symbol, a sign that he had arrived at the top, not a means of getting there.

ARMY OFFICERS

During this period 208 army officers sat in the House of Commons. This figure does not include militia officers nor those who served as volunteers in time of war, but only regular army officers whose names appear in the semi-official army lists. Roughly speaking, one out of every ten Members of Parliament held a commission in the regular army at some period during his service in the House, which seems a very high proportion for a nation which had no tradition of militarism and had for a long time withstood the creation of a standing army. Perhaps it can partly be explained by the fact that the army was still in the eighteenth century a very amateurish service. Once commissioned, an officer remained on the army list unless he resigned or was dismissed for misconduct, though in fact he may have been a soldier in name only, seeing no service and receiving no military employment. For men of good family, promotion in the junior grades was quick, facilitated by the purchase system; and a young man with good connexions who entered the army at the age of eighteen might look forward to being a lieutenant-colonel before he was thirty. Thereafter promotion would be much slower, dependent mainly on seniority, and once an officer had passed beyond the stage of regimental duty his chance of employment lessened. With no elaborate staff organization, there were few posts available for senior officers; and many a major-general or lieutenant-general held nothing but his rank.

Here is the military career of one officer who sat in the House of Commons: Charles Moore, 6th Earl of Drogheda in the Irish peerage, M.P. for Horsham 1776–80. Drogheda was given his first commission in the 12th Dragoons at the age of fourteen, and at twenty-five was lieutenant-colonel of the 1st Horse. During the seven years' war he raised a regiment of light dragoons at his own expense, and in 1762 was promoted colonel and appointed colonel of the 18th Light Dragoons. From 1770 to 1797 he was master-general of the Ordnance in Ireland, an office which he owned as much to his being an Irish peer as to anything else. His promotion in the army followed regularly as a matter of seniority, until in 1821, shortly after his ninety-first birthday, he became a field-marshal. He had been in the army for more than seventy years and had seen no active service.

Drogheda's military career was exceptional only because he lived to such a great age, and it will hardly be contended that the four years he spent in the House of Commons helped to gain him promotion. In fact, it would have made no difference if he had never sat in Parliament; the most important factors in his military career were his wealth and social position, not his membership of the House of Commons. He reached the top because he came from the class which expected to fill the highest positions in the army. Yet the belief persisted that Parliament was the quickest road to military promotion. 'If your inclinations are to push forward in the army', a friend wrote to James Mure Campbell in 1751, 'undoubtedly being in Parliament is the only way.' Campbell duly entered the House as M.P. for Ayrshire in 1754, when he was a major in the 11th Dragoons, and his seat in Parliament undoubtedly helped to obtain for him a company in the 3rd Foot Guards in 1756. Among the mass of junior officers struggling for promotion, those who were Members of Parliament stood out and might expect speedier promotion than the average. But both George II and George III held a tight control over service appointments, and Members of Parliament who expected to jump over the heads of officers senior to themselves were more often than not disappointed. And above lieutenant-colonel, the Member of Parliament had no advantage as far as mere rank was concerned.

Amongst junior officers, the most coveted appointments were to the command of a company or a battalion in the Foot Guards and their equivalents in the Household cavalry. Rank in the Guards carried with it correspondingly higher rank in the army: thus a lieutenant in the Guards was a captain in the army, a captain in the Guards a lieutenant-colonel in the army, &c. For senior officers, the plum appointments were colonelcies of regiments and governorships of forts. These were strictly military appointments, but as far as Members of Parliament were concerned political considerations entered into them. A Member of Parliament in opposition could not expect a regiment or a governorship, or promotion to a more lucrative appointment. On the other hand, demotion or loss of rank in the army, or worse, was usually independent of politics and resulted from military misconduct leading to conviction by court-martial. The outstanding example is provided by Lieutenant-General Lord George Sackville, a Member of the House from 1741 to 1782, who disobeyed orders to bring up the cavalry at the battle of Minden, 1 August 1759, was dismissed the service and declared by court-martial unfit to hold any military command whatsoever. How he escaped the death penalty is not clear: certainly the King expected no lesser sentence. In the new reign, Sackville was given office in the first Rockingham Administration; regained his position as a front-rank debater in the House of Commons; and disastrously for his own reputation, became secretary of state for the colonies with responsibility for the American war. He ended his career in the House of Lords. The only soldier whose military career was broken for political reasons in this period was Sir Henry Erskine, M.P. for Anstruther Easter Burghs, who was dismissed the army by order of the King in 1756 for voting with Pitt and the Prince of Wales's friends against the subsidy treaties. Erskine's harsh treatment was prompted by the King's jealousy of the Prince of Wales and by the fact that the subsidy treaties had been concluded by the King himself to ensure the defence of Hanover.

In the earlier part of the period appointments in the army, as distinct from rank, were considered by the Government almost as the military equivalent of political office, and were liable to be forfeited by Members who went into opposition. In November 1763 Major-General William Ashe A'Court, M.P. for Heytesbury, was deprived of his appointment as lieutenant-colonel of the 2nd Foot Guards for voting with the Opposition on the Wilkes case, and Lieutenant-Colonel Isaac Barré, M.P. for Chipping Wycombe, was dismissed from the place of adjutant-general and the governorship of Stirling castle for the same offence. In 1764 a parliamentary controversy was aroused by the dismissal of Lieutenant-General Henry Seymour Conway, M.P. for Thetford, from the colonelcy of the 1st Dragoons for voting against the Government over general warrants. The Opposition contended that the colonelcy of a regiment was a military appointment which could be lost only for military misconduct, and was not to be considered in the same category as a political office or a place at court. Though the King never explicitly acknowledged this, the practice of dismissing officers for their votes in Parliament ceased. Lieutenant-General John Burgoyne, M.P. for Preston, though he greatly offended the King by precipitately going into opposition in 1778 and censuring the Government's conduct of the war, was allowed to retain his regiment and his governorship. The Government took its revenge upon him in another way by ordering him back to America (he was a prisoner-of-war on parole), upon which Burgoyne promptly resigned his military appointments.

By the end of the period it was tacitly understood that an officer who voted against the Government would not be dismissed from strictly military appointments. But it by no means followed that he would not thereby lose promotion in the army. Colonel Alexander Stewart, M.P. for Kirkcudbright Stewartry, having failed to secure a regiment from the younger Pitt, voted against him over the Regency. When, after the King's recovery, Stewart again applied for promotion, Henry Dundas sharply reminded him that his political conduct had not been satisfactory. 'If political support is to be any foundation for military preferment', Dundas wrote on 18 June 1789, 'these occurrences must of necessity have produced other pretensions not inferior to yours.' The implication plainly is that the Government intended to distribute army appointments, as they did civil appointments, to those officers who supported them in the House of Commons. It could hardly be otherwise, when the distinction between military and political appointments was by no means clear.

General Burgoyne, who had been appointed commander-in-chief in Ireland by the Rockingham Administration in March 1782, was advised by his political friends not to resign with them when Shelburne became minister. The office of commander-in-chief in Ireland, wrote Portland to Burgoyne, was purely military, and he continued: 'I could see no objection to your retaining it, and in carrying on the most violent opposition to the court at the same time in a political line.' But in January 1784, after Fox's dismissal and Pitt's accession to office, Burgoyne resigned what he now professed to believe was a political office. 'The trust of commander-in-chief', he wrote to Lord Sydney, Home secretary, required 'the most confidential connexion with his Majesty's ministers on both sides of the water.' Similarly, General Conway, commander-in-chief in England, held that his post was a purely military one, and did not resign when Shelburne took office. Under the Fox-North coalition he withdrew from the cabinet, thus dissociating himself from responsibility for the Government's political decisions. But in December 1783, believing that Pitt's assumption of office was unconstitutional, he resigned what he had hitherto regarded as a purely military office.

Parliament's authority over the army was based on its control over finance and did not extend to military promotions and appointments. The secretary at war, who generally answered for the army in the House of Commons, was the King's military secretary, never sat in the Cabinet, and in the House was mainly concerned with finance. Lord Barrington, secretary at war 1755–61 and 1765–78, probably the most conscientious man to hold the office during this period, said in the Commons on 9 December 1770:

A secretary at war must obey the King's orders signified by a secretary of state or resign. The secretary at war is not a Cabinet Councillor. He is only a ministerial officer. He is not a proper judge of the propriety of a measure.

Nor did he see fit to resign his office when, in 1776, he disagreed with the strategy of trying to reduce the rebellion in America by offensive warfare.

The effective head of the army in 1754 was the Duke of Cumberland, the King's second son, who held the appointment of captain-general. Cumberland's political adviser, Henry Fox, was secretary at war, and between them Cumberland and Fox directed a group in the House of Commons composed mainly of army officers. In Lord Dupplin's list of 1754 the Cumberland-Fox group comprises 26 Members, while there were also 20 other army officers in the House who looked to Cumberland as the source of professional favours. After Cumberland's resignation in 1757 this group disintegrated, and henceforth the army officers were so many individuals in the House, without any political direction from the head of their profession.

Field Marshal Lord Ligonier, M.P. 1748–63, and commander-in-chief of the army 1757–66, was insignificant in the House of Commons. His successor, Lord Granby, M.P. 1741–70, was politically connected with Chatham, and resigned in January 1770 when Chatham went into opposition. From 1770 to 1778 the post of commander-in-chief was vacant; when it became necessary to fill it during the American war, the office was given to Lord Amherst, a distinguished soldier who never sat in the House. Henry Seymour Conway, M.P., was commander-in-chief from March 1782 to December 1783, when the office was again allowed to become vacant and it was not until war broke out with France in 1793 that a fresh appointment was made. Clearly it was felt that there was no necessity to have a commander-in-chief in time of peace, nor, when there was one, for him to be in the House of Commons.

Three times during this period the House of Commons took it upon itself to inquire into the failure of military operations: in April 1757, on the loss of Minorca; in April 1779, on the conduct of the Howe brothers in America; and in May 1779, on the failure of Burgoyne's expedition. The Minorca inquiry was a political move, led by Charles and George Townshend, supported by the Tories, encouraged by Pitt, and aimed at Henry Fox and the Duke of Newcastle. The Howe and Burgoyne inquiries were granted at the request of those officers, all three Members of Parliament, who had served without success in America, had returned home disgruntled with Administration, and wished to justify their conduct. A mass of documents was laid before the House and a great deal of information elicited from witnesses, but, inevitably, no conclusions were arrived at. The debates tended to take a political turn, for, in fact, the House of Commons was not a suitable body to inquire into the conduct of military operations.

Of the 208 army officers who sat in the House during this period 56 (more than one quarter) were Scots. The Scots formed a much higher percentage of army Members than they did of the House as a whole or of any other group. Here are the numbers of army officers returned at each general election:

1754	49 including 13 Scots
1761	56 13
1768	68 12

1774	64 including 16 Scots
1780	54 13
1784	54 17

The general election of 1768, when the highest number of army officers entered the House, was a peace-time general election; the two general elections held in time of war, 1761 and 1780, produced a comparatively low number of army officers.

The following table shows the ranks held by army Members when they first entered the House during this period, the Scots being again differentiated. Army officers who entered Parliament before 1754 are omitted.

Rank	English, Welsh, and Irish	Scots	Total
Lieutenant or below	16	2	18
Captain	34	9	43
Major	8	5	13
Lieutenant-Colonel	29	15	44
Colonel	18	11	29
Major-General	8	2	10
Lieutenant-General	2	2	4

50 per cent of the English officers were below the rank of lieutenant-colonel when they first entered Parliament, but only 30 per cent of the Scots. Again the figures suggest that the army was more of a profession in Scotland than in the remainder of Great Britain. The number of Members who became colonels of regiments also bears out this conclusion: 74 of the 152 English officers (43 per cent), and 39 of the 56 Scottish officers (69 per cent).

66 of the English, Welsh, and Irish officers served in the Foot Guards (43 per cent); only 12 of the Scots (21 per cent); and of all the Members who served as officers in the Guards 51 per cent eventually obtained regiments (the figures are no different for the Scots than for the others). It is clear, however, that in this respect the Guards were not specially favoured. A slightly higher proportion, 54 per cent, of those who did not serve in the Guards obtained regiments.

The army Members were overwhelmingly upper class. 38 per cent of the English Members and 30 per cent of the Scottish Members came from aristocratic families, and most of the remainder from old-established landed gentry. Heirs to peerages and great estates went into the army, but not into the navy, the law, or the church; and the upper ranks of the army were chockful of peers. There was a higher percentage of aristocratic Members in the army group than in any other occupational group, and only one out of these 208 Members can be described as a self-made man. This was Major-General William Phillips, M.P. for Boroughbridge 1775–80, born of humble parents, who made a distinguished career in the Royal Artillery. Through a brother officer Henry Clinton, later commander-in-chief in America during the revolutionary war, Phillips became friendly with the 2nd Duke of Newcastle, electioneered on behalf of the Duke's son at Westminster in 1774, and was returned on Newcastle's interest at Boroughbridge. He spent but a few months in the House of Commons before going on service in America, where he died in 1781.

There were only two specialized corps in the eighteenth-century army, the artillery and the engineers, and these were not officered from the classes which aspired to a seat in Parliament. Phillips is the only artillery officer known to have sat in the House during this period, but there was also one ex-artillery officer: Harry Burrard, M.P. for Lymington 1780–8, who had left the artillery for the more fashionable 60th Foot four years before he entered Parliament. The only engineer officer was Archibald Campbell, M.P. for Stirling Burghs 1774–80 and 1789–91, who became chief engineer at Bengal in the service of the East India Company and afterwards transferred to the infantry.

NAVAL OFFICERS

The navy as compared with the army was very much a professional service. Army officers received no formal training before being commissioned, and learnt their trade after having joined their regiments. But the potential naval officer underwent a rigorous training in seamanship and navigation before taking up his commission. An army officer only needed to know how to ride a horse; a naval officer had to sail a ship. Those who made the navy their career (even if they came of the most aristocratic families) went to sea as boys, generally before they were fourteen. If a boy came of a good family or had relatives with influence at the Admiralty, he could expect his lieutenant's commission by the time he was twenty. At about twenty-five he would be promoted captain;

and then would follow a long wait, of perhaps twenty years, before he achieved flag rank. Further promotion would depend upon seniority.

There were few places available for naval officers: a few semi-sinecures, such as the governorship of Greenwich or Chelsea hospitals; the senior ranks in the marines; and, at the very top, seats on the Board of Admiralty. Five naval officers (Lord Anson, Sir Charles Saunders, Sir Edward Hawke, Lord Keppel, and Lord Howe) held the post of first lord of the Admiralty during this period; and at least one, and usually two, of the junior lords were naval officers (two of them without being in Parliament). There were no appointments in the navy equivalent to those of colonelcies of regiments and governorships of forts in the army. The naval officer's most lucrative opportunities came in time of war, through the capture of enemy ships and a share in the prize money. These, though comparatively infrequent, brought expectations of gain far beyond the reach of the officer in the army.

In time of peace the naval estimates were reduced, ships were laid up, seamen were discharged, and most naval officers (those, at least, who had reached the rank of captain) went into what amounted to retirement. There were a few guard ships in harbour, but no fleet was brought together until war threatened again. Yet officers continued to be promoted according to their seniority, and when war came those who had been captains would now be admirals, and instead of commanding ships would be destined to command fleets. They emerged from retirement, rusty and ill-equipped for service, like the ships they sailed. Thus, Rear-Admiral Lord Howe, in 1775 appointed naval commander-in-chief in American waters, had not been to sea since 1763. Vice-Admiral Augustus Keppel, who had reached flag rank at the end of the seven years' war, had not been to sea for fifteen years when in 1778 he was appointed to the command of the Channel fleet and charged with the task of preventing a Franco-Spanish invasion. When Keppel struck his flag in 1779, having lost all confidence in Lord Sandwich, first lord of the Admiralty, Sir Charles Hardy, M.P. for Plymouth, was named to the command of the Channel fleet. The appointment was severely criticized by the Duke of Richmond in the House of Lords: 'Sir Charles Hardy had not been at sea for almost twenty years. He was arrived at a period of life little calculated for active service [he was sixty-five].' And Richard Kempenfelt, one of Hardy's captains, wrote about him: 'There is a fund of good nature in the man, but not one grain of the commander-in-chief . . . My God! what have your great people done by such an appointment?'

The presence of so many naval officers in the House of Commons was detrimental to the service in time of war. Service rivalries were fought out on the floor of the House, and political quarrels originating in Parliament were carried over into the fleet. Lord Sandwich, first lord of the Admiralty during the American war, had a reputation for jobbery which was not ill founded. It was felt that under him naval appointments were determined less by merit than by political considerations, and that he did not ask whether an officer could handle a fleet well but whether he voted on the right side in the House of Commons. Those who did not, such as Howe and Keppel, went to sea suspicious of Sandwich's intentions and uneasy lest he betray them behind their backs. Controversy raged high both in the navy and in Parliament when in 1779, after the indecisive battle off Ushant, Keppel, the commander-in-chief, was court-martialled at the request of his second-in-command Sir Hugh Palliser, Sandwich's leading assistant at the Admiralty Board. Since Keppel was a leading member of the Opposition and of very high standing in the navy, it was no wonder that feeling amongst naval Members was aroused. Palliser's ill-judged demand for a court-martial on his superior officer was believed to have been backed by Sandwich for political reasons, and Keppel's acquittal was hailed as a triumph by the Opposition.

The only naval officer in the House to be tried by court-martial and found guilty of misconduct on active service was Admiral John Byng, M.P. for Rochester, who was sentenced to death for negligence in the defence of Minorca and shot on the quarter-deck of the *Monarque* in Portsmouth harbour, 14 March 1757. Byng's condemnation has been represented as an attempt by Henry Fox and the Duke of Newcastle to shift from their own shoulders the blame for the loss of Minorca. There was a strong movement in the House of Commons in favour of commuting the death penalty, and a bill was introduced to allow the officers who had tried Byng to explain their reasons for condemning him. It seems probable that the failure of the bill was due to pressure exerted by the King and the Duke of Cumberland, both of whom were hostile to Byng.

A total of 79 serving naval officers sat in the House during this period, and the number entering Parliament at each general election is as follows: 16 in 1754, 22 in 1761, 19 in 1768, 16 in 1774, 14 in 1780, and 23 in 1784. These figures seem to be purely adventitious. The general election which returned the highest number of naval officers, 1784, was in peace time; but the general election of 1761, which returned 22 naval officers, only one less than the figure for 1784, was in war time, as was also the general election of 1780, which returned the lowest number of naval officers.

The ranks held by naval officers on their first entry into the House during this period are shown below (officers who sat before 1754 are not included):

Lieutenant	2
Commander	1
Captain	53
Rear-Admiral	6
Vice-Admiral	10
Admiral	4

The two naval officers who entered as lieutenants were James Luttrell (for Stockbridge in 1775) and Eliab Harvey (for Maldon in 1780). Both owed their seats to their family connexions. The four officers who entered at the rank of admiral were George Clinton, Henry Osborn, Sir William Rowley, and Isaac Townsend. Two were brought in by Government for Admiralty boroughs: Clinton at Saltash in 1754, and Townsend at Portsmouth in 1757. In all, eighteen out of these 79 officers sat for Admiralty boroughs.

The navy was much less popular in Scotland than in England: only 9 of the 79 naval officers were Scots. The aristocratic representation was high, about 25 per cent, but much less than among the army officers. But without exception all the naval officers who came from noble families were younger sons: the navy was a hard life, even for the officers, and it did not attract those who expected to inherit great estates. A good many officers came from families which had a naval tradition, and some had quite a humble origin. Samuel Cornish entered the navy as an able seaman and rose to be vice-admiral and a baronet; Robert Kingsmill, an Irishman, was the son of a captain in the army; John Macbride, another Irishman, was the son of a Presbyterian minister; and so on. Most revealing for the educational background to a naval officer's life is a letter of Admiral Thomas Pye (who came of good gentry family) to Lord Sandwich, 28 April 1773:

Give me leave my Lord to make one observation more and I have don—and that is when you peruse Admiral Pyes letters you will please not too scrutinise too

close either to the speling or the grammatical part as I allow my self to be no
proficient in either, I had the mortification to be neglected in my education,
went to sea at fourteen without any, and a man of war was my university . . .
I therefore attempt to state facts only and value myself upon nothing but my
integrity and zeal . . . ever makeing my own interest a secondary consideration,
have therefore only to brag though poor am honest.

COUNTRY GENTLEMEN

In theory every Member of the House of Commons in this period was a
country gentleman, since all had to swear to the possession of landed
property before they could take their seats in the House. In practice the
expression had both a social and a political meaning. In the list of the
newly-elected Parliament drawn up by Lord Dupplin for Newcastle after
the general election of 1754, the Members were classified according to
political and professional groups: followers of the Prince of Wales, for
instance, in the first category, and in the second, army officers, naval
officers, lawyers, placemen, &c. Those who could not be placed in one of
these groups were called country gentlemen, or, if they were in opposition
to the Government, Tories. They followed no profession, they belonged
to no party, they were independent in the sense that they brought themselves into Parliament and did not acknowledge the leadership of any
political patron.

The ownership of land did not by itself qualify for the description
of country gentleman. No one would have dreamed of calling Edmund
Burke a country gentleman, though he owned an estate in Buckinghamshire
and engaged in farming as a means of supporting his family. Burke was
obviously a politician, and one who was closely attached to a party leader.
George Augustus Selwyn, though he owned estates in the country, was too
much a man-about-town to be styled a country gentleman, and in any
case the sinecures he held would have disqualified him for the appellation.
Irish peers, such as Lord Verney or Lord Upper Ossory, sitting in
Parliament on their own interest and holding no office, had moved beyond
the country gentlemen and were half-way to the aristocracy. What, then,
did the eighteenth century mean by the term country gentleman? What
were his distinguishing characteristics, and what his peculiar role in
politics?

A country gentleman was first and foremost a landowner who was not
a member of a peerage family. Second, and just as essentially, he sat in

Parliament on his own interest, either for a county, a considerable borough, or for his own pocket borough. Since he was obliged to no one for his seat in the House, neither to the Crown nor to a political patron, it followed that he was independent in his political attachments. This was the distinguishing mark of the country gentleman: he had no personal ambitions or close political affiliations, and could approach every political problem with an independent judgement. For in theory, the House of Commons was composed of men of property (and therefore immune from pecuniary influence), neither biased in favour of the Crown nor against it, who considered every question brought before them on its merits and gave an honest vote according to the dictates of their consciences. In practice, this was a visionary state which had never existed or could possibly exist; and already by 1754 the influence of the Crown and the growth of parties had gone some way towards bringing about the situation with which we are familiar today, of a number of Members voting regularly with the Government and a number voting regularly in opposition. But there still remained throughout this period a large group of Members—roughly about 200 strong—who were uncommitted to either side, and who held the real balance of power in the House. They were the country gentleman, the floating voters of the eighteenth-century House of Commons. As a political phenomenon, they are extinct today and have been for some years.

Richard Polwhele in his *History of Cornwall*, published early in the nineteenth century, wrote about Sir William Lemon, M.P. for Penryn 1770–4 and for Cornwall 1774–1824: 'In him we justly admire the old country gentleman, faithful to his King without servility, attached to the people without democracy.' No country gentleman could have asked for a nobler epitaph, and the very term country gentleman was one to be proud of. Richard Hippisley Coxe, M.P. for Somerset 1768–84, spoke of himself in the House on 12 February 1770 as one who desired 'the character of a plain, honest country gentleman'. The phrase gave added weight to what a Member had to say. On 27 February 1784 William Hussey, M.P. for Salisbury, when urging Pitt and Fox to unite, described himself as 'one of those independent country gentlemen who had never attached themselves to any party'. His plea for union was strengthened by his standing as an independent Member, uninfluenced by considerations of political advantage.

During the debate on the Yorkshire petition for parliamentary reform,

8 May 1781, Viscount Feilding, M.P. for Bere Alston, a supporter of North's Administration, described how in recent years a new third party had emerged in the House, independent of the Government and of the Opposition.

The balance of power in that House [Feilding continued] was taken out of the hands of the minister, and placed in those of the country gentlemen ... men neither to be frowned into servility nor hussaed into faction. By the support of these men, and not as had been asserted, by the low arts of corruption, did the present minister stand.

The country gentlemen as a group were disposed to give any minister appointed by the Crown a fair trial (which partially accounts for the fact that only one Administration during this period—that of Shelburne in 1783—resigned as the result of a defeat in the House of Commons), and yet to watch Administration with a critical eye. They would not allow themselves to be used by Opposition leaders for what the country gentlemen regarded as factious ends; nor would they vote for a policy which they disapproved, out of regard for a minister. Sir Roger Newdigate, M.P. for Oxford University, in many ways the pattern of a country gentleman, wrote shortly after the accession of George III: 'I like the King and shall be with his ministers as long as I think an honest man ought, and believe it best not to lose the country gentleman in the courtier.' And though Newdigate in general supported Administration, he never hesitated to vote against them when he thought they were wrong.

This disposition to give Administration a fair trial, to put the best possible interpretation upon their conduct, helps to account for the ineffectiveness of the country gentlemen as a political group. For ineffective they were: though they held the balance of power in the House, they never became the third force Lord Feilding had described them as being in 1781. To have been a force in politics they would have needed a leader and a degree of organization—to have become in other words a political party— which was clearly impossible for independent country gentlemen. Thus by the very nature of things these Members could never be anything but an adjunct to one party or the other, able to tip the balance in critical times. Moreover, the country gentlemen were at best but amateur politicians, irregular in their attendance at the House, and few of them making much impression in debate.

Thus, on the majority of political questions the country gentlemen did not vote as a group and their votes cancelled each other out. On general warrants in 1764, on the Middlesex election in 1769, on the American war, the country gentlemen were divided, which left the advantage with the Government. They sympathized with the Opposition's programme of economical reform, which accounts for North's defeats on Burke's bill and Dunning's motion in the spring of 1780; but on the American war the majority of them supported the Government. It was only after Cornwallis's surrender at Yorktown, when North admitted in the House that the Government no longer intended to prosecute the war in America, that the country gentlemen deserted him. On 18 March 1782, Thomas Grosvenor, M.P. for Chester, one of the most upright and independent country gentlemen in Parliament and hitherto a firm supporter of the Government's American policy, told North 'in his own name and in those of some other country gentlemen',

That, being now convinced that the present Administration cannot continue any longer, they are of opinion that vain and ineffectual struggles tend only to public mischief and confusion, and that they shall think it their duty henceforward to desist from opposing what appears to be clearly the sense of the House of Commons.

The floating voters had turned against North, and his Administration was doomed.

The most important attempt of the country gentlemen to act as a group during this period was in January 1784, shortly after Pitt had taken office. A group of 78 Members met at the St. Alban's Tavern 'with a view to conciliate differences and to forward a union of the contending parties in Parliament'. All but five sat for English or Welsh constituencies, nineteen for English counties, and practically all had held themselves aloof from close party connexions. Fear of a premature dissolution of Parliament was one factor in urging them to promote a union between Pitt and Fox, but more important was the old belief that the King's Administration should be formed of the best men of all parties and that party differences were a source of weakness to the nation. Thomas Grosvenor took the chair at the first meeting, but the two leading men in the movement were Charles Marsham, M.P. for Kent, and Thomas Powys, M.P. for Northamptonshire. On 26 January 1784 the meeting passed a resolution 'to support the party who should in the present distracted moment manifest a disposition to union'. The St. Alban's Tavern group, wrote the *Morning Chronicle* on 28 January, 'assert in the finest manner the supreme importance of the landed interest. Their characters, personally speaking, will be looked up to as the political saviours of their country.'

Of course nothing came of the St. Alban's Tavern resolution. Pitt and the Duke of Portland (the titular leader of Fox's party) professed all respect and concern for the country gentlemen and promised to do all they could to promote a union of the parties. But Pitt said it must be done 'with principle and honour', and Portland said that Pitt having obtained office unconstitutionally must first resign; and so the two politicians engaged in a sparring match, neither probably having the least belief in a successful outcome to the negotiations but each manœuvring to put the other in the wrong. At this moment, the St. Alban's Tavern group, had they been united, could have turned the scale. But they were not united. When the negotiations finally broke down, 45 of the group went with Pitt and 30 with Fox. The independent country gentlemen preserved their right to vote according to their own judgement, with the result that they lost all the weight which their apparent union had given them.

John Strutt, M.P. for Maldon 1774–90, an Essex country gentleman of decided opinions and obstinate temperament, was the only Member of Parliament to oppose the vote of thanks to Admiral Keppel on 12 February 1779. The *English Chronicle*, an Opposition newspaper, commenting in 1780 on this 'singular dissent from the united voice of the British legislature', attributed it to 'the hereditary characteristics of a country squire—considerable ignorance, under the guidance and direction of strong prejudice, without any mixture of deliberate malignity whatever'. The picture here hinted at of the typical country squire, though unflattering, has some tincture of the truth about it. The country gentleman claimed to be the eighteenth-century equivalent of the ordinary 'man in the street'—without expert knowledge of the problems of government and judging them by political prejudices rather than by a political faith—yet whose co-operation and support was essential if government was to be carried on at all. And what the country gentlemen primarily demanded from government was that it should be cheap and leave them a free hand to manage local affairs themselves. 'The chief business of a Government', wrote Soame Jenyns, M.P. 1741–80, in his *Reflections on Several Subjects*, 'is to hinder those who are under its care from doing mischief to themselves.' Socially and politically conservative, the country gentleman was opposed to fundamental changes in the constitution. To be acceptable to him, reform must appear in a conservative guise. The success during this period of the movement for economical reform and the failure of that for parliamentary reform, were due to the fact that one appeared as a purification of the constitution, a return to its original state, while the other was plainly an attempt to alter the constitution. The favourite minister of the country gentlemen was one like George Grenville, careful of the nation's expenditure, prepared to reform abuses, yet opposed to fundamental changes.

Two examples conclude this survey of the country gentlemen, one sitting for a pocket borough and the other for a county. George Hunt succeeded to the Cornish estates of his uncle Henry, 3rd Earl of Radnor, and to the control of one seat at Bodmin; which he held in Parliament from 1753 to 1784, when he was succeeded by his brother. The *English Chronicle* wrote about him in 1780:

George Hunt Esq. is a gentleman of independent fortune, and resides in the neighbourhood of this borough .... He has had the honour of representing it above thirty years during which period he has never condescended to accept any favour nor to become the creature of any Administration. He is attached to no set of political tenets in particular, but following the dictates of an independent and upright mind has uniformly voted for or against such a system as he thought any way advantageous or inimical to the real interests of his country .... He can neither be said to possess the shining qualities necessary for constituting a public orator, nor the systematic solidity requisite in a great statesman, but is nevertheless eminently qualified for the important trust he holds, *viz.* the honest representative of a free people.

Hunt's parliamentary record fully bears out this character of him. In Bute's list of the Parliament elected in 1761 he was marked: 'without connexion of Government otherwise than inclination'; and though he voted steadily against North's Administration he received no office when the Opposition came to power in 1782. He attended the House regularly but is not known to have spoken, and his name hardly ever occurs in the correspondence of the party leaders.

Sir George Savile, M.P. for Yorkshire 1759–83, was one of the most respected Members to sit in the House during this period—the John Hampden of the eighteenth century. A close friend of Lord Rockingham, he refused to stand on Rockingham's interest at York or Higham Ferrers;

nor would he accept office from Rockingham in 1765 or 1782. Though he acted with the Rockinghams in politics, he never belonged to the party; and on certain questions (for example, East India affairs and parliamentary reform) he took his own line, greatly to Rockingham's embarrassment. Savile had a moral attitude towards politics, and was revolted by Fox's alliance with North in 1783. Burke, though he admired and respected Savile, was too good a party man to sympathize with Savile's independent attitude; and in November 1783 he refused to sign the letter from the Yorkshire Members requesting Savile not to vacate his seat in the House. Indeed, there was good sense behind Burke's refusal, for although Savile was almost the ideal of what the eighteenth century thought a Member of Parliament should be, had the House been composed entirely of men of his independence parliamentary government would have been almost impossible.

EAST INDIANS

In 1754 the East India Company was a business organization trading to India and China, and enjoying monopoly rights under a charter from the Crown. By 1790, in addition to its commercial interests, it had acquired sovereignty over a large part of India, which it exercised under the direction of the British Government. The story of how this change was brought about does not belong to this survey, but many of the men who helped to shape the destiny of India during these years sat in the House of Commons and the affairs of the Company became increasingly the concern of Parliament. As a political problem India ranked second only to America. Clive's victories, in alliance with native rulers, against the French during the seven years' war ensured that Britain would be the dominant European power in India; and his assumption of the financial administration of Bengal in 1764 gave the Company its first territorial responsibilities. The boom in East India stock which followed and the reports of maladministration in India, led to a parliamentary inquiry in the winter of 1766–7 and the Government's first intervention in the Company's affairs: for a limited period the Company was forbidden to increase its dividend and compelled to pay an annual sum to the state. This agreement was reached after acute political controversy both within the Company and in the House of Commons; and controversy broke out afresh when, following the collapse of East India stock in 1772, Lord

North's Administration drew up a new plan for the government of Bengal. Henceforth the Company would administer its territories on lines laid down by the state.

In the later part of the period there were many points of controversy in the Indian problem. There was the straightforward clash between the Government, compelled to assume some of the responsibility for India, and the Whig Opposition, concerned to prevent any increase in the influence and authority of the Crown. There were disagreements between the Company's servants in India (the cases of Warren Hastings and Lord Pigot are obvious examples), which led to the formation of factions at East India House and to attempts to find support in the House of Commons. Officials in India took sides in disputes between Indian native rulers, and the repercussions of these disputes were felt in the House and influenced the policy of both the Government and the Opposition. Men went out to India to make their fortunes and returned intent on a seat in Parliament, either as a symbol of their newly-acquired wealth or as a safeguard against official inquiries into their conduct. So many men with so many different purposes makes it impossible in this period to talk of an East India interest as if it were a pressure group with a clearly defined aim.

Members connected with the East India Company can be roughly classified into five groups. First, the directors of the Company, generally big London merchants and bankers, interested in it from a commercial and financial point of view, and who did not go out to India. Next, former members of the East India Company's naval service and officers of the Royal Navy who had served in Indian waters; then, officers of the Bengal army, together with regular army officers who had served in India. The fourth group comprises Members who had been in the Company's civil service in India; and the fifth group, Members who held large amounts of stock and whose interest in the Company was usually purely financial. These groups overlap a good deal: the Company's civil and military services, for example, were not exclusive; and Company servants returning from India sought and obtained seats on the board of directors.

At the general election of 1754 only two Company directors were returned to Parliament: Henry Crabb Boulton, who had been a Company official for nearly thirty years and was now interested in East India shipping; and Robert Jones, a London merchant. There were three former directors: Sir William Baker, Zachary Philip Fonnereau, and Thomas Walpole, all London merchants; and at least two Members, both large proprietors of stock, who were shortly to join the direction: George Amyand and Sir George Colebrooke. The only two Members returned in 1754 who had been to India were Robert Clive, elected for Mitchell, but unseated on petition the following year, and Gabriel Hanger, who had been a factor in the Company's service in India, had resigned in 1725 on succeeding to the family estates and had taken no further part in the Company's affairs.

At the general election of 1761 three directors were returned: George Amyand, Henry Crabb Boulton, and Robert Jones; and four Members who were shortly to become directors: Sir George Colebrooke, Peregrine Cust, George Dempster, and John Stephenson. Clive himself, now a very rich man, was returned for Shrewsbury; and during this period began to build up a following in the House composed of men whose fortunes he had helped to make. John Walsh, his henchman in India and a cousin of Lady Clive, was elected for Worcester at the general election; and in 1763 George Clive, Robert Clive's cousin, who had been with him in India, was elected for Bishop's Castle, shortly to become a Clive borough. Three other men who had been in India (or 'nabobs', as the eighteenth century called them) entered the House during this Parliament: Robert Palk, governor of Madras 1763–1767, elected for Ashburton in December 1767; Sir George Pigot, Palk's predecessor at Madras, for Wallingford in January 1765; and Laurence Sulivan, who was to head the opposition to Clive at East India House and for the next twenty years to be one of the leading men in the Company. There were also a number of Members during this Parliament who were, or were shortly to become, large proprietors of East India stock: William Burke, Sir Matthew Fetherstonhaugh, Alexander Hume, William Hussey, Sir Edward Turner, Lord Verney, Thomas Walpole, to name only the most considerable. When Company affairs came before Parliament in 1766 there was a nucleus of Members who in different ways and for different purposes had an interest in the Company; and Chatham's inquiry, though it did little to determine Government policy, gave the House an insight into the Company's problems and helped to create parliamentary opinion on India.

The Parliament of 1768 saw a significant increase in the number of East Indians in the House. Thirteen directors of the Company sat in this

Parliament, including seven who had been in India; while a further twelve Members, former military or civil servants of the Company, had also been in India. How did these men get into the House, and what type of constituency did they represent?

Twelve of these nineteen nabobs first entered the House during the Parliament of 1761, only four of them for constituencies with which their families had long been connected: Henry Fletcher for Cumberland (the only nabob before 1784 to sit for an English county), William Frankland for Thirsk, Hector Munro for Inverness Burghs, and Henry Vansittart for Reading. Robert Gregory had been recommended by Lord Rockingham to Lord Aylesford and sat on Aylesford's interest at Maidstone; and Eyre Coote fought a hard contest at Leicester, where he was a stranger, on a joint interest with the brother of Lord Stamford, a leading Leicestershire magnate. The remaining nabobs came in for venal boroughs, and their intrusion into this type of constituency is an interesting social and political phenomenon.

In November 1770 there was a by-election at New Shoreham, a venal borough which put itself up for sale to the highest bidder. All three candidates were nabobs: William James and John Purling were former naval commanders in the Company's service and now directors, and Thomas Rumbold had been a member of the council of Bengal. Richard Smith, who had recently retired from the Bengal army, was also a candidate for a time, but his offer of £3,000 for the seat was considered by the group which ran the borough to be too low, and Smith withdrew from the contest. Purling was returned but unseated on petition in favour of Rumbold, but the scandal attending this election was so great that the House of Commons instituted an inquiry. As a result New Shoreham was reformed by extending its franchise to include the neighbouring freeholders, which effectively barred the nabobs for the future.

Cricklade, the second borough to be reformed during this period, also suffered from the attentions of the nabobs. Sir Robert Fletcher, a contumacious officer of the Bengal army who had been cashiered by Clive in 1766, was the first East Indian to be returned for Cricklade (in 1768). At the general election of 1780 Paul Benfield and John Macpherson, both of whom had been concerned in the deposition of Lord Pigot, governor of Madras, and to whom a seat in Parliament was a matter of urgency, secured their election for Cricklade by bribery so flagrant and notorious that the House of Commons intervened and reformed the borough on the lines of New Shoreham. Hindon, another venal Wiltshire borough, narrowly escaped reformation in 1775 after Richard Smith, the nabob who had tried for a seat at New Shoreham in 1770, had been convicted of bribery: Smith lost his seat and suffered a term of imprisonment, but the bill to reform Hindon was dropped. Hindon was saved because there were two old-established interests in the borough, although both were somewhat in eclipse. At this stage, until about 1774, the nabobs generally sought out boroughs which were amenable to the influence of money; they had not as yet threatened any well-nurtured interest based on the ownership of property.

Before 1774 other boroughs in which the nabobs tried to establish a permanent influence were Shaftesbury and Worcester. Both were expensive and difficult constituencies, and though each had patrons the patrons had no strong hold on their boroughs. Francis Sykes, a close friend of Clive, was first returned for Shaftesbury in 1771 on the interest of Lord Shaftesbury, who together with Lord Ilchester had hitherto controlled the borough. Sykes then built up his own interest, secured control of the corporation, and in 1774 stood jointly with the nabob who had been seated for New Shoreham in 1770, Thomas Rumbold, against Hans Winthrop Mortimer. Lords Ilchester and Shaftesbury now began to find the borough too hot for them (it had never been easy to control, but with the nabobs in the field it had become more uncertain than ever); and a tremendous struggle developed between Sykes and Mortimer. Finally Sykes, after having been convicted for bribery and fined £11,000, sold his property at Shaftesbury to Paul Benfield, while Mortimer ended his days a prisoner for debt.

Worcester, a large freeman borough with an electorate of about 2,000, had from the beginning of this period a strong East Indian element in its representation. Henry Crabb Boulton, director of the East India Company, whose family seems to have had a Worcestershire origin, sat for Worcester 1754–73; and John Walsh, Clive's henchman, 1761–1780. The border country between England and Wales was pre-eminently Clive's territory, which may account for Walsh's introduction to Worcester and also for that of another nabob, Thomas Bates Rous, on the death of Boulton. Rous was a former officer in the Company's naval service and a director of the Company, and stood professedly on Clive's interest. He was successful in 1773, was unseated on petition for bribery the following year, and regained the seat at the general election of 1774. Worcester politics were dominated by the conflict between the corporation and the independent party, and the nabobs made common cause with the corporation; but it was also a venal borough, which must have favoured the nabobs against the local gentry.

In the last three Parliaments of this period the number of East Indians in the House increased, as is shown by the following table (the figures include those returned at by-elections as well as the general election but do not include army and naval officers not in the service of the East India Company who visited India in the course of their duty):

Parliament	Directors who had not been in India	Directors who had been in India	Nabobs	Total
1774–1780	4	5	17	26
1780–1784	4	5	22	31
1784–1790	9	3	33	45

Even these figures fall short of the actual number of Members who were directly concerned with East India affairs, for leading proprietors are not included nor politicians such as Edmund Burke and Henry Dundas who were particularly interested in the Indian problem. But they are sufficient to show that the House which passed Pitt's India Act and which voted the impeachment of Warren Hastings had a much higher percentage of Members with experience of the problems of India than the House which first inquired into the state of the Company in 1766.

From 1768 to 1784 more directors who had seen service in India were returned to Parliament than those who had not. In the Parliament of 1784 there is an important change, and the number of directors who had not been in India far exceeds those who had. Old India hands, such as Henry Fletcher, Robert Gregory, John Purling, and Thomas Rumbold, drop out of the direction, and the leading men in the East India Company after 1784 more closely resemble the prominent London merchants who had composed the majority of the direction before 1768. But there is a difference: the men of 1784 were far more aware of their responsibilities, both commercial and political, and were of a more sober cast of mind. They included Francis Baring, head of the great house of Baring Brothers, a recognized authority on trade and finance; Samuel Smith, of the firm of Nottingham bankers; and John Thornton, leading Evangelical, friend of Wilberforce, and disciple of Adam Smith. Gone were the days when the chairman of the East India Company would conceal from the shareholders the real state of its affairs in order to job the stock, as Sir George Colebrooke had done in the crisis of 1772.

Until about 1774 the chief reasons for the nabobs' entering the House seem to have been social. They were mostly self-made men, who without performing Clive's services had emulated him in one particular and returned from 'India's plundered land' with sizeable fortunes, intent on enjoying the prestige and social standing their wealth would give them. A seat in Parliament, like an estate in the country, was a symbol of success. They more or less followed the prototype of Clive, who hoped to make a great figure in Parliament and to achieve a British peerage. (Some nabobs obtained baronetcies, but Clive and Pigot alone secured peerages—Irish peerages.) They gravitated towards the venal boroughs: it required time and patience to build up a parliamentary interest in a non-venal borough, and the nabobs had plenty of money and were in a hurry. Few of them reached the front rank in the House: even Clive, though he acquired a parliamentary following of about a dozen Members, played a defensive role in Parliament, concerned mainly to defend his reputation and his Indian wealth.

In the second half of the period the nabobs began to intervene in the non-venal boroughs and attempted to oust old-established interests or to revive with new wealth and energy the dormant influence of their own families. James Amyatt, who had been in the Company's naval service and subsequently a free merchant in India, came of a family long prominent at Totnes and was returned there at the general election of 1774. John Call, of a Cornish family, after thinking of buying Humphry Morice's interest at Launceston and Newport, finally settled on Callington, near his estate, and in 1784 wrested one seat from the Orford interest. Robert Palk bought burgages at Ashburton and secured control over one seat; Sir George Pigot settled in Staffordshire and cultivated the neighbouring borough of Bridgnorth; and George Vansittart successfully contested Berkshire in 1784, which his father had represented 1757–74. Richard Barwell, Hastings's ally on the supreme council of Bengal, on his return home had to depend on the Treasury for a seat in Parliament; but in 1790 he went into the electoral market and purchased the boroughs of Winchelsea and Tregony.

One method of making a fortune in India was by lending money to native princes on the security of their territorial revenues. This resulted in Englishmen becoming involved in Indian quarrels, and the disputes and feuds arising therefrom being taken to the House of Commons. The dispute between the Nawab of Arcot and the Raja of Tanjore bedevilled East India Company politics during the latter part of this period and even affected party divisions in Parliament, for as Lord Pigot and William Burke were supporters of the Raja, their friends in the Opposition felt bound to espouse his cause. In 1775 Pigot, M.P. for Bridgnorth, finally obtained the governorship of Madras, which he had been soliciting for years. In India he took the part of the Raja against the Nawab, and in 1777 was deposed from his governorship by a majority of his council, who were creditors of the Nawab and who stood to lose financially by Pigot's action.

The leader of the group who opposed Pigot, George Stratton, was recalled to England and immediately sought a seat in Parliament. He found a powerful patron in Lord Sandwich, first lord of the Admiralty, and in December 1778, at Sandwich's recommendation, was returned on the Orford interest at Callington. Stratton's main reason for being in Parliament was to try and prevent an inquiry into his conduct in India, and his only two speeches in the House were in reply to attacks made against him. But Stratton's membership of the Commons did not save him from punishment, and in February 1780, he was tried in the King's bench and fined £1,000. In October 1782, when Stratton was reported to be selling his estate in Oxfordshire and about to go abroad, John Call expected him to vacate his seat in the House 'since the object of his being in Parliament is partly if not wholly at an end'. But in fact Stratton remained a Member of Parliament until the dissolution of 1784.

Another creditor of the Nawab of Arcot, deeply implicated in the conspiracy against Lord Pigot, was the notorious Paul Benfield, who had made a fortune by moneylending and had twice been dismissed the service of the East India Company for disobedience. After an inquiry into the events in Madras, Benfield was again suspended and ordered home; and in 1780 he began his campaign for reinstatement by bribing the electors of Cricklade to return him to Parliament. Naturally he voted with Administration, and so successfully did he win their favour that in October 1781 he was reinstated in the Company's service and returned to India. Lord Cornwallis, appointed governor-general of Bengal in 1786, found much to censure in Benfield's conduct; and in 1789 Benfield was again back in England and a candidate for a seat in Parliament—which he obtained in February 1790 at Malmesbury.

For Indian governors a charge of maladministration was an occupational hazard; they sought seats in the House of Commons to defend
themselves. Thomas Rumbold, who had succeeded the unfortunate Pigot
as governor of Madras, at the height of the American conflict involved
the East India Company in war with the powerful native ruler Hyder Ali.
On his return to England in January 1781 he faced a storm of criticism
and the demand for a parliamentary inquiry, so in April he bought a
seat in the Isle of Wight borough of Yarmouth. The committee which
investigated the causes of the war in the Carnatic recommended his
prosecution, and a bill of pains and penalties against him was introduced.
But the difficulties of obtaining evidence for such a prosecution were
immense and the case was eventually dropped. The story that Rumbold
bribed Henry Dundas, the chairman of the parliamentary committee,
obviously cannot be proved and perhaps ought not to be taken seriously;
but there were other ways in which Rumbold could soften the hearts
of his prosecutors. 'If a judgment were to be formed from yesterday',
wrote Charles James Fox to the King on 10 May 1782, 'it must be that
there was real tenderness for the person accused, which if it be the
real temper of the House at large must make it impossible to carry on
the prosecution with effect.' A seat in Parliament was of inestimable
advantage to Rumbold in that it gave him the opportunity to state
his case himself; perhaps unconsciously, the House was loth to entertain
accusations brought against one of its own Members unless there was
overwhelming evidence.

Indeed, it may even be doubted whether Warren Hastings would ever
have been impeached had he been a Member of the House of Commons.
Certainly Hastings realized the importance of a seat in the House, in
view of the accusations likely to be brought against him, if not for
himself at least for a friend who would speak for him. At the general
election of 1784 he bought for £4,000 a seat at West Looe for his
former aide-de-camp John Scott, and throughout the Parliament Scott's
role was that of Hastings's defender. But he greatly over-played his
part, so much so that the House grew weary of his long speeches and
his excessive zeal in defence of his master; and it might almost be said
that Hastings was impeached because he picked the wrong man to defend
him in the House of Commons. Philip Francis, Hastings's great adversary
in the Bengal council, also obtained a seat at the general election of
1784, with a view to gratifying his animosity against his old enemy.

But just as Scott was too much the professional advocate for Hastings, so Francis was too much the *advocatus diaboli*; and though the House voted Hastings's impeachment it refused to name Francis one of the managers. James Adams, M.P. for West Looe, was voicing the opinion of many when he said on 11 December 1787: 'It was not becoming the honour and dignity of their proceedings for that House to appoint for one of their managers . . . the only one of its Members who had . . . had a personal quarrel with Mr. Hastings.' At all times the House of Commons had a strong sense of justice and fair dealing to an accused.

One other group of East Indians deserves special mention: those who acted as agents in Britain for Indian princes. In 1775 Lauchlin Macleane, M.P. for Arundel 1768–71, who had ruined himself (and a good many others) in East India speculations, and had been sent out to India to try and retrieve his and his creditors' fortunes, became agent in England for the Nawab of Arcot; and in 1778 William Burke, Edmund Burke's friend and self-styled cousin, who had also been involved in East India speculations, became agent for the Raja of Tanjore. Thus both these Indian princes, at odds with each other, had their agents to press their case with the East India Company and the British Government. On Macleane's death in 1777 he was succeeded as the Nawab's agent by John Macpherson, who had been involved in the intrigue which resulted in the deposition of Lord Pigot. Macpherson also undertook to act as agent for Warren Hastings, and on his return to England in 1779 purchased a seat at Cricklade in order to promote the interests of his two masters. Since Lord Rockingham's party supported Pigot and the Raja of Tanjore, Macpherson naturally cultivated the North Administration and in 1781 succeeded in getting himself appointed to the Bengal council.

There were also in the House two of the Nawab's principal creditors. Richard Smith, whose début at New Shoreham and imprisonment for bribery at Hindon have already been mentioned, was one. At the general election of 1780 he bought two seats at Wendover from Lord Verney, one for himself and the other for his son. In the House Smith attached himself to the Rockingham party, and in 1781 was chairman of the Opposition-controlled select committee on East India affairs. The other of the Nawab's creditors was Sir Samuel Hannay, M.P. for Camelford 1784–90, a London merchant with large East India shipping interests and closely associated with John Macpherson.

Much has been made, and rightly, of the extortion and corruption which marked Company rule in India. It was difficult for the Company to control their servants, and an official dismissed for misconduct, as was John Johnstone in 1763, could make a party matter of it at East India House and secure his reinstatement by a vote of the court of proprietors. 'Few fortunes acquired in the East will bear a very minute investigation', wrote George Dempster in 1778; but the remedy for misconduct and corruption in India—strengthening the powers of the governor-general in Bengal and making him responsible to the Government in London—was adopted in 1784.

WEST INDIANS AND NORTH AMERICANS

Economically, the West Indies were the most valued part of the British empire in the eighteenth century. Sugar, cultivated at low cost by slave labour and marketed in Europe, was a great source of wealth; and the provisioning of the islands with slaves and almost every necessity of life, an important branch of British commerce. Many of the West Indian planters, including some of the biggest, were absentee landlords, at least for a large part of their lives. They left their estates in the hands of managers, content if their revenues did not decrease, and lived as country gentlemen in Britain. Even if they resided in the islands, they invariably sent their children to be educated in Britain. They formed no attachments with the West Indies which could not be broken. Britain was not to them the mother country, as it was to the North Americans; it was their home, and if business forced them to return to the islands they did so unwillingly. For these reasons it is to be expected that the number of West Indians sitting in the British Parliament will be higher than the number of North Americans.

In calculating the number of West Indians in the House a distinction must be drawn between those who were born in the islands or had resided there, and those who owned large plantations in the islands but never visited them. The Lascelles family of Harewood, Yorkshire, ancestors of the Earls of Harewood, owned large estates in Barbados, and had an interest in the firm of Lascelles and Maxwell, sugar factors, of Mark Lane, London. Three members of the family sat in the House during this period: Edwin Lascelles, his brother Daniel, and his cousin and eventual heir Edward. In addition to controlling one seat at

Northallerton, Edwin Lascelles was of sufficient standing to represent Yorkshire for nearly twenty years. Neither he nor his kinsmen seem ever to have visited the West Indies or to have been more than sleeping partners in the family business. They were country gentlemen, ambitious of the honours of the peerage, and their West Indian estates were merely one of the sources of their wealth. To take another example: William Fitzherbert, the friend of Dr. Johnson, prided himself on being an independent country gentleman, though he admitted in the House that he depended 'in a great measure' on the income from his plantations in Barbados. These men were much concerned when West Indian affairs came into the House of Commons, as were many others whose stake in the islands was by no means as great, but socially they do not form part of the group known as the West Indians.

That group was never as large as contemporaries seem to have imagined. On an average there were never more than about a dozen West Indians in the House at any time, as the following table shows:

Parliament	West Indians returned at general election	West Indians returned at by-elections	Total
1754–1761	13	2	15
1761–1768	11	0	11
1768–1774	7	6	13
1774–1780	8	6	14
1780–1784	13	0	13
1784–1790	8	1	9

The most considerable West Indian proprietor to be returned at the general election of 1754 was William Beckford, alderman of London, twice lord major, and from 1754 until his death in 1770 one of its representatives in Parliament. Beckford owned large estates in Jamaica and is sometimes described by contemporaries as a West Indian merchant, but he seems to have been no more than a planter: he was representative of the popular party in the City of London, not of its business community. He owned an estate in Wiltshire and cultivated a parliamentary interest at Salisbury, where his brother Julines Beckford was returned in 1754. Another brother, Richard Beckford, was invited to contest Bristol by the local Tories. He was absent in Jamaica at the time of the election, and William Beckford successfully conducted his campaign.

A certain group arrangement is to be found among the West Indians sitting in the House, based on family ties and connexions with particular boroughs. One such group connected the families of Dawkins, Morant, and Pennant, all of whom had estates in Jamaica, and involved the boroughs of Hindon, Chippenham, and Southampton. James Dawkins was returned for Hindon in 1754 on the interest of William Beckford; his brother, Henry Dawkins, came in at a by-election for Southampton in 1760, succeeding another Jamaican, Anthony Langley Swymmer. Henry Dawkins bought an estate in Wiltshire, and in 1768 he contested Salisbury, which Julines Beckford, another West Indian, had represented 1754–64; defeated at Salisbury, Dawkins next tried Chippenham, and built up such an interest in the borough that in 1784 he was able to retire in favour of his son. Dawkins had two cousins in the House: Edward Morant, a former member of the Jamaica assembly, who was first returned for Parliament in 1761 on the Beckford interest at Hindon; and Richard Pennant, son of a Liverpool merchant and grandson of a chief justice of Jamaica, who was returned in 1761 for Petersfield, where William Jolliffe, the patron of the borough, had placed one seat at the disposal of William Beckford.

The relationship between these West Indian families was social rather than political. The three West Indians who owed their entry into the House to Beckford did not follow him in politics, and once in Parliament began to cultivate separate and independent electoral interests. James Dawkins was an active Jacobite before he entered Parliament, and his brother Henry was an independent with no close political connexions. Edward Morant became a friend of the Duke of Bolton, whom he followed politically and upon whom he depended for a seat in the House. Richard Pennant became connected with Sir William Meredith, M.P. for Liverpool and a leading member of the Rockingham group; with Meredith's support, he successfully contested Liverpool in 1767, and, joining the Rockinghams in the House of Commons, remained faithful to them even after Meredith had left them.

The West Indians, in fact, did not form a separate and distinguishable group in the House of Commons: they were part of English society, both politically and socially. Mostly rich men, they could afford to take an independent line in politics; and, unlike the East Indians, they kept clear of the venal boroughs and preferred to cultivate constituencies near their estates, using the traditional means. When questions came into the

House of Commons affecting the economic interests of the West Indies, there was a tendency for the West Indian Members to act together, and they would be joined by other Members with West Indian interests. In 1788, when the slave trade was debated by the House, it is not surprising to find Richard Pennant and Bamber Gascoyne junior speaking against abolition, one a West Indian proprietor and both Members for Liverpool, one of the principal centres of the trade in England.

George Grenville's Stamp Act concerned the West Indies as much as it did the mainland colonies, but it was from those Members interested in North America that the opposition to the stamp tax came in the House of Commons. On the division on the repeal of the Stamp Act, 22 February 1766, three of the ten West Indians in the House are known to have voted against the repeal (no list survives of those who voted for the repeal). Two of these Members were politically connected with Grenville (William Mathew Burt and James Edward Colleton) and the third (Samuel Martin) was a follower of Bute: all three voted according to their party inclinations, irrespective of their interests as West Indian proprietors. Those who are known to have voted for the repeal include Rose Fuller, at this time politically connected with Newcastle and Rockingham and a leader of the movement for repeal; William Beckford, an ally of Pitt, who had opposed the Stamp Act and denied the right of Great Britain to tax the colonies; and Charles Barrow, a close friend of William Dowdeswell, chancellor of the Exchequer. On this question, of special concern to the West Indians but also of general constitutional significance, the West Indians divided according to their particular allegiances and connexions, exactly as did other Members of Parliament.

In December 1775, after fighting had broken out in America, Lord North introduced a bill prohibiting trade with the colonies in rebellion. Nathaniel Bayly, M.P. for Westbury, a Jamaica planter, denounced the measure as ruinous to the West Indies:

He was well informed, nay he was fully convinced, that the inhabitants of those islands must be starved; and though they should not, their crops must be left, as they had not nearly lumber enough to save the present; that such being the case, the proprietors must be ruined, and the consequences would in the end reach the merchants, so as, he feared, to bring on a general bankruptcy among those in any manner concerned or interested in the West India trade.

Bayly was answered by John St. Leger Douglas, M.P. for Hindon, who 'though he had a considerable estate in the West Indies' yet thought the bill 'a wise and salutary measure'—'It was better to suffer temporary inconveniences than sacrifice the British empire in America to the local interests of any of its constituent parts.' But the majority of West Indians in Parliament opposed the Government on the American war: of those who sat in the Parliament of 1774–80, eight voted regularly with the Opposition and only four with the Government, while the attitude of two others is doubtful. Still, none of those who had been in Parliament before war broke out changed their political attitude when war came. The West Indian interest was primarily an economic, not a political, one.

The British reply to the American slogan of 'no taxation without representation' was the theory of virtual representation and the idea (held by Government and Opposition alike) that there was no part of the British dominions which was not under the authority of Parliament. The suggestion that America should be allowed to send Members to the House of Commons never reached the realm of practical politics. There were not merely the difficulties resulting from slow communications and a separation of three thousand miles, but political and psychological objections of even greater weight: the Americans regarded Great Britain as their mother country but not as their homeland, and accepted the authority of the House of Commons in the abstract rather than in the concrete. Over thirty men, born and nurtured in the West Indies, gained seats in the House of Commons during these years, but only four, or possibly five, from North America. These were Daniel Moore, John Huske, Henry Cruger, and Staats Long Morris; while Barlow Trecothick, though he spent a good part of his life in America and is sometimes described in contemporary correspondence as an American, was probably born in England or at sea.

Daniel Moore, who represented Great Marlow 1754–1761, was the son of John Moore, attorney-general of Pennsylvania, and settled as a merchant in Barbados. Little is known about him, and he was not prominent during the short time he sat in the House of Commons. John Huske, M.P. for Maldon 1763–73, who came from New Hampshire, was a far more prominent figure, though of very doubtful reputation. He came over to England about 1748 and attached himself to the family of Lord Townshend. An energetic and ruthless man, Huske contested the populous borough of Maldon in 1763, and after a storming campaign gained a runaway victory. In the House he was a frequent speaker on American problems, and though popularly credited in America with being a supporter of the Stamp Act, seems in fact to have opposed it. He certainly voted for its repeal in 1766. In 1767 he was consulted by his friend Charles Townshend, chancellor of the Exchequer, on the duties to be laid on the American trade; and though the exact part Huske played cannot be traced, it is clear that he, an American, did not object to the principle of the Townshend duties. After an absence of twenty years from America, he was hardly able to appreciate the strength and degree of opposition to parliamentary taxation in his native land, yet Huske responded to that feeling once it had materialized. In December 1768 he presented to the House the petition from the Pennsylvania assembly against being taxed by the British Parliament, and urged the House to accept it. And he collaborated with the colonial agents on American affairs, until in 1769 he was compelled to flee to France to escape prosecution for deficiencies in his accounts as deputy treasurer of the chamber. He died there in 1773.

Henry Cruger, born in New York of a merchant family long prominent in provincial politics, illustrates in his career the tragedy of the American revolution. Cruger came to England in about 1757, settled as a merchant in Bristol, married the daughter of a Bristol merchant, and engaged as a radical in local politics. In 1766 he was one of the deputation of Bristol merchants who came to London to press for the repeal of the Stamp Act, and in 1774, after a visit to America, was elected for Bristol together with Edmund Burke. Cruger sympathized with American grievances, thought the policy of the British Government unwise and even unjust, but was not prepared to deny that Great Britain had a case or that the Americans had not been provoking. His theory of empire was similar to that of his colleague Burke (with whom, incidentally, Cruger was on bad terms). Cruger said in his first speech in the House, 16 December 1774:

I acknowledge that there must exist a power somewhere to superintend and regulate the movements of the whole for the attainment and preservation of our common happiness; this supreme power can be justly and adequately exercised only by the legislature of Great Britain.

And his approach to the problem of taxation was that of a practical man, concerned with consequences rather than abstract principles:

When Great Britain derives from her colonies the most ample supplies of wealth by her commerce, is it not absurd to close up those channels for the sake of imposing taxes, which ... never have and probably never will defray the expense of collecting them?

He held on as long as he could to the belief that the Americans could be persuaded by concessions from Great Britain to revoke the Declaration of Independence, and when that illusion was shattered urged that Britain should treat with America as an independent state. Defeated at Bristol at the general election of 1780, Cruger returned to America for a visit after the conclusion of peace and was elected *in absentia* for Bristol in 1784. In March 1790, while still a Member of the British Parliament, he went to live in America permanently, in 1792 was elected to the senate of New York, and died at New York in 1827.

Staats Long Morris, the fourth American to sit in the House during this period, was a different type of man altogether. Like Cruger he was a New Yorker, a half-brother of Gouverneur Morris, the revolutionary leader; but unlike Cruger, having settled in Britain, he identified himself completely with his adopted country. An army officer, he came over to England in 1755 with despatches, and had the good fortune to captivate the dowager Duchess of Gordon, more than ten years his senior, whom he married in 1756. She promoted his career in the British army, and in 1774 had him brought into Parliament on the Gordon interest for Elgin Burghs. Morris was a careerist pure and simple, and in Parliament was a steady supporter of North's American policy. His only speech in the House, on 7 December 1775, was to defend the conduct of the British troops at the battle of Bunker Hill.

Barlow Trecothick, M.P. for London 1768–74, spent his youth and early manhood in America, settled in London as a merchant in about 1750, and in 1766 became colonial agent for the New Hampshire assembly. In 1766 he gave evidence before the House of Commons in favour of the repeal of the Stamp Act, and after he had entered Parliament attached himself to the Rockingham party and took a pro-American line. Paul Wentworth, who represented Saltash for a few weeks in 1780, belonged to the Wentworth family of New Hampshire, but it is uncertain whether or not he was born in America. He spent most of the American war as a British intelligence agent in Paris, highly esteemed by Lord North; and his seat at Saltash was part of the Government's reward for his services. There were also three other Members who had lived for a long time in North America: Charles Ogilvie, M.P. for West Looe 1774–5, a Scot who emigrated to South Carolina after the '45 and lost his property there during the revolution; Richard Penn, M.P. for Appleby 1784–90, one of the proprietors of Pennsylvania, who in 1775 presented the petition from the Continental Congress to the King; and Denys Rolle, M.P. for Barnstaple 1761–74, who went to found a settlement in East Florida.

This survey has taken no account of the numerous army and navy officers who visited America in the course of their service, or of those who went as colonial governors. It is difficult to summarize the impressions they brought back of America or to estimate for how much these counted in determining their conduct in the House of Commons. Naturally, they saw the American problem from the British point of view; and even with those who were sympathetic to America, British party connexions and attitudes counted for more than a sober appreciation of American realities. Isaac Barré, Lord Shelburne's chief follower in the House of Commons, who had served under Wolfe during the seven years' war, spoke out on behalf of the Americans during the debate on Grenville's stamp tax, 6 February 1765. 'There are gentlemen in this House from the West Indies', Barré said, 'but there are very few who know the circumstances of North America'; and he continued, with reference to the proposed tax: 'The people, I believe, are as truly loyal as any subjects the King has, but a people jealous of their liberties and who will vindicate them if ever they should be violated.' Barré was recognized in America as a good friend to the colonies, but even he came out in favour of the Boston port bill. 'Now is your time to try in a civilized manner your power over the Americans', he said in the debate of 14 March 1774; but at the same time he asked for a conciliatory gesture towards the colonies, and pressed for the repeal of the duty on tea.

Army officers who had seen service in America had a low opinion of the fighting qualities of the Americans. This was partly the professional soldier's disdain for the volunteer, but it also reflected an inability to comprehend the spiritual strength of the American cause, which was not confined to the professional soldiers. James Grant, M.P. for Tain Burghs, who had served in America during the seven years' war and afterwards had been governor of East Florida, boasted in the House on 2 February 1775 that with 5,000 regulars he could march from one end of America to the other. Even Barré thought little of American troops. 'If it is necessary', he said on 23 March 1774, 'I have no doubt but that a small part of our force would reduce the Americans.' Grant, after having fought against the Americans in the war of independence, recanted his contemptuous views—'He never saw better troops than some of the rebel regiments were', he said in the House on 8 December 1779. Understanding came too late. Hence the constant British under-valuation during the war of the authority of Congress and the undue reliance on the strength of the Loyalists, which made it impossible for the British Government to devise a military strategy or political policy comfortable to reality.

What emerges most clearly of all from a study of the parliamentary debates on America is the extent of Parliament's ignorance of the people over whom it claimed to exercise supreme authority. The North Americans who sat in the House were too few to present the American case effectively, and their long residence in Britain had isolated them to some extent from American opinion. The service officers and colonial governors who had been in America saw matters from the point of view of British authority, and the merchants trading with America were concerned mainly for their trade. The only men who could speak authoritatively for the Americans were the colonial agents, and they did not carry sufficient weight to impress the British Government and Parliament.

Nine colonial agents sat in the House of Commons during this period. John Sharpe and Lovell Stanhope were agents for West Indian islands, and Brook Watson for New Brunswick 1786–93; the remainder were agents for North American mainland colonies. James Abercromby by the time he entered Parliament in 1761 had relinquished all of his agencies except that for the council and governor of Virginia. The following five Members held agencies during the period when the American problem was dominant: Edmund Burke, for the New York assembly 1771–5; Charles Garth, for the South Carolina assembly 1762–75, and for the Maryland assembly 1766–75; John Sargent, special agent for the New York assembly 1765–6; John Thomlinson and Barlow Trecothick, joint agents for the New Hampshire assembly, Thomlinson 1763–7, Trecothick 1766–74.

The main work of the colonial agents was to represent the views of the provincial assemblies to the British Government and its departments. Charles Garth described himself to the South Carolina assembly as the 'minister of the province' in Britain—a kind of eighteenth-century high commissioner. But to whom was Garth responsible for his conduct in Parliament: to the South Carolina assembly or to the electors of Devizes, the borough he represented? That was a question to which there was no clear-cut answer, and posed a dilemma which each agent solved according to his convictions. Garth, for example, voted against the Stamp Act on 6 February 1765, and on almost every issue of American policy during the next few years his vote was given in accordance with the wishes of the assembly of South Carolina. But when in 1774, after the Boston tea party, North introduced punitive legislation against the colonies, Garth voted with Administration and continued to do so until he left Parliament in 1780. At the critical moment, he supported the authority of Great Britain against his American 'constituents'.

John Sargent, a close friend of Benjamin Franklin, though thanked by the New York assembly for his services over the repeal of the Stamp Act, counted himself a follower of George Grenville, the author of the Stamp Act. And Edmund Burke, who worked hard and loyally on behalf of the New York assembly, spoke on American affairs in the House as a member of the Rockingham party not as a representative of New York. Indeed, it could hardly be otherwise. The Member of Parliament who acted as a colonial agent could perform many services for his American 'constituents', but at the height of the dispute between Great Britain and the colonies he could not speak for the American people. There were in the British House of Commons men who knew America and loved her people, representatives of her assemblies and even men born and educated in America, but there were few who called themselves Americans and none who had been sent there by the American people.

IRISHMEN

About 80 Irishmen or Anglo-Irishmen (it is not easy to distinguish between them) sat in the House of Commons between 1754 and 1790. The following table indicates the numbers in each Parliament:

Parliament	Returned at the general election	Returned at by-elections	Total
1754–1761	13	9	22
1761–1768	17	8	25
1768–1774	29	7	36
1774–1780	22	8	30
1780–1784	25	5	30
1784–1790	20	5	25

The Irish sat for almost every type of constituency. Two represented English counties: Lord Ludlow, M.P. for Huntingdonshire 1768–96, and Henry Lawes Luttrell, M.P. for Middlesex 1769–74; while several sat for the larger English boroughs (Lord Lucan for Northampton, Andrew

Robinson Bowes for Newcastle-upon-Tyne, John Baker Holroyd for Coventry, Robert Nugent for Bristol, &c.) Only one sat for a Scottish constituency: Sir George Macartney, M.P. for Ayr Burghs 1774–6, who was a son-in-law of the Earl of Bute, joint patron of the constituency; and only one for a Welsh constituency: Whitshed Keene, M.P. for Montgomery 1774–1818.

The Irish who sat in the British House of Commons can be fairly evenly divided into two groups: the upper-class Irish, with interests in both countries, and those who may be called 'adventurers': men who came to England to seek their fortunes, and who won in their adopted country a status they had not enjoyed in their native land.

The upper-class Irish were mostly landowners in both countries, either Irish peers or commoners who also sat in the Irish House of Commons. Among them were such great Anglo-Irish families as the Fitzmaurices, Earls of Shelburne and the Ponsonbys, Earls of Bessborough; and others, not so great, whose political interests were concentrated mainly in one or the other of the two countries. Wills Hill, Earl of Hillsborough in the Irish peerage and a large Irish landowner, sat for Warwick from 1741 to 1756, when he was created a peer of Great Britain. He had no electoral interest in England, but controlled nine seats in the Irish Parliament; yet his political career was spent almost entirely in England where he twice held the office of secretary of state. On the other hand, Thomas Conolly, M.P. for Malmesbury 1759–68 and for Chichester 1768–80, said to have been the richest commoner in Ireland, was of little note in the British Parliament but of considerable importance in the Irish. It was almost impossible for a man to become a leading figure in both Parliaments, simply because he could not be in two places at once. A man with a seat in both Parliaments could be but a nominal member of one of them, and in almost all cases he chose to concentrate on the British House of Commons.

Only one man entered the British House of Commons after having made a considerable reputation in the Irish: Henry Flood, after a distinguished career of over thirty years in Irish politics, who was returned for Winchester in 1783 on the interest of the Duke of Chandos. But Flood's first speech was a failure, his style of oratory was unsuited to the British House of Commons, and he formed no close connexions with British politicians. He had made his reputation in Ireland as a champion of Irish rights against England, but he never tried to play the part of the Irish patriot at Westminster. Though there was a strong nationalist movement in Ireland, which culminated in 1782 in the repeal of Poynings's Law and the emancipation of the Irish Parliament from the control of the British, there was no such thing as an Irish party in the British House of Commons. The Irish Members were completely assimilated; they were to be found on both sides of the House and in all parties, but they never appear as a group even when Irish affairs were under discussion.

Moreover, the Irish Members who sat in the British House of Commons were far more concerned to help Ireland economically than to promote the cause of Irish nationalism. Some of these Members possessed property in both countries; others, who had achieved success and honour in Britain, still had close ties with Ireland. They regarded themselves as a bridge linking the two countries. 'Ireland cannot be separated one moment from England without losing every source of her present prosperity and even hope of her future', wrote Edmund Burke, and in this he was speaking for almost all the Irish Members in the House of Commons. For Irish constitutional demands, Burke had little sympathy; yet he felt deeply the misery of the Roman Catholics, and the economic grievances of a people whose trade and commerce were crippled in the interests of England. Despite the opposition of his constituents at Bristol, he supported North's policy of commercial concessions to Ireland, and was libelled in the English press as a disguised Catholic, a pupil of St. Omer, and one who preferred the interests of Ireland to those of the city he represented in Parliament.

Another Irishman who advocated commercial concessions to Ireland, and one who has never received his due from historians, was Robert Nugent, Burke's predecessor as Member for Bristol. The common people of Ireland, Nugent said in the House on 16 December 1778, were suffering 'every species of misery and distress human nature was capable of bearing'. 'The Irish . . . were now ripe for any revolution', he said on 29 April 1779, 'as they could not possibly change their masters to a disadvantage.' Nugent, like Burke, saw the prosperity of the two countries inseparably intertwined and had no wish to separate them. 'Give Ireland everything she can ask', he argued in the House on 6 December 1779, 'which may promise to produce substantial benefit to that country, but which will not touch or materially affect the interest of this.' Among the few English Members to take up the grievances of

Ireland was Viscount Beauchamp, who sat fifteen years in the Irish House of Commons and had served as chief secretary to his father Lord Hertford, lord lieutenant of Ireland 1765–6. Beauchamp advocated the repeal of the penal laws and the removal of Irish commercial restrictions; as the heir to great estates in Ireland, he had an interest in Irish prosperity and quiet, and direct personal experience of the facts of Irish life. Still, the usual attitude of the English Members towards the Irish was of contempt for the Catholics and fear of the Protestants; there was little feeling of community between the two peoples, and concessions to Ireland by the British Parliament were never made willingly.

There were about 40 Members during this period who may be labelled Irish 'adventurers', and among them some of the most remarkable personalities in the House. The word 'adventurers' is not used to imply anything unworthy or reprehensible in their conduct. They were adventurers in the sense that they set forth from their native land, with few advantages of birth or wealth, to seek fame and fortune in England. Two of them— Edmund Burke, son of a Dublin attorney, and Richard Brinsley Sheridan, son of an Irish actor and teacher of rhetoric—became outstanding figures in the House of Commons, and their names are known today wherever the English language is spoken. Among other Irishmen who achieved distinction in both politics and literature were John Courtenay, the poetical biographer of Dr. Johnson, esteemed in his day as one of the wittiest men in the House; John Baker Holroyd, the devoted friend of Gibbon and first editor of his autobiography; Robert Nugent, poetaster and patron of Goldsmith; and Robert Wood, under-secretary of state and one of the leading Homeric scholars of his age. The men of letters form a much higher proportion of the Irish Members in the House than they do of any other national group.

An adventurer in the pejorative sense was Andrew Robinson Bowes, M.P. for Newcastle-upon-Tyne 1780–4, who speculated in the marriage market. His first wife had a fortune of over £20,000, which Bowes retained after her death; his second, whose family name he took, was the daughter and heiress of George Bowes, M.P. for County Durham 1727–60, and widow of John Lyon, 7th Earl of Strathmore. She was one of the richest heiresses of her day and one of the most scatterbrained, but fortunately for her and her children she had the wit to convey her property into the hands of trustees. Bowes, after bullying and tormenting her so that she was forced to leave him, finally had her kidnapped in Oxford Street; but she was rescued and took divorce proceedings against her husband. Bowes ended in the Fleet prison.

Five Irish Members were prominent in the East India Company. In the first rank were Laurence Sulivan, a director for more than twenty years and probably the greatest administrator the Company had during this period, and Sir Eyre Coote, second only to Clive in the Company's military service. John Carnac, of mixed Irish and Huguenot extraction, had served with Clive in India and subsequently sat on the council of Bombay; Robert Gregory, after having been in India as a free merchant, became a director and eventually chairman of the Company; and Lauchlin Macleane busied himself in the underworld of speculation and intrigue.

Few of the Irish had any electoral interest of their own. The Earl of Shelburne commanded two seats at Calne and one at Chipping Wycombe, but then Shelburne was a great English landowner and hardly thought of himself as an Irishman. Other Anglo-Irish families had a certain fleeting interest in English boroughs: the Damers had large estates in Dorset and throughout this period held one seat for Dorchester; Arnold Nesbitt, a London merchant, had an uncertain interest at Winchelsea; and Lord Egmont had some influence at Bridgwater. Robert Nugent acquired from his second wife control over one seat at St. Mawes. But the only Irish family who deliberately set about cultivating a parliamentary interest in England during this period were the Luttrells of Luttrellstown.

Simon Luttrell of Luttrellstown, co. Dublin, came of a family which had been settled in Ireland since the fifteenth century, but claimed kinship with the old English family of the Luttrells of Dunster and when raised to the Irish peerage took his titles from estates of the Dunster family. About 1757 Luttrell bought the estate of Four Oaks in Warwickshire, and began to foster a parliamentary interest at Tamworth and Wigan. At Tamworth he faced formidable opposition from Lord Weymouth and Lord Townshend, and in 1765 gave up his attempt on the borough; at Wigan, which he represented 1761–8, he was finally driven out by the Duke of Portland. In 1774 he set up his standard at Stockbridge, a venal borough, and by lavish expenditure secured both seats and held them, though not without trouble, for the remainder of this period.

The Luttrell family made a great noise in politics. Four of Simon Luttrell's sons sat in the House of Commons, and his daughter Anne married the Duke of Cumberland, George III's younger brother. Henry Lawes Luttrell, the eldest son, a regular supporter of whatever Administration happened to be in power, volunteered to stand against John Wilkes as the Government candidate for Middlesex in 1769. Luttrell had no property in the county and stood no chance of defeating Wilkes on the poll, but no one else was prepared to become a candidate and the Government regarded it as essential that Wilkes should be turned out of his seat. Luttrell was duly defeated at the election and then seated by a vote of the House of Commons (thus becoming the second Irishman during this period to sit for an English county). For many years he was one of the most unpopular men in the House: the Opposition despised him, even Government supporters thought little of him, his father quarrelled with him, and his younger brothers took the opposite side in politics.

One of those younger brothers, Temple Simon Luttrell, returned for Milborne Port in 1775 on the interest of Thomas Hutchings Medlycott, became notorious in the House for violent abuse of Lord North and Lord Sandwich. There was something about the Luttrells which made them unpalatable to the parties in the House of Commons, and Temple Simon Luttrell was very much a lone wolf in opposition. In 1780 Lord North, determined to be rid of him, offered Medlycott £3,000 if he would drop Luttrell at the forthcoming general election and return a Government candidate instead. Luttrell got wind of the transaction and charged North in the House of Commons with corruption, which North blandly denied; the Opposition, who had listened for five years to Luttrell's wild charges and abusive threats against North, thought it was just another of his stories and refused to support him, and even the Opposition press, usually so ready to take up a scandal against a minister, would not believe it coming from Luttrell. The House voted *nem. con.* that the accusations against North were 'ill founded and injurious'. At the general election of 1780 Luttrell stood at both Milborne Port and Reading and was defeated at both places.

Simon Luttrell's younger sons in general followed their father in politics, went with him into opposition in 1775 and returned to the Government fold in 1780. The family were constantly at odds with each other and the course of their politics was often unpredictable. But what chiefly emerges from a study of the Luttrells is the amazing number of constituencies they contested. Old Simon Luttrell had influence at Tamworth and Wigan, and sat in the House for Mitchell, Wigan,

Weobley, and Stockbridge; while Henry Lawes Luttrell depended entirely on the Treasury for a seat in Parliament. The younger sons at various times sat for or contested Stockbridge, Milborne Port, Reading, Petersfield, and Dover, and in 1768 were reported to be nibbling at Colchester. And in 1774 James Luttrell backed his brother-in-law Lord Waltham's attempts at Maldon and in Essex. So many and such a range of constituencies, and the only one in which they took root was Stockbridge, where money counted for more than anything.

SCOTSMEN

The 45 seats allotted to Scotland by the Act of Union were insufficient during this period for the number of Scots who wished to enter the House of Commons. In point of population, Scotland, which sent only about one-twelfth of the Members to the House of Commons, was under-represented. The Scottish constituencies were almost entirely the preserve of Scotsmen (only five Englishmen and one Irishman represented a Scottish constituency during this period), and in addition more than sixty Scots sat for English or Welsh constituencies. But the under-representation of Scotland is not sufficient by itself to account for this overspill of Scots into England and Wales. To begin with, eldest sons of Scottish peers were debarred from sitting for Scottish constituencies; and if a Member for a Scottish constituency became, as he would if his elder brother died, the eldest son of a Scottish peer, his seat in Parliament was vacated. A curious case occurred in 1787 when Francis Charteris, M.P. for Haddington Burghs, became the eldest son of a Scottish peer whose peerage had been forfeited by attainder in 1746. Charteris's father, on the death of his elder brother, assumed the title of Earl of Wemyss (though the attainder had never been reversed), and Charteris was held to have become the eldest son of a Scottish peer and therefore incapable of sitting for a Scottish constituency.

Again, there were Scotsmen who sat for English constituencies in right of property held by their families. John Stuart, 3rd Earl of Bute, George III's minister, married the daughter of Edward Wortley Montagu, who inherited from her father control over one seat at Bossiney; and two of Bute's sons represented Bossiney during this period. In this case it is rather absurd to speak of Bute's sons as Scots representing an English constituency: on their mother's side they were English, and it was their mother's family borough which they represented in Parliament. Similarly, John Campbell of Calder inherited considerable property in Wales, through his mother, the heiress of the Lort family of Stackpole Court, Pembrokeshire. Campbell himself represented Pembrokeshire 1727–47; his son, Pryse Campbell, Cardigan Boroughs from March to December 1768; and his grandson, John Campbell, Cardigan Boroughs 1780–96. The Campbells of Calder were Scots in Scotland and Welsh in Wales; and old John Campbell felt obliged to remind his family not to forget their ancestral home. 'If my grandson sees with my eyes', he wrote, 'nothing done here [Stackpole Court] will make him insensible to the natural beauties of Calder, or slight that ancient, honourable, and agreeable seat of the family.' To take another example: should Lord Archibald Hamilton, M.P. for Lancashire 1768–72, be described as Scots or English? He was the son of a Scottish duke and eventually succeeded to the dukedom of Hamilton in 1799. Yet he owned estates in Lancashire and made his home there, and to sit in Parliament for an English county was in the eighteenth century the absolute and certain mark of an Englishman. In short, there was so much intermarriage between English and Scottish families as to make national distinctions almost meaningless.

The Scot who wished to enter Parliament and could not find a seat in his native country took his chance in England just as the English did. If he were a Government supporter, he might be brought in for some borough at the disposal of Government as was Lord Lorne at Dover in 1765, Francis Holburne at Plymouth in 1768, or Thomas Erskine at Portsmouth in 1783. If he had money, he could try his luck at a venal borough, as did Sir Patrick Craufurd at Arundel and Alexander Macleod at Honiton in 1780 (unfortunately both disbursed their money with more zeal than discretion and were unseated for bribery), or he could buy a seat from a borough-monger, as Henry Drummond did at Wendover in 1774. Scotsmen closely connected with English politicians were returned to Parliament by their patrons: Alexander Forrester, rejected by Edinburgh in 1761 as being too anglicized (he had spent most of his life in England) was brought in by the Duke of Bedford at Okehampton; William Gordon sat for Woodstock and Heytesbury on the interest of the Duke of Marlborough; Alexander Wedderburn for Bishop's Castle and Okehampton on the interest of Lord Clive; &c. And even some of the larger English boroughs welcomed Scots for their representatives, provided they were men of substance, since the choice of an outsider was a good way of letting the local landowners know that the borough was determined to be independent of their influence. When in 1761 William Mayne contested Canterbury, a very dignified and independent constituency, he was met with the cry 'No Scotch, no foreigner', and came bottom of the poll; but Mayne did not give up the borough and in 1774 he was returned. And two English pocket boroughs were purchased by Scots during this period: Richmond by Sir Lawrence Dundas in 1762, and Gatton by William Mayne in 1774.

In 1754 the Act of Union between England and Scotland was less than fifty years old. That union had been essentially one of two legislatures, and had not affected the Scottish legal system or ecclesiastical establishment. Nor had it removed the long-standing national animosities of the two peoples. Dr. Johnson's prejudice against the Scots was not characteristic of the Tories alone, but was shared by the leaders of the Whigs. In 1755, when Newcastle was searching for a chancellor of the Exchequer, he thought of appointing John Campbell of Calder. 'He is an old corps man', wrote the Duke to Lord Hardwicke, 'but he is a Scotchman and a Campbell. The King will be uneasy.' And in 1760, when Pitt suggested James St. Clair, M.P. for Fife, for the post of commander-in-chief, Newcastle again objected. 'I declared my opinion against St. Clair and nothing shall make me alter it', he wrote to Hardwicke. 'Certainly no great general, certainly a Scotchman who would fill the army with all Scotch, a low Scotchman... Lady Yarmouth assures me positively that the King [George II] will not have St. Clair.'

Perhaps nothing contributed so much to Bute's unpopularity as the fact that he was a Scot. Certainly this was so in the metropolitan area, where so-called public opinion was often nothing more than the rationalization of partially avowed and dimly realized prejudices. Even when Bute was all powerful with the King, the dislike of having Scotsmen in office was as prevalent as ever in parliamentary and official circles. Sir Henry Erskine, M.P. for Anstruther Easter Burghs, who had been dismissed from the army by George II for having voted with Pitt against the subsidy treaties, hoped for employment in a civil capacity in the new reign but found his having been born in Scotland an obstacle to his success. In March 1763, when Bute was on the point of resigning, Henry Fox suggested that James Oswald, M.P. for Dysart Burghs, should be appointed chancellor of the Exchequer in the new Administration—

'His abilities are so great', wrote Fox, '. . . that nobody will think he was made because he is a Scotchman.' Bute and the King concurred in the opinion that Oswald was eminently fitted for the office (as indeed he was), but feared that 'his being born on the other side of the Tweed might cause some more abuse', and Oswald was not appointed. Nor was the prejudice against Scots limited to the time when Bute was in office, or confined to Government appointments. In 1777 the directors of the East India Company turned down the Government's recommendation of Alexander Mackay to be commander-in-chief in India because they 'objected to gentlemen of North Britain for commands-in-chief'. And here is another example of anti-Scottish prejudice from a quarter where one would not expect to find it. On 20 August 1780 Edward Eliot, having offered the Opposition the nomination to three vacant seats in his Cornish boroughs, wrote to the Duke of Portland on receiving the names of the candidates: 'I have not the least objection to either of the three names you mention, unless the baronet is a North Briton.' The Opposition had been complaining for years that the Scots Members were but tools and hirelings of the minister, yet even when they took the right side in politics they were not welcome.

Anti-Scottish feeling in England was the eighteenth-century equivalent of anti-Semitism. It was widespread, though sometimes only half-avowed, and the impression remains that those who professed it were secretly ashamed of it. Superficially at least, reasons could be given for it, but these reasons were not the cause of anti-Scottish feeling any more than a dislike of hooked noses is a cause of anti-Semitism today. But anti-Scottish feeling had no deep psychological roots and was bound to pass away in time, as the more thoughtful Scots recognized. Gilbert Elliot, M.P. for Selkirkshire, one of the ablest Scottish Members in the House, wrote to his friend David Hume, the historian and philosopher, on 22 September 1764:

We are both Englishmen; that is true British subjects. Am I not a Member of Parliament with as much liberty to abuse ministers . . . as if I had been born in Wapping? . . . Had it not been for the clamour of 'a Scot', perhaps indeed I might have been in some more active but not more honourable or lucrative situation. This clamour . . . will in time give way to some other equally absurd.

There is no doubt that had Elliot been an Englishman he would have achieved a much higher position in Administration. Yet by the end of the period Scotsmen were beginning to take their natural place in politics and Scottish birth was no longer the handicap it once had been. Henry Dundas, in effect deputy leader of the House of Commons and minister for Indian affairs, wrote to Sir Archibald Campbell, governor of Madras, in March 1787:

I need not tell you that the powers with which you are invested and the feelings of disappointed men will create in them those little jealousies and malevolencies which are the concomitants of little minds. I am a little involved in the kind of attacks that are whispered about. It is said with a Scotchman at the head of the Board of Control [for India] and a Scotchman at the government of Madras, all India will soon be in their hands and that the county of Argyll will be depopulated by the emigration of Campbells to be provided for by you at Madras. These kind of whispers are to be neither noticed nor regarded when they come in competition with any matter of the smallest importance. At the same time, when I recollect that Mr. Wilkes by such nonsense almost created an insurrection in this country, I do not think that even nonsense is at all times to be disregarded.

Dundas recognized the essentially emotional and irrational nature of anti-Scottish feeling. Yet some rational basis for it could be found, at least by the Opposition, in the belief that Scottish Members went to Westminster primarily to provide for themselves, their families, relations, and constituents, and that they would therefore support any Administration, without regard to its politics, so long as it provided for them. A superficial glance at the division lists during the last years of North's Administration, when the Scottish Members voted overwhelmingly with the Government, appears to confirm that view. Nor are there wanting other signs of confirmation.

Before the Industrial Revolution, Scotland was economically a poor country compared to England, as was recognized by Robert Rickart Hepburn, M.P. for Kincardineshire 1768–74, in a letter of 29 March 1783 to Sir Robert Murray Keith, M.P. for Peeblesshire 1775–80:

It is natural for people who can afford it to get near the seat of Government; in England . . . you feel you are in a better country . . . amongst a richer and happier people . . . All this strikes one with a damp whenever you cross the Tweed, and everything relating to the Government here seem things . . . that we have little concern in. The only objects of the common people is to be free of patronage . . . and of the gentlemen a good or bad crop . . . We are only fit to supply England with inhabitants, and very few of those that can help it will ever return except for a visit.

l

In fact the Scots did return, after having made their fortunes in England, in the army or the navy, in India or the colonies, and re-established their families with new wealth. Then so did the English: for every Scot who came back rich from India or the colonies, there were at least two Englishmen; but to many of the English it seemed that the Scots were interlopers. 'The noblest prospect a Scotchman sees', said Johnson, 'is the high road that leads him into England'; though by the end of this period the time was fast approaching when the 'noble prospects' in Scotland would lead the Englishman to migrate northwards.

About 1754, when real political issues were few and politics appeared little more than a struggle for power, the Scots Members naturally took the side of the Government. There was no sense in belonging to the Opposition unless the Opposition symbolized a cause for which it was worth fighting. Gilbert Elliot, who first attracted the attention of the House by a brilliant speech against a Government bill to perpetuate the practice of appointing Scottish sheriffs-depute at pleasure, wrote to his wife on 22 February 1755: 'I impute the notice I have met with very much to its being a thing a little uncommon, from Scotland, for a young man, supported by none of the great, to take up a point of the constitution upon as high a key as any English Member of Parliament.' Clearly the implication is that only English Members could afford the luxury of opposing the Government even on a political issue. But during the next two years, when the system of foreign policy and the competency of Newcastle's Administration to wage war were the real issues of politics, there were proportionally quite as many Scots in opposition as English.

When Bute became first lord of the Treasury in the new reign it was only natural that the Scottish Members should rally to him: Bute was, after all, the first Scot to become head of Administration since the Union. So, too, the Scots could not be expected to support the cause of John Wilkes, who had blackguarded their nation in the London gutter press. The harm Wilkes did in sowing discord between the two peoples can be seen from an incident soon after his arrest. At Michaelmas 1763 the freeholders of Elginshire, under their praeses Sir Robert Gordon of Gordonstoun, affirmed their support of Administration on the Wilkes issue and their approbation of the conduct of Bute and his brother James Stuart Mackenzie. These resolutions were reprinted in the London press and increased anti-Scottish feeling to such an extent that Stuart Mackenzie was compelled to inform the Elginshire freeholders of the 'immense impropriety' of such well meant, but embarrassing, actions. The good Wilkes did, he did accidentally and without meaning it; but the evil he did deliberately.

On Wilkes's case (both over general warrants in 1764 and over the Middlesex election in 1769) and on the issue of American policy, there was a disposition in most Scottish Members to be on the side of Government. The Scots were more authoritarian than the English (probably because their ecclesiastical discipline was more rigorous than that of the Church of England) and less ready to see the significance of constitutional issues. This was recognized by the more far-seeing Scottish Members. Thus William Strahan, the printer, later M.P. for Malmesbury and Wootton Bassett, wrote about the Government's position on 26 June 1770, soon after North had taken office:

In Scotland they make a national cause of it and are quite unanimous in favour of Government: and their union upon this occasion is easily accounted for, as the Jacobite party, now their old cause is extinguished, from the very nature of their principles remain firm friends of monarchy, in opposition equally to anarchy and republicanism.

And George Dempster, M.P. for Perth Burghs and a prominent member of the Rockingham party, wrote on the eve of the American war:

In Scotland, myself and a very few more excepted, the whole body of the gentry and of the independent and enlightened class of people are to a man on the side of Administration . . . There is a principle against America as well as for her, insomuch that it would not be easy for a ministry more favourable to her to bring the bulk of the House over to their opinion.

John Hope, M.P. for Linlithgowshire 1768–70, who during the short time he sat in the House of Commons had taken a very independent part, wrote of Scotland in 1780 as 'a country where it is regarded as a kind of treason to speak of the measures of Government with the smallest contempt'.

The table overleaf compares the percentage of Members for Scottish constituencies voting with the Opposition, on certain specific issues throughout the period, with the percentage of the House as a whole.

When Lord Dupplin drew up his classification of the Parliament elected in 1754, John Mackye was the only Member from Scotland whom he listed as with the Opposition—and even about Mackye it is by no

Year	Issue	Percentage of Scottish Members with Opposition	Percentage of whole House with Opposition
1754 (March)	Newcastle's Administration	2%	26%
1764	General warrants	13%	42%
1769	Middlesex election	11%	32%
1780	Economical reform	13%	45%
1782 (March)	North's Administration	15%	44%
1783 (February)	Shelburne's peace preliminaries	40%	40%
1783 (November)	Fox's East India bill	15%	25%
1784 (March)	Pitt's Administration	38%	46%
1788	Pitt's Regency bill	31%	40%

means certain that Dupplin was correct. Scotland was practically unanimous in support of the Government. On most issues during the next thirty years there was always a small body of Scots, not more than 15 per cent (that is, not more than nine Members) who voted with the Opposition, while in the House as a whole between 32 per cent and 45 per cent voted with Opposition. But after the downfall of North's Administration, the percentage of Scottish Members voting with the Opposition does not vary very much from that of the House as a whole. This confirms the conclusion reached after a study of the general election of 1784 (in section 2 of this survey), that after 1782 party had come to stay and affected Scotland to the same extent as it did England. In regard to the administrations of Shelburne, Portland, and the younger Pitt, the Scottish Members divided in the same way and in roughly the same proportions as the English Members. Paradoxically, therefore, the advent of party, which the eighteenth century always feared would disrupt national unity, had a unifying effect. Members began to think of themselves less as Englishmen or Scotsmen, and more as followers of Pitt or Fox: party replaced national allegiance as the bond between Members. England and Scotland were becoming one nation.

Because the electorates in the Scottish constituencies were small, the Treasury, the only electoral machine in existence during the eighteenth century, had proportionally more influence in Scotland than it had in England or Wales. Yet it does not appear that that influence was a predominant factor in deciding the political allegiance of Scottish Members. If party feeling was sufficiently strong, it was possible to defy the Treasury; and there were in Scotland, as in England, Members who brought themselves into Parliament and were independent of both Government and party. George Dempster, M.P. for Perth Burghs 1761–8 and 1769–90, described by Wraxall as 'one of the most conscientious men who ever sat in Parliament', wrote to his friend Sir Adam Fergusson on 26 January 1775:

I have long thought . . . that unless one preserves a little freedom and independency in Parliament to act in every question and to vote agreeably to . . . one's own mind, a seat in Parliament is a seat of thorns and rusty nails. That this cannot be attained without some ease in your affairs . . . either you must be very rich or very frugal.

Here was a factor which counted for more than the influence of the Treasury in deciding the political allegiance of Scottish Members. Independence was a political luxury reserved for the more wealthy Members: the independent Member had to be able to afford to bring himself into Parliament, and to maintain himself there without office or the prospect of office. If there were more independent Englishmen than Scotsmen in the House, it was because England was the richer country and the English Members could better afford it. The independent Scots, like the independent English, were wealthy men, but there were more of them in England than in Scotland.

Here are a few of the independent Scottish Members. James Duff, Earl Fife, M.P. for Banffshire 1754–84 and for Elginshire 1784–90, had been a follower of George Grenville, but after Grenville's death connected himself with no party. 'I wish to God party were at an end', he wrote after the fall of Shelburne's Administration, 'and that they would care for the country. I care not twopence for either of them.' And a little later: 'Thank God I am connected with no faction or party.' Alexander Garden of Troup, M.P. for Aberdeenshire 1768–85, was described in 1781 by the *English Chronicle*, an Opposition newspaper by no means well disposed towards the Scots, as 'the only Scotch Member who never asked a favour', and by his brother as 'a truly independent country gentleman.' Sir James Johnstone of Westerhall, M.P. for Dumfries Burghs 1784–90, was one of the most independent Members to sit in the House during this period. 'He had never been at St. James's since 1761 nor at Carlton House in his life', he said at the time of the Regency crisis. 'A man might be a good Member of Parliament . . . without cringing at court or sacrificing to the rising sun. On all questions Johnstone followed his own judgement, and a bare recital of the causes he espoused confirms his individuality and independence: while generally supporting Pitt, he voted against his plan to increase fortifications; supported universal toleration and the abolition of the slave trade; advocated complete uniformity between English and Scottish law; and though he voted for parliamentary reform, opposed the reform of the Scottish burghs. He came out strongly in favour of the impeachment of Warren Hastings and Sir Elijah Impey, and was indeed particularly prone to take up an indictment against anyone in authority. 'He would suspect whom he pleased', he said on one occasion. 'He would suspect the Speaker, the bishops, every man in the House. He was sent there to suspect them and he dared to do his duty.' Suspicion of authority, by whomever it was exercised, was the true mark of the independent Member.

There was also a third factor which worked against the independence of the Scottish Member. The spirit of the clans was still vigorously alive in Scotland, and the Scottish M.P., to a much higher degree than the English, regarded himself in the House more as a representative of his family than of his constituency. There were no popular constituencies in Scotland, and every Scottish Member, who had not won his seat by bribery, was chosen because of the strength of his family interest. John Hope, who belonged to a junior branch of the family of the Earl of Hopetoun, was elected for Linlithgowshire in 1768 after a bitter contest with James Dundas of Dundas. Hope, who had spent a good deal of his life in Holland, had a different view of politics from that of most Scottish Members. He followed the Opposition line over the Middlesex election, which greatly disturbed his family: Dundas of Dundas had brought a petition against Hope's election, and if Hope voted with the Opposition the Government might throw its weight behind Dundas. But Lord Hopetoun was less concerned about whether Wilkes or Luttrell was the legally elected Member for Middlesex, as about whether the Hopes or the Dundases should control Linlithgowshire. Eventually Hope himself realized this:

As to my action against the inclinations of Lord Hopetoun [he wrote] ... I was sensible that in Parliament I was but a creature of his making, but still I considered myself as a free agent and one of the representatives of the commons and not of the peers of Great Britain.

The argument would have been sound had his constituents had much

share in his election: but in fact there were less than forty freeholders
on the Linlithgowshire roll in 1768, and some of these held fictitious
qualifications. Hope had stood as a representative of the Hopetoun
interest, and without the support of that interest he would never
have been elected. 'The honour of the family interest in the county
was the chief purpose of giving me the seat in Parliament', he wrote,
shortly before Dundas's petition came up for decision. '... I ought
therefore to have done nothing without their advice and approbation.'
On 27 March 1770 Hope was unseated, a blow to the family interest
which Lord Hopetoun never forgot and for which he never forgave
his nephew.

At various times in the eighteenth century there existed a 'minister
for Scotland', who was charged with the distribution of Scottish
patronage and was responsible for the attendance of Scottish Members in
the House and for ensuring that they voted with the Government. In
1754 this office was held by Archibald, 3rd Duke of Argyll, popularly
known as 'the viceroy' or 'the uncrowned King of Scotland', who had
enjoyed his power ever since Sir Robert Walpole's day.

Patronage in England was the responsibility of the first lord of
the Treasury, and the 'viceroy' system in Scotland worked well when
the first lord of the Treasury and the minister for Scotland were
close political allies. But when their aims diverged, the system did
not work at all; and there was always a minority in Scotland, jealous
of the viceroy's power, and ready to instigate the 'English ministry'
against him. Thus in March 1754 General Bland, commander-in-chief
in Scotland, urged Newcastle and Hardwicke to appoint Robert
Dundas, M.P. for Edinburghshire, lord advocate and minister for
Scotland. 'The business of the Crown suffers', Bland wrote, 'by not
having an able man ... who is solely attached to the King and
owes his preferment purely to the English ministers and not to any
of the leading men here.' The Duke of Argyll, a great Scottish peer,
co-survivor with Newcastle and Hardwicke from Sir Robert Walpole's
Administration, was able to play an independent part in politics, to
intrigue against Newcastle and if need be to break with him; but Robert
Dundas would owe everything to Newcastle and his loyalty could be
depended upon.

Newcastle agreed to the appointment of Dundas as lord advocate
but not as minister for Scotland: Argyll had given no sign of any

disposition to oppose the English ministers, and his authority in Scotland was too deep-rooted for him to be replaced without a political crisis of the first order. In 1756, when Newcastle was hoping to reconstruct his ministry to take in Pitt, he played with the idea of leaving out Argyll, who was considered to be too close to Henry Fox, and drew up lists of Scottish Members who would or would not follow Argyll if he were out of office. But the real threat to Argyll's position came not from Newcastle but from another quarter. In 1756 both George II and Argyll himself were over seventy, and politicians in England and Scotland were anticipating who would have the disposal of affairs when the King and his viceroy died. The answer was obvious: on the death of the King, the Earl of Bute, Argyll's nephew and the Prince of Wales's favourite, would take over in both countries.

In England Bute bided his time and waited as patiently as he could until the death of the King should herald his assumption of power: he could do nothing in England, after Newcastle and Pitt had come together, while George II was alive. In Scotland, however, as preparations began for the forthcoming general election, Bute tried to supplant his uncle. It was part of the viceroy's responsibilities to ensure that Scotland sent Members to Parliament favourably disposed towards the Government, and in addition to his authority as viceroy, Argyll was a great territorial magnate. In 1759 Argyll, who controlled two of the five burghs in the constituency of Ayr Burghs, endorsed the candidature of his cousin Lord Frederick Campbell for the general election; Bute, who controlled one burgh, and whose ally Lord Eglintoun controlled another, put forward Patrick Craufurd. The ensuing quarrel dominated Scottish politics during the next twelve months, but after the death of George II in October 1760, Argyll, realizing his position had weakened, accepted a compromise. In April 1761, in the middle of the general election, Argyll himself died.

Bute now took over the position of minister in Scotland, as he was shortly to do in England, and delegated his authority to his brother James Stuart Mackenzie. In April 1763, when Bute resigned the Treasury, he took steps to ensure that Stuart Mackenzie should remain minister for Scotland; and the King insisted that Grenville, the new head of the Treasury, should in Scottish affairs take 'all recommendations from Mr. Mackenzie'. There were now two patronage ministers, George Grenville for England and James Stuart Mackenzie for Scotland.

It seems unlikely that such a system could ever have worked: certainly Bute, in recommending it, showed no appreciation of the realities of power in the House of Commons. Grenville, as leader of the House, could well have delegated Scottish affairs to a deputy, provided that the deputy was a man of his own creation, upon whom he could rely. But Stuart Mackenzie, as minister for Scotland, was responsible directly to the King, and Grenville, though charged with the conduct of the House of Commons, had no authority to deal with Scottish Members. Grenville's jealousy of Bute's influence over the King increased after Bute's attempt in August 1763 to replace the Grenville Administration. Meanwhile, Stuart Mackenzie continued to consult Bute on Scottish appointments; honest and conscientious and no party man, he tried to distribute patronage according to merit while Grenville wanted it to be used to strengthen his ministry's position in Parliament. In the clashes between Grenville and Stuart Mackenzie, the King invariably supported Mackenzie. He wrote to Bute after one such clash:

I am glad there has been this struggle of the ministers, for I will show them who recommends Scotch offices. I have ever declared Mr. Mackenzie for that department; I will settle that matter instantly and if they have not understood my orders on this occasion it is not for want of explaining the thing clearly.

There could be but one end to this dispute. In May 1765 Grenville forced Stuart Mackenzie's dismissal, abolished the post of minister for Scottish affairs, and concentrated all authority in the House of Commons into his own hands. For almost twenty years there was no minister for Scotland. The Rockingham Administration considered reviving the post, and offered it first to Lord Kinnoull, and next to Robert Dundas, lord president of the court of session, but neither would accept it. It was not until Henry Dundas joined Pitt in 1783 that there was again a minister for Scotland. But the post held by Dundas was very different from that of Stuart Mackenzie. He was professedly Pitt's deputy, linked to him by close personal and political ties, not possessed of an independent authority as Stuart Mackenzie and the Duke of Argyll had been. Dundas was closely allied in electoral affairs with the Duke of Buccleuch, while William Adam and Sir Thomas Dundas of Aske managed Scotland for the Opposition. Thus by 1784 not only were Scottish Members divided in the House along party lines, but there were in Scotland itself rudimentary party organizations.

WELSHMEN

There is little to be said about the Welshmen who sat in Parliament during these years. The twenty-four Welsh constituencies seem to have been sufficient for the number of Welshmen who wished to enter the House of Commons: few of them contested constituencies outside Wales, and on at least six occasions during the period Englishmen or Irishmen found seats in Welsh boroughs. Only four Welsh Members ever held political office which was not of a strictly local nature; and in the list of merchants, professional men, and service officers the Welsh Members form proportionally the lowest of the national groups. Most of them were country squires whose political horizon did not extend much farther than their own locality. They did not form close party connexions at Westminister, and the development of party in Wales lagged behind that in England and Scotland. Politically speaking, Wales was backward; and though the country had been linked to England for hundreds of years, and ever since the sixteenth century had sent Members to Parliament, the Welsh had retained their distinctive characteristics and were less integrated into the general community of the kingdom than the Scots.

Here is one example of Welsh exclusiveness and their absorption in local affairs. The Owen family of Orielton had considerable electoral influence in Pembrokeshire and Pembroke Boroughs, and between 1722 and 1774 Sir William Owen, 4th Bt., represented one or the other constituency. Practically every one of his many letters to the Duke of Newcastle and Lord Hardwicke is concerned with local patronage, and there is hardly any mention of national affairs or wider political issues. He apparently never spoke in the House (at least not during this period), and his vote on the land tax division of 27 February 1767 is the only one recorded in the twenty years between 1754 and 1774.

A second example is provided by the Morgan family of Tredegar, referred to in section 1 of this survey, who controlled three seats in the House of Commons, and who went over to Lord North in 1770 in return for the lord lieutenancies of Breconshire and Monmouthshire. But more striking is the behaviour of Sir Watkin Williams Wynn, 4th Bt., M.P. for Shropshire 1772–4 and for Denbighshire 1774–89, the son of the great Tory leader of the early half of the century. During his first few years in the House Wynn voted with the Opposition. Then, in 1775, the lord lieutenancy of Merioneth became vacant, and Wynn applied for the office. The King replied to Lord North's recommendation: 'I consent to Sir Watkin Williams being lieutenant of Merioneth if he means to be grateful, otherwise favours granted to persons in opposition is not very political.' Wynn was appointed, and showed his gratitude by changing to the Government side in the House of Commons. But in 1778 the Treasury's plan to inquire into the encroachments on Crown lands in Wales, which was bitterly resented by Welsh landowners, led him to desert the Government and rejoin the Opposition. These years were dominated by the greatest problem the British Parliament was called upon to solve during this period, yet the American war seems to have counted for less in Wynn's political thought than his attempt to re-establish his family interest in Merioneth or his contest with Lord Powis in Montgomeryshire.

SUICIDES AND MADMEN

During this period the King, George III, suffered at least once from an attack of insanity, and one of his ministers, the Earl of Chatham, appears also to have been a victim of the same illness. It may be well therefore to end this survey of the Members of the House of Commons by briefly stating the facts regarding mental instability and suicide in the House, without venturing upon sociological deductions which lie outside the province of the parliamentary historian. Eight men, all Members of Parliament at the time, are known to have committed suicide during this period: Sir John Bland; Robert, Lord Clive; John Damer; William Fitzherbert; George Hay; Robert Mayne; Jenison Shafto; and Hans Stanley. Hay and Shafto were certainly insane at the time of their deaths, while there was a strain of mental instability in Stanley's family (his father also had committed suicide). Bland killed himself after having incurred heavy gambling debts, while Mayne, a banker, had become bankrupt and had apparently been defrauding his clients. Various reasons were ascribed by contemporaries to account for the other suicides, none of which can be held to be certain.

In addition to these eight, five other Members who sat during this period committed suicide. One was John Calcraft junior, whose death took place in 1831; the other four, all of whom died before 1790, were not Members of Parliament at the time of their deaths. These were

Herbert Lloyd; John Murray, 3rd Duke of Atholl; Charles Powlett, 5th Duke of Bolton; and William Skrine. A further three Members (Thomas Bradshaw, Charles Yorke, and Samuel Touchet) are reported by contemporaries to have committed suicide. Bradshaw almost certainly did so, and Yorke with equal probability did not; in Touchet's case it is difficult to know what degree of credence to give to the report of his suicide. Thus, of the 1,964 men who sat in the House of Commons between 1754 and 1790, thirteen certainly committed suicide and three may have done so.

Ten Members are known to have been insane at some period of their adult lives (including two who committed suicide): Thomas Alston; James Coutts; Richard Hippisley Coxe; Estcourt Cresswell; William Finch; Sir Charles Hanbury Williams; George Hay (a suicide); Thomas Scrope; Jenison Shafto (a suicide); and Charles Wilkinson. Hardly anyone who reads the biography of Lord George Gordon will doubt that he too was insane, and it also appears probable that Robert Paris Taylor was. About another Member who is said to have been insane, Charles Whitworth, the evidence is inconclusive.

4. THE HOUSE OF COMMONS

More than the aggregate of its individual Members is the House of Commons itself, an institution with a corporate life and personality of its own. The men whose life-stories are related in these volumes are not so many individuals who happen to have flourished at about the same time: their lives are inter-linked, and the highest common factor in their careers is their membership of the House of Commons. From that they derived, or expected to derive, certain advantages: the right to be heard in the great council of the nation, the social prestige which this gave them, preferences in their careers which they might not otherwise have obtained, &c. And to it they severally contributed something which, as far as individuals are concerned, it is difficult to evaluate or even define, but which collectively formed the corporate personality of the House.

The majority of Members in the eighteenth century were not professional politicians, representing their constituents on a party basis and realizing in their party's assumption of office the culmination of their political efforts. Instead, they claimed to be a representative selection of the upper classes of their time, summoned to Westminster primarily to vote the supplies and to be a check upon the executive power of the state, and in the performance of their duties representative of the nation at large. Their standards of rectitude differed in some respects from ours. To a modern reader it is surprising to learn that in 1767, when the House was inquiring into the affairs of the East India Company, the chancellor of the Exchequer was himself speculating in East India stock. Even Edmund Burke, who carried into public life the highest principles of morality, was not disturbed by the fact that his 'cousin', William Burke, engaged in similar speculations, while holding the office of under-secretary of state. Even more reprehensible, if true, is the conduct of Robert Wood, who in 1770 as under-secretary of state and closely concerned in the negotiations with Spain over the Falkland Islands, was reputed to be working for war and speculating in the funds accordingly. Members who were commissaries or paymasters made fortunes during the seven years' war, and holders of Government balances had golden opportunities to enrich themselves. On this latter practice the attitude of the House changed after 1782, and other forms of dubious conduct became increasingly frowned upon by public opinion. However, in matters touching its own privileges and dignity, or which offended against its code of expected behaviour, the House was characteristically sensitive.

Pride of place among those Members who suffered the displeasure of the House must be given to John Wilkes, though whether he is to be described as a rogue or a political martyr must be left undecided—probably he was a little of both. Wilkes was first expelled the House on 19 January 1764 for publishing a seditious libel against the King in the *North Briton*; he was expelled a second time on 4 February 1769, for a libel against Lord Weymouth, secretary of state, but the expulsion was strongly opposed, and his subsequent re-election for Middlesex involved the House in prolonged controversy which did not end even when Wilkes's defeated opponent was declared duly elected. Apart from Wilkes, the only other Member expelled the House during these years was Christopher Atkinson, M.P. for Hedon, expelled on 4 December 1783 after having been found guilty and sentenced to twelve months' imprisonment for perjury.

Three Members were imprisoned by the House. On 8 February 1771 Colonel George Onslow, M.P. for Guildford, instigated the House to take action against the printers of the London newspapers who had committed a breach of privilege by publishing reports of debates. When the House sent a messenger to arrest the printer of the *London Evening Post*, three City magistrates (Wilkes; Brass Crosby, M.P. for Honiton and lord mayor of London; and Richard Oliver, M.P. for London) committed the messenger to prison. For this offence Crosby and Oliver were sent to the Tower for the remainder of the session, but the House refrained from proceeding against Wilkes. Historically the case is important as the last occasion on which the House took action against those who published reports of its debates.

The third Member to be imprisoned by the House was John Roberts, M.P. for Taunton, in 1781. It was the custom during this period, when important business was to be considered, to enforce attendance by means of a call of the House. On the day for which the call was fixed, every Member had to be in his place and answer his name, unless previously excused for reasons of health or private business. Roberts was absent from the call of the House ordered for 31 January 1781; was again absent when ordered to attend on

15 February; and was committed to the custody of the serjeant-at-arms. His imprisonment was short: on 19 February, after apologizing to the House and explaining that it was illness not contempt which had occasioned his absence, he was released.

What changes took place in the House of Commons during this period? Lord North entered the House at the general election of 1754 and remained there without a break until he succeeded to his father's peerage shortly after the general election of 1790. His career in the House spans the whole of our period. Changes occurred, but possibly not all of them were clearly perceived by North on an intellectual level for they were gradual, their total effect cumulative, and the process of adaptation unspectacular. The eighteenth century was not like the seventeenth a period of great constitutional changes, affecting the authority of the House and its relations with the Crown; nor, like the nineteenth century, was it a period when the composition of the House and its relations with the electorate altered fundamentally. The principal developments during these years may be grouped under three headings: the emergence of a new attitude towards the conduct of elections and the determination of election petitions; a change in the type of legislation coming before the House; and the growth of party. These developments in turn reflect deeper changes in the life and thought of the nation at large which are beyond the province of the parliamentary historian.

At the beginning of this period election disputes were decided by the House as a whole, and the first session of a new Parliament was occupied by little else than voting the supplies and determining election petitions. It was a slow and tedious process, involving much detail which would have been better left to a small committee than to a body of 558 Members; and often the issue was decided with little respect to the merits of the question. One of the most controversial election petitions of 1754 was that from Oxfordshire, where, after an expensive and bitter contest, a double return had been made of two Whigs and two Tories. Sir William Meredith, who at the time was reckoned a Tory, wrote subsequently of the Oxfordshire election case:

39 in 40 of the judges (the Members) knew nothing of the matter, and therefore voted as they liked best. . . . Nor, to this hour, can either side tell which had the majority of legal votes, nor any Member of Parliament who noted that question give any other reason for his vote but as he stood inclined for the *old* or *new* interest of Oxfordshire.

The two Members eventually declared duly elected, who had stood on the new or Whig interest, owed their seats in effect not to the freeholders of Oxfordshire but to the Whig majority in the House of Commons. Indeed, had the House been prepared to act as an independent and impartial tribunal, it would have found it difficult to do so: the House as a whole was not the place to examine minutely the qualifications of hundreds of freeholders and decide whether or not they had a legal right to vote.

When no party issue was involved in the trial of an election petition, as was usually the case from 1754 to 1770, it became a matter of lobbying for the support of friends and the friends of friends—again, often with little respect to the merits of the case. Yet it should not be assumed that under the old system of trying election petitions justice was always foiled by the big battalions. In 1768 for instance, Sir James Lowther, a Government supporter, was unseated for Cumberland in favour of Henry Fletcher, a member of the Opposition. Lowther's case was weak, he himself was personally unpopular, and the Government did not exert itself on his behalf: all these factors contributed to effect a just result. Still, the absence of any one of them might have tipped the scale the other way. The determination of controverted elections by the House of Commons was at best a chancy business.

In 1769, after John Wilkes had been three times elected for Middlesex despite being expelled the House and declared incapable of being re-elected into that Parliament, the Grafton Administration was driven to embrace a desperate expedient for getting rid of him. Henry Lawes Luttrell was induced to stand against Wilkes, and though beaten by an overwhelming majority was declared by the House on petition to be the duly elected Member. The Opposition were not slow to point out that Luttrell owed his seat not to the freeholders of Middlesex but to the Government majority in the House of Commons—exactly as the successful Whig candidates for Oxfordshire had done in 1754. Moreover, argued the Opposition, what was to prevent the Government doing this in other cases, and using their majority to deprive of his seat any member of the Opposition who had made himself peculiarly obnoxious to them? What then became of the rights of electors to choose their Members freely? And what safeguard was there for the independence of Parliament and its claim to speak for the nation at large?

From the controversy over the Middlesex election there emerged a new way of deciding controverted elections. In 1770 George Grenville introduced a bill which provided that each election petition should be referred to a committee of the House chosen by lot. A rather complicated procedure was drawn up for choosing the committee: Members over the age of sixty or who had already served on an election committee that session were excused; from the remainder the Speaker drew forty-nine names by lot; each of the petitioners nominated one Member and then struck off one name alternately until the number was reduced to thirteen. The committee's decision was by majority vote, and the chairman had the casting vote. The bill was originally introduced as a temporary measure but was made permanent in 1774, despite the opposition of Lord North's Administration.

Grenville's Act won great praise from contemporaries, probably more than it deserved. Its supreme virtue was that it made it almost impossible for the Government to determine a controverted election along party lines, for the committee could hardly be packed. But it did nothing to remove the other objection to the trial of election petitions by the House of Commons, namely that Members of Parliament were not in general fit and proper persons to judge the complicated issues involved. After 1770 election petitions received a fairer trial, or at least appeared to do so, but election committees occasionally produced some whimsical verdicts. Here are two examples.

At Helston the right of election was assumed to be in the corporation. The borough was controlled by the Godolphin family, and on the death of Francis, 2nd Earl of Godolphin in 1766 it passed to his grandson Francis, Marquess of Carmarthen. Then followed disputes in the corporation, which seriously weakened the Godolphin interest, until in 1774 Lord Carmarthen secured a new charter, reserving to the corporation the right to co-opt new members. He then proceeded to oust his opponents and pack the corporation with men on whom he could depend. At the general election of 1774 the anti-Godolphin voters who had been turned out of the corporation put up two candidates to oppose those on Carmarthen's interest, knowing full well that they would be defeated but resolved to try their luck with a House of Commons election committee. The manœuvre succeeded, for the committee which tried the petition set aside the new charter and declared that the six voters ousted by Carmarthen in 1774 were the only legal voters of Helston. This decision was confirmed by another committee in 1781, by which time the number of voters at Helston had fallen to three; and it was only in 1790, when the electorate had been further reduced to one old man of over eighty, that the right of election was at last declared to be in the corporation.

Election committees were not bound by precedents, or rather could be led by a clever lawyer to accept as a precedent what had not hitherto been regarded as one. Though they generally began with declaring that they would not hear evidence as to the right of election, in one instance during this period they arbitrarily changed the right of election against all recent precedents. At Pontefract the right of election was in the burgage holders, and though there was a strong party which contended that it should be in the inhabitant householders, the point was decided against them by election committees in 1768 and 1775. In 1783, with parliamentary reform in the air, the party of the householder franchise made their third attempt to get a candidate elected; and this time the House of Commons committee ignored the decisions of 1768 and 1775, ignored also previous determinations of 1699 and 1715 in favour of the burgage holders, and adopted a House of Commons determination of 1624 in favour of the inhabitant householders. In effect the committee declared that for eighty-four years Pontefract had been returning Members on the wrong franchise, and that the decisions of previous committees could not bind their successors. In view of such a resolution, could there be said to be such a thing as law in the determination of election petitions? Similarly in 1787 in the case of Saltash, where the right of voting was assumed to be in the corporation, the House of Commons committee allowed the votes of the freeholders and in effect altered the borough franchise.

The great curse of eighteenth-century elections was their expense. To the average elector the vote was not a trust, not an element in the process of choosing a Government; and it was rarely cast in accordance with a clearly-defined political outlook: it was a privilege attendant upon property or social position and was expected to yield suitable returns. Even the most independent voters expected to be treated by the candidates and in some populous constituencies to receive a token of the candidates' regard—half a guinea for a single vote or a guinea for a double vote, or tickets exchangeable for drink at public houses. The eighteenth century did not regard this as bribery, any more than it did candidates' paying municipal expenses or helping to foot the bill for schemes of public welfare. Obviously, the line between treating and bribery was a very fine one, yet there was a distinction between the two: that the voters should receive something by way of expenses was admitted, but the buying and selling of votes was illegal, and if detected was punished.

In individual cases, bribery was hard to prove, but when it was openly practised and extended to the electorate as a whole, the House could take action. It did so twice during this period, in respect of two constituencies: New Shoreham in 1771 and Cricklade in 1782. Each constituency received the same treatment: the delinquent voters were disfranchised, and the right of voting was extended to 40 shilling freeholders in the neighbouring hundreds. Thus Cricklade and New Shoreham became in effect miniature county constituencies, preserves of the country gentlemen, with influence replacing bribery. And there was nothing reprehensible about influence: it was the natural way for property to exert itself, while bribery was the perverse way. Action against bribery was action in defence of property.

The second development, the change which came over the type of legislation introduced into the House, was a gradual one. The second half of the eighteenth century was not a period of violent social changes: rather it was a time when forces were slowly building up beneath the surface, to break through at the turn of the century in both a political and a social direction. The class composition of the House changed little throughout the period, and the impetus to reform came not from new classes entering Parliament but from a heightened social consciousness in the old-established classes.

Two subjects of social legislation had long concerned the House: the poor law and the relief of insolvent debtors; and throughout this period they took up a great deal of parliamentary time. The problem of imprisonment for debt was never tackled as a whole: there was too much opposition from the commercial interests for any attempt at changing the system to stand much chance of success, and all that could be done was to pass periodical acts, often in the teeth of strong opposition, for the relief of insolvent debtors. The poor law was primarily a matter for the local authorities, and almost all the attempts to improve its administration during this period were the work of one man, Thomas

Gilbert, M.P. for Newcastle-under-Lyme 1763–8 and for Lichfield 1768–94, a protégé of Lord Gower and in politics a member of the Bedford group.

Gilbert's first poor law bill, which grouped parishes together for purposes of organized relief, passed the Commons in April 1765 but was defeated in the Lords (largely because of the opposition of the Newcastle and Rockingham Whigs, whose principal objection to the bill was that it was a measure of the Bedford party); and it was not until 1782 that Gilbert was able to get his bill on the statute book. It was, wrote Sidney and Beatrice Webb, 'the most elaborate and perhaps the most influential' poor law measure of the eighteenth century; and two of its provisions—the union of parishes to build workhouses and the sanctioning of outdoor relief—were of great consequence in the future development of the poor law. Behind poor law legislation were two factors: the desire for increased administrative efficiency and less expense, and sympathy with the hardships of the poor. As might be expected in a Parliament composed mainly of landowners, the first factor counted more than the second; but there were in the House Members who had a real understanding of the hardships of the poorer classes, and who recognized a connexion between poverty and crime. One of them, Robert Nugent, said in a debate of 2 March 1774:

If we do not alter our laws of settlement we shall depopulate this country. This country could contain and maintain twice the number that is in it. The quantity of executions at Tyburn owe part of their origin to our poor laws. There are more executions in our capital than in the capitals of all other kingdoms.

Crime, and the savage measures taken to repress it, were two of the greatest social evils of the age, practically unrecognized by the parties which struggled for supremacy in the House of Commons but increasingly the concern of a few individuals drawn from all quarters of the House. From about 1770 onwards there was a small but vocal movement for penal reform, which, however, achieved little because of the opposition of the House of Lords. In 1770 Sir William Meredith, M.P. for Liverpool, moved for an inquiry into the state of the criminal law, from which there resulted a bill reducing the number of offences punishable by death. Meredith's speech against capital punishment for minor offences, 13 May 1777, was reprinted in pamphlet form as late as 1831, and is mentioned in the preface to Dickens's *Barnaby Rudge*. Others associated with him in this work were Sir Thomas Charles Bunbury, who helped to found the Derby and was the owner of the first winner of the race; Sir George Savile; Reginald Pole Carew, the friend of Bentham; Alexander Popham, who tried to improve conditions in prisons; John Glynn, the friend and colleague of Wilkes; William Eden, who studied the subject of transportation; and Edmund Burke, who, if he had not been diverted by other aims, might have made a great penal reformer.

Horace Walpole once said that every abuse in England was a freehold, and the chief obstacle during the period to any kind of social reform was that there was always an institution or a class which had an interest in the maintenance of the existing system and which cherished that interest as a right of property. From the parliamentary reformers downwards, every reformer had to face this difficulty and few of them managed to overcome it. The conscience of the nation was difficult to arouse, for the circulation of newspapers was small and the urbanized middle class was only just emerging into political consciousness and making its voice heard. In June 1785 Archibald Macdonald, solicitor-general, moved for a bill to reform the police in the London area. Macdonald had realized that an inefficient and corrupt police force was a factor making for the increase of crime, and he proposed to appoint three full-time commissioners of police and establish a system of regular patrols. But his plan was opposed by the City of London, on the ground that it was an infringement of their chartered rights, and Macdonald was forced to withdraw it.

The Parliament of 1784 was occupied with measures of reform in all spheres—political, administrative, and social—a remarkable contrast to the record of previous Parliaments. On almost every subject from weights and measures to Parliament itself, there was some Member ready to press the case for reform. One of the most interesting schemes hatched during this Parliament, but one which was never permitted to grow wings, was put forward on 30 April 1787 by John Rolle, M.P. for Devon. Speaking 'at the express desire of his constituents', who felt themselves oppressed by the weight of the poor rates, Rolle proposed something like a scheme of social insurance to be financed by employers and employed. There would be 'one general club or fund throughout the kingdom, with permanency to the body and security to the capital . . . to be raised by obliging the rich in a certain limited proportion to become contributors to the benefit of the poor, and to oblige the poor, whilst young and in health, to contribute towards their own support when disabled by sickness, accident, or age'.

More significant for the immediate future, was the motion of Sir William Dolben, M.P. for Oxford University, on 21 May 1788, for a bill to improve the conditions of negro slaves being transported to the West Indies. Oxford in the late eighteenth and early nineteenth centuries is popularly supposed to have been a centre of opposition to reform of all kinds, and it is forgotten that the first move in the British Parliament for regulation of the slave trade came from one of the representatives for Oxford University. Dolben's motion was followed on 12 May 1789 by Wilberforce's motion against the slave trade: the first act of a campaign to which he was to devote his parliamentary career.

Throughout the period private legislation continued to occupy a large part of the time of the House. It is amazing how numerous were the actions in life which required a private Act of Parliament before they could be legally performed: divorces, alterations of marriage settlements, schemes for enclosures, for turnpike roads, for paving the streets of towns, for selling entailed property, for building jails and town halls, &c. When the House did get down to public business its main work was financial, not legislative. 'The first duty of the House', said Sir John Riggs Miller, M.P. for Newport, in 1788, 'was to watch over and economize the public expenditure'—a sentiment which might have been repeated at any time during the century. The idea that Parliament should enact a legislative programme each session was completely unknown: legislation, when necessary, was conceived of as supplementing the existing common and statute law and bringing it up to date. Nor was it the purpose of Parliament to supply the King with ministers. Indeed, old-fashioned Members saw a clear distinction between the functions of the executive and the legislature, which could be maintained in theory but no longer corresponded to practice. Welbore Ellis, admittedly a man of rigid mind, conservative and unresponsive to change, said in the House on 25 May 1778: 'He did not think the House of Commons an assembly calculated for the discussion of state affairs. It was the business of Parliament to raise supplies, not to debate on the measures of Government.' And George Forster Tufnell, M.P. for Beverley, who generally voted with the Opposition, asserted on 25 April 1780 during a debate on the militia that the House 'had no right to interfere with the executive power'. For the eighteenth century held that the function of the executive was limited and its power restricted—'Providence has so ordered the world', wrote Lord Shelburne in his autobiography.

'that very little government is necessary.' Hence the belief could still be entertained and professed that Parliament had nothing to do with state affairs—a theory which always broke down when state affairs touched the pockets or consciences of the Members. This brings us to our third major development, the growth of party.

When Members were sorely troubled in their minds about affairs of state, when there were deep divisions in the nation on issues of principle or policy, they came together to form parties, and the theoretical distinction between the functions of the executive and the legislature was forgotten. The House of Commons did not ask in February 1782 whether it had a right to condemn Lord North's conduct of the American war: it proceeded to do so as the grand tribunal of the nation, representative of all persons and property in Britain, whose deliberation comprehended the whole range of the nation's affairs. Its function was not merely to vote supplies but also to redress grievances, which implied an authority to consider the work of any department of the executive. But in the happy days around the beginning of this period the work of the British Government was virtually restricted to preserving the constitution (which meant doing nothing in home affairs) and conducting foreign policy. To the Duke of Newcastle 'home affairs' meant patronage, not legislation, and it was over foreign policy (including the conduct or misconduct of war) that political disputes, which must be distinguished from the struggles for power which go on at all times in every institution, arose. It is with the restricted function of Government in mind that any consideration of the state of parties in 1754 must begin.

According to Lord Dupplin's classification of the Parliament elected in 1754, almost every Member of the House of Commons was either a Whig or a Tory. This happy anticipation of nineteenth-century conditions, when every person in the land was said to be either a Liberal or a Conservative, presents the appearance of a two party system which, if viewed superficially, can be deceptive. It is true that on closer examination the 410 Members classed as Whigs in 1754 resolve themselves into followers of the Duke of Newcastle, the Duke of Bedford, the Prince of Wales, and of half a dozen smaller party leaders; and that their political behaviour could never be depended upon even by their own leaders. As for the 106 Tories, they did not profess to acknowledge any leader, but were independent Members, voting according to their own lights whether of principle or prejudice. Still, the words Whig and Tory must have meant something or Dupplin would not have used them, and an examination of the Members individually may help us to uncover their meaning.

But first, a word of warning. When the names Whig and Tory were first used as party labels in English politics in the late seventeenth century they denoted two different attitudes towards a particular set of political circumstances. It by no means follows that in 1754, when political circumstances had changed, that those attitudes remained the same or that the words Whig and Tory meant what they had done in 1679. To give a similar example from current politics: the words Conservative and Labour denote two different attitudes in politics today just as they did at the death of Queen Victoria, but those attitudes have changed a good deal in the intervening sixty years. Two world wars, the social changes resulting from them, scientific and intellectual developments, have brought changes in the political thinking of both parties, and the problems facing them in the 1960s are entirely different from those of 1901. It is true that the Conservative party remains the party of private enterprise and the Labour party that of public control, but these broad general attitudes have not the same meaning as in 1901. The Conservative does not stand for unrestrained private enterprise nor Labour for complete public control: there are shades of meaning within the parties, there is a large area where neither party applies its principle wholeheartedly, and it is precisely in that area that the most acute political controversies arise. In whatever way historians may regard these controversies, they present themselves to the politicians not as conflicts between abstract principles of government but as attempts to find solutions to current political problems. Political parties do not exist in a void nor are political principles academic intellectual exercises in logical thought. A history of parties is meaningless which does not relate them to the specific political questions they were called upon to solve.

With these considerations in mind, let us return to Dupplin's list of Tories elected in 1754. To the 106 he names, three more might be added: Valentine Knightley, M.P. for Northamptonshire, omitted apparently through oversight; Julines Beckford, seated after a double return; and Sir John Philipps, who replaced William Beckford at Petersfield (Beckford having been returned for two constituencies). Of these 109 Members, 100 sat for English constituencies, comprising more than one-fifth of the English Members; eight sat for Welsh constituencies—one-third of their representatives; and only one—John Mackye—sat for a Scottish constituency (why Dupplin included Mackye among the list of Tories is by no means clear). Of the 80 English county Members, 38 were classed as Tories; and only one among them was the son of a peer: Lord Harley, M.P. for Herefordshire. The remaining 37 Tory knights of the shire were the élite of the county families: eleven were baronets when first returned; sixteen had been preceded in the representation of their counties by their fathers; and many of their descendants continued to sit for generations. To name but a few of those elected in 1754: an Egerton of Tatton and a Cholmondeley of Vale Royal were returned for Cheshire; a Molesworth of Pencarrow and a Buller of Morval for Cornwall; an Isham of Lamport and a Knightley of Fawsley for Northamptonshire; a Courtenay for Devon, a Long for Wiltshire, a Bagot for Staffordshire, a Noel for Rutland, a Curzon for Derbyshire, a Wodehouse for Norfolk, &c. There was an extraordinary permanency in their tenure of seats; few had ever been to the poll, only one was ever defeated, and only three suffered any interruption in the tenure of their seats. Their average term of service for their counties was 24 years—far longer than the average for other constituencies; and there was none of the shifting about from constituency to constituency so common among Members who owed their seats to the Treasury or to borough-owners.

The remaining Tories sat for large boroughs in their own counties or for complete pocket boroughs owned by themselves or close friends or relatives. Hardly any of the Tories had been in the professions (one was a naval officer and three were at the bar), and only a handful were merchants. None held office in 1754 and most never were in office. In short, the Tories were pre-eminently the landed gentry, unconnected with the court—a social group rather than a political party.

It is possible to compile a similar list of Tories returned at the general election of 1761, and their numbers would be about the same. But from about 1763 onwards it is increasingly difficult to differentiate between Whigs and Tories, for politics were no longer carried on in those terms. Even between 1754 and 1763 the task is not easy; often there is no infallible test and the issue depends on the balance of probabilities. Men who knew the House of Commons well could not always agree. Among those classed as Tories by Dupplin in 1754 was William Edwardes, M.P. for Haverfordwest, who was also classed as a Tory by

Henry Fox in February 1755. Yet two years earlier Fox had recommended Edwardes to Henry Pelham as a good Whig, and in 1761 Newcastle treated him as a Whig who was to receive the Treasury whip. In 1761 Newcastle classed Sir Robert Ladbroke, M.P. for London, as a Tory; but in Bute's list of that Parliament he is marked as 'elected by [the] Presbyterian interest'—surely a mark of Whiggism. About John Morton, returned for Abingdon in 1754, party managers could never make up their minds: Richard Neville Aldworth, M.P., a Berkshire neighbour, told the Duke of Bedford that Morton was no Tory and was disposed to attach himself to the Bedford party, and Dupplin in 1754 classed him as a Whig. But in the Oxfordshire election of 1754 Morton voted for the Tory candidates and spoke on their side during the hearing of the election petition. Jarrit Smith, M.P. for Bristol 1756–68, though a foundation member of the Steadfast Society, the group of Bristol Tories, and returned at Bristol on the Tory interest, was summoned to the meeting of Whigs, 2 November 1761, to consider the choice of a Speaker. And many other examples could be added.

The extent to which the words Whig and Tory had lost their political connotations can be seen from the Essex by-election of 1759. The Whigs, having no suitable candidate to propose for the vacancy, hit upon the happy idea of nominating a Tory and calling him a Whig. Sir William Maynard was approached, secured the consent of Lord Maynard, the leader of the Essex Tories, and agreed to stand on the Whig interest. The Duke of Newcastle gave the scheme his hearty approval: 'Sure the Whigs should give Sir William all the support in their power', he wrote to Lord Rochford, leader of the Essex Whigs, 'and make him the Whig candidate.' And so Maynard, a Tory, was returned unopposed on the Whig interest. As the time of the university boat race approaches, boys at school wear dark blue or light blue cockades, and become fervent partisans of Oxford or Cambridge, without knowing anything about rowing or having any connexion with either university. In the same way, in about 1754 men were either Whigs or Tories with just as much reason for their choice. Oxford or Cambridge, Rangers or Celtic, Tottenham Hotspur or Arsenal, Whig or Tory—taking sides and supporting one's team is natural in gregarious rivalry; and politics in the eighteenth century absorbed much of the enthusiasm and partisanship which now goes into organized sport.

It was universally recognized around 1754 that the old party denominations of Whig and Tory no longer corresponded to political realities and that the issues which formerly distinguished them were dead. The Tories, who in the earlier part of the century had been excluded from court and office, were making their way back long before George II died. Horace Walpole, in his *Memoires of the reign of King George III*, wrote that the 'moment of his accession was fortunate beyond example. The extinction of parties had not waited for, but preceded the dawn of his reign'; and the King himself admitted in February 1762 that there were no party divisions in the House of Commons. Pitt cultivated the support of the Tories and eased the process of their return to court: he encouraged them to accept commissions in the militia, a substitute for office, and interceded on their behalf for favours and honours. Lord Talbot wrote to Newcastle on 23 January 1758 in favour of William Harvey, Tory M.P. for Essex, 'that during the time whilst the constellation is in the ascendant under the influence of which the Members of Tory counties may dare to receive marks of ministerial regard ... Mr. William Harvey might receive a favour and the Duke of Newcastle bestow it'. And here is another example, concerning an M.P. of the most undoubted Tory antecedents: Richard Grosvenor, M.P. for Chester 1754–61, who not only came out strongly in support of Pitt but in November 1758 gave public approbation of the Newcastle-Pitt Administration by seconding the Address at the opening of the session—a Tory Member seconding the Address of a Whig ministry. George III did not set out to abolish party distinctions: they had disappeared, the result of changing political conditions, before he came to the throne.

The durability of parties depends less on the ideas they represent than on the strength and coherence of party organizations. There were no party organizations in 1754, apart from the Treasury, which acted as a kind of party organization for the Whigs, though its influence was limited to those Members whom it provided with seats or who looked to it for favours. The Tories had not even a leader who could command the confidence of the whole: Sir John Philipps, M.P. for Petersfield, formerly prominent in their ranks, now possessed little influence outside Wales, and William Beckford, M.P. for London, though invariably classed as a Tory seems to have considered himself a Whig. The Tories, in so far as any organization at all is to be found in their ranks, grouped themselves on a regional basis, and there was little intercourse between the Tories say of Devon and Cornwall and those of the Midland counties. With such flimsy organizations to support them, it is no wonder the parties crumbled and disintegrated. Yet something intangible remained, unaffected by the dissolution of the two old parties: political ideas survived, without the protection of party organizations, and took root in strange and wonderful places. What these ideas were, and where they finally flowered, may be seen from a glance at some typical Tories of 1754.

But first, let us note the fact that one Member only, of the 1,964 who sat in the House from 1754 to 1790, is known to have referred to himself as a Tory. Humphrey Sibthorp, M.P. for Boston 1777–84, wrote to his friend John Strutt on 4 January 1784, shortly after Pitt had taken office: 'I am, I freely own it, not so much any man's friend as I am the King's, nor do I wish in these times at least to purge off all Tory blood.' Sibthorp had been a supporter of North's Administration, and for all his professions of devotion to the King had heartily disliked the King's intervention against Fox's East India bill. Nor was he favourably disposed towards Pitt's Administration; in fact this self-styled Tory was much more inclined to support Charles James Fox, who regarded himself as the leader of the Whigs.

Sir Roger Newdigate, M.P. for Middlesex 1742–7 and for Oxford University 1751–80, would in 1754 have been selected as the archetype of the Tories. Devoted to the interests of the Church of England, zealous in defence of its privileges and prerogatives; a constant opposer of what he called 'Hanoverian measures', by which he meant continental wars and foreign subsidies; an opponent of standing armies, Government influence over the House of Commons, and Whig measures in general— were not these the hall-marks of the Tory about the middle of the century? Though Newdigate supported the militia (the Tories' alternative to the regular army) and enthusiastically discharged his duties as a militia officer, he never quite fell for the blandishments of Pitt, the great advocate for the militia, as some other Tories did. On 19 April 1757 he opposed a series of resolutions granting a subsidy to the King of Prussia: 'Gave my negative to every proposition', he wrote in his diary, 'no British measure.' In the new reign he went to court and kissed the King's hand (which he had never done under George II), yet still maintained a certain attitude of detachment. 'I like the King', he wrote, 'and shall be with his ministers as long as I think an honest man ought, and believe it best not to lose the country gentleman in the courtier.' It was an attitude he preserved throughout his parliamentary career.

Newdigate supported North's American policy, and during at least the early years of North's Administration regularly received the Treasury whip. During the '70s his Tory opinions, which he rigidly maintained, led to a curious pattern of cross voting. On the question of religious toleration, he adhered to what might be called the right wing of the Government and opposed all concessions to the Dissenters; yet he regularly voted for shortening the duration of Parliaments, a measure supported only by the extreme left wing of the Opposition. His Toryism, in short, led him to become both an arch-Tory and a radical at the same time. And when in 1780, dejected at the ill conduct of the American war, he decided to leave Parliament, he, who had uniformly supported North's American policy, denounced North's Administration in terms which might have been used by a Rockingham Whig. In his letter of resignation to the vice-chancellor of Oxford University, he ascribed the nation's disasters to 'majorities implicitly following the dictates of the ministers of the day, changing their opinions as the minister was changed' (a remarkable, albeit probably unconscious, echo of Burke), and, in the true radical vein, denounced the corruption of both Parliament and Administration—'the people at large more corrupt than even the representative body, and that more corrupt than even the minister himself'.

George Cooke, M.P. for Middlesex 1750–68, another of those whom Dupplin classed as a Tory in 1754, was described by Horace Walpole as a 'pompous Jacobite'. Cooke had been politically connected with Newdigate, but their ways began to diverge during the seven years' war when Cooke became a fervent adherent of Pitt. The conflict between his Tory principles, which led him to oppose continental warfare, and his support of Pitt, in 1761 the great advocate of the continental war, resulted in contradictions: thus on 9 February 1761 he opposed the payment of a subsidy to Hanover, yet on 13 November spoke for continued British participation in the German war—which could hardly be done without the payment of subsidies. By 1765 the former Jacobite had become entirely devoted to Pitt; and while Newdigate was strongly anti-American, Cooke was one of the few Members who agreed with Pitt's contention that Great Britain had no right to tax the colonies.

In short, the fact that a Member was classed as a Tory in 1754 or 1761 is no guide to what his subsequent conduct would be or what attitude he would take when the American problem came before Parliament. For the Tories were essentially independents, and once Toryism as a political creed had lost its *raison d'être*, there was no party organization to keep the Tories together. All the various parties of the late '60s had a sprinkling of former Tories among them. To give some examples: Marshe Dickinson went with the Bedfords; Edward Kynaston and Thomas Howard with the Grenvilles; William Beckford, George Cooke, and Thomas Prowse with Chatham; Charles Barrow, Sir William Meredith, and Sir William Codrington with the Rockinghams. William Dowdeswell, leader of the Rockingham party in the Commons from 1766 till his death in 1775, was a former Tory. It is ironical that the Rockinghams should have regarded themselves as the heirs of the Whigs and should have labelled their opponents as Tories, when they were led during their formative years by an ex-Tory who had never renounced his Tory principles.

The Rockinghams, as the main Opposition party during the American crisis, inherited much of the political thinking of the Tories. What Professor Butterfield has called the stock Opposition programme of the eighteenth century—a series of measures designed to reduce the influence of the Crown over the House of Commons—could be employed against Lord North as well as against Sir Robert Walpole or Henry Pelham; and the Rockinghams, who carried these measures into effect in 1782, are the true spiritual heirs of the Tories. But indeed Tory principles were not the property of the Tories only: they may be found in the mouths of many Members who by no stretch of the imagination could be labelled as Tories. Lord Fife, a highly independent Scottish Member and a former follower of George Grenville, expressed typical Tory sentiments in a letter to his factor on 20 April 1773: 'In the present times of low credit, avert war, say I. Stock jobbers, Jews, and contractors make by that, but you and I are out of pocket.' And Lord Hardwicke wrote to his nephew in 1782 about Sir Henry Peyton, a candidate for the forthcoming by-election in Cambridgeshire: 'Sir Henry Peyton dislikes many of the things we do, short Parliaments, new modes of election, &c., is no violent American, and shook his head about losing our authority in Ireland.' Almost all of these sentiments would have been subscribed to by Burke and the Rockingham Whigs, yet Hardwicke ended: 'I rather take Sir Henry to be a moderate Tory.' Even the Tory feeling against a standing army was taken up at the end of the period and paraded as a Whig principle. James Martin, M.P. for Tewkesbury, a radical both in politics and religion, said in the House on 27 February 1786 during the debate on the Duke of Richmond's fortifications plan: 'The adoption of that system would make an increase of the standing army necessary, a matter he was too much of a Whig to give consent to.'

The Whigs in the late seventeenth century had been the party opposed to the Crown: they had tried to exclude the Duke of York from the succession in 1679 and had opposed the Tory principle of an hereditary, indefeasible right to the Crown. There were still a few Whigs of the old breed left in 1754. One of them was Robert More, M.P. for Shrewsbury, described by Horace Walpole as 'a Whig of the primitive stamp', who thought of himself as politically and spiritually descended from the parliamentarians of 1641. Another was Newcastle's great friend John White, M.P. for East Retford, a Dissenter, described by Walpole as 'an old republican who governed Newcastle'. Other old-style Whigs, close friends of Newcastle, were John Page, M.P. for Chichester, and John Thornhagh (who later took the name of Hewett), M.P. for Nottinghamshire. But these men never held political office under Newcastle nor joined the crowd of eager, expectant place hunters who thronged his levees. The old Whigs were as jealous of their independence as any Tory, and they supported Newcastle as the representative of an old political tradition, not for what they could get out of him. Page in 1758 told the Duke of Richmond that though he had spent £15,000 on parliamentary elections he had never held 'any employment under the Crown nor any private pecuniary reward from any minister, though in general a friend to them'. And Newcastle wrote to Hewett on 12 July 1766: 'You never asked anything of me but such trifles as I should be ashamed to refuse'; to which Hewett replied: 'Almost all I've asked has been with a view to support myself in this county.'

Another old Whig, so independent and disinterested that in Bute's list of 1761 he was classed as a Tory, was Edward Montagu, M.P. for Huntingdon 1734–68, husband of the literary lady Mrs. Elizabeth Montagu. On 22 October 1761 Lord Sandwich replied to Newcastle's request for Montagu's attendance at the opening of the session: 'As to my cousin Mr. Montagu, I much fear he never will (as he never yet has) give his countenance to any Administration.' And when, shortly after the accession of George III, his wife asked if she might go to court, Montagu replied:

The principal reason of my absenting myself ever since I was Member of Parliament was that I did not concur in the measures that were then taking, and the principal members of the Opposition thought they had no business at St. James's.... I have for many years lived in a state of independency, though I may truly call it of proscription...

No wonder Bute mistook him for a Tory! The above passage could well have been written by Newdigate; indeed, something very similar was written by Newdigate at about the same time:

I can't answer your question what my party is. I am only sure it is neither Cumberland nor Pelham. Landed men must love peace, men proscribed and abused for fifty years together [should] be presented with fools caps if they make ladders for tyrant Whigs to mount by.

It is pertinent to ask, in the light of these passages, what were the differences between the old Whigs, and the old Tories? As far as political principles were concerned, there was very little difference: Montagu was a Whig because his ancestors had been Whigs and he sat for a pocket borough under the control of a Whig peer; while Newdigate was a Tory because he came of a Tory family and sat for the traditionally Tory university of Oxford. The real political alignments were on an entirely different basis from those of Whig and Tory.

Lord Waldegrave, governor to George III as Prince of Wales, wrote in his *Memoirs*, composed about 1757:

When the Hanover succession took place, the Whigs became the possessors of all the great offices and other lucrative employments; since which time, instead of quarrelling with the prerogative, they have been the champions of every Administration.
However, they have not always been united in one body, under one general, like a regular and well-disciplined army; but may be more aptly compared to an alliance of different clans, fighting in the same cause, professing the same principles, but influenced and guided by their different chieftains.

Party struggles in the last years of George II and the early years of George III were essentially struggles for office, with political principles used as shibboleths, a means of distinguishing friend from foe. The Whig and Tory parties had been destroyed, said Bamber Gascoyne in the House on 11 December 1761, and 'personal parties [had been] substituted in their stead'. Party existed in the House only, and was rarely found in the constituencies. There were as yet few political issues to grip the imagination of the nation at large and to divide it on a party basis. When such issues do arise, party divisions seem inevitable, and then there is no need to justify the existence of party as Burke tried to do in 1770 in his *Thoughts on the Cause of the Present Discontents*. When political issues come home to men's business and bosoms, party divisions require no justification: the need Burke felt to defend them in 1770 is a proof of their essential artificiality at that time. This was clearly seen by Lord Holland, grandson of Henry Fox and nephew of Charles James Fox, who in his *Memoirs of the Whig Party* distinguished between the 'parliamentary cabals' of the first twelve years of George III's reign as 'mere struggles for favour and power' and the 'great questions of policy and principle which arose on the American war'. For neither general warrants nor Wilkes's election for Middlesex in 1769 was a 'great question of policy and principle': all parties agreed that the legality of general warrants had never been determined, and the point of dispute about the Middlesex election was one of law rather than of policy. And until 1774 American policy was only occasionally an issue of dispute between the parties.

Some idea of the state of parties under the Chatham Administration can be obtained from three lists of the House of Commons drawn up independently of each other in the winter of 1766–7. One, compiled in November 1766, is among the papers of Lord Rockingham, the leader of the largest Opposition party; the second, which from internal evidence can be assigned to January 1767, is among the papers of Charles Townshend, Chatham's chancellor of the Exchequer; while the third, dated 2 March 1767, was compiled by the Duke of Newcastle, then closely allied with Rockingham in opposition. The classifications used in these lists are not the same: Rockingham and Newcastle, both highly neurotic personalities fixated on the past, used the old terms of Whigs and Tories, while Townshend attempted a more realistic phraseology and employed the term 'country gentlemen' instead of 'Tories'. The table on p. 282 attempts to compare these three lists.

A schematic analysis of this kind is misleading in so far as it conceals the discrepancies between the different classifications, which tend to cancel each other out and produce uniform results. A more careful examination of the three lists reveals the fact that for a large number of Members the compilers could not agree on a classification.

List	Govern-ment party	Rocking-ham party	Gren-ville party	Bedford party	Tories (Newcastle and Rockingham); country gentlemen (Townshend)	Doubtful or absent	Un-classified
Rockingham	225	121	17	35	86	69	5
Townshend	212	65	56	24	34	69	98
Newcastle	232	101	54[1]		91	69	11

[1]Newcastle did not distinguish between the Grenville and Bedford parties.

Thus George Hunt, a thoroughly independent Member, was listed by Rockingham as one of his party; by Townshend as a Government supporter; and by Newcastle as 'doubtful or absent'. Eight Members were classed by Rockingham as Whigs and by Newcastle as Tories. Of the 121 Members classed by Rockingham as belonging to his own party, Newcastle, his close friend and ally, accepted only 77. I repeat here what I wrote in *The Chatham Administration* about Rockingham's and Newcastle's lists:

Putting these results in another way, more than one third of Rockingham's list of friends was rejected by Newcastle, and about a quarter of Newcastle's list was rejected by Rockingham. Yet the two lists were drawn up within three months of each other. Here, then, are the leaders of a party unable to agree upon who were their followers. What value can be given to their lists of the other parties if they do not know their own? And what kind of a party was it whose leaders did not know their own followers?

Still, certain facts do emerge from this table. The Government party was about 220 strong; the combined Opposition parties about 150; and about 180 Members were attached to neither Government nor Opposition. Rockingham greatly exaggerated the size of his own party and under-estimated that of his most formidable rival, Grenville. Townshend's list is the most realistic, in frankly admitting that there were nearly 100 Members who could not be classified. And the balance of power in the House is clearly with the independents—whether styled Tory, country gentlemen, or doubtful: the men uncommitted to any party. The picture bears no resemblance to that of the present day House of Commons, but it is similar to that of the present day British electorate: there are two large blocs, always voting in their own ways, and between them a mass of uncommitted voters holding the balance.

What can be learnt from · the speeches of Members about party divisions? The obvious thing that strikes anyone who reads through the biographical volumes is the number of Members who disclaimed party. It was the favourite gambit on the hustings. Sir Wilfred Lawson at the Cumberland by-election of 1761 declared that he would be the better able to discharge the trust imposed upon him 'as he did not look upon himself as particularly obliged to any particular party', and Samuel Eyre in his address to the electors of Devizes in February 1765 promised to be 'steady, uniform, and independent, not biassed by interest, not attached to party'. Rear-Admiral Lord Hood wrote in 1783 when invited to contest Westminster: 'I shall ever most carefully and studiously stand clear . . . of all suspicion of being a party man; for if once I show myself of that frame of mind . . . I must . . . expect to lose every degree of consideration in the line of my profession.' In the constituencies anything which seemed to be a party measure was damned. Henry Duncombe, M.P. for Yorkshire 1780–96, attended a meeting at York in September 1770 to consider what further steps should be taken to secure redress of grievances arising from the Middlesex election. Though strongly opposed to the Government's policy, Duncombe refused to concur in the measure suggested by the Rockingham party. 'I had the misfortune to differ from my associates', he wrote subsequently to Christopher Wyvill, 'as things seemed then to me to carry too much the air of a party spirit, which I totally disclaimed.' The highest compliment which could be paid to a Member of Parliament was to say that he was unconnected with party. The *Public Ledger*, an Opposition newspaper, wrote in 1779 about Francis Annesley, M.P. for Reading: 'A very conscientious Member of Parliament, means well, votes with the Opposition, but not attached to any party.' And the number of Members who in debate disclaimed party connexions is legion. Here is one example, out of hundreds. Richard Wilbraham Bootle, M.P. for Chester, described by the *English Chronicle* in 1780 as 'one of the most independent Members in the House', said in the debate of 21 February 1783, on Shelburne's peace preliminaries: 'He had seen so much injustice transacted in that House through the influence of party while he sat in the gallery and before he was a Member, that when he came into the House he had washed his hands of party for ever.' And Wilberforce in 1785 described party as the evil 'from which our greatest misfortunes arose'.

Even those Members who were generally considered to belong to parties, denounced party as an unhealthy element in political life. Let us take a few examples from the Rockinghams, perhaps the most party-conscious group in the House. Lord John Cavendish, one of Rockingham's most trusted advisers, who owed his seat at York to Rockingham's influence, said in the House on 2 April 1770 that he 'wished all cursed distinctions of party to be done away'. Charles Turner, Cavendish's colleague at York and also elected on Rockingham's recommendation, did not consider himself as belonging to a party: he was, in his own words, 'a country gentleman who meant to act entirely for the service of his constituents'; and on another occasion he described himself as 'no party man' but 'an old-fashioned Whig'——a curious association of phrases, with the implication that the Whigs were no longer a party. Sir George Savile, M.P. for Yorkshire, to whose friendship and alliance Rockingham was indebted for his supremacy in Yorkshire politics, and of whom Burke wrote in 1773 that 'much of the strength of our cause has arisen from its having his support', wrote to his nephew on 12 January 1783, at the close of his political life: 'What man can say he is conscientiously using the best of his judgment on any great state point, when he is ... sticking to a party in order to ... get ... a reward for his fidelity?'

And here is another example concerning another Member connected with the Rockingham party. Robert Gregory, for many years a director of the East India Company, was a friend of Rockingham who in 1768 had recommended him to Lord Aylesford for a seat at Maidstone. Gregory voted with the Opposition and was specially interested in East India affairs, on which he acted as one of Rockingham's advisers. It would be natural to class him as belonging to the Rockingham party, were it not for an incident which took place in the House on 9 April 1781, during an East India debate. After Lord North had described the grave situation in India provoked by Hyder Ali's invasion of the Carnatic, Gregory declared he would support whatever measures the Government should take to meet the crisis. Burke, who followed him, pledged himself, Gregory, and 'those in opposition with whom he had conversed on the subject' to support North 'in everything that should appear to them conducive to the joint interest of the Company and the kingdom'. What followed may be described in the words of the parliamentary reporter:

Mr. Gregory got up again; and with warmth observed that as no man was more ready to support the noble Lord in everything reasonable than he was, yet he requested the honourable Member would only pledge himself and nobody else for

the support of the measures that might be proposed; he said he stood connected
with no party, nor with the honourable Member who had spoken last; he would
give his opinion freely, and his support where he thought it due; but still
regardless of the promises of others, he being as independent in his principles and
his seat as any man in the House ...

Mr. Burke was hurt ... and observed that as the honourable gentleman thought
proper to renounce any connexion with him, he was very welcome to do it.

Clearly, Gregory valued his independence to speak his mind freely,
and was not prepared to allow a party to speak for him. Burke, however,
who depended on Rockingham for a seat in the House, felt differently.
Many years earlier he had outlined the case for party, arguing with
reason and irrefutable logic:

How men can proceed without any connexion at all is to me utterly incomprehens-
ible. Of what sort of materials must that man be made ... who can sit whole years
in Parliament with five hundred and fifty of his fellow citizens ... without
seeing any one sort of men whose character, conduct, or disposition would lead
him to associate himself with them, to aid and be aided, in any one system of
public utility?

But Burke's devotion to the Rockingham party satisfied a deep emotional
need in his nature, and time after time he sacrificed his own opinion to the
judgement of his party leaders. And there is clearly a difference between
Members associating together on a voluntary basis, reserving their right
to differ from the group if they wish, and Members who have to follow the
party line or else find another party which suits them better. The essential
basis of party in the eighteenth century was voluntary; party decisions
could not bind the individual Members, who preserved their independence
as the most dearly cherished privilege of a Member of Parliament.

That this was so can be underlined by citing a few declarations by
Members whose political conduct proved their independence. Lord
Strange, M.P. for Lancashire, who for nine years held the office of
chancellor of the duchy of Lancaster without drawing the salary, said
in August 1765, when asked if he would support the newly-appointed
Rockingham ministry, 'that a Whig Administration I should always
approve of, and if such a one was appointed I should certainly vote
with them whenever I thought them right, and that I would go no further
with any Administration.' About the same time, John Campbell of Calder,
M.P. for Corfe Castle, an old Whig who remembered Sir Robert Walpole,
wrote to Newcastle:

Though an honest man may often comply with things not quite agreeable to him, rather than give any advantage against an Administration which he approves, yet there are some things in which he must follow his own judgment, such as he has, without regard to persons.

William Fitzherbert, M.P. for Derby, who, from being partisan of Wilkes had become his enemy, thus defended himself in the House on 14 December 1770: 'I am a private gentleman in employment, without connexions, without hopes, without fears. I am independent from temper... I shall never be ashamed to say what I think.' Nicolson Calvert, M.P. for Tewkesbury, though a follower of Chatham, voted for the Government on the Spanish convention, 13 February 1771, because he thought Great Britain had been the aggressor in the quarrel over the Falkland Islands: 'I stand a free man. No man shall ever lead me.' General John Burgoyne, M.P. for Preston, normally a Government supporter, voted with the Opposition over the Spanish convention, and described the rule of his political conduct as 'to assist Government in my general line of conduct, but that in great national points... I would ever hold myself at liberty to maintain my own opinion'. Robert Walsingham, who represented the Duke of Devonshire's borough of Knaresborough, normally voted with the Opposition but refused to concur in their attack on the naval administration of his friend Lord Sandwich: 'He was an independent man', he said on 19 April 1799, 'and was ready to put the smiles or frowns of either side of the House equally at defiance.'

Despite these examples, it may be objected that solemn assertions of independence were often no more than lip-service to an accepted idea. Even if this were so, it would prove, nevertheless, that independence, rather than devotion to a party, was the expected conduct of a Member of Parliament. But the number of real independents will come as a surprise even to some of those best acquainted with the period; and still more so, the number of Members who, though as a rule voting with Government or a party, would deviate from their normal line and act according to their own judgement and conscience. At the very outset of this period, on 3 October 1754, William Pitt wrote about the newly elected House of Commons: 'They are not disciplined troops, and he must be an able general indeed who can answer for them.' And almost at the end, when the younger Pitt, despite his brilliant electoral victory of 1784, was running into difficulties with the House, Daniel Pulteney, M.P. for

Bramber, wrote to his patron the Duke of Rutland, 4 March 1785:

The explanation to all this is neither more nor less than that the House of Commons, being at present perhaps *too independent* ... has many whims and caprices, and will decide against any minister, sometimes without ill-will to him in the main.

There it is in a nut-shell: 'too independent', 'whims and caprices'. No wonder that experienced electoral and parliamentary managers were often unable to gauge the attitude of Members, especially when they were mute. And no wonder that Governments were frequently defeated: their majorities depended largely on the support of the independents, and that support could always be withdrawn. Four divisions in which North's Administration was defeated will serve as examples, none of them concerned with its American policy. (It will be noticed that the Government would have had a clear majority on each occasion if all those who normally supported Government had done so in these divisions.)

Date	Division	Government vote	Opposition vote	Number of normal Government supporters voting with Opposition
9 February 1773	Petition of naval officers for an increase in half pay	45	154	70
25 February 1774	Motion to make permanent Grenville's Act for deciding controverted elections	122	250	115
12 February 1779	Jennings Clerke's bill to debar Government contractors from sitting in the House	143	158	30
6 April 1780	Dunning's motion against the influence of the Crown	215	233	39

We should be clear as to what the eighteenth century meant by independence. An independent Member could act with a party or even hold office under the Crown without thereby forfeiting his independence. The crucial test was the tenure by which he held his seat in the House. If he sat for a Treasury borough, or depended on Government assistance (financial or otherwise), or if he owed his seat to a patron, he could not be truly independent; for his political conduct had necessarily to be acceptable to those who brought him into Parliament, and if it was not he faced the prospect of losing his seat. But if he sat for a county or a populous borough, or for his own pocket borough, or if he had bought his seat, then he was truly independent, responsible only to his constituents (if he had any). Sir George Savile, who represented the 20,000 freeholders of Yorkshire, or Thomas Pitt, who represented the seven burgages of Old Sarum, were both, in eighteenth-century eyes, independent; Edmund Burke, who when he sat for Malton represented nobody but Lord Rockingham, was not.

In the last analysis the real test of independence was an economic one. Sir Gregory Page Turner, M.P. for Thirsk 1784–1805, claimed that 'whatever his abilities were ... his property rendered him independent, and he always delivered his sincere sentiments according to his conscientious opinion'. When in 1756 Rose Fuller, a rich Jamaica planter, was looking for a seat in the House, a friend wrote to Lord Hardwicke: 'Mr Fuller ... is of too much property to desire to be brought in by any interest that should entirely restrain the freedom of his vote.' A cousin of Ralph Payne thus recommended him to the Duke of Grafton for a seat at the general election of 1768: 'He has a very strong attachment to Lord Chatham and the present Administration ... but as he is willing to be at a large expense to get into Parliament ... he hopes to be allowed a perfect independency ... and means to act on all occasions on the best convictions of his own understanding only.' And the *English Chronicle* wrote about William Plumer, M.P. for Hertfordshire, in 1781: 'Having little to wish ... and nothing to fear, he is governed by no consideration but his own conviction.'

The connexion between financial security and political independence is clearly stated in the following extract, written in October 1757, from the diary of Sir John Gordon, M.P. for Cromartyshire:

Thank God I still have between £800 and £900 per annum, subject to a debt only of about £7,000, besides the salary of my office ... I am now able to stand against ministerial close fistedness for I am not obliged to be equally dependent as formerly when my situation subjected me to slights at their hands.

A Member might also be restrained in his independence by the circumstances of his family. When Thomas Pelham was elected for Sussex in 1780 the *English Chronicle* wrote that it was doubtful which way he would give his vote in Parliament. Pelham was strongly inclined to the Opposition and thought Lord North 'a most abominable minister', yet he hesitated to vote against Administration lest his father be dismissed from his court sinecure in consequence. He wrote to his father on 8 August 1781: 'I am sure that with a very large nominal estate, you must at present feel a dependence on your emoluments from Government, and that the least turn in affairs would make your situation very uncomfortable.' He compromised between his convictions and his interest, by voting against the American war but supporting North on motions of confidence in his Administration. The contrary fate befell Lord Herbert, first returned to Parliament in 1780 for his family's borough of Wilton, who wished to vote with the Government but was afraid of offending his father Lord Pembroke, a red-hot oppositionist. Three weeks after taking his seat, Herbert wrote to a friend:

I have lately discovered what has long been known, that in this blessed country nobody sits on principle, being all biassed by connexions, either friendly or family interest, &c. For my part I have been on three divisions in the House and out of those three times have only voted once according to my opinions, and did that *en cachet* for fear my *family connexions* should get hold of it. And after all this, the world are pleased to call me a free Englishman and a member of a free Parliament!

Few patrons were generous enough to allow their dependants to vote as they pleased in the House. The three line whip already existed during this period, but it was sent by the patron not by the party. On 28 February 1755, when the House was occupied with the struggle over the Mitchell election petition, the Duke of Newcastle wrote to his cousin James Pelham, M.P. for Hastings:

Dear Jemmy,
    I should not trouble you with desiring you to attend the Mitchell election this night, if I did not think I had a right to insist with my own family to attend, where my situation as one of the principal ministers is greatly concerned ... and if this is the case what an appearance would it have for you to be absent.

'Dear Jemmy' however did not attend, and the tone of the Duke's next communication changed abruptly:

Sir,
    You will not be surprised that after the letter I wrote you I should be much disappointed and concerned that you did not attend the Mitchell election. I am

convinced that it was not your age or infirmities that occasioned your absence, but some attachment separate from and independent of me. Since that is the case I should advise you, for your own sake as well as mine, to quit your seat in Parliament, that I may choose one at Hastings upon whom I may entirely depend.

Pelham managed to pacify the Duke and convince him that ill health alone was the reason for his absence. One of the very few exceptions to the rule that a patron's politics governed his dependant's took place in 1787, when Lord Spencer allowed Humphrey Minchin, who sat on his interest at Okehampton, to go over to Pitt; still, at the next general election Minchin felt obliged to obtain a seat elsewhere.

With so many Members independent of Administration, why did the House almost invariably support successive Administrations of different political complexions, which has earned it the reputation of subserviency from historians and contemporaries alike? One reason is that the independents were politically ineffective: not being bound by a community of views, interest, or purpose, they could not form a body capable of political manœuvre—to do that they would have had to become a party. Except on rare occasions, when a powerful wave of public feeling swept the country (as for instance towards the end of the American war) the independents, by dividing more or less evenly between Government and Opposition, cancelled each other out, and thus enabled a comparatively small but compact Treasury group to tip the balance decisively in favour of Administration. Moreover, the attendance of placemen, mostly resident in or near London, or even of those closely identified with political parties, was more regular than that of the independents, who were not professional politicians.

A second reason is that on controversial issues there was a tendency on the part of the independents to give the Government the benefit of the doubt. To vote with the Opposition smacked of faction, and the independent Member would not do so unless the issue touched his conscience. Herbert Mackworth, M.P. for Cardiff Boroughs, declared during the debate on the expulsion of Wilkes, 3 February 1769: 'My mind is distressed to give a vote ... I shall go against his Majesty's ministers, but my principle is to support them.' And Sir Thomas Clavering, M.P. for Durham county, said on 19 March 1770, when attacked for changing his mind on the Middlesex election: 'I think Administration acted wrong, but when the majority of this House thought otherwise it was my duty to submit to it.' The principle of giving the Government the benefit of the doubt was expressed by Sir Gregory Page Turner, M.P. for Thirsk, when he said in the debate on Pitt's commercial propositions, 12 May 1785, that 'he did not understand the resolutions, but could vote with a clear conscience from his confidence in the right honourable gentleman'.

Burke and other Opposition politicians frequently denounced those Members who were prepared to vote with every Administration, whatever its political complexion; but the existence of a court party followed logically from the fact that the Government, through the Treasury and the Admiralty, controlled a number of pocket boroughs, and was able to secure the nomination to many more under private patronage. A court party existed, not through deliberate intent, but by the force of electoral circumstances; and what might be called a court political philosophy also existed. The Crown, the head of the executive, naturally attracted those who were ambitious of office, especially if they had no parliamentary interest of their own. Here was another factor which retarded the growth of party in the political sense.

It has been shown in an earlier section that the electoral influence of the Crown decreased during this period. The fundamental cause of that decrease seems to have been the growth of party feeling in the House of Commons, which was itself a consequence of the emergence of political questions which deeply divided the House and the politically conscious part of the nation. The history of the House of Commons can only be understood as part of the political history of Great Britain; still, it is beyond the scope of this survey to tell the story of the political developments of these years. All that can be done is to show their effect upon the House of Commons, and the changes in the party composition of the House between 1754 and 1790.

In 1754, according to Lord Dupplin's calculations, the Government party under the leadership of the Duke of Newcastle, numbered 368 Members. But most of those Members owed allegiance to Newcastle not as party leader but as first lord of the Treasury, and did not follow him when he went into opposition in 1762. Bute had as big a majority as ever Newcastle had, and in December 1762, after Bute's victory on the peace preliminaries, it seemed that a new stability had been reached in terms of the new reign. There was a new King and there was a new minister, but essentially the political system remained unchanged.

The period of short-lived ministries, from 1762 to 1770, was pre-
eminently a period of personal politics. Each successive minister—Bute,
Grenville, Rockingham, Chatham—was able in office to build up his own
party and to lead it into opposition after he had left office, but the
longer he remained in opposition the smaller his following grew. Grenville,
when he became first lord of the Treasury in April 1763, had no followers
in the House of Commons; when he left office in July 1765 there was a
group of about 70 Members who looked to him as their political leader.
By July 1766, when Chatham took office, this group had been reduced to
about 30, and when Grenville died in November 1770 the number of
his followers in the House did not exceed 20. Shortly after his death his
two principal lieutenants, Lord Suffolk and Alexander Wedderburn,
made overtures to the court, and in January 1771 most of Grenville's
friends rejoined Administration. Parties which were essentially personal
in their nature could not survive the natural or political death of their
leader. Bute's group broke up after his retirement from politics in 1766;
the Duke of Bedford's group merged into the Government party after
the Duke's death in January 1771; while Chatham, who did not bother to
cultivate a party, had never more than a handful of followers in the House.

Personal parties grew in size at the expense of the Government party.
However much Members in office or who aspired to office might protest
that their political allegiance was to the sovereign alone, and however
much they might deplore the growth of party, they were nearly all sooner
or later engulfed by the parties: they could not for ever swim against the
current of the age. Welbore Ellis, who had held office continuously from
1747 to 1765 and from 1770 to 1782, protested to the King in March
1783: 'I have been in Parliament forty-two years, and in this long
course of service I can say what few can, that I never was a part of any
concerted system of Opposition.' Yet he was in opposition to Pitt from
1783 to 1794, and like a fish out of water: Sir Gilbert Elliot in 1787
described him as 'out of his place in a hopeless opposition'. Lord Granby,
on his return from Germany in February 1763, declared to the King that
he would in future support Bute as he had hitherto supported Newcastle.
'Lord Granby's language to me was full of duty and attachment', wrote
the King to Bute, 'saying . . . his inclination as well as duty would make
him ever attached to my person, and subsequently support my measures
and ministry as at present composed or however I should form it.' For
the next three years Granby's conduct conformed to his profession, but in

July 1765, when the King dismissed Grenville and gave the Treasury to Rockingham, his language began to change. 'If your Majesty orders me to continue in office', he told the King, 'I have only to obey, but, Sir, I hope you will permit me to continue unconnected with your ministers.' Granby was now much more the politician and much less the servant of the Crown, and five years later he resigned his offices and went with Chatham into opposition. Despite all his professions of political allegiance to the Crown, he had become a party man.

The era of personal parties came to an end about 1770. Bute had retired; Chatham was in the House of Lords; Grenville and Bedford were shortly to die. With Lord North as first lord of the Treasury the court party had again a leader in the House of Commons, and as the agitation over the Middlesex election died away a new stability was achieved in the House, not to be disturbed until the disasters of the American war.

One party only survived the era of personal parties: that led by Lord Rockingham. When Rockingham left office in July 1766 he had about 70 Members in his party. Their numbers probably increased during the following three years, years of weak leadership by Administration and of increasing party conflict in the House. By January 1770, when North took office, Rockingham had about 100 followers and was the only party leader in the Opposition with any considerable following. Chatham and Shelburne, his rivals in the Opposition, disclaimed the idea of party and drew their support mainly from the independent Members; while the handful of radicals in the House were as yet unorganized. These years saw a certain hardening of party lines, an acceptance of party as a normal element in the life of the House of Commons, which is symbolized by the fact that in the Parliament of 1768–74 Members are noted as taking their seats according to their political inclinations. There had long been a Treasury bench; now there began to be an Opposition front bench; and the practice of sitting regularly on one or the other side of the House spread to the back benches. It was by no means universal: Richard Rigby, paymaster general from 1768 to 1782, always sat on the Opposition side of the House. Still, the fact that Rigby was thought to be eccentric in this, indicates what was coming to be the accepted custom; and in 1778 George Johnstone used the expression 'cross the floor' in the sense of changing one's political allegiance. Yet party allegiance, as contrasted with political inclination, was confined to a minority of Members only. Chatham told the Duke of Richmond in 1771 that 'there were many eccentric men who would not belong to a party' and that they were 'the real strength of Opposition'. It could not be otherwise so long as the majority of Members were returned independent of party organizations.

The Rockinghams were pre-eminently an aristocratic party. Lord George Cavendish was speaking Rockingham's sentiments when he told Horace Walpole in February 1783 that 'he liked an aristocracy and thought it right that great families with great connexions should govern'. They had no roots in the nation at large: no follower of Rockingham ever sat for London or Westminster (Charles James Fox was a political leader in his own right), and Burke's attempt to capture Bristol for the Rockinghams proved a failure. Their belief that 'great families with great connexions should govern' was alien to the spirit of urban radicalism. They looked back to an imaginary golden age of Whig rule and lacked inspiration for the future. Rockingham wrote on 20 December 1772 to one of his followers, James Murray, who was contemplating leaving Parliament: 'I cannot wonder that you and others should be tired out with the drudgery of Parliament and in continuing a system of politics which affords little prospect of success.' And even after fighting had broken out in America, when Burke was trying to rouse the party to face the greatest political crisis of their time, Rockingham thought nothing could be done until 'a degree of experience of the evils' had brought about 'a right judgement in the public at large'. Burke, in despair at the sloth and procrastination of his leaders, wrote to Charles Fox on 8 October 1777: 'A great deal of activity and enterprise can scarcely ever be expected from such men, unless some horrible calamity is just over their heads or unless they suffer some gross personal insults from power.' The failure of the Rockinghams to appeal to the nation at large, to develop a positive political faith, was a brake on the development of party in the constituencies.

The era of political parties, as contrasted with personal parties, dates from about 1775, though the two types overlap: personal parties had political questions thrust upon them and had to adapt themselves accordingly. Parties were shaped by the great issues of the American war and of reform, and from 1775 to 1782 five groups can be distinguished in the House of Commons, each differentiated on a political basis.

First was the Government party, led by Lord North, which stood for the prosecution of the American war and was opposed to both economical and parliamentary reform. Its numbers were between 150 and 200: it was at its highest in 1775 and 1776 when enthusiasm for the war was at its greatest, and began slowly to decrease from 1780 as it became clear that the aims for which the war had begun were not to be attained. Allied to the Government party was a group of independent Members, who supported North on the American war but opposed him over reform. In John Robinson's survey for the general election of 1780 above twenty Members are noted as voting with the Government on the American war but with the Opposition on economical reform. Here are Robinson's comments on some of them:

I put Lord Ongley [M.P. for Bedfordshire] down for, because he generally is so except in some of the questions of economy and reformation . . .

Mr. Hungerford [M.P. for Leicestershire] most generally with, except upon very popular questions.

Sir Horace Mann [M.P. for Maidstone] is canvassed against, because on the popular questions he has gone against, but he is often for, and inclines to support Government and the present constitution.

Mr. Daniel Lascelles [M.P. for Northallerton] is only put hopeful, because in these late popular questions he has gone against, but he is a friend to Government . . .

Sir H. P. St. John [M.P. for Hampshire] is often with us, but in the late questions was against or shirked.

All the Members classed by Robinson under this heading sat for large open constituencies (nearly half of them for counties) or for pocket boroughs entirely under their own control: they were as a group closely in touch with their constituents and responsive to public opinion. From the evidence of division lists it would appear that Robinson under-estimated their number, and that the group comprised at least 50 Members.

Looked at quantitatively, the Opposition consisted of one large party, a number of smaller groups, and a mass of independent Members. Rockingham's party did not exceed a hundred in number; and the smaller Opposition groups—those of Lord Shelburne, the Duke of Rutland, and Sir James Lowther—contained only a handful of Members. The number of independent Members who voted with Opposition was increasing after 1779 and by the time of North's fall probably numbered about 100. Split as it was into a number of groups, it was difficult for the Opposition to formulate a policy which would reconcile them all. In fact, there were at least three different policies in the Opposition, which frequently produced discord and led after 1782 to a complete re-alignment of parties.

The Rockingham group favoured an immediate end to the American war by acknowledging the independence of the United States; it advocated economical reform, but was opposed to parliamentary reform. What might be called the Shelburne policy, in which he was supported in varying degrees by Rutland, Lowther, and many independents, was also opposed to the American war but desired if possible to preserve the sovereignty of Great Britain over the colonies and disliked the idea of unconditional recognition of American independence. Shelburne laid much less emphasis on economical reform than Rockingham: he was more interested in overhauling the antiquated administrative system than in reducing the influence of the Crown, and he was more sympathetic towards parliamentary reform. Lastly, there were the radicals, whose ideas cut sharply across those of the other parties.

The radicals never numbered more than a dozen Members, most of them sitting for the metropolitan constituencies. They did not form a coherent group in the House, but were mixed with and permeated all parties. Wilkes had a little following of his own; James Townsend and John Sawbridge adhered in the main to Shelburne; while others, such as Sir Joseph Mawbey and James Martin remained aloof from close party connexions. There could as yet be no radical party in the House, for it was a firm article of the radical creed that a Member must vote according to the wishes of his constituents. Radicals elected for London took a pledge to this effect, and in the metropolitan constituencies it was the practice to hold meetings at frequent intervals to vote instructions to the Members. To such an extent did some Members carry this principle, that in March 1790 James Martin declared in the House that he would vote against the repeal of the Test and Corporation Acts, contrary to his own convictions, because it was the wish of his constituents. But by the time Pitt had taken office, even the metropolitan radicals were beginning to withdraw from this position. Nathaniel Newnham, M.P. for London, said in the House on 18 June 1784:

Upon all local questions, upon all oppressive internal taxes, and every case that related to them in particular, the constituents' instructions ought .., to be implicitly obeyed; but where the character, talents, and views of ministers were matters under consideration, where measures affecting the general interests of the nation at large were to be discussed and decided upon, there he thought the representative ought to be left to himself to act as his own judgement ... should direct him.

Some idea of the radical programme can be seen from the election address issued at the general election of 1774 by the four radical candidates for London—John Sawbridge, Frederick Bull, Brass Crosby, and George Hayley. They pledged themselves to work for shorter Parliaments, a place bill, an oath against bribery to be taken by all candidates for Parliament, parliamentary reform, the annulment of the Commons' resolutions on the Middlesex election of 1769, and measures for conciliation in America. Some of this was common to the ideas of the Tories about 1754, and it is easy to see how an old Tory like Sir Roger Newdigate came to vote for radical measures. On social questions the radicals were lukewarm, if not reactionary, and none of the great social reform movements of this period—penal reform or the abolition of the slave trade—owed anything to them. They were also strongly opposed to the extension of religious toleration to Roman Catholics. Nathaniel Polhill, returned for Southwark as a Wilkite radical in 1774, was a leading member of Lord George Gordon's Protestant Association, and his only speech in the House, 26 May 1780, was in support of the Association's protest against the Catholic Relief Act of 1778. Frederick Bull, M.P. for London 1773–84, a follower of Wilkes, was another radical who belonged to the Protestant Association. Such was the feeling amongst the radicals against the Roman Catholics, that at the general election of 1780 John Sawbridge had to issue an assurance that he had opposed the Catholic Relief Act.

The news of Cornwallis's surrender at Yorktown, received in England in December 1781, united all the Opposition parties on the practical issue of putting an end to the war in America, and won for them the support of so many independent Members as to make Lord North's position precarious and eventually untenable. His fall was heralded by General Conway's motion on 22 February 1782 against the further prosecution of the war, which the Government survived by a majority of only one vote; on a second motion in similar terms on 27 February the Government was beaten by 234 to 215. The Opposition then moved in for the kill, and on 8 March Lord John Cavendish proposed a motion of no confidence in the Government. This, however, was defeated by 226 to 216; and on 15 March a motion of censure against the Government, moved by Sir John Rous, M.P. for Suffolk, was also beaten, by 236 votes to 227.

An extraordinary situation resulted from these divisions. The House of Commons had repudiated the American war yet had expressed its confidence in the minister; it had condemned his policy yet had supported his continuance in office. In part this was the result of North's declaration that he would re-shape his policy in accordance with the successful motion of 27 February, and his introduction the following day of a bill to enable the Government to make peace with the colonies. In part also it resulted from a feeling among the independent Members, which can be summed up in a remark by Philip Yorke, M.P. for Cambridgeshire, who had voted with the Opposition against the continuance of the war: 'I should be sorry that it should be attended with the consequences of putting Mr. Fox in Lord North's situation, to which I by no means wish to be an accessory, and yet I could not avoid voting for the address.' Yorke, and others like him, did not consider it to be the duty of the House of Commons to prescribe to the King who his ministers should be.

An analysis of the division lists for the last weeks of North's Administration shows that there were 241 Members who supported Government, 237 who voted with the Opposition, and 31 who concurred with the Opposition on the American war yet opposed any censure of North's Administration. It was the Members of this latter group who enabled North to retain office, despite the condemnation of his policy by the House of Commons, and it was when a number of them intimated to North that they would no longer oppose what seemed to be the sense of the House that he determined to resign. Thus a relatively small body of Members held the balance in the House, just as today a relatively small number of voters holds the balance in the electorate.

The part public opinion played in the downfall of North can to some extent be measured from the table overleaf. This analyses the voting of Members from different types of constituencies, first on Dunning's motion against the influence of the Crown (6 April 1780) and next on Rous's motion of censure against the Government (15 March 1782). Members who paired are included. The biggest constituencies (the English counties and the large boroughs), the ones least amenable to the influence of patrons, voted overwhelmingly against the Government, whose main support came from the Members for the small English boroughs and Scotland (the constituencies with the smallest electorates).

In the two years which followed North's resignation there were four Administrations: those of Rockingham, Shelburne, the Fox-North coalition, and the younger Pitt. On Rockingham's death, the bulk of

Type of Constituency	Dunning's motion (6 April 1780)		Rous's motion (15 March 1782)	
	Government	Opposition	Government	Opposition
English counties	10	58	14	56
Large English boroughs	12	41	13	45
Medium English boroughs	21	18	24	22
Small English boroughs	137	95	147	94
Universities	1	2	3	1
Wales	9	16	13	10
Scotland	27	5	30	7
	217	235	244	235

his followers joined with the bulk of North's followers to form a party under the nominal leadership of the Duke of Portland but really directed by Charles James Fox. After the general election of 1784, when Pitt had consolidated his power, the House settled down on something like a two-party basis, superficially resembling the House of today. On the one side was Pitt, holding a position like that of a modern prime minister; on the other was Fox, holding the position of a modern leader of the Opposition. Between 1780 and 1784 there had been a consolidation of parties; the smaller groups had disappeared; and every Member of the House appeared to have taken sides, either for Pitt or for Fox. The names of Whig and Tory had long since ceased to have any meaning, or rather were in the process of acquiring entirely different meanings from those they had held in 1754; and the speculative historian can see in Pitt the founder of the modern Conservative party, and in Fox the inspirer of the Liberal party of the nineteenth century. Moreover, this consolidation into two parties had affected the whole of the nation—Scotland as well as England. Are we then to conclude that by 1784 party had become an established part of the British political scene?

To this conclusion certain qualifications must be made. In 1784, just as in 1754, the politicians professed to decry party and to wish for an Administration formed from the best of all parties. Lord John Cavendish, when moving the motion of censure against Shelburne's peace pre-liminaries, 21 February 1783, defended the coalition between Fox and North by comparing it with the Pitt-Newcastle coalition of 1757—

'Nothing but a union of great and able men could save the country', he said. Benjamin Hammett, M.P. for Taunton, spoke for many independent Members when he told the House on 19 December 1783, the day Pitt assumed office, that 'he liked those ministers who were gone out, and those who were coming in', 'was really sorry that such divisions prevailed in the House', and wished that 'a coalition, taking in the abilities of all parts of the House, might take place'. Such also was the wish of the seventy Members who gathered at the St. Alban's Tavern to forward the idea of a union between Pitt and Fox; and Pitt and Fox, however sceptical they might feel about the possibilities of such a union, had at the least to profess to take it seriously. The difficulty was that there could be only one leader of the House of Commons, and neither Pitt nor Fox was prepared to yield this place to the other; and also that the King had shown his decided preference for Pitt. Had there been any essential change since 1754 when Henry Fox and the elder Pitt had contended for the position which was now the object of their sons' ambition? Was it not still the basic problem of politics to find a minister who could command the confidence of the Crown and of the House of Commons? Parties had been consolidated but the problem remained.

Nor had the political structure of the House changed much by the end of the period. A computation undertaken in 1788 on behalf of a group of independent Members gave Pitt's Administration 281 supporters (186 of whom were described as the party of the Crown 'who would probably support his Majesty's Government under any minister not peculiarly unpopular'), the Opposition 155 votes, and classed 108 Members as 'independent' or 'unconnected'. Thus the independents still formed a large group between two opposing parties, although their numbers had decreased since Lord North's day. And independence, rather than allegiance to a party, was still the proudest boast of a Member of Parliament. Even Pitt did not regard himself as the leader of a party but rather as the servant of the House. On four occasions during the Parliament of 1784–90 he brought forward measures which were rejected by the House (the Westminster) scrutiny, parliamentary reform, the Irish commercial propositions, and the plan for fortifying the dockyards at Plymouth and Portsmouth), and on each occasion he accepted the decision of the House without feeling that it indicated a lack of confidence in himself. And some of the most momentous questions which came before the House during this Parliament—the impeachment of Warren Hastings, parliamentary reform, the abolition of the slave trade, the repeal of the Test and Corporation Acts—were not party issues. They indicate a heightened social consciousness in the British political nation, a different standard of social and political morality from that prevailing about 1754; but their appearance as issues of political controversy was not the result of the growth of party feeling, nor was there anything which might be regarded as a party line regarding them. A Member of Parliament still sought the approval of his constituents (or the patron of the borough which he represented—in Gibbon's words his 'great constituent') not of his party, for it was to his constituents not to his party that he owed his seat.

It was also true at the end of the period, as at the beginning, that the influence of the Crown was greater than the influence of party in the choice of a leader of the House of Commons. The younger Pitt, who depended on the Crown, triumphed over Fox, who relied upon party; and Fox's only chance of obtaining office after 1784 was when the King's illness seemed about to place the authority of the Crown in hands more favourable to him. Pitt held the double post of minister for the Crown in the House of Commons and minister for the House of Commons in the King's Closet: the post held by all great eighteenth-century statesmen, the key office in politics. Government was a partnership between the Crown and the House of Commons, and it was fortunate for Great Britain that on the American problem, the most intractable political question of the period, the Crown did not attempt to find a solution independent of the House of Commons. By identifying himself with the will of the House, George III preserved intact the system of mixed government which was ultimately to develop into the system of constitutional government. For that, he deserved well of his people; but the price the nation had to pay for the preservation of its system of government was the loss of the American colonies.

APPENDICES

DATES OF PARLIAMENTS

Year	Date for which summoned	Dates of sessions	Date of dissolution
1754	31 May 1754	31 May–5 June 1754	
		14 Nov. 1754–25 Apr. 1755	
		13 Nov. 1755–27 May 1756	
		2 Dec. 1756– 4 July 1757	
		1 Dec. 1757–20 June 1758	
		23 Nov. 1758– 2 June 1759	
		13 Nov. 1759–22 May 1760	
		26 Oct.–29 Oct. 1760	
		18 Nov. 1760–19 Mar. 1761	20 Mar. 1761
1761	19 May 1761	19 May 1761	
		3 Nov. 1761– 2 June 1762	
		25 Nov. 1762–19 Apr. 1763	
		15 Nov. 1763–19 Apr. 1764	
		10 Jan.–25 May 1765	
		17 Dec. 1765– 6 June 1766	
		11 Nov. 1766– 2 June 1767	
		24 Nov. 1767–10 Mar. 1768	11 Mar. 1768
1768	10 May 1768	10 May–21 June 1768	
		8 Nov. 1768– 9 May 1769	
		9 Jan.–19 May 1770	
		13 Nov. 1770– 8 May 1771	
		21 Jan.–9 June 1772	
		26 Nov. 1772– 1 July 1773	
		13 Jan.–22 June 1774	30 Sept. 1774
1774	29 Nov. 1774	29 Nov. 1774–26 May 1775	
		26 Oct. 1775–23 May 1776	
		31 Oct. 1776– 6 June 1777	
		20 Nov. 1777– 3 June 1778	
		26 Nov. 1778– 3 July 1779	
		25 Nov. 1779– 8 July 1780	1 Sept. 1780

Year	Date for which summoned	Dates of sessions	Date of dissolution
1780	31 Oct. 1780	31 Oct. 1780–16 July 1781 27 Nov. 1781–11 July 1782 5 Dec. 1782–16 July 1783 11 Nov. 1783–24 Mar. 1784	25 Mar. 1784
1784	18 May 1784	18 May–20 Aug. 1784 25 Jan.– 2 Aug. 1785 24 Jan.–11 July 1786 23 Jan.–30 May 1787 15 Nov. 1787–11 July 1788 20 Nov. 1788–11 Aug. 1789 21 Jan.–10 June 1790	11 June 1790

SPEAKERS OF THE HOUSE OF COMMONS

31 May 1754	Arthur Onslow
3 Nov. 1761	Sir John Cust
22 Jan. 1770	Sir Fletcher Norton
31 Oct. 1780	Charles Wolfran Cornwall
5 Jan. 1789	William Wyndham Grenville
8 June 1789	Henry Addington

CHAIRMEN OF WAYS AND MEANS

19 Nov. 1754	Job Staunton Charlton
17 Nov. 1761	Marshe Dickinson
15 Feb. 1765	John Paterson
14 Nov. 1768	Sir Charles Whitworth
30 Nov. 1778	John Ord
31 May 1784	Thomas Gilbert

FIRST MINISTERS AND LEADERS
OF THE HOUSE OF COMMONS

The office of Prime Minister as it exists today was unknown during this period, though the term was sometimes used. But in each Administration there was one minister who stood above the others, was generally recognized as its head, and was usually described as 'the Minister', 'the First Minister', or 'the Prime Minister'. He might be the first Lord of the Treasury (as were Grenville, North, and the younger Pitt) or might hold some other important political office (Chatham, as lord privy seal, was First Minister from 1766 to 1768). But sometimes other arrangements were made, dictated by the political circumstances of the time. Thus, from July 1757 to October 1761 Newcastle and Pitt shared the Administration; the Duke of Cumberland, the King's uncle, was the head of the so-called Rockingham Administration from its formation in July 1765 till his death in October; and from March to July 1782 Rockingham and Shelburne ranked equally as First Minister. The subject is one of general constitutional rather than of purely parliamentary interest, and cannot be treated here at length. But a list of the successive Administrations may be useful, describing them by the names used in the biographies and constituency histories.

When the head of the Administration was a commoner, he also led the House; when the head of the Administration was a peer, the lead in the House of Commons was not attached to any particular office, though it was exercised by a senior Government spokesman generally known as 'His Majesty's Minister in the House of Commons' and in virtue of that position a member of the Cabinet.

Date	Administration	First Lord of the Treasury	Leader of the House of Commons
Mar. 1754	Newcastle	Duke of Newcastle	Sir Thomas Robinson (secretary of state, southern department) Henry Fox (secretary of state, southern department) from Oct. 1755
Nov. 1756	Pitt-Devonshire coalition	Duke of Devonshire	William Pitt (secretary of state, southern department)
July 1757	Pitt-Newcastle coalition	Duke of Newcastle	William Pitt (secretary of state, southern department)
Oct. 1761	Bute-Newcastle coalition	Duke of Newcastle	George Grenville (treasurer of the navy)
May 1762	Bute	Earl of Bute	George Grenville (secretary of state, northern department) Henry Fox (paymaster general) from Oct. 1762
Apr. 1763	Grenville	George Grenville	George Grenville
July 1765	1st Rockingham	Marquess of Rockingham	Henry Seymour Conway (secretary of state, southern department; April 1766, northern department)
July 1766	Chatham	Duke of Grafton	Henry Seymour Conway (secretary of state, northern department) Lord North (chancellor of the Exchequer) from Jan. 1768
Oct. 1768	Grafton	Duke of Grafton	Lord North (chancellor of the Exchequer)
Jan. 1770	North	Lord North	Lord North
Mar. 1782	2nd Rockingham	Marquess of Rockingham	Charles James Fox (secretary of state, Foreign affairs)
July 1782	Shelburne	Earl of Shelburne	Thomas Townshend (secretary of state, Home affairs)
Apr. 1783	Fox-North coalition	Duke of Portland	Charles James Fox (secretary of state, Foreign affairs)
Dec. 1783	Pitt	William Pitt the younger	William Pitt the younger

INDEX

Parliamentary constituencies and Members of the House of Commons have in general been excluded from this index. For the constituencies see volume I, pp. 205–512, for Members see volumes II and III, of the three-volume edition.